WHAT HOME BUYERS REALLY WANT

2024 EDITION

NAHB®
National Association of Home Builders

What Home Buyers Really Want, 2024 Edition

BuilderBooks, a Service of the National Association of Home Builders

Patricia Potts	Senior Director
Kristie McCauley	Copywriter
Design Central	Cover Design
Robert Brown	Composition

James W. Tobin III	Chief Executive Officer
Robert Dietz	Senior Vice President and Chief Economist, Economics and Housing Policy
Paul Emrath	Vice President, Economics and Housing Policy
Rose Quint	Assistant Vice President, Survey Research, Economics and Housing Policy

Published in the United States of America

27 26 25 24 1 2 3 4 5

ISBN-13: 978-0-86718-813-4
eISBN-13: 978-0-86718-814-1

For further information, please contact:
National Association of Home Builders
1201 15th Street, NW
Washington, DC 20005-2800
BuilderBooks.com

Table of Contents

Acknowledgments

What Home Buyers Really Want, 2024 Edition is produced by the NAHB Economics & Housing Policy Group. The primary objective of this study is to provide builders, manufacturers, architects, and the residential construction industry in general, a thorough analysis of what buyers are looking for in their homes and communities, the amenities that are trending, and the ones that are fading in popularity. Because of the inherent diversity in home buyers' backgrounds, the study provides granular specificity on what different groups of buyers want in a home, based on demographic factors such as generation, geographic location, race/ethnicity, income, and price point.

The study was prepared as housing affordability buckled under the weight of 30%+ increases in home prices and the highest mortgage rates in more than 20 years. In response, new questions were introduced to understand the choices and compromises buyers are making to reach homeownership despite the deterioration in housing affordability.

What Home Buyers Really Want, 2024 Edition was prepared under the direction of Robert Dietz, Ph.D., NAHB Chief Economist and Senior Vice President. The following staff participated in producing the final report:

Paul Emrath, Vice President – Survey and Housing Policy Research
Rose Quint, Assistant Vice President – Survey Research
Ashok Chaluvadi – Senior Economist
Eric Lynch – Economist

The study would not have been possible without the generous support of NAHB's Sustainability & Green Building Department.

Results presented throughout this study come from a survey based on a consumer research panel maintained by Home Innovation Research Labs. For more information about the consumer research panel, or other market research services offered by Home Innovation Research Labs, contact Ed Hudson at (800) 638-8556, ext. 6305.

Executive Summary

The 2024 Edition of *What Home Buyers Really Want* continues the NAHB commitment to be at the forefront of research on home buyer preferences. The primary objective of this study is to provide builders, manufacturers, architects, and the general residential construction industry with a thorough analysis of what buyers are looking for in their homes and communities, the amenities that are trending, and the ones that are fading in popularity. Because of the inherent diversity in backgrounds of home buyers, the study provides granular specificity on what different groups of buyers want in a home based on demographic factors such as generation, geographic location, race/ethnicity, income, and price point.

Although the national health emergency caused by the COVID-19 virus may have subsided, the pandemic that forced millions of Americans to work, attend school, and socialize virtually from home continues to have a lasting impact on how we use our homes and, by extension, on what buyers want today. The pandemic also led to fiscal and monetary policies that continue to reverberate in the economy and the housing industry. Housing affordability, for example, has buckled under the weight of 30%+ increases in home prices and the highest mortgage rates in over 20 years. As a result, *What Home Buyers Really Want, 2024 Edition* includes new questions to understand the choices and compromises buyers make to reach homeownership despite the deterioration in housing affordability.

A comprehensive, nationwide survey of recent and prospective home buyers, selected and weighted to represent the actual universe of homeowners in the country by geographic distribution, age, income and race/ethnicity, is the basis for *What Home Buyers Really Want, 2024 Edition.*

The survey was conducted in two phases using consumer panels maintained by the Home Innovation Research Labs in 2023. The first phase used screening questions to identify recent homebuyers (who purchased a home in the last three years) or prospective homebuyers (those expecting to buy a home in the next three years). In the second phase, those identified in phase one received a detailed questionnaire. The reported results are from 3,008 responses to the questionnaire.

KEY FINDINGS

- A single-family detached home remains the top preference for most home buyers (67%). Far fewer want to purchase a townhouse (16%) or a multifamily condo (10%).

- Assuming location, size, and quality were the same, the typical buyer who prefers a single-family detached home would need a discount of nearly 30% to accept buying a townhome instead.

- The desirability of newly built homes continues to grow: 61% of buyers would prefer to buy a new home over an existing home—the most since 2007.
- Buyers have diverse preferences for the architectural style of their homes: 34% want a traditional style, 26% contemporary, 17% modern, and 12% transitional.
- Only 37% of buyers would like wood to be the framing material for their exterior walls. Instead, most would prefer concrete (25%) or steel (23%), which is an extraordinary finding, given that 94% of the homes in the U.S. have wood frames.
- Buyers expect to pay (or recently paid) a median of $307,061 for a home. About 42% expect to pay between $250,000 and $499,999.
- In an environment where the 30-year fixed mortgage rate surpassed 7% for the first time in over 20 years, buyers were asked about the maximum rate they would accept on a loan to buy a home. For the typical buyer, that threshold is 4.46%.
- Buyers want a median of 2,067 square feet of finished space. This finding reveals that the ideal home size is smaller now than the 2,260 square feet it was in 2003.
- 87% of buyers care about the lot size of their home. Of those, 47% are satisfied with lots of ½ acre or less, 23% want 1 acre, and 18% prefer 2+ acres.
- Home buyers prefer open layouts: 76% want an open floor plan between the kitchen and the dining room, 72% between the kitchen and the family room, and 65% between the dining and the family room.
- Most buyers (54%) would prefer to live in a one-story home, while 38% prefer a 2-story home. Wealthier buyers purchasing homes for $500,000+ are significantly more likely to want multiple stories (54%) than those buying modest homes below $150,000 (37%).
- For 60% of buyers, the washer and dryer belong on the first floor.
- Two of every three buyers want some form of basement: 34% prefer a full basement and 32% a half basement. That leaves roughly one-third of buyers with no interest in having a basement.
- The typical buyer wants three bedrooms. A non-trivial minority of 30% wants at least four bedrooms, however.
- Buyers have diverse opinions on parking space. While 35% would prefer a two-car garage, 33% would be happy with a carport (for one or two cars), 16% want a one-car garage, and 12% a 3+ car garage.

- 45% of buyers would like to buy a home designed for multiple generations. This preference is significantly stronger among minorities (72% of Hispanics, 71% of Asians, and 61% of African Americans) than Caucasian buyers (37%).

- Buyers rated over 200 home and community features on the level of influence each would have on their purchase decision using the following scale:
  - *Essential/must have:* unlikely to buy a home without the feature.
  - *Desirable:* would seriously influence their purchase decision.
  - *Indifferent:* would not influence their purchase.
  - *Do not want:* not likely to buy a home with the feature.

- A laundry room and a patio tie as the top two most wanted of all 200+features, with 86% of buyers rating them essential or desirable. In all, 13 features are wanted by at least 80% of buyers, including three more exterior features (exterior lighting, a front porch, and landscaping), ENERGY STAR windows and appliances, hardwood flooring, a full bath on the main level, ceiling fans, garage storage, and a walk-in pantry and table space in the kitchen.

- At the opposite end of the scale, the presence of 11 features would cause at least 33% of buyers to reject a potential home. The 'do not want' list is led by an elevator (47%), glass walls (42%), and a wine cellar (41%).

- If buying a new home, 71% of buyers would pay extra to upgrade to a gourmet kitchen (e.g., high-end appliances, cabinets, counters), and 65% would pay to upgrade the master bath (e.g., freestanding tub, rainfall shower). Fewer than half would pay for any other major upgrade.

- The kitchen (especially since the pandemic) serves multiple functions for cooking, working, studying, and entertaining, sometimes simultaneously. It's not surprising then that buyers want a well-equipped kitchen. The top five kitchen features are a walk-in pantry (80%), table space for eating (80%), double sink (78%), drinking water filtration (75%), pull-out shelves and a central island (tied at 74%).

- Bathrooms also have a strong influence on home buyers. At the top of their wish list are four features of the primary bath: a shower stall and tub (78%), a linen closet (76%), a private toilet compartment (70%), and a double vanity (67%).

- The typical home buyer wants to have two bathrooms. A substantial minority of 21%, however, would prefer at least three bathrooms in the home.

- The top three choices for windows have energy efficiency top of mind: Energy Star windows (83%), triple-pane insulating glass (77%), and low e-insulating glass (67%). Preference for these three window types and materials increases significantly with the buyer's age.

- For exterior doors, over 50% of buyers would be positively influenced by sliding patio doors, hinged/French patio doors, an entry door with decorative glass panels, and a double main entry door.

- The majority of buyers (81%) want hardwood flooring for the living spaces of the main level of the home.

- More than any other decorative feature, home buyers want a ceiling fan (81%), followed by built-in shelving (72%) and ceiling crown molding (64%).

- Out of 18 specialty rooms in the house, the four most influential on the purchase decision are the laundry room (86%), great room (72%), dining room (69%), and home office (68%). The latter is particularly popular among wealthier buyers: 80% of those with an income of $150,000 or more want a home office, compared to "only" 55% of those with incomes below $50,000.

- For the number and size of home offices, most buyers are interested in having only one home office (66%), and most want it to be between 100 and 150 square feet (59%).

- While 40% of buyers overall want a delivery vestibule, the share is higher among younger, minority, and high-income buyers. Among those under 35, 55% want a delivery vestibule compared to 32% of buyers 65 and older; 63% of Hispanics favor it, compared to 34% of Caucasians; and 55% of those earning $150,000+ want a delivery vestibule vs. 30% of those with income below $50,000.

- Out of 11 specialty features, garage storage takes the top spot (81%), followed by soundproof walls/floors and recessed lighting (tied at 66%) and a drop zone for keys and coats (62%).

- The most wanted accessibility feature is a full bath on the main level of the home (80%), followed by non-slip floor surfaces (74%), doorways at least 3' wide (73%), and hallways at least 4' wide (71%).

- Outdoor features are in high demand, especially post-pandemic. In this study, for the first time, all outdoor features are rated essential/desirable by more than 50% of buyers, led by a patio (86%), exterior lighting (82%), a front porch (81%), and landscaping (80%).

- Brick and stone are the two most popular materials for the front exterior wall, rated essential/desirable by 71% and 70% of buyers, respectively. The desirability of stucco increases with the price point of the home.

- Although 80% of buyers are concerned about the environment, only 18% are willing to pay more for an environmentally friendly home. That 18%, however, is the highest share willing to pay since 2003.

- Many more buyers are willing to pay extra upfront for an environmentally-friendly home if that investment translates into annual savings of $1,000 in utility costs: 58% will pay upwards of $5,000 extra, and of those, 23% will even pay $15,000 or more. On average, buyers will pay $12,314 to achieve a $1,000 reduction in utility costs, which is an 8.1% annual rate of return.

- While ENERGY STAR remains the only green certification program recognized by more than half of home buyers (73%), awareness about all other programs is increasing. The share of buyers who know about LEED for Homes, for example, has grown from 24% in 2018 to 36% in 2023.

- Given buyers awareness of the program, it is not surprising to see ENERGY STAR ratings among the most wanted features in a home. Of 30 green features, the three most popular are ENERGY STAR-rated items: windows (83%), appliances (80%), and rating for the whole home (78%), followed by energy conservation features (triple pane windows, efficient lighting, and high insulation). As buyers see it, a green home is primarily an energy-efficient home.

- Preferences are shifting toward electricity and away from gas to power homes. From 2020 to 2023, the share of buyers who prefer electricity rose for all three basic systems: air heating/cooling (up 7 points to 59%), water heating (up 9 points to 49%), and cooking (up 3 points 42%). Importantly, however, a plurality of 48% of buyers still want gas in their stoves.

- The top reasons buyers choose a particular energy source for cooking are safety (60%), reliability (46%), and cost (41%).

- For the first time, we asked buyers if they would be willing to buy an all-electric home (one not connected to a gas line). Nationally, 60% would do it, but there are notable geographic differences. While 71% of buyers in the Pacific division would buy an all-electric home, the share is only 46% in the East North Central division.

- On a series of trade-offs between a green and a non-green alternative, a majority of buyers favor the green option in four out of seven cases (finishes made of durable/more expensive materials, a right-sized heating/cooling system, a home-oriented to make efficient use of the sun, and low maintenance landscaping). Preferences for these green options grow with the buyer's age.

- Nonetheless, in the trade-off question that directly asks buyers to choose between upgraded interior finishes (e.g., flooring, counters, trim) and green features (e.g., energy/water efficiency/indoor air quality), aesthetic appeal wins for 54% of buyers. The least popular green trade-off is interconnected streets with efficient traffic flow–favored by only 31% of buyers.

- Of 19 technology features, all but three are rated essential/desirable by 50% or more. Buyers want technology primarily to help them feel safe at home and to save energy by controlling the inside temperature efficiently. The top five most wanted technology features are programmable thermostat, security cameras, video doorbell, wireless home security system, and multi-zone HVAC system.

- Although not among the topmost wanted technology features, 49% of buyers do rate a charging station for electric cars as essential/desirable, up from 38% in 2020 and from 23% when first asked in 2012.

- 63% of prospective and recent home buyers plan to watch virtual home tours (or did so if bought a home in the last three years). The popularity of virtual home tours increases with income and price points.

- 53% of buyers would prefer to live in the suburbs, either outlying (29%) or close-in (24%); 25% would prefer a home in a rural area; and 23% in the central city, either right in downtown (13%) or outside of downtown (10%). Millennials are significantly more likely than Boomers to prefer the central city over the suburbs.

- The typical home buyer is willing to commute a median of 11.3 miles to work.

- Working from home is common among homebuyers: 43% report being able to work remotely at least two days a week.

- The onset of the COVID-19 pandemic shone a light on the importance of community features, as many households began making use of public spaces in their neighborhoods. Findings show that an ideal community offers convenience, walkability, and a quintessential suburban feel. Of 29 community features, the top five most wanted (by more than 60%) are being near retail space, a park, walking/jogging trails, a walkable environment (connecting homes, shopping, and public spaces), and a typical suburban neighborhood (all single-family detached homes).

- Gen Z and Millennials are significantly more likely than Boomers to want 28 of the 29 community features (being near retail space is popular irrespective of age), particularly a daycare center, baseball/soccer fields, playgrounds, mixed-use (near office/commercial space), and good public elementary/secondary schools.

- To be able to afford a home, the most likely compromises buyers are willing to accept are a smaller lot (39%), fewer exterior amenities (36%), farther from the urban core (36%), and a smaller home (35%). The least likely compromise is denser development (14%).

- The 35% of buyers willing to take a smaller home in exchange for affordability were asked where specifically they would prefer to cut down on square footage. Most would do it by shrinking the home office (53%) and the dining room (52%). They are least open to downsizing the kitchen and the closets. Interestingly, willingness to accept smaller closets is significantly higher among younger buyers (46% of Gen Z vs. 17% of Boomers).

- 68% of buyers prefer the base price of the home include all amenities and features, as opposed to buying a home where all amenities are offered as options at extra cost (32%).

- In a trade-off pitting size vs. amenities, the latter holds more weight: 63% prefer a smaller house with high-quality products and amenities rather than a bigger house with fewer amenities (37%).

ORGANIZATION OF THE STUDY

The following 12 chapters discuss the results of the survey in more detail, including newly added questions on the choices buyers are making to reach homeownership despite worsening levels of housing affordability. Throughout the study, cases are illustrated where preferences vary significantly by geography (Census divisions), buyer type (first-time vs. repeat buyer), age of the buyer, generation, household composition (e.g., married couples with children vs. one-person households), race/ethnicity, income, and price expected to pay for the home. Appendix A contains detailed tables showing responses to every question broken down by each of these categories.

Chapter 1

Home Type, Price & Size

TWO-THIRDS OF BUYERS PREFER SINGLE-FAMILY DETACHED HOMES

When it comes to structure type, a single-family detached unit remains the top preference for most home buyers, as two out of three say it is their first purchase option. This finding shows an equilibrium between current and future desire for detached single-family homes since the same share of buyers (66%) currently live in this type of home. On the other hand, more buyers would like to live in townhomes than currently do (16% vs. 12%) and fewer want to move to a multifamily unit than live there now (10% vs. 14%). There is little difference between the share of buyers who live in a manufactured home (6%) and those who would like to buy one (5%) (Fig. 1-1).

Figure 1-1. Structure Type

(Percent of Respondents)

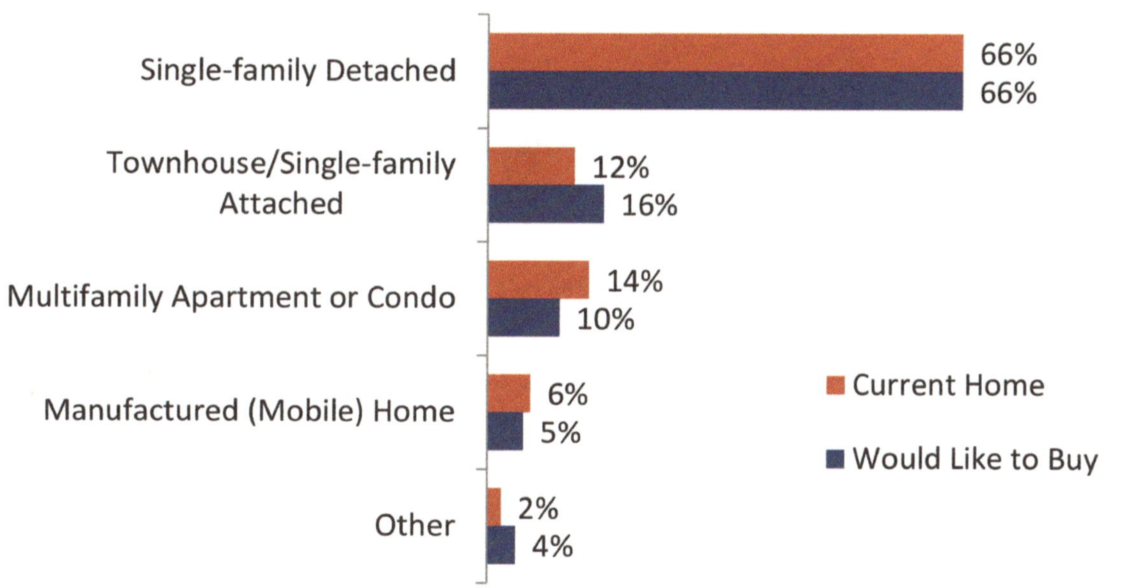

Historically, single-family detached homes have been the most desired home type in the NAHB series, with over 60% of buyers reporting it as their first preference in every iteration of the study since 2003 (Fig. 1-2). Although townhouses have typically been the first choice of only a minority of home buyers, that share has been increasing slowly for over a decade, from 10% in 2007 to 16% in 2023. A multifamily unit is generally the top choice for only a single-digit minority, but in 2023 a full 10% of buyers declared it their top preference. As the least preferred structure type, manufactured homes have been the first choice of a mere 2% to 6% of home buyers since the inception of the series.

Figure 1-2. History of Buyers' First Preference for Structure Type

(Percent of Respondents)

	2003	2007	2012	2015	2018	2020	2023
Single-family Detached	71	63	71	65	77	67	66
Townhouse/Single-family Attached	13	10	11	11	13	15	16
Multifamily Apartment or Condo	5	4	3	8	4	8	10
Manufactured (Mobile) Home	3	3	2	5	4	6	5
Other	8	20	13	10	3	4	4

Statistics for the entire population, however, can hide differences that may exist among different sub-populations. As Figure 1-3 illustrates, there are important differences across the nine Census Divisions in the country. For example, in the East South Central, West South Central, South Atlantic, and East North Central Divisions, over 70% of buyers prefer a single-family detached home, while only 9% to 16% would choose to buy a townhouse. In the other five divisions, preferences for a detached unit are less dominant. In the West North Central Division, 'only' 43% prefer a single-family detached home vs. 29% a townhouse; in New England, the shares are 52% vs. 18%; in the Mountain Division, 60% vs. 22%; in the Pacific, 63% vs. 17%; and in the Middle Atlantic, 64% vs. 18%.

According to the analysis described in Chapter 12, the percentages in the West North Central, East South Central, and Mountain divisions are statistically different from the percentages in the default South Atlantic Division. In addition to geography, the detailed tables in Appendix A provide a breakdown of all findings by various home buyer demographic characteristics.

Figure 1-3. Top Preference for Structure Type by Census Division

(Percent of Respondents)

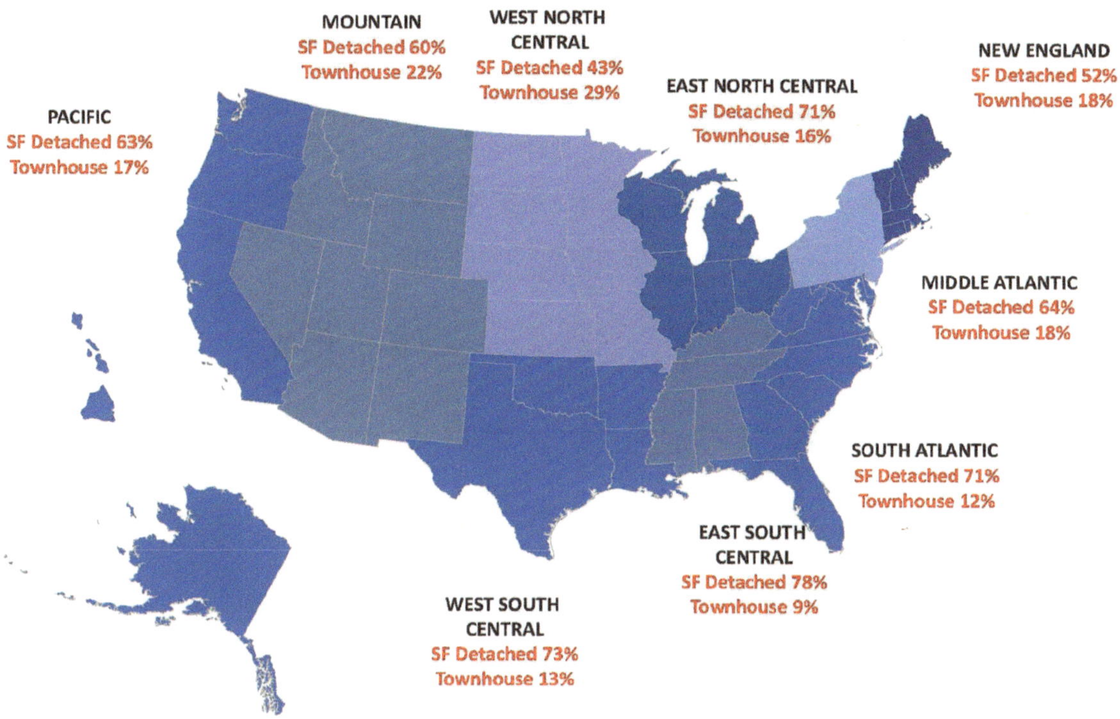

ONLY A DEEP DISCOUNT WOULD SHIFT BUYERS FROM DETACHED TO ATTACHED

Buyers for whom a single-family detached home is their first purchase choice were asked a hypothetical question: If location, home size, and finish quality were the same, what price discount would be a strong enough incentive to buy a townhouse instead of the preferred detached single-family home? Results provide evidence of how deep preferences for a detached home run: the typical buyer would need the townhouse to be about 29.7% less expensive than a detached home to accept the substitution. In fact, for 28% of buyers, no price discount would persuade them to give up a detached unit. Another 20% say the discount would have to be "more than 30%" (Fig. 1-4).

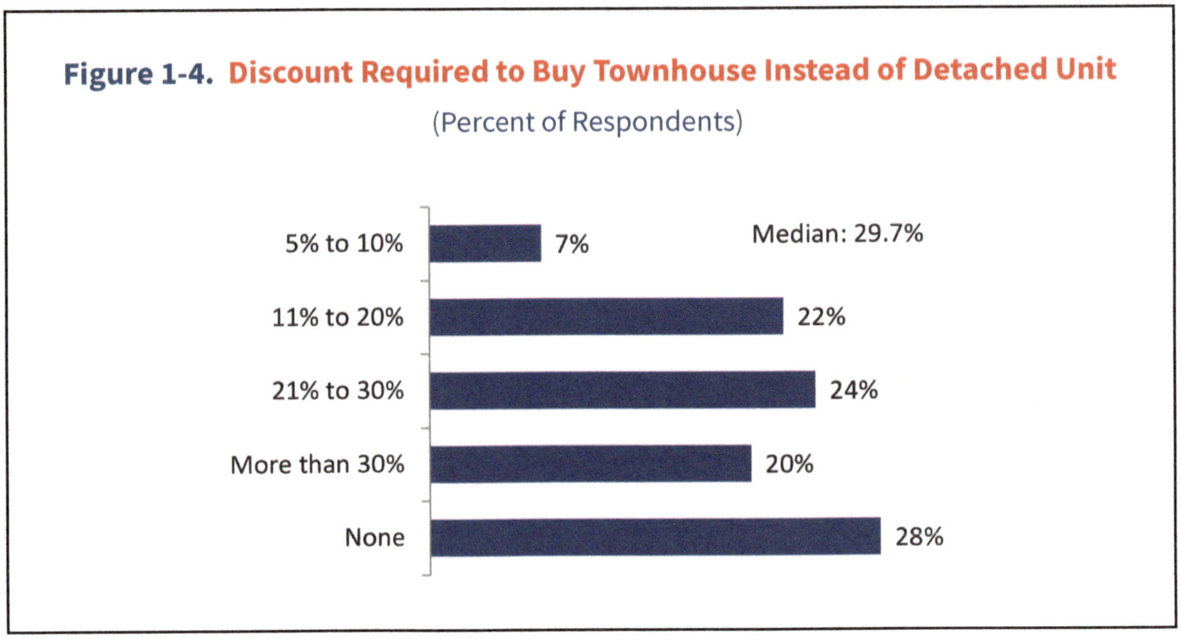

PREFERENCE FOR NEW HOMES KEEPS GROWING

Faced with the alternative of choosing between an existing home and a newly built home, 61% of home buyers indicate their first preference would be a new home – the highest the new home percentage has been since 2007 (Fig. 1-5). The finding shows the desirability of new homes continues to grow. In 2018, 54% of buyers preferred a new home. In 2020, during the COVID-19 pandemic, the share jumped to 60%, driven by a lack of existing home inventory and fears of touring occupied homes in person. In 2023, higher mortgage rates have led millions of existing homeowners with mortgages under 4% to postpone plans to

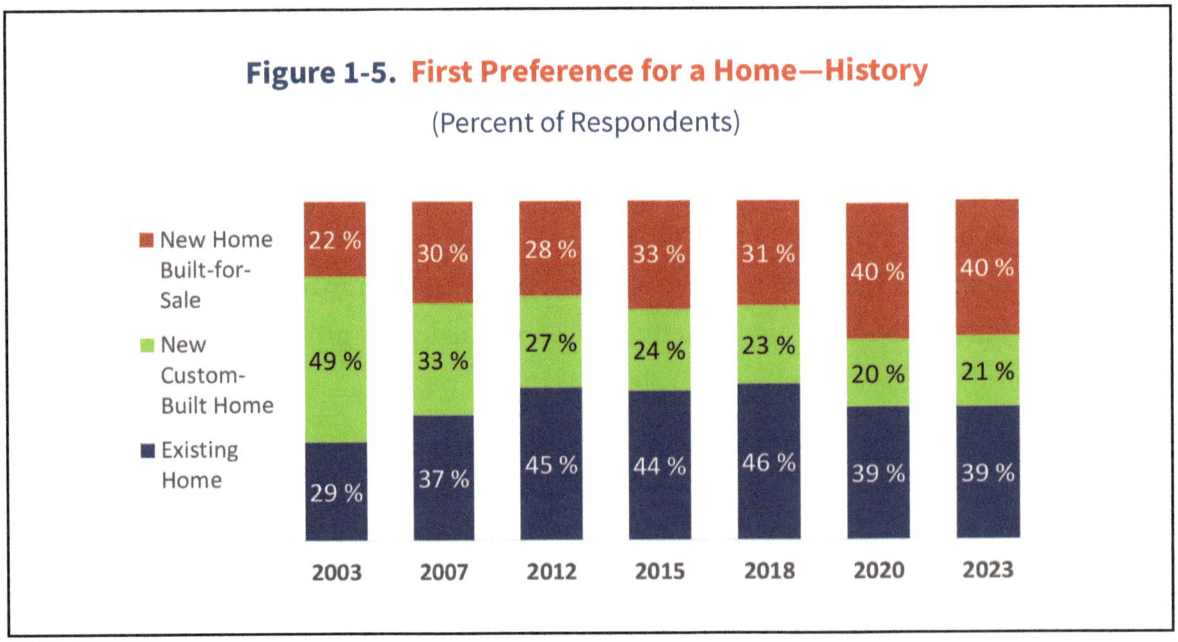

list their homes for sale, and for many buyers, that supply vacuum has left new homes as the only game in town.

New homes can be custom-built on the buyer's lot or they can be built-for-sale (including the land). Over the last two decades, the NAHB study shows a rising trend in the share of buyers who would prefer a new home built-for-sale, from 22% in 2003 to 40% in 2023. In contrast, during the same period, the share who would prefer a custom-built home declined from 49% to 21%.

Some types of households are significantly more likely than others to prefer a new home built-for-sale over a custom-built or existing home. Among married couples with children, for example, a majority of 53% rank a new home built-for-sale as their first preference, compared to 34% of single parents, 30% of married couples without children, and only 25% of one-person households (Fig. 1-6). The analysis described in Chapter 12 shows there is a very strong statistical difference between the percentage of married couples with children and the percentage of other home buyers.

One last point about this topic: despite the evidence supporting buyers' strong preference for newly built homes, the reality is that they often need to compromise (i.e., buy an existing home instead) so they can afford a home purchase. In 2022, existing homes accounted for roughly 88% of the 5.1 million universe of new and existing homes sold. In the last 20 years, the share has ranged from a low of 83% in 2003 to a high of 93% in 2011[1].

Figure 1-6. Share of Buyers Who Prefer a New Home Built-For-Sale by Household Composition

(Percent of Respondents)

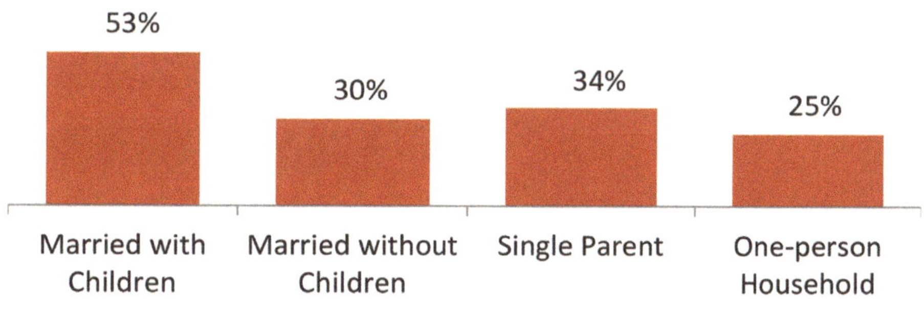

[1] US Census Bureau, Survey of Construction, New Residential Sales & National Association of Realtors, Existing Home Sales.

NO CONSENSUS ON EXTERIOR DESIGN

The 2023 NAHB study, for the second time in its history, asked buyers about their preferences for the exterior design of their next home using descriptions and broad visual representations of four specific options (Fig. 1-7), namely:

- ***Modern*** – bold, boxy, flat roofs
- ***Contemporary*** – clean lines, sloped roofs, expansive windows
- ***Traditional*** – rooted in historic styles
- ***Transitional*** – contemporary design with traditional cues

Figure 1-7. Examples & Descriptions of Exterior Designs

Modern *Photo by* *Tsutsumida Pictures*	**Contemporary** *Photo by* *ImageArts Productions*	**Traditional** *Photo by* *Donald Stasenka*	**Transitional** *Photo by* *Mark Boisclair Photography*

Results show that buyers have interestingly diverse preferences for the architectural style of their homes. Evidence of this is the complete lack of consensus around a single, most preferred exterior design. Instead, a plurality of 34% prefer a "traditional" home, and 26% prefer a "contemporary" home. Smaller minorities want a "modern" home (17%) or a "transitional" one (12%). Overall, only 8% of buyers report "no strong preference" for a particular exterior design, which means that over 90% feel strongly about their specific (and diverse) exterior design preference (Fig. 1-8).

Figure 1-8. Preference for Home Exterior Designs

(Percent of Respondents)

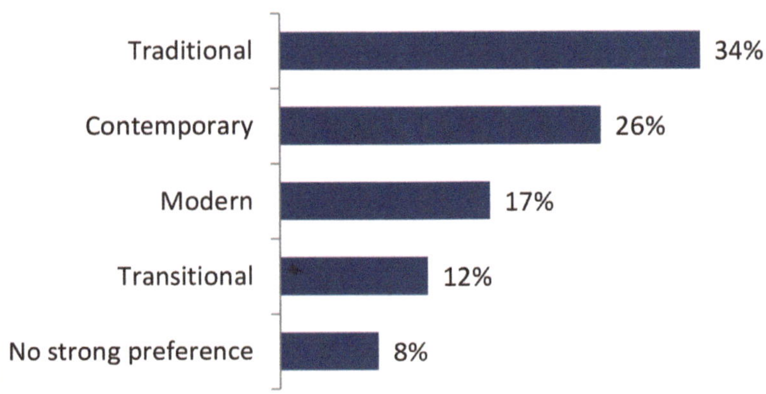

Looking at the top two exterior design preferences by generation shows older buyers are more likely to prefer a traditional design. The latter appeals to 26% of Gen Z buyers (those born in 1997 or later), 28% of Millennials (1981 to 1996), 34% of Gen X buyers (1965 to 1980), and 37% of Boomers (1946 to 1964) (Fig. 1-9). Meanwhile, the share of buyers interested in a contemporary design drops slightly from 30%-31% among the younger two generations to 25% among the older two cohorts. The statistically significant effect of age on exterior design preference is illustrated in Chapter 12.

Figure 1-9. Top Two Exterior Designs by Buyers' Generation
(Percent of Respondents)

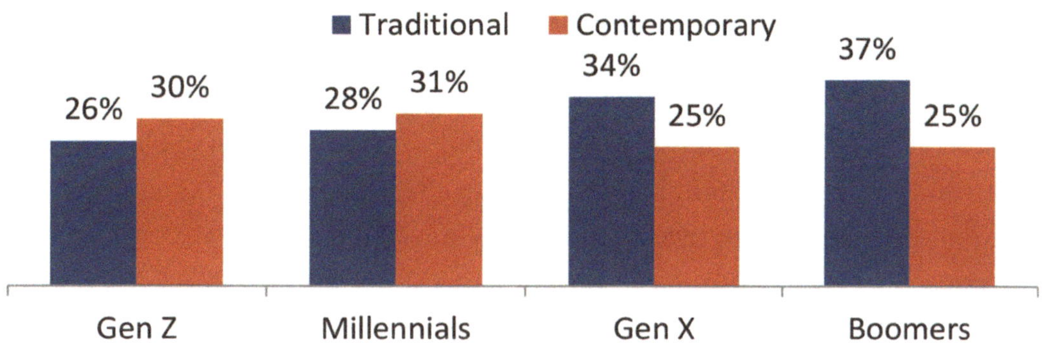

MOST BUYERS PREFER STEEL OR CONCRETE AS FRAMING MATERIAL, NOT WOOD

When NAHB surveyed builders in early 2023 about what they would most like to ask a large cross-section of home buyers, one of the items at the top of the list was the material buyers wanted to frame the exterior walls of their homes. Given that an overwhelming majority of homes completed in the U.S. are framed with wood (94% in 2022[2]), it is an extraordinary finding that only 37% of buyers want wood to frame the exterior walls of their homes. Instead, the majority of buyers want one of the two alternatives: 25% would prefer concrete framing (despite the additional $35,000 cost) and another 23% would prefer steel (despite the additional cost of $15,000). For 15% of buyers, the framing material of their home's exterior walls is irrelevant and therefore they have no preference (Fig. 1-10).

[2] U.S. Census Bureau, Survey of Construction, Characteristics of New Housing.

Figure 1-10. Preference for Exterior Walls' Framing Material

(Percent of Respondents)

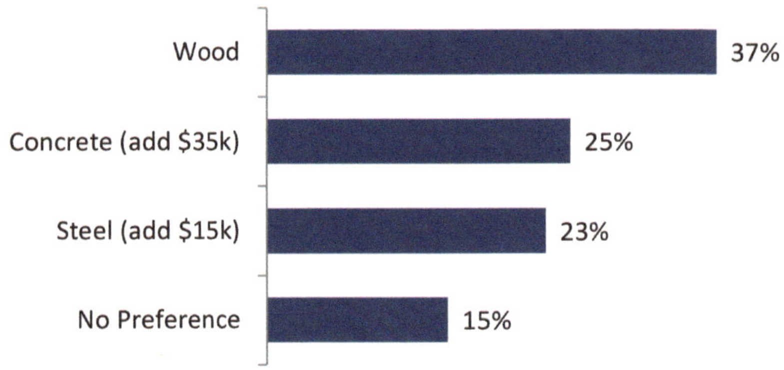

The popularity of wood as the desired framing material is inversely related to the price buyers expect to pay for the home (or paid if the home was bought in the last three years). Among buyers with a price point below $150,000, 43% prefer wood as their home's framing material, compared with 37% of those paying $150,000 to $249,999, 35% of those paying $250,000 to $499,999, and 33% of those paying $500,000 or more. Meanwhile, the combined desirability of concrete and steel rises from 40% of buyers at the low end of the price spectrum to 54% at the top end (Fig. 1-11). This is entirely consistent with the analysis described in Chapter 12, showing that choice of the more expensive framing materials is highly correlated with income, which in turn is highly correlated with the price buyers expect to pay.

Figure 1-11. Preference for Exterior Walls' Framing Material by Home Price

(Percent of Respondents)

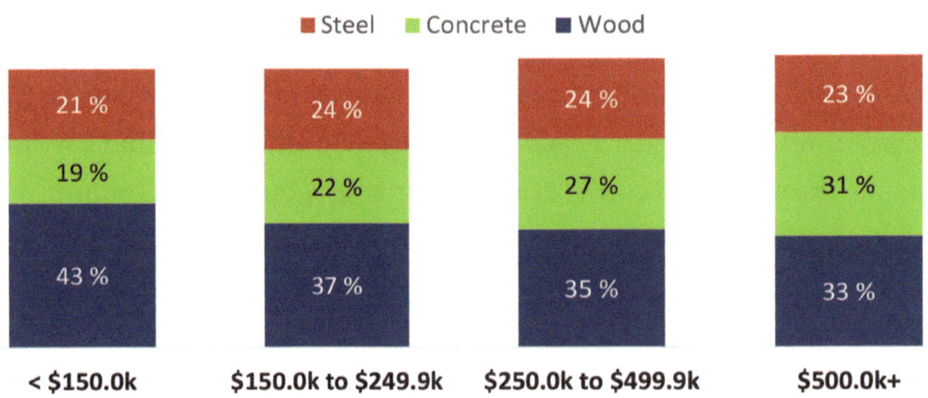

BUYERS' EXPECTATIONS FALL SHORT OF ACTUAL PRICE INCREASES

The median price buyers in the study expect to pay for their next home (or paid recently) is $307,061. Twenty-one percent of buyers expect to pay $250,000 to $349,999, another 21% expect to pay $350,000 to $499,999, and 20% $500,000 or more. About one-fifth (19%) expect to pay under $150,000 (Fig. 1-12).

Figure 1-12. How Much Buyers Expect to Pay for Next Home

(Percent of Respondents)

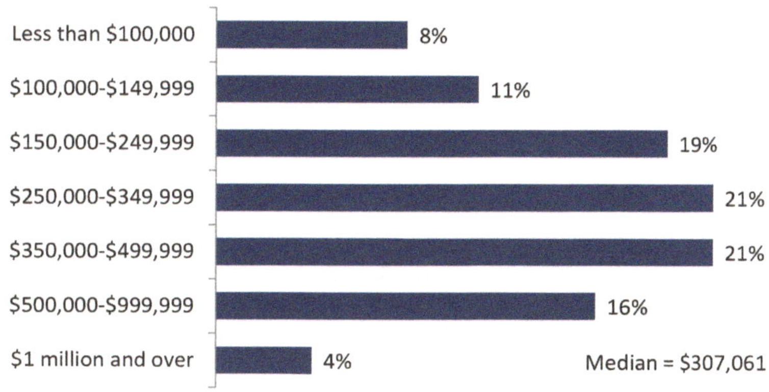

Throughout the history of the NAHB study, the median price home buyers have expected to pay has only decreased once, between 2007 and 2012, when it dropped by 12%. Between all other iterations of the study, the price buyers expect to pay has increased: 31% from 2003 to 2007, 8% from 2012 to 2015, 16% from 2015 to 2018, 4% from 2018 to 2020, and 16% from 2020 to 2023 (Fig. 1-13).

In those same years, the price buyers expected to pay and actual national price indexes for existing and new homes moved in the same directions, but the magnitudes of the changes sometimes varied. For example, between 2012 and 2105, the price buyers expected to pay grew by 8%, substantially less than the increases reported during the same period for existing (22%) and new (16%) homes. In contrast, between 2015 and 2018, the 16% increase in the price buyers expected to pay closely resembled the 17% or 18% increase shown by the price indexes for new and existing homes.

The latest NAHB study once again shows a large disparity. Between 2020 and 2023, the price home buyers expect to pay for a home rose by 16%, only about half the increases reported during the same period in the national price indexes for both new (31%) and existing (38%) homes.

Figure 1-13. Median Price Buyers Expect to Pay—History

(Percent of Respondents)

	2003	2007	2012	2015	2018	2020	2023
Price Buyers Expect to Pay ('000s)	$175.9	$230.9	$203.9	$219.9	$254.1	$264.6	$307.1
% Change		31%	-12%	8%	16%	4%	16%
Change in Quality Adjusted Price Indexes							
Existing Homes Sold		35%	-22%	22%	18%	10%	38%
New Homes Sold		22%	-7%	16%	17%	6%	31%

For existing homes, the index is the S&P/Case-Shiller® U.S. National Home Price Index. For new homes, the index is the U.S. Census Bureau's Quality Adjusted Price Index for New Single-family Homes sold. The Case-Shiller index uses repeat sales of the same homes, and the Census Bureau uses regression methods, to control for differences in the quality of homes sold. The percent changes are based on annual index numbers, except for 2023, which uses the monthly indexes for July 2023, the latest available at the time of this writing.

The price buyers expect to pay for their home varies significantly by the buyer's type and age. The typical first-time buyer, for example, expects to pay $199,154, about 38% less than the typical repeat buyer ($321,033). Among generations, Millennial buyers expect to pay the most for their next home, a median of $324,166. In comparison, Gen Z buyers expect to pay $217,046 (33% less than Millennials); Boomers expect to pay $299,882 (7% less), and Gen X buyers expect to pay about the same $316,537 (only 2% less) (Fig. 1-14). The age differences remain statistically significant even after controlling for the buyer's income.

Figure 1-14. Median Home Price Buyers Expect to Pay By Buyer Type & Generation (000's)

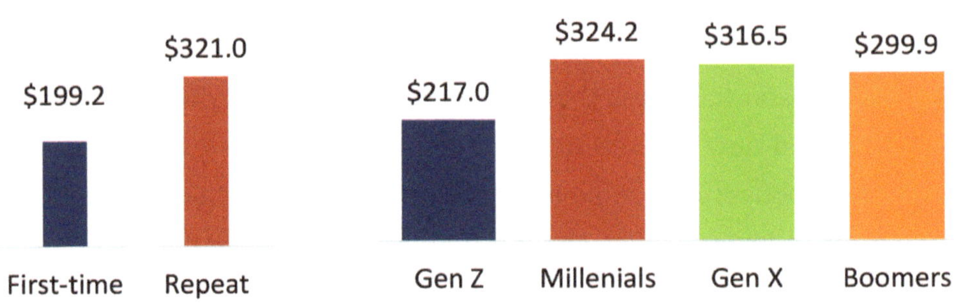

4.46% IS THE SWEET SPOT FOR MORTGAGE RATES

In 2022, with inflation running hot at a 40-year high, the Federal Reserve Bank embarked on a sustained campaign to bring prices under control through multiple rounds (10+) of interest rate hikes. In short order, the 30-year fixed mortgage rate more than doubled from historic lows (2%-3%) during the pandemic to 7% in the fall of 2022, before settling in the high 6% range throughout much of the first half of 2023 and returning to the 7% range in late summer of that year. The interest rate effect can be quite significant. According to NAHB's priced-out analysis, an increase in mortgage rates from 3.5% to 7.0% prices roughly 18 million American households out of the market for a median-priced new home[3]. This is the backdrop for a new question in the latest NAHB study asking buyers about the maximum mortgage rate they are willing to accept on a loan to buy a home.

For a typical buyer, 4.46% is the maximum acceptable mortgage rate. Although 12% say that interest rates do not play any role in their home buying decision (likely cash buyers) and another 5% are willing to accept mortgages at 7.0% or more, the maximum rate 40% of buyers (the plurality) will accept is somewhere between 3.0% and 4.9%. Another 30% will accept a rate between 5.0% and 6.9%, if that is what it will take to reach homeownership. Most home buyers understand the era of ultra-low mortgage rates is in the rear-view mirror, as a mere 14% say the maximum rate they would accept is below 3% (Fig. 1-15).

Figure 1-15. Maximum Acceptable Mortgage Rate to Buy a Home
(Percent of Respondents)

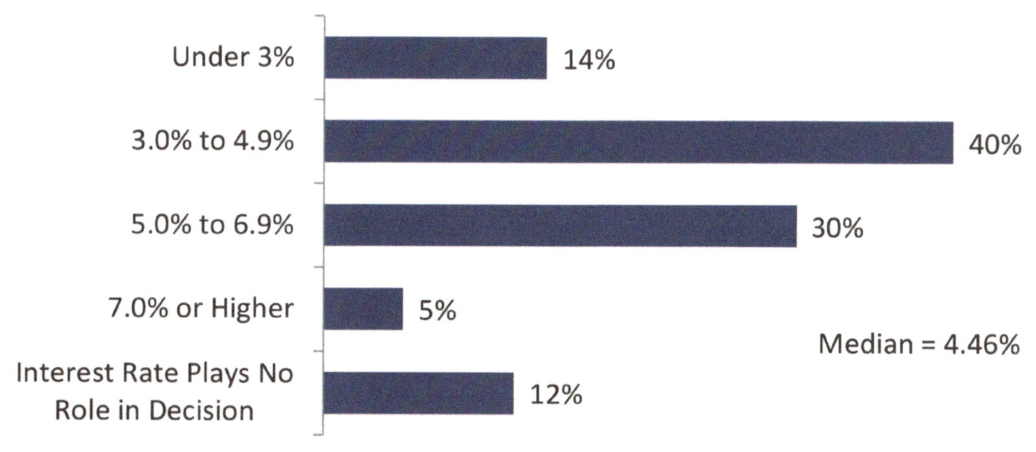

[3] National Association of Home Builders, Households Priced Out by Higher House Prices and Interest Rates.

More granular analysis reveals that buyers of different income levels have different pain points for the maximum mortgage rate they are willing to accept, and the differences are statistically significant. The typical buyer whose income is below $50,000 will accept a maximum rate of 3.96%. But as Figure 1-16 shows, that rate increases steadily with income, reaching 4.98% for buyers with income of $150,000 or more.

Figure 1-16. Maximum Acceptable Mortgage Rate to Buy a Home by Buyers' Income

(Percent of Respondents)

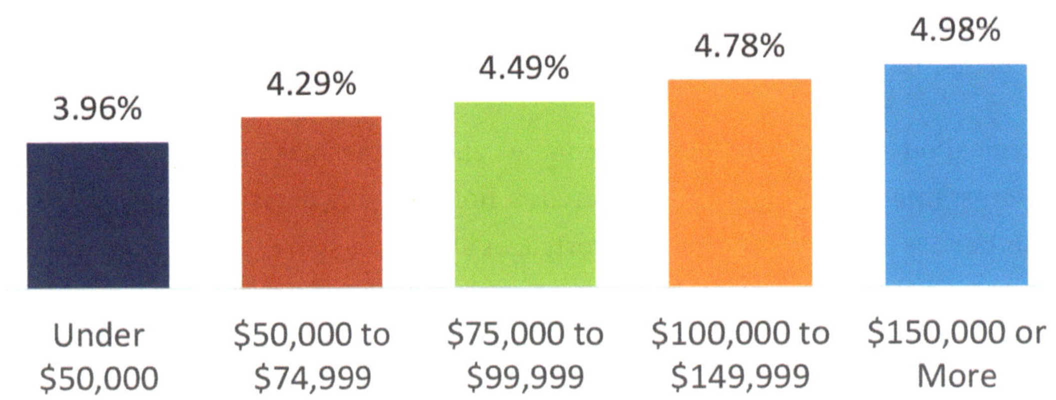

BUYERS ARE LOOKING FOR MORE SPACE

The typical homeowner in this study lives in a 1,802-square-foot-home but would rather live in one with 2,067 square feet. That translates into a 15% increase in finished space. As Figure 1-17 illustrates, more owners currently live in homes with less than 1,600 square feet (40%) than would like to do so (26%). For larger home sizes, results show slightly more owners want them than currently have them. For example, 39% currently live in homes between 1,600 and 2,499 square feet, compared with 43% who want a home in that size range. Similarly, 12% live in homes with 2,500 to 2,999 square feet but 16% would like to do so. Finally, 10% of owners' current homes have at least 3,000 square feet of space, yet 14% want a home of that size.

The median 2,067 square feet of space desired by homeowners in this study falls between the median size of existing homes and the median size of new homes being built in the U.S. In 2021, the median size of existing homes was 1,800 square feet for detached single-family units and 1,380 square feet for attached ones[4]. That same year, the median size of all new single-family homes completed was 2,273 square feet[5].

Figure 1-17. Square Footage of Finished Area Buyers Have & Would Like to Have

(Percent of Respondents)

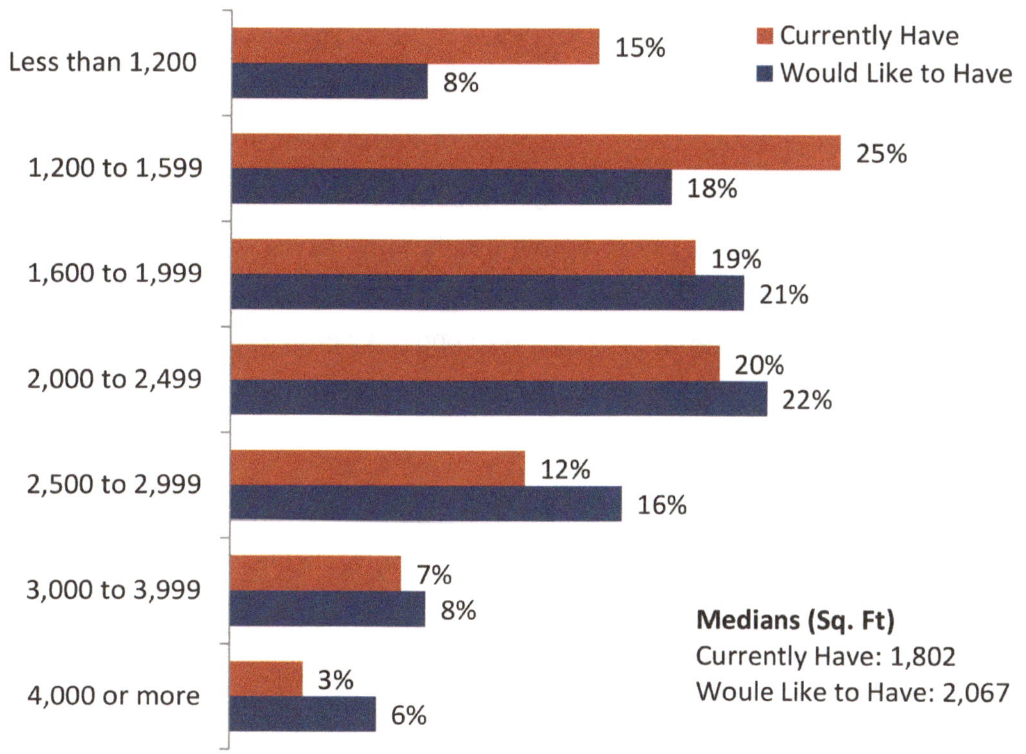

In the last 20 years, there has been a clear shift downward in the amount of space buyers want. NAHB studies from 2003 to 2012 reveal that the typical buyer during this period wanted a home with at least 2,200 square feet of finished area. Starting in 2015, however, buyers' preferences shifted toward smaller homes. That year, and then again in 2018, 2020, and 2023, the typical buyer decided a home with around 2,000 to 2,075 square feet was enough (Fig. 1-18). Among the possible explanations behind the shift in size preferences are high home and land prices and the desire to save on heating and cooling costs.

[4] U.S. Census Bureau, 2021 American Housing Survey, www.census.gov/programs-surveys/ahs

[5] U.S. Census Bureau, Characteristics of New Housing, www.census.gov/construction/chars

Figure 1-18. Median Square Footage of Finished Area Buyers Would Like to Have

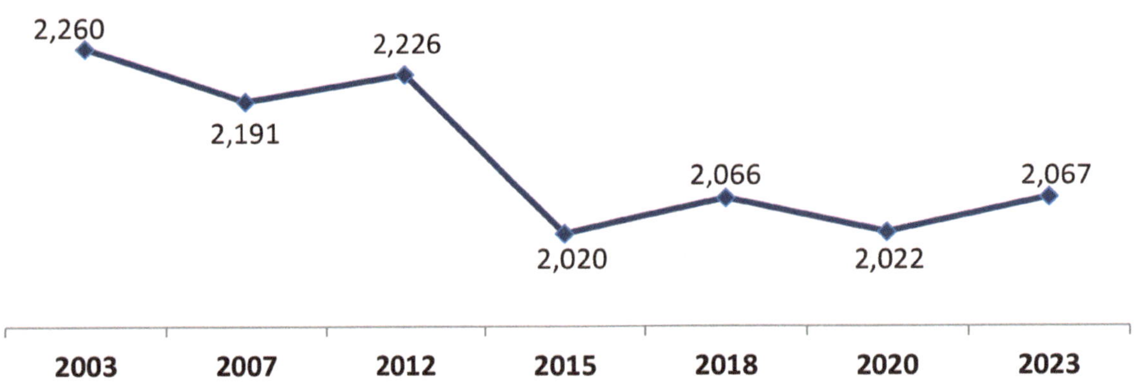

As can be expected, the amount of space home buyers want increases in a statistically significant way with the amount of money they plan on paying for the home. For example, buyers looking to spend less than $150,000 for their next home want a median of only 1,617 square feet; those who plan to pay $150,000 to $249,999 want 1,775 square feet; buyers paying $250,000 to $499,999 want 2,149 square feet; and those who will pay half a million dollars or more want a median of 2,581 square feet (Fig. 1-19).

Figure 1-19. Median Square Footage Buyers Have & Would Like to Have by Home Price

(Percent of Respondents)

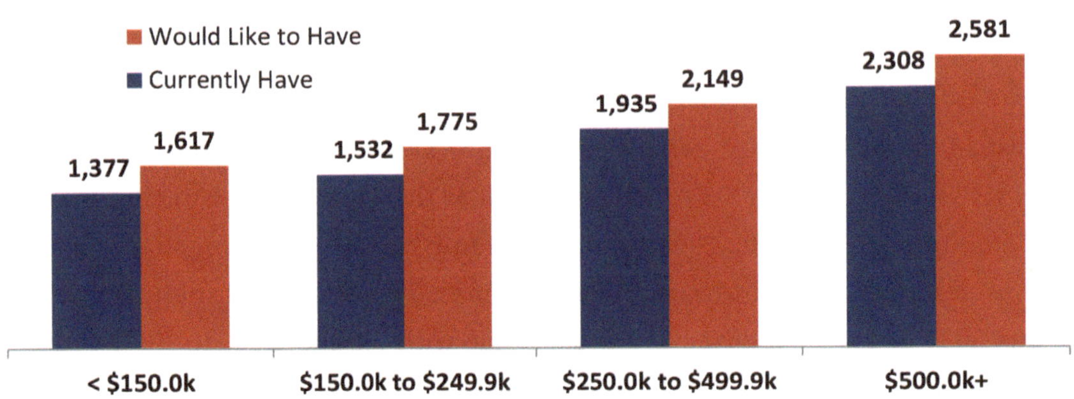

A HALF ACRE IS ENOUGH TO SATISFY 47% OF BUYERS

The size of the lot their home is built on matters to most buyers – 87% of them to be exact. The other 13% have no preference and so the size of the lot is irrelevant to them. For those who care, only 9% prefer a small lot of 1/8 acre; about twice that share – 17% – prefer a slightly larger lot of ¼ acre, while 21% would rather have ½ acre. Together, 47% of buyers will be satisfied with lots of ½ acre or smaller. Still, a non-trivial share of buyers prefer large lots, 23% 1 acre and 18% 2 acres (Fig. 1-20).

The figure also breaks down lot size preferences by generation, showing that Boomers are significantly less likely than the younger three generations to want large lots. While only 32% of Boomers are interested in lots of 1+ acres, the share is 51% among Gen Z buyers, 47% among Millennials, and 49% among Gen X buyers. This finding is not entirely surprising, as older buyers are less likely to need yards for children or want to maintain them. The analysis described in Chapter 12, however, shows that the effect of age on lot size preferences persists and remains statistically significant even after controlling for other factors, including household composition.

Figure 1-20. Lot Size Preference by Generation

(Percent of Respondents)

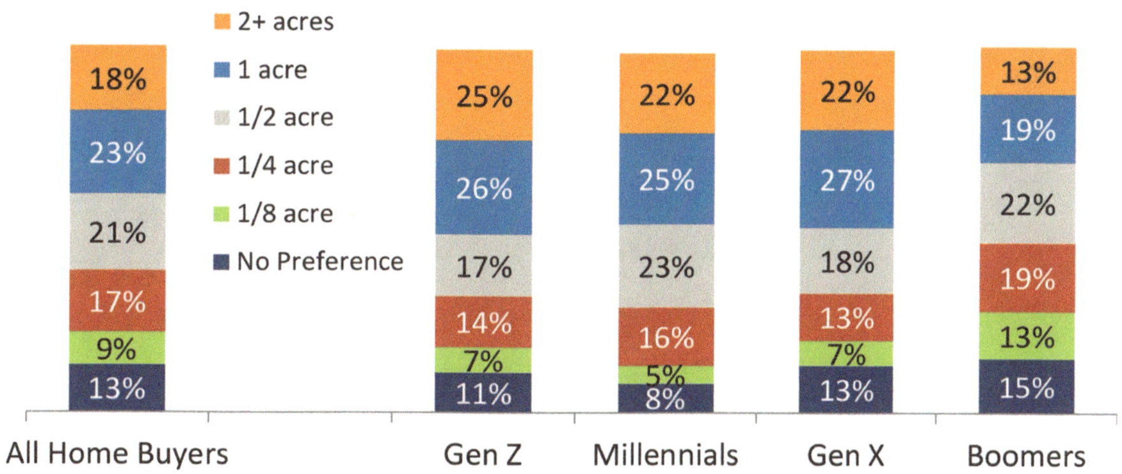

Chapter 2

Room Layout & Design

BUYERS WANT OPEN LAYOUTS, ESPECIALLY TO THE KITCHEN

The 2023 NAHB survey contained several questions on the basic layout of common areas of the home. Most home buyers prefer open layouts, especially around the kitchen. For example, 76% prefer an open kitchen-dining room layout, either completely open (46%) or only partially separated by a half wall, arch, or counter (30%). A minority of 15% want the kitchen and dining room to be in separate areas of the house. Seven percent prefer the kitchen and dining room are side-by-side but separate, and 3% do not want a dining room (Fig. 2-1).

Figure 2-1. Buyers' Preferred Room Layout

(Percent of Respondents)

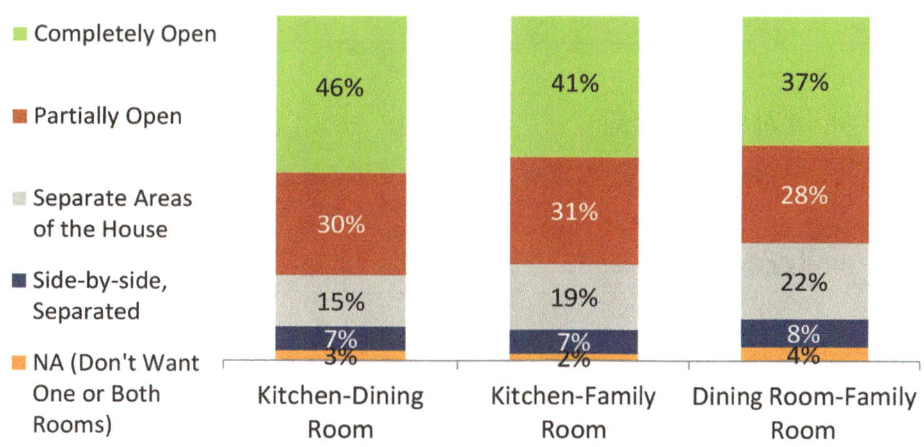

Preferences for open kitchen-family room layouts are nearly as strong. Forty-one percent of buyers want the kitchen-family room combination to be completely open, and 31% prefer it partially open. Nineteen percent prefer the kitchen and family room to be in separate areas of the house, 7% prefer separate but side-by-side, and 2% do not want a family room. The survey did not offer the option for a home without a kitchen because the International Residential Code requires a kitchen area in every dwelling unit.

Switching to a layout that does not involve the kitchen, somewhat larger minorities prefer the non-open options. Twenty-two percent of buyers prefer the dining room and family room to be separate areas of the house, and another 8% want them separate but side-by-side. Four percent prefer a home that does not include one or both rooms, which leaves the majority of buyers (65%) who prefer the dining and family rooms to be open to each other: 37% completely and 28% partially.

Compared to 2020, the 2023 results show a modest shift away from open layouts toward rooms in separate areas of the house. But despite the shift, a completely open layout remains the favorite, with partially open second. Other sources of trends data (e.g., NAHB surveys of builders and buyers), however, provide evidence that demand for open layouts has strengthened — not weakened — in recent years. As of this writing, therefore, the current data on changes in layout preferences is at best mixed (Fig. 2-2).

Figure 2-2. Buyers' Preferred Room Layout: History

(Percent of Respondents)

	2015	2018	2020	2023
Kitchen-Dining Room				
Completely Open	45	49	50	46
Partially Open	41	37	35	30
Separate Areas of the House	3	3	3	15
Side-by-side, Separated	9	8	9	7
Home without a Dining Room	3	3	3	3
Kitchen-Family Room				
Completely Open	32	43	46	41
Partially Open	38	38	33	31
Separate Areas of the House	16	8	6	19
Side-by-side, Separated	11	10	12	7
Home without a Dining Room	4	2	2	2
Dining Room-Family Room				
Completely Oopen		38	41	37
Partially Open		32	29	28
Separate Areas of the House		12	9	22
Side-by-side, Separated		12	17	8
Home without One/Both Rooms		6	5	4

MOST WEALTHY BUYERS PREFER MULTIPLE STORIES

When asked about the number of stories they prefer, assuming the same floor space and excluding the basement, most home buyers (54%) would choose a single-story home, while 38% prefer a two-story structure. Only 6% want a three-story and 2% a split-level home (Fig. 2-3).

Figure 2-3. Preferred Floor Plan by Home Price (000's)
(Percent of Respondents)

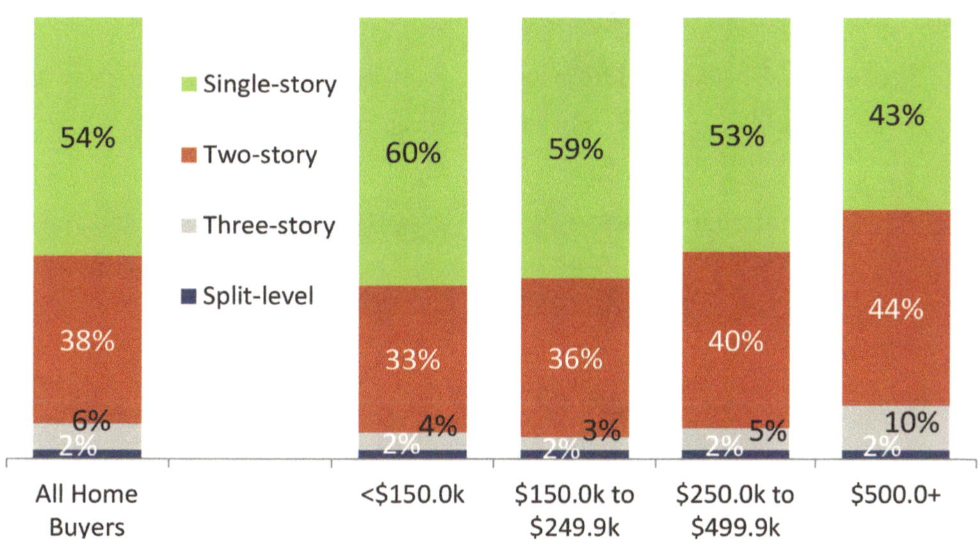

Split-level construction (a structure with floors on more than one level when the difference in some floor levels is less than a full-story) was more common in the past than now. According to the Census Bureau's published statistics, split-level structures dropped from over 10% of single-family homes completed in the late 1970s, to less than .5% by 2005. As a result, the Census Bureau stopped reporting on new split-level homes and instead began providing data on new single-family homes with three or more stories. NAHB tabulation of the latest Census data shows that, in 2022, three-plus-story structures accounted for 5% of single-family starts.

A breakdown of results by price point shows most wealthy buyers prefer more than one story. Among those whose price point is $500,000 or higher, 54% want multiple stories (44% two and 10% three), while a minority of 43% would prefer a single-story home instead. At the most modest end of the scale (buyers with price points below $150,000), only 37% express desire for multiple stories, while a solid majority of 60% would be content with a single-story home (Fig. 2-3). The differences are highly significant, according to the statistical analysis described in Chapter 12.

LAUNDRY ON THE FIRST FLOOR

Whether they prefer a home with one or multiple stories, most buyers (60%) agree that the washer and dryer should be on the first floor of the home. For other possible locations, 17% prefer the laundry equipment to be in the basement, 15% in the garage, and 7% on the second or higher floor (Fig. 2-4).

Figure 2-4. Preferred Location for the Clothes Washer & Dryer

(Percent of Respondents)

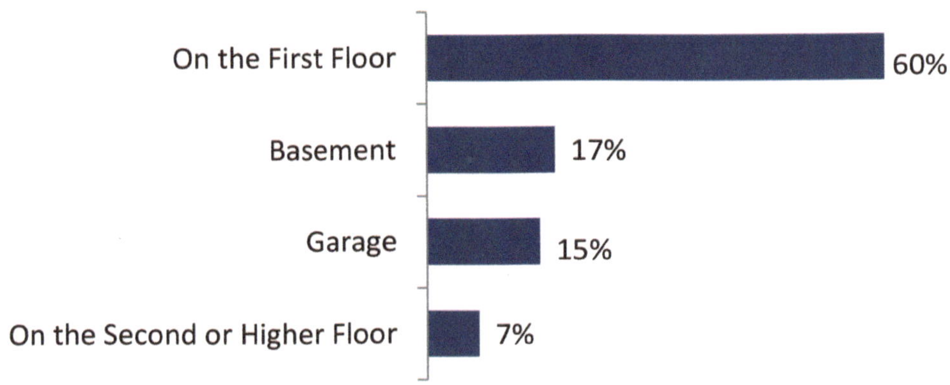

BASEMENTS MORE POPULAR IN COOLER CLIMATES

The NAHB survey also asked buyers about their preference for a basement, taking cost differences into account. The questionnaire provided cost estimates of $22,500 for a half basement and $45,000 for a full basement. NAHB developed these estimates based on cost per square foot for an average single-story home reported in the RSMeans Residential Costs publication, adjusted for inflation using the Consumer Price Index, and multiplied by the average square footage of a single-story home in the HUD/Census Bureau American Housing Survey.

Results show that two out of every three buyers in the study want some form of basement: 34% would prefer a full basement and another 32% a half basement, which leaves roughly one-third of buyers (34%) who report no interest in having a basement (Fig. 2-5).

Figure 2-5. Buyer Preferences for a Basement Taking Price Difference into Account

(Percent of Respondents)

But nationwide percentages mask important regional differences, which are statistically significant based on the analysis described in Chapter 12. In the northern Census divisions (those that do not extend all the way to the southern border of the continental U.S.), more than 75% of buyers want a basement (either full or partial). Specifically, 90% of buyers in New England, 82% in West North Central, 81% in the Middle Atlantic, and 76% in the East North Central divisions indicated that they wanted a basement, even taking the extra cost into account. Preference for a basement is lower in all other divisions of the country: 44% in West South Central, 55% in South Atlantic, 62% in Mountain, 63% in Pacific, and 68% in the East South Central divisions (Fig. 2-6). In northern climates, homeowners are accustomed to single-family homes with basements because, historically, codes in these climate zones required footings so deep that the extra cost of converting the foundation to a basement was not that great.

Additionally, preference for a basement is directly related to income. Among buyers earning less than $50,000 a year, 55% want a basement. The share rises to 64% among those earning $50,000 to $74,999, to 69% among those earning $75,000 to $99,999, 70% of those earning $100,000 to $149,999, and to 76% of buyers earning $150,000 or more (Appendix A, page A-39). Again, these differences are statistically significant to a high degree.

Figure 2-6. Share of Buyers Who Want a Basement (Full or Partial) by Census Division

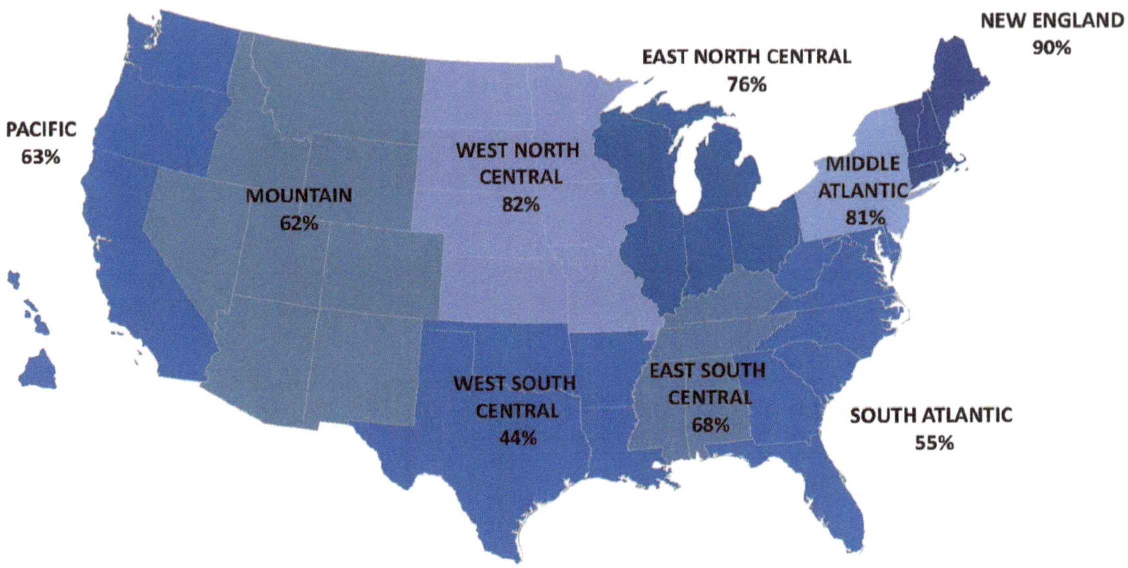

Historically, the share of buyers interested in a full basement is significantly lower in 2023 (34%) than in 2003 (54%). Preference for a half basement, on the other hand, has nearly doubled during this period, from 17% to 32%. The share of buyers who do not want a basement has been volatile over the years, ranging from a low of 29% in 2003 to a high of 44% in 2018 (Fig. 2-7).

Figure 2-7. Buyer Preferences for a Basement: History

(Percent of Respondents)

	2003	2007	2012	2015	2018	2020	2023
Full Basement	54	46	46	37	32	32	34
Half Basement	17	16	20	21	25	27	32
No Basement	29	38	34	43	44	41	34

TYPICAL BUYER WANTS THREE BEDROOMS

Although a sizable share of buyers (30%) would prefer to buy a home with 4+ bedrooms, the plurality (45%) would be satisfied with three bedrooms, while about a quarter (26%) would prefer only one or two bedrooms (Fig. 2-8). The median number of bedrooms desired is three.

Figure 2-8. Number of Bedrooms Preferred, by Household Composition

(Percent of Respondents)

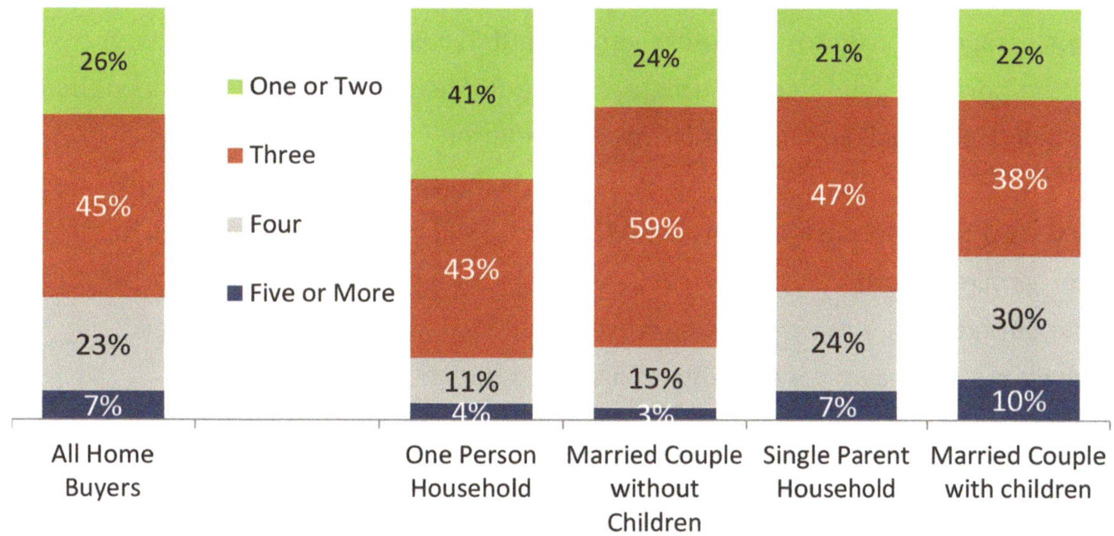

The composition of the household—particularly the presence or absence of children—has a strong influence on the desired number of bedrooms. For example, 40% of married couples with children and 31% of single parents want a home with at least four bedrooms, compared to only 15% of one-person households and 18% of married couples without children. The differences are statistically significant, even after controlling for the differences in home buyer characteristics like age and income.

Over the past two decades, NAHB home buyer surveys show a moderate trend in preference toward homes with fewer bedrooms. In 2003, 38% of buyers preferred 4+ bedrooms; by 2023, that share had trended down to 30%. Meanwhile, during the same period, the share for one or two bedrooms rose from 19% to 26% (Fig. 2-9).

Figure 2-9. Number of Bedrooms Preferred: History

(Percent of Respondents)

	2003	2007	2012	2015	2018	2020	2023
One or Two	19	13	13	21	20	23	26
Three	44	47	47	49	49	46	45
Four	30	31	32	24	25	24	23
Five or More	8	9	8	6	6	8	7

JUST OVER ⅓ OF BUYERS WANT A TWO-CAR GARAGE

The survey listed several parking options and the cost associated with each choice: $10,000 for a single-vehicle carport, $18,000 for a double-vehicle carport, $30,000 for a one-car garage, $50,000 for a two-car garage and $70,000 for a three-car garage. NAHB based the parking facility cost estimates on the RSMeans Residential Costs publication, with a relatively small adjustment for overall inflation.

Given the options and costs, a plurality of buyers (35%) would prefer to buy a home with a two-car garage. Another 20% of buyers would opt for a two-vehicle carport, 16% prefer a one-car garage, 13% a one-vehicle carport, while 12% want the 3+ car garage. Only 5% of buyers do not want a parking facility of any kind (Fig. 2-10).

Figure 2-10. Buyer Preferences for a Parking Facility

(Percent of Respondents)

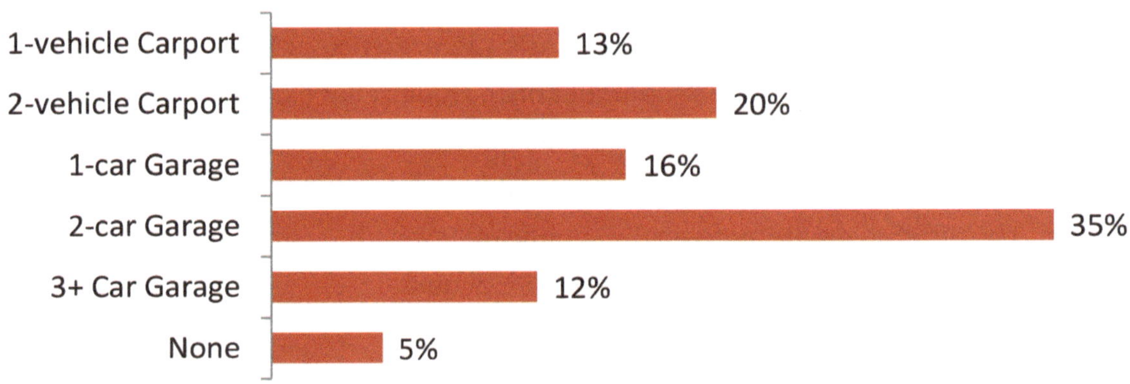

Looking at historical data for the past 20 years shows buyers increasingly willing to choose less expensive parking options. For example, in 2003, only 5% of buyers preferred the one-vehicle carport; by 2023, the share had nearly tripled to 13%. Similarly, those who prefer a two-vehicle carport jumped from 7% to 20% during this period. Meanwhile, the opposite trend is evident for two and 3+ car garages. The share of buyers wanting the former dropped from 49% in 2003 to 35% in 2023, and for the latter, from 25% to 12% (Fig. 2-11). The long-term trend suggests large garages are becoming a feature that buyers are willing to compromise on to achieve homeownership.

Figure 2-11. Buyer Preferences for a Parking Facility: History

(Percent of Respondents)

	2003	2007	2012	2015	2018	2020	2023
1-vehicle Carport	5	5	4	9	8	11	13
2-vehicle Carport	7	10	11	10	10	14	20
1-car Garage	11	7	8	14	13	18	16
2-car Garage	49	50	53	48	48	42	35
3-car Garage	21	22	19	n/a	n/a	n/a	n/a
4-car Garage	4	4	3	n/a	n/a	n/a	n/a
3+ Car Garage	n/a	n/a	n/a	15	14	12	12
None	3	2	2	4	5	4	5

MOST MINORITY BUYERS PREFER MULTIGENERATIONAL HOMES

Overall, across a representative sample of all types of home buyers in the country, 45% would prefer to purchase a home designed to house multiple generations. While 36% reject the idea, 19% are simply not sure. However, buyers are not homogeneous, and this preference varies significantly among buyers of different racial/ethnic groups, income levels, age, and household composition.

Figure 2-12 illustrates one example. Minority buyers are significantly more likely to prefer a multigenerational home than Caucasian buyers. Where solid majorities of Hispanic (72%), Asian (71%), and African American (61%) buyers want a home where multiple generations can live together, the share is barely 37% among Caucasian buyers. Another stark contrast exists across income levels: only 38% of buyers with incomes below $75,000 want this type of home, compared to 60% among those with income of $150,000 or more (Appendix A, Page A-45). The differences across income brackets and racial/ethnic categories are statistically significant in a model that controls for both, as well as other home buyer characteristics.

Figure 2-12. Would You Prefer a Home Designed for Multiple Generations? By Buyer's Race/Ethnicity

(Percent of Respondents)

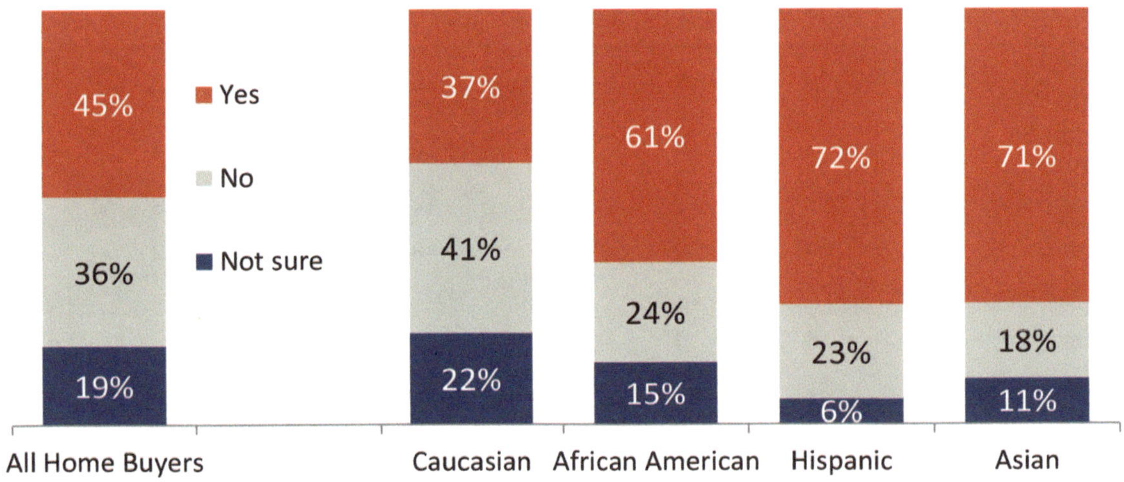

The multigenerational home question is a newer question on the NAHB study, so only two data points exist. This limited time horizon shows the overall preference for this type of home grew from 39% of buyers in 2020 to 45% in 2023, while the share not interested dropped from 39% to 36% and the unsure from 23% to 19% (Fig. 2-13). Two factors are likely behind the rise in popularity of multigenerational homes: high housing costs and the recent pandemic. Sharing a home makes housing more affordable to all involved, plus living in close proximity facilitates intra-generational support for child and adult care.

Figure 2-13. Buyers' Preference for a Multigenerational Home: History

(Percent of Respondents)

	2020	2023
Yes	39	45
No	39	36
Don't Know/Not Sure	23	19

Chapter 3

The Most Wanted & Unwanted Features

86% OF BUYERS WANT LAUNDRY ROOMS & PATIOS

A useful section of NAHB's home buyer preference surveys is an extensive list of features that buyers rate on the same scale, allowing the items on the list to be compared in a consistent manner and ranked. The 2023 survey asked recent and prospective buyers to rate 200+ home and community features using a four-tier scale that emphasizes how each feature influences the buyer's purchase decision:

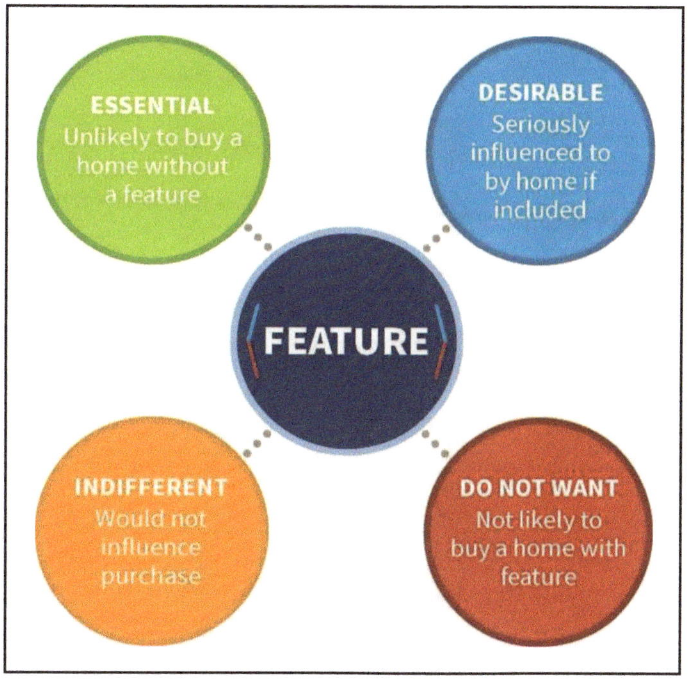

Figure 3-1 shows the "most wanted" features, based on the percentage of buyers rating them either desirable or essential. The chart includes the thirteen features that were rated essential (unlikely to buy a home without it) or desirable (would be seriously influenced to buy home if included) by at least 80% of the buyers. At the top of the list are a laundry room and patio, each rated essential or desirable by 86% of home buyers. ENERGY STAR-rated windows (83%) were second, and exterior lighting (82%) third. After that, four features (ceiling fan, garage storage, front porch and hardwood flooring) are tied at 81%, and five more are tied at 80%.

Four of the 13 most wanted items in Fig. 3-1 are exterior amenities covered in detail in Chapter 7. Landscaping debuted on the 'most wanted' list after its introduction to the NAHB study in 2023. The list also includes two features in the kitchen (walk-in pantry and table space for eating) and two related to energy efficiency (ENERGY STAR windows and appliances).

Figure 3-1. The Most Wanted Features

(Rated Essential or Desirable by At Least 80% of Home Buyers)

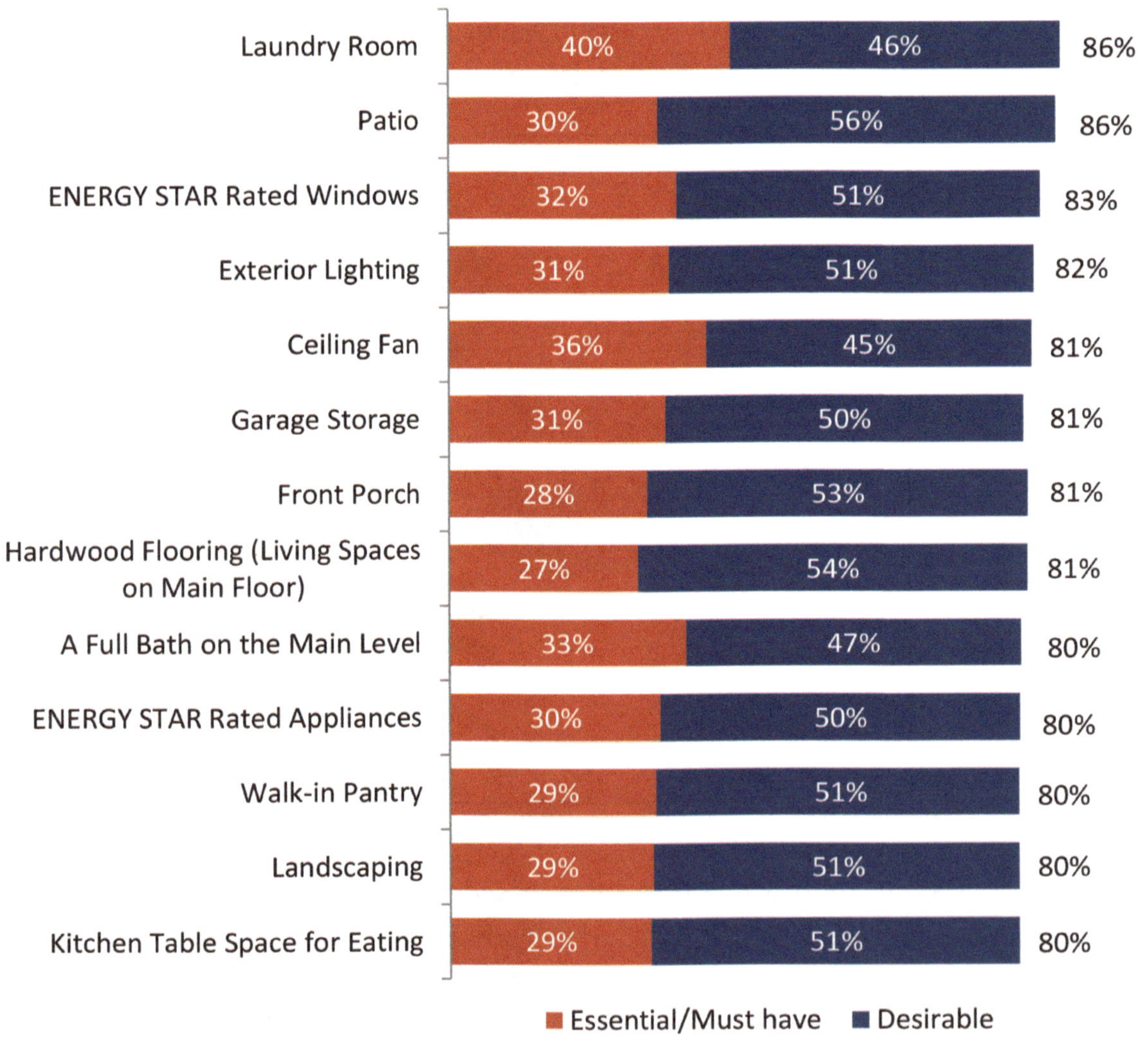

THE MOST WANTED LIST HAS BEEN RELATIVELY STABLE SINCE 2003

The features on the most wanted list have not experienced significant changes over the last 20 years. A laundry room has consistently placed at the very top of the list, and all the features cited as desirable or essential by at least 80% of home buyers in 2023 have remained relatively popular since being included in the survey. None of the essential/desirable shares have been trending upward recently. The share for a patio increased from 73% in 2003 to 86% in 2023. The share for a bathroom on the main level increased from 75% to 80% over the same period. In both cases, however, the increase occurred before the last two surveys (Fig. 3-2).

Four of the 2023 most wanted features reached new historic low points in 2023. The laundry room and ENERGY STAR appliances each edged down one percentage point from its previous low in 2020. Exterior lighting was three points below its previous lows in 2003 and 2018 (85%). The ceiling fan was one point below its previous low recorded in 2003. In all four cases, the percentage changes are modest. These features remain popular among most home buyers.

Figure 3-2. History of the 2023 Most Wanted Features
(Percent of Buyers Rating the Features Essential or Desirable)

	2003	2007	2012	2015	2018	2020	2023
Laundry Room	94	93	93	92	91	87	86
Patio	73	81	83	84	87	82	86
ENERGY STAR-Rated windows	n/a	88	89	87	89	83	83
Exterior Lighting	85	86	90	90	85	87	82
Ceiling Fan	82	85	88	86	85	83	81
Garage Storage	n/a	n/a	86	81	85	77	81
Front Porch	82	79	80	79	79	81	81
Hardwood Flooring (for Living Spaces on the Main Level)	n/a	n/a	n/a	82	83	81	81
Full Bath on the Main Level	75	74	81	83	79	80	80
ENERGY STAR-Rated Appliances	n/a	88	94	90	86	81	80
Walk-in Pantry	83	85	85	80	83	81	80
Landscaping	n/a	n/a	n/a	n/a	n/a	n/a	80
Kitchen table space for eating	n/a	n/a	n/a	80	78	78	80

LAUNDRY ROOMS ARE ESSENTIAL, ALTHOUGH LESS SO WITH ASIAN BUYERS

Many of the most wanted features shown in Fig. 3-1 made the list on the strength of buyers saying the feature was desirable, rather than essential. Hardwood on the main floor's living spaces, for example, is rated at least desirable by 81% of home buyers, but essential by "only" 27%. In some cases, builders may be interested specifically in features that many home buyers consider essential — meaning they are unlikely to buy a home without it.

The laundry room also ranks first by this measure, rated essential by 40% of home buyers, followed by ceiling fan with 36%. In total, ten of the 200-plus features included in the NAHB survey were rated essential by at least 30% of home buyers (Fig. 3-3).

Many features appear on the "most essential" list in Fig. 3-3 and the generally "most wanted" list in Fig. 3-1, but this is not true across the board. A double kitchen sink and a primary bath with both a shower stall and tub are considered essential by at least 30% of buyers but do not make it on the generally most wanted list. On the other hand, five of the most wanted features in Fig 3-1 (front porch, hardwood flooring, walk-in pantry, landscaping, and kitchen table space for eating) did not make it on the most essential list in Fig. 3-3.

Perhaps surprisingly, Asian home buyers are somewhat less likely than others to rate the top two features in Figure 3-3 essential. For example, only 22% of Asian buyers rate the laundry room as essential, compared to 42% of Caucasian and African American buyers, with Hispanic buyers falling halfway in between. Similarly, 24% of Asian buyers rate a ceiling fan essential, compared to over 30% of buyers in the other three tabulated racial/ethnic categories (Fig. 3-4). According to the analysis described in Chapter 12, the difference between Asian and other home buyer preferences for the two features is highly significant. The difference between Hispanic and other home buyers is significant at a lower level for the laundry room.

Figure 3-3. The Most Essential Features

(Rated Essential/Must Have by At Least 30% of Buyers)

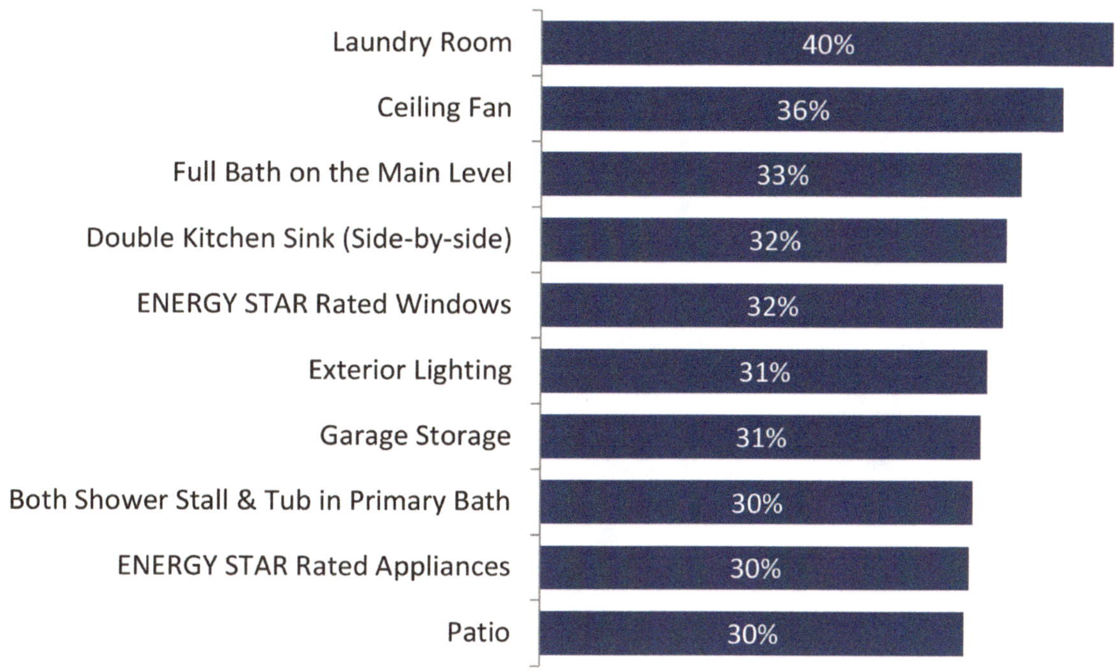

Figure 3-4. Essential Ratings for a Ceiling Fan & Laundry Room by Home Buyer's Race & Ethnicity

(Percent of Buyers Rating Features as Essential)

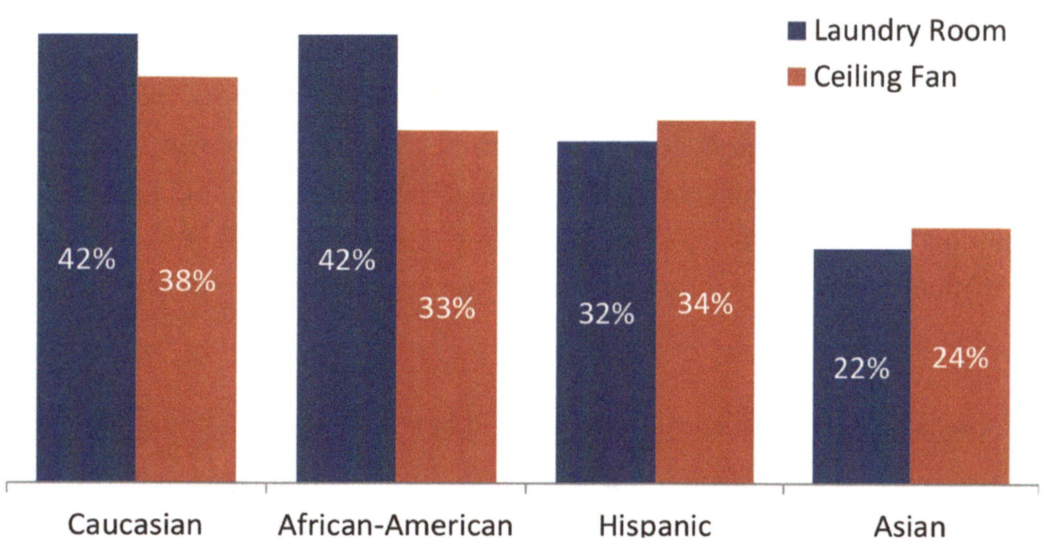

Preferences for a ceiling fan also show one large and statistically significant geographic difference—in the New England Census division. Only 22% of home buyers in New England rated a ceiling fan as essential compared to over 30% in the other eight divisions (Fig. 3-5).

Figure 3-5. Share of Buyers Who Rate a Ceiling Fan Essential by Census Division

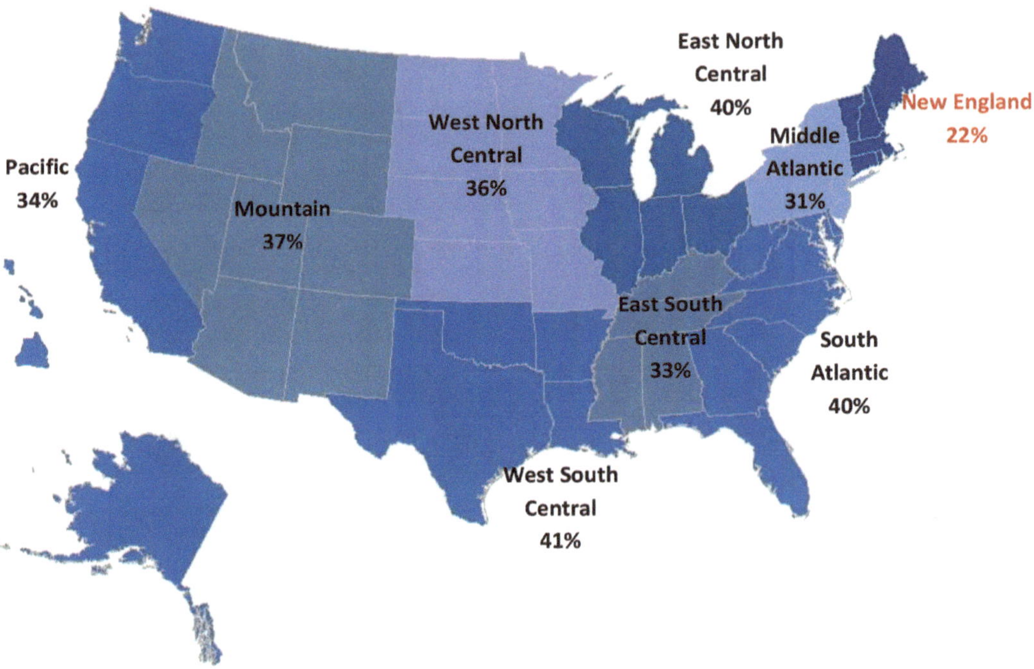

MOST BUYERS WOULD PAY TO UPGRADE THEIR KITCHENS & BATHS

A new question on the 2023 NAHB survey asked home buyers to check the top three areas they would pay more to upgrade. At the top, 71% of buyers would pay extra for a gourmet kitchen (e.g., high-end appliances, cabinets, counters). The majority (65%) would also pay to upgrade the master bath (e.g., freestanding tub, rainfall shower). Chapter 4 discusses preferences for kitchen and bath features. Fewer than half would pay to upgrade the remaining features listed, including 49% for outdoor features, 43% for hardwood flooring throughout the entire house, 36% for a finished basement, and 24% for upgraded exterior material on the front of the house (Fig. 3-6).

Looking at results across the various demographic sub-populations in the study shows that the two most popular upgrades buyers are willing to pay for are a gourmet kitchen and the master bath. This is across geographic divisions, generations, buyer type, household composition, race/ethnic group, income level, or price point (Appendix A, Pages A19-A21).

Figure 3-6. What Are the Top Three Features You Would Pay to Upgrade?
(Percent of Respondents)

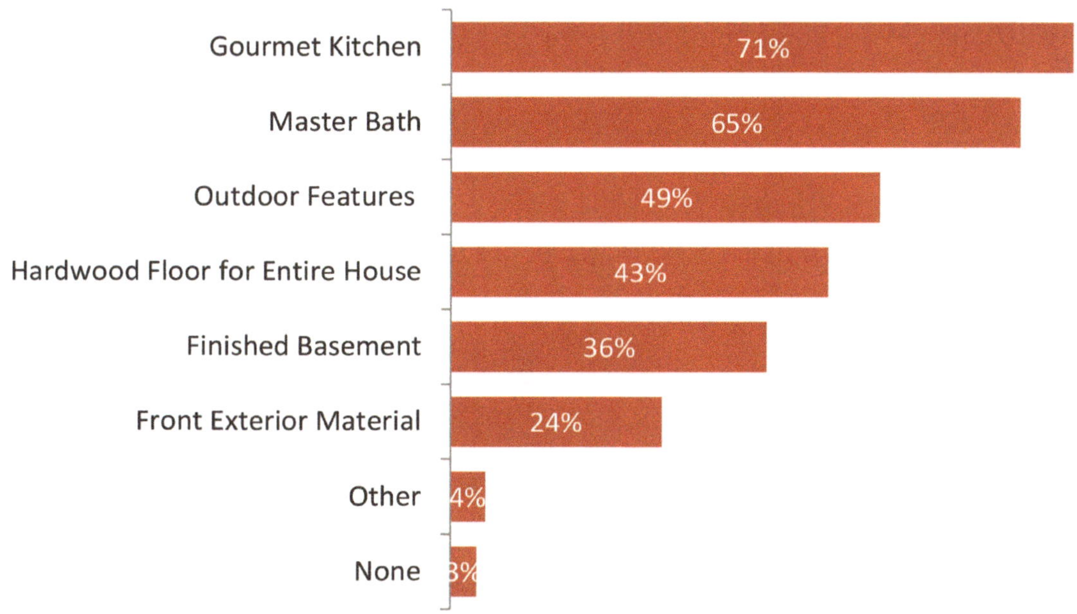

ELEVATORS, GLASS WALLS & WINE CELLARS TOP THE UNWANTED LIST

In addition to features home buyers want, builders should also be able to identify features that a large proportion of their buyers do not want. Figure 3-7 shows the most unwanted features based on the share of buyers rating the item "do not want." Again, a "do not want" rating means buyers are unlikely to purchase a home if it has the feature.

By this criterion, an elevator ranked as the most unwanted feature, explicitly rejected by 47% of buyers, followed by glass walls at 42% and a wine cellar at 41%. These three specialty features (discussed in Chapter 6) are the only items rejected by over 40% of home buyers. Further down the unwanted scale are a group of eight features rated "do not want" by 33% to 35% of buyers: a home in a golf course community, a two-story family room, a home in a community with a daycare center, a pet washing station, a home in a community with a homeowners association, a plant-covered roof, dual toilets in the primary bath and cork flooring for living spaces on the main floor (Fig. 3-7). Three of the eight are community features discussed in Chapter 10.

It's important to remember, however, that a niche market usually exists even for an item as generally unpopular as an elevator. Despite the large share of buyers who do not want elevators, glass walls, or wine cellars, at least one-third of buyers think each of these three features is desirable or better— 12% even rated each one essential. Among the features in Figure 3-7, the pet washing station is the one rated essential or desirable by most buyers (42%).

Figure 3-7. The Most Unwanted Features

(Features Rated "Do Not Want" by at Least 33% of Home Buyers)

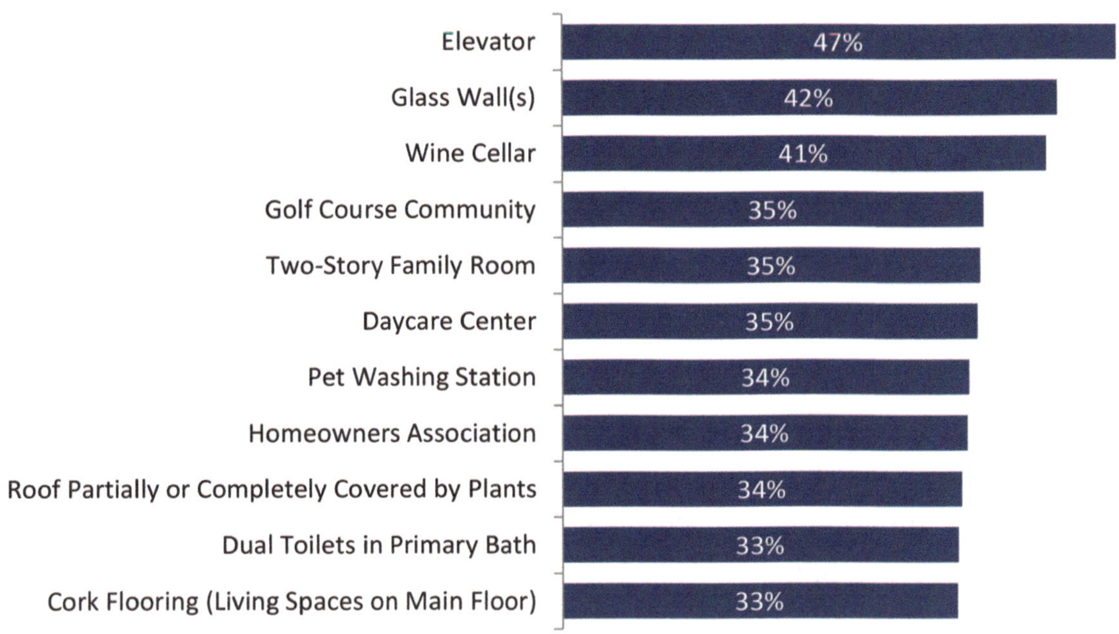

It should probably come as little surprise that buyer resistance to some features often declines among buyers in higher income brackets. One of the reasons buyers may say they do not want a particular feature is fear that it will cost too much, a fear that is naturally more intense among buyers at the lower end of the income distribution. For all three of the most unwanted features in Fig. 3-7, the "do not want" percentage shrinks systematically as the home buyer's income rises. In each case, the spread between buyers with incomes under $50,000 and buyers with incomes of at least $150,000 is 27 or 28 percentage points. For example, 57% of buyers with incomes under $50,000 "do not want" an elevator, compared to only 30% of buyers with incomes of $150,000 or more, and the pattern is similar for glass walls and wine cellars (Fig. 3-8).

Figure 3-8. The Most Unwanted Features by Home Buyer's Income Bracket
(Percent of Buyers Rating the Features "Do Not Want")

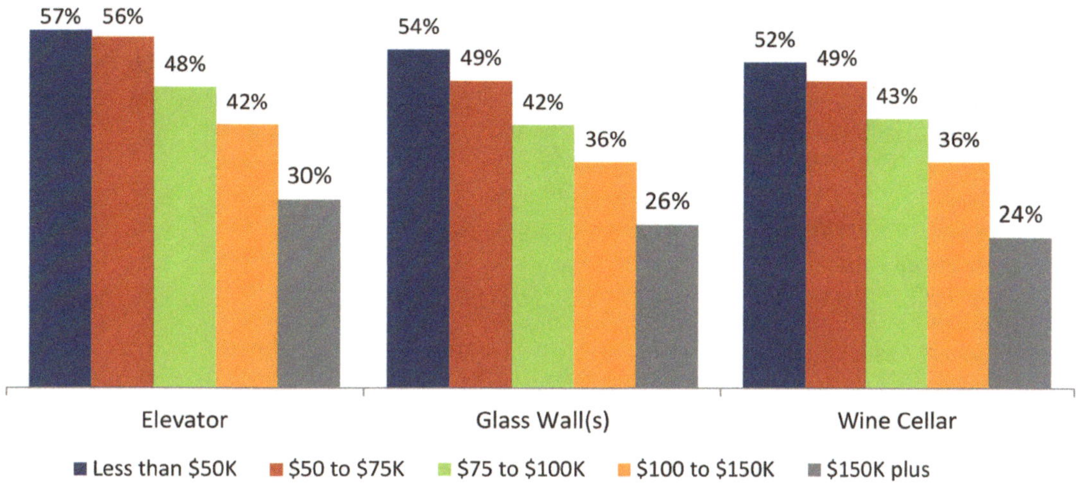

RESISTANCE TO EXOTIC FEATURES IS FADING OVER TIME

Not all the items on the 2023 most unwanted list appear on previous iterations of NAHB's home buyer preference survey back to 2003, as NAHB has added items to the questionnaire over the years. Often, these are newer, more exotic items that have only recently appeared on builders' and buyers' radar screens. For example, pet washing stations were added to the survey in 2015 and glass walls in 2020. Sometimes, buyers assign low ratings to features like these when the features are first introduced, and they end up on the most unwanted list.

Interestingly, buyer resistance to virtually all of the features on the 2023 most unwanted list has faded noticeably over time (Fig. 3-9). For example, the share of buyers who "do not want" an elevator reached a low point of 63% in 2015, then declined more, to 56% percent in 2020 and 47% in 2023. Similarly, the share of buyers who "do not want" a home in a golf course community reached a low point of 53% in 2015, then declined further — to 47% in 2018, 46% in 2020, and 35% in 2023. In fact, all but one of the items on the 2023 most unwanted list reached historic low points in 2023. The sole exception is a two-story family room, which was two points off its historic low in 2023.

Figure 3-9. History of 2023's Most Unwanted Features

(Percent of Buyers Rating the Features "Do Not Want")

	2003	2007	2012	2015	2018	2020	2023
Elevator	69	70	70	63	66	56	47
Glass Wall(s)	n/a	n/a	n/a	n/a	n/a	54	42
Wine Cellar	n/a	n/a	n/a	53	57	48	41
Golf Course Community	73	54	66	53	47	46	35
Two-story Family Room	n/a	33	43	47	47	37	35
Daycare Center	n/a	n/a	n/a	52	50	50	35
Pet Washing Station	n/a	n/a	n/a	54	49	47	34
Homeowners Association	n/a	n/a	n/a	n/a	n/a	n/a	34
Plant Covered Roof	n/a	n/a	n/a	n/a	50	46	34
Dual Toilets in Primary Bath	n/a	n/a	n/a	44	48	40	33
Cork Flooring (for Living Spaces on the Main Floor)	n/a	n/a	n/a	45	47	41	33

Chapter 4

Kitchen & Baths

BUYERS WANT KITCHENS LOADED WITH AMENITIES

The kitchen has typically been the central gathering place of a home, serving more functions than just a place to prepare food. During the COVID-19 pandemic, the kitchen became more prominent, commonly multitasking as an office for remote workers, a classroom for families, and a place for entertaining especially when lockdowns were prevalent. Given its continued importance in the home, NAHB asked buyers to rate 28 kitchen features on the four-tier scale first described in Chapter 3 (essential/must have, desirable, indifferent, or do not want). Results show that buyers want well-equipped kitchens, as more than 50% rated 21 of the 28 features either essential or desirable — every feature from the top of Figure 4-1 down to a trash compactor.

A walk-in pantry and table space for eating are the two most wanted features in a kitchen, given that 80% of buyers rated both as either essential or desirable. After the top two, five features are wanted by more than 70% of buyers: a double-sink (side-by-side) (78%), drinking water filtration (75%), pull-out shelves and central island (each at 74%), and granite or other natural stone countertop (73%). Not far behind, four features are rated essential/desirable by at least two-thirds of all buyers: recessed lighting (69%), customized backsplash (68%), quartz/engineered stone countertop (67%), and special-use storage, such as wine racks and spice drawer (66%).

Figure 4-1. Kitchen Features Rated Essential or Desirable
(Percent of Respondents)

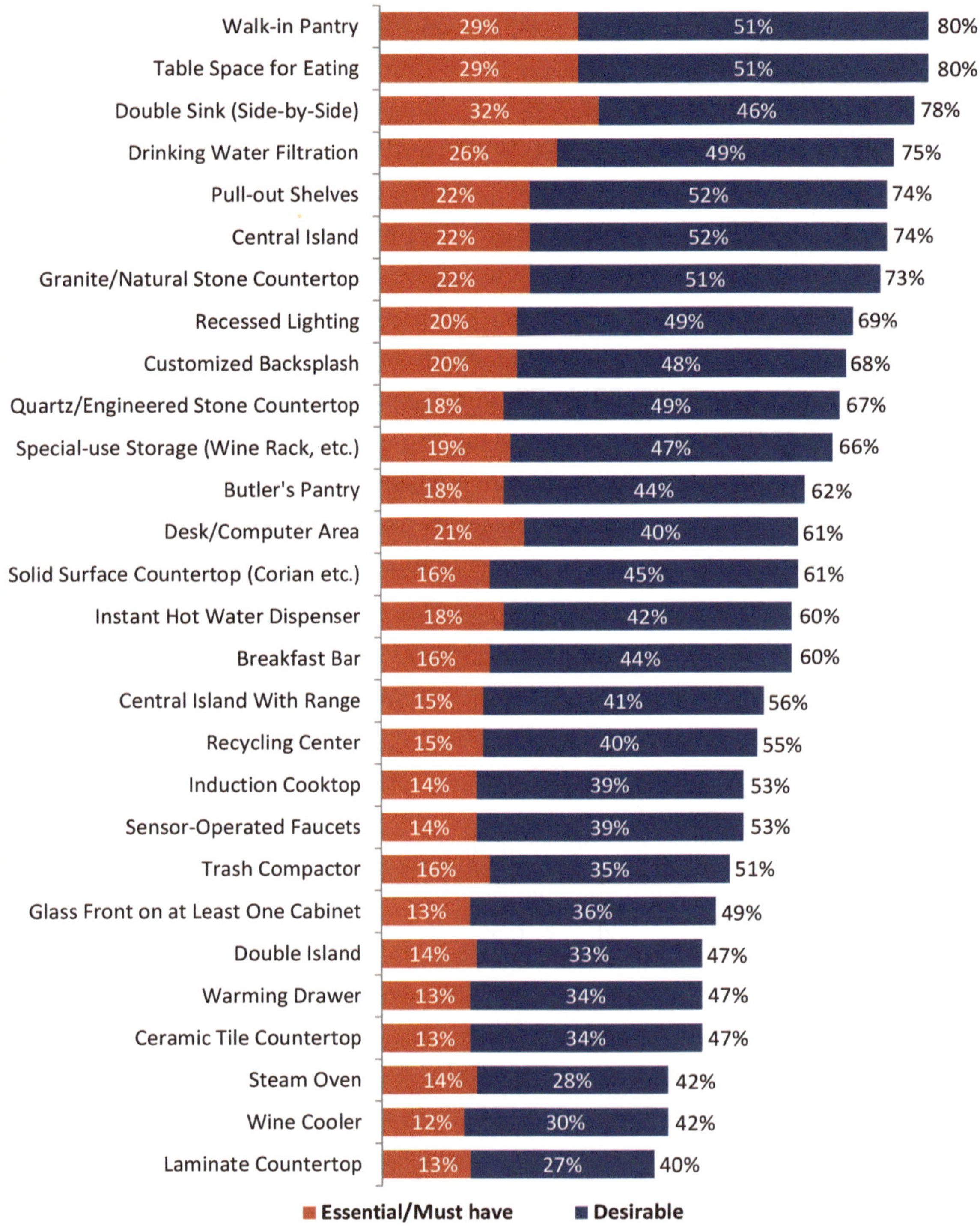

Analyzing how home buyers have rated kitchen features since 2003 helps to demonstrate how the kitchen has increased in importance over the past two decades, given the rising share of buyers who think of these kitchen features as essential or desirable (Fig. 4-2). Below are the kitchen features whose popularity increased by at least 20 percentage points between 2003 and 2023:

- Desk/computer area, up 30 points from 31% to 61%.
- Instant hot water dispenser, up 28 points from 32% to 60%.
- Recycling center, up 27 points from 28% to 55%.
- Trash compactor, up 23 points from 28% to 51%.
- Drinking water filtration system, up 21 points from 54% to 75%.

Many of the features in Figure 4-2 appeared on the survey in 2015, and some of them have already shown rising desirability trends as well. At the top of this list, with increases of at least 15 percentage points between 2015 and 2023, are:

- Butler's pantry, up 20 points from 42% to 62%.
- Double island, up 19 points from 28% to 47%.
- Warming drawer, up 17 points from 30% to 47%.
- Sensor-operated faucets, up 15 points from 38% to 53%.
- Wine cooler, up 15 points from 27% to 42%.

MILLENNIALS MORE LIKELY THAN BOOMERS TO PREFER SOME KITCHEN FEATURES

When analyzing by generation, Millennial (born 1981 to 1996) home buyers are more likely to want certain kitchen features than Boomers (born 1946 to 1964) (Fig. 4-3). A steam oven is desirable or essential to 62% of Millennials but only to 30% of Baby Boomers – a 32-point difference between these age groups. Likewise, a home with a double kitchen island (66%) and wine cooler (61%) influences Millennials to buy a home, compared to only 36% and 33% of Boomers, respectively. On the other hand, Gen X (born 1965 to 1980) home buyers are in the middle since they rank steam oven (48%), double island (53%), and wine cooler (46%) in between their Millennial and Boomer counterparts. As for the youngest generation, Gen Z (born 1997 or later), 57% favor all three features, slightly lower preferences than among Millennials. Six additional kitchen features show a similar dynamic. Millennials are significantly more likely than Boomers (by at least 20-points) to want laminate countertops, ceramic tile countertops, warming drawer,

Figure 4-2. Kitchen Features History
(Percent of Buyers Rating the Features Essential or Desirable)

	2003	2007	2012	2015	2018	2020	2023
Walk-in Pantry	83	85	85	80	83	81	80
Table Space for Eating	n/a	n/a	n/a	n/a	78	78	80
Double Sink (Side-by-Side)	n/a	n/a	n/a	79	81	81	78
Drinking Water Filtration	54	69	69	70	68	76	75
Pull-out Shelves	n/a	n/a	n/a	67	73	68	74
Central Island	74	79	76	77	76	77	74
Granite/Natural Stone Countertop	n/a	70	71	71	75	73	73
Recessed Lighting	n/a	n/a	n/a	69	69	69	69
Customized Backsplash	n/a	n/a	n/a	66	68	69	68
Quartz/Engineered Stone Countertop	n/a	44	43	49	60	60	67
Special Use Storage (Wine Rack, etc.)	59	65	56	57	63	60	66
Butler's Pantry	n/a	n/a	n/a	42	57	52	62
Desk/Computer Area	31	37	65	61	51	60	61
Solid Surface Countertop (Corian etc.)	64	60	62	58	54	61	61
Instant Hot Water Dispenser	32	43	52	54	47	59	60
Breakfast Bar	n/a	n/a	n/a	60	56	64	60
Central Island with Range	48	61	45	45	48	50	56
Recycling Center	28	40	43	48	48	49	55
Induction Cooktop	n/a	n/a	n/a	n/a	42	48	53
Sensor-operated Faucets	n/a	n/a	n/a	38	44	53	53
Trash Compactor	28	34	38	38	38	49	51
Glass Front on at Least One Cabinet	n/a	n/a	n/a	45	39	47	49
Double Island	n/a	n/a	n/a	28	35	40	47
Warming Drawer	n/a	n/a	n/a	30	34	40	47
Ceramic Tile Countertop	33	46	31	35	31	39	47
Steam Oven	n/a	n/a	n/a	n/a	25	33	42
Wine Cooler	n/a	n/a	n/a	27	30	38	42
Laminate Countertop	29	23	20	23	24	34	40

Figure 4-3. Kitchen Features Rated Essential/Desirable by Generation
Largest Margins Between Millennials and Boomers
(Percent of Respondents)

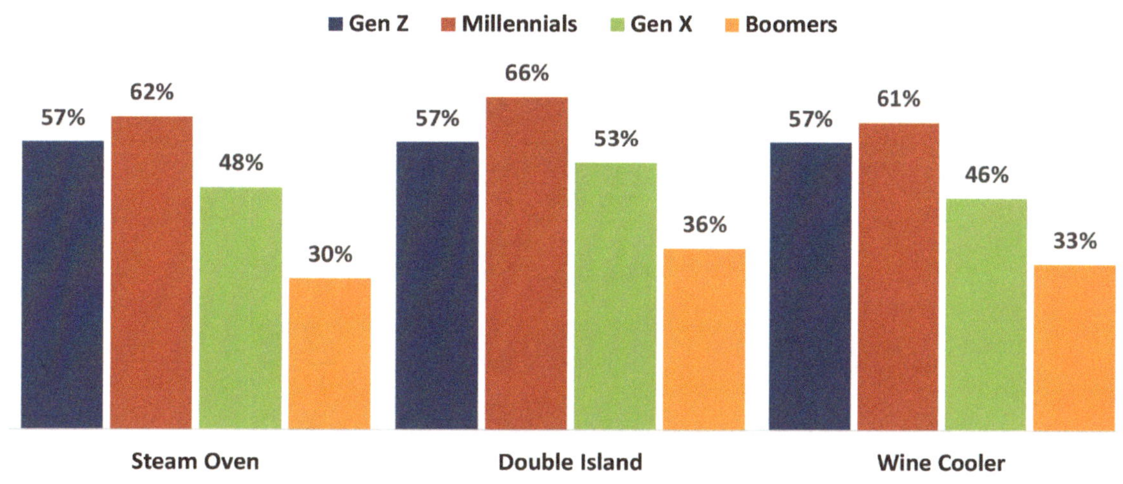

central island with range, trash compactor, and sensor-operated faucets (Appendix A, Pages A79-A81). In every one of these cases, age has a statistically significant impact on buyer preferences, even after controlling for differences in income and other factors, as explained in Chapter 12.

APPROXIMATELY ONE-THIRD DO NOT WANT LAMINATE COUNTERTOPS

As explained in the previous chapter, buyers responding to the survey also had the option to rate features 'do not want' in cases when they are unlikely to purchase a home if it included that feature. Looking exclusively at the kitchen, laminate countertops is the most likely item to be rejected by buyers (32% do not want it), followed closely by a wine cooler (31%). This is consistent with where these items fell in Figure 4-1 (i.e., the bottom portion). Another four kitchen features are rejected by at least 20% of buyers: ceramic tile countertop (25%), steam oven (23%), glass front on at least one cabinet (22%), and double island (20%) (Fig. 4-4).

Figure 4-4. Kitchen Features NOT Wanted by Home Buyers
(Percent of Respondents Rating Features "Do Not Want")

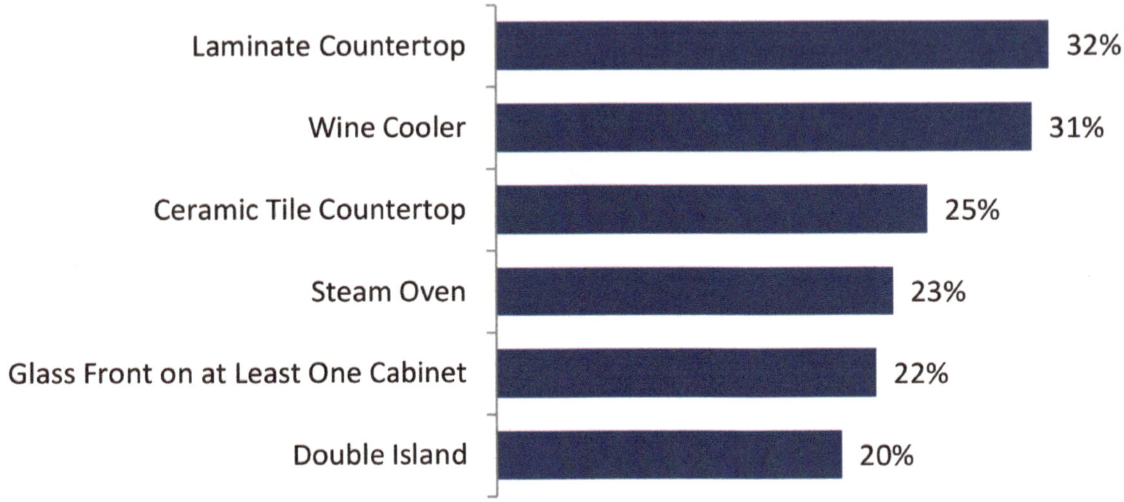

HOME BUYERS WANT LOTS OF AMENITIES IN PRIMARY BATH

Results from the 2023 NAHB survey show the importance of bathrooms, especially the primary bathroom, to home buyers. Of the 18 bath features buyers were asked to rate on the essential/desirable/indifferent/unwanted scale, 14 received an essential or desirable rating from more than 50% of buyers — every feature from the top of Figure 4-5 down to a skylight in primary bath.

At the top of buyers' wish list for bathrooms are three for the primary bath: a shower stall and tub (78%), a linen closet (76%), and a private toilet compartment (70%). Slightly lower majorities also want the primary bath to have a double vanity (67%), multiple shower heads (63%), body spray panel (60%), and a whirlpool tub (59%). Other bath features that positively influence the purchase decision of more than 60% of home buyers include a white toilet, tub, and sink (67%), ceramic tile walls (65%), and a granite vanity (64%).

Figure 4-5. Bathroom Features Rated Essential or Desirable
(Percent of Respondents)

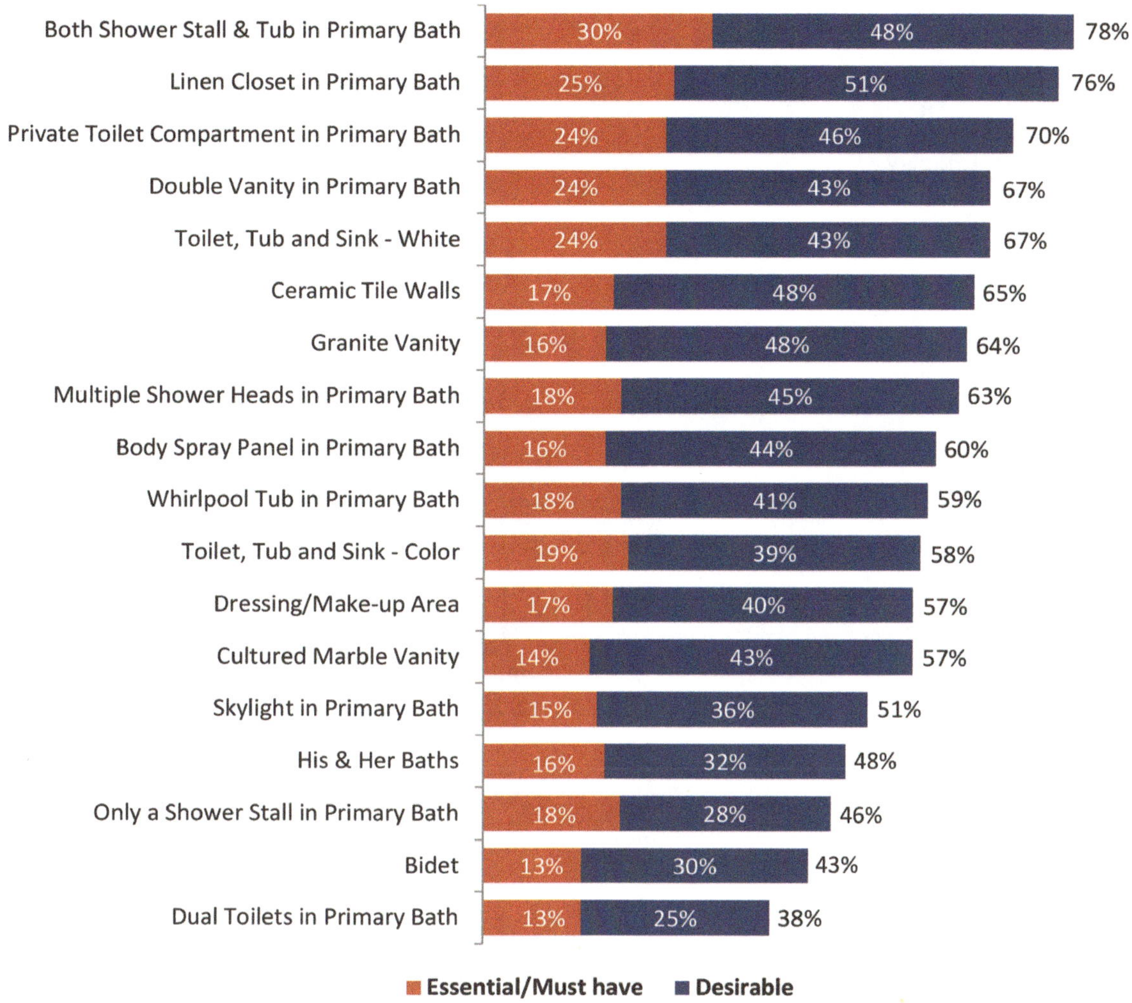

Figure 4-6 shows that a shower stall & tub and a linen closet in the primary bath have consistently been the two most wanted bathroom features for 20 years. Other primary bath features have gained significance for buyers over time. For example, a toilet compartment is wanted by 70% of buyers in 2023, compared to 54% in 2003. Similarly, preference for multiple shower heads is at 63%, up from 50% in 2003.

Figure 4-6. Bathroom Features History
(Percent of Buyers Rating the Features Essential or Desirable)

	2003	2007	2012	2015	2018	2020	2023
Both Shower Stall & Tub in Primary Bath ^	73	81	82	79	73	74	78
Linen Closet in Primary Bath*^	89	90	90	75	78	76	76
Private Toilet Compartment in Primary Bath*^	54	61	59	62	65	67	70
Toilet, Tub, & Sink - White	34	49	34	54	63	65	67
Double Vanity in Primary Bath^	n/a	n/a	n/a	69	71	69	67
Ceramic Tile Walls	56	68	65	63	62	62	65
Granite Vanity	n/a	n/a	n/a	59	61	65	64
Multiple Shower Heads in Primary Bath^	50	55	55	55	57	59	63
Body Spray Panel in Primary Bath^	n/a	n/a	n/a	n/a	56	56	60
Whirlpool Tub in Primary Bath*^	56	60	61	53	54	56	59
Toilet, Tub, & Sink - Color	34	49	34	36	47	44	58
Dressing/Make-up Area	50	58	48	49	53	52	57
Cultured Marble Vanity	n/a	n/a	n/a	47	48	55	57
Skylight in Primary Bath^	n/a	n/a	n/a	45	47	47	51
His & Her Baths	n/a	n/a	n/a	28	34	40	48
Only a Shower Stall in Primary Bath^	n/a	n/a	n/a	32	36	44	46
Bidet	n/a	n/a	n/a	n/a	n/a	37	43
Dual Toilets in Primary Bath^	n/a	n/a	n/a	22	24	34	38

* Prior to 2015, the questionnaire did not specify that the feature was in the master bath.
^ Prior to 2020, the questionnaire referred to "master" instead of "primary."

SOME BATH FEATURES BECOME MORE POPULAR AS PRICE POINT INCREASES

Generally, the more buyers expect to pay for a home, the fancier they expect the bathrooms to be. For some features, the positive correlation is particularly strong. Figure 4-7 showcases the three bath features where the difference in preference between those expecting to pay the least (less than $150,00) and most ($500,000 or more) is at least 14 points: double vanity (58% vs. 77%), private toilet compartment (62% vs. 76%) and granite vanity (59% vs. 73%) (fig. 4-7). The statistical analysis described in Chapter 12 indicates each of these differences is highly significant.

Figure 4-7. Bathroom Features Rated Essential/Desirable, With 14+ Point Difference by Price Point
(Percent of Respondents)

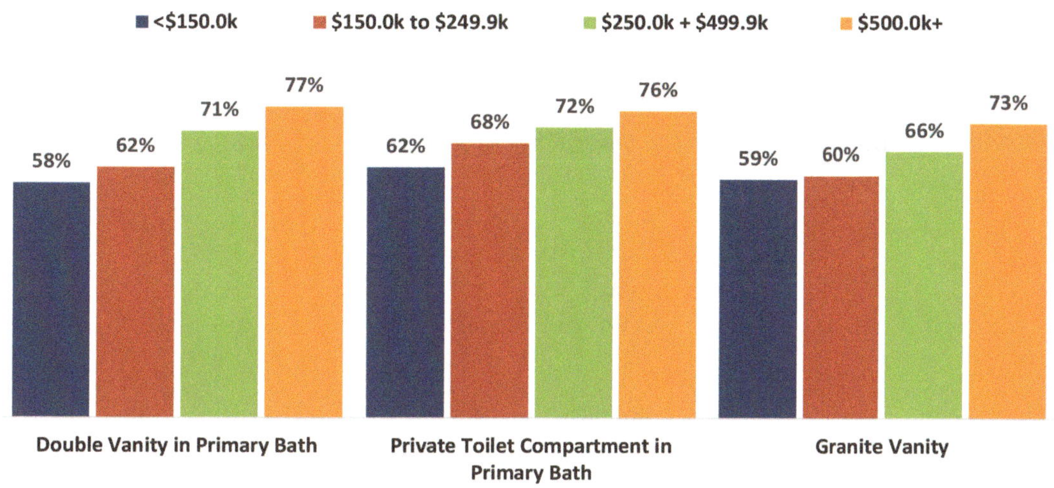

ONE-THIRD OF BUYERS DO NOT WANT DUAL TOILETS IN PRIMARY BATH

Five of the 18 bathroom features in the survey received a 'do not want' rating from more than 20% of buyers, indicating they would be unlikely to purchase a home with dual toilets in primary bath (33%), a bidet (27%), His & Her Baths (24%), and only a shower stall (23%) and a skylight (22%) in the primary bath (Fig. 4-8).

Figure 4-8. Bath Features NOT Wanted by Home Buyers
(Percent of Respondents Rating Features "Do Not Want")

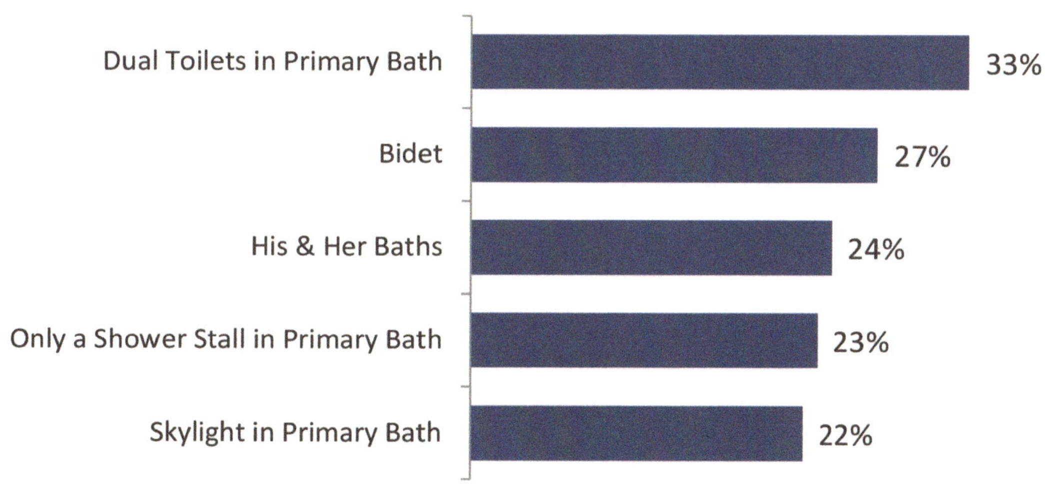

TYPICAL HOME BUYER WANTS TWO BATHROOMS

The NAHB survey also asked buyers how many bathrooms they would like in their homes, considering the additional cost of $25,000 for each full bathroom. Results show that a typical home buyer prefers a home with two bathrooms. Overall, 16% want one or one-and-a-half baths, a plurality of 39% want two baths, 24% prefer two-and-half, 12% prefer three, and 9% want more than three (Fig. 4-9).

Figure 4-9. Number of Bathrooms Preferred, by Price Buyers Expect to Pay for the Home
(Percent of Respondents)

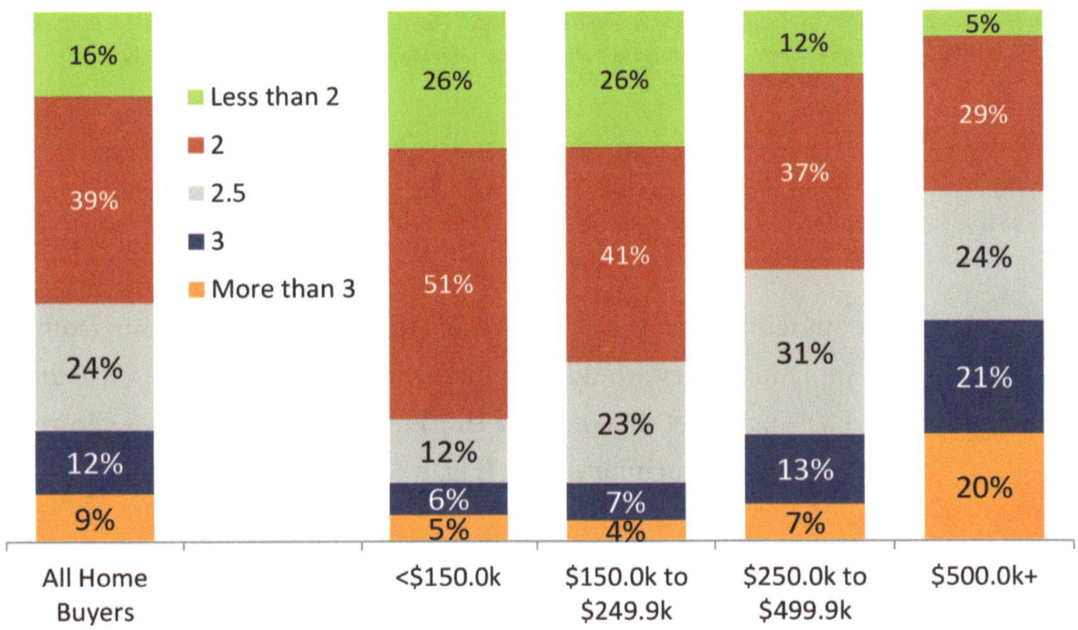

In general, the higher the price buyers expect to pay for the home (or paid recently), the more bathrooms they want. One way to see this is by looking at the share of buyers who want at least three full baths by house price, which is 11% of those expecting to pay less than $250,000, 20% of those expecting to pay $250,000 to $499,999, and 41% of those expecting to pay $500,000 or more (Fig. 4-9). Again, the analysis of Chapter 12 shows that these effects are statistically significant.

PERCENTAGE OF HOME BUYERS WANTING TWO BATHROOMS AT ALL-TIME HIGH

Figure 4-10 shows the history of responses to the question on preferred number of bathrooms. The share whose first preference is to have two baths reached a series high of 39% in 2023 after rising from 37% in 2020. On the other hand, the share of buyers interested in 3+ baths dropped from 26% to 21% since the 2020 survey, while the share who prefer one or one-and-a-half baths remained essentially unchanged, going from 17% to 16%.

Figure 4-10. Number of Bathrooms Preferred: History
(Percent of Respondents)

	2003	2007	2012	2015	2018	2020	2023
1	3	1	1	3	3	5	5
1 1/2	18	10	10	14	11	12	11
2	34	36	35	38	35	37	39
2 1/2	27	28	30	26	29	21	24
3	11	14	13	10	12	13	12
3 1/2	4	7	6	5	5	6	6
4 or more	3	3	4	3	4	7	3

Chapter 5

Windows, Doors, Flooring & Decorative Features

ENERGY STAR RATED WINDOWS RANK HIGH AMONG BUYERS

Using the same four-tiered scale of essential/desirable/indifferent/unwanted first introduced in Chapter 3, home buyers rated various window types and materials for their home. Their top three choices demonstrate that energy efficiency is the main deciding factor for windows. The most wanted window type, by 83% of buyers, is ENERGY-STAR rated windows (32% essential; 51% desirable), followed by tripled-pane insulating glass, wanted by 77% of home buyers (23% essential; 54% desirable); and low e-insulating glass, preferred by 67% of home buyers (19% essential; 48% desirable). The remaining window options were essential or desirable to smaller majorities of buyers, except for gas filled (argon or krypton) insulating glass, which appeals to 47% of buyers (Fig. 5-1).

Figure 5-1. Window Features Rated Essential or Desirable

(Share of Respondents)

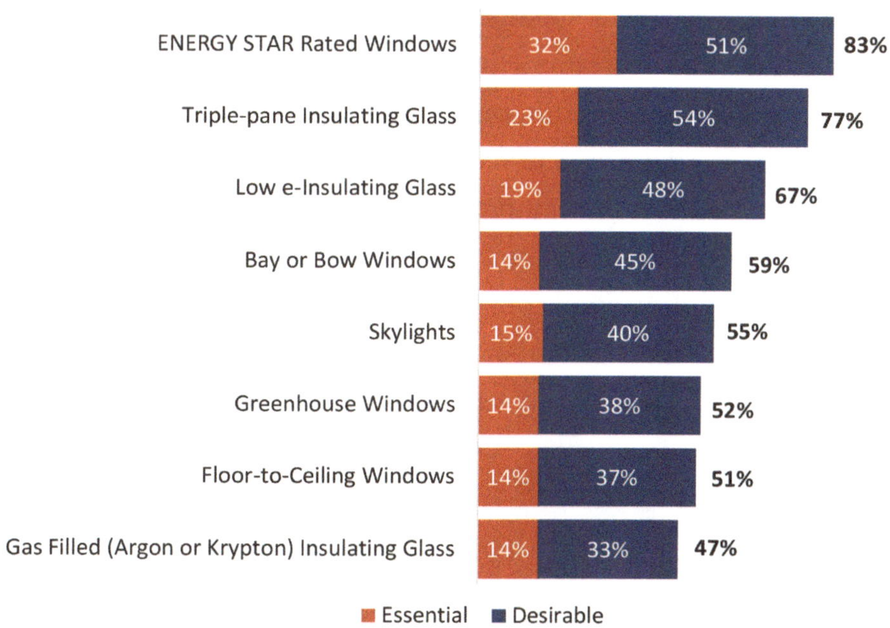

In fact, ENERGY STAR windows ranked third most wanted out of a list of over 200 home features, as discussed in Chapter 3. Looking at changes in window preferences from 2020 to 2023, only one stands out: the share of buyers interested in greenhouse windows rose 7 points, from 45% to 52%. Longer term, the appeal of triple-pane insulating glass has grown significantly over the past 20 years, going from 47% of buyers considering it essential/desirable in 2003 to 77% in 2023 (Fig. 5-2).

Figure 5-2. Windows Features – History

(Percent of Respondents Rating Essential or Desirable)

	2003	2007	2012	2015	2018	2020	2023
ENERGY STAR Rated Windows	n/a	88	89	87	89	83	83
Triple-pane Insulating Glass	47	n/a	69	70	77	73	77
Low e-Insulating Glass	n/a	n/a	n/a	66	62	65	67
Bay or Bow Windows	59	60	58	59	52	57	59
Skylights	43	52	52	53	48	54	55
Greenhouse Windows	19	27	32	38	36	45	52
Floor-to-Ceiling Windows	n/a	n/a	n/a	n/a	n/a	48	51
Gas Filled Insulating Glass	n/a	n/a	n/a	47	43	44	47

ENERGY EFFICIENT WINDOWS ARE PARTICULARLY IMPORTANT TO OLDER BUYERS

Although energy-efficient window types and materials are wanted by the majority of buyers of all age groups, the desirability of these features grows significantly with age. In fact, there is at least an 18-point difference in the share of buyers under 35 who rate them essential/desirable and those 65 or older. ENERGY STAR windows, for example, are wanted by 64% of buyers under 35, compared with 87% of those in the 65+ group. Similarly, preference for triple pane insulating glass jumps from 62% among the youngest cohort to 81% among the oldest, while for low e-insulating glass, the shares rise from 55% to 73%, respectively (Fig. 5-3). As described in Chapter 12, the effect of the buyer's age on these window preferences is statistically significant.

Figure 5-3. Preference for Energy Efficient Windows by Buyer's Age

(Percent of Respondents Rating Essential or Desirable)

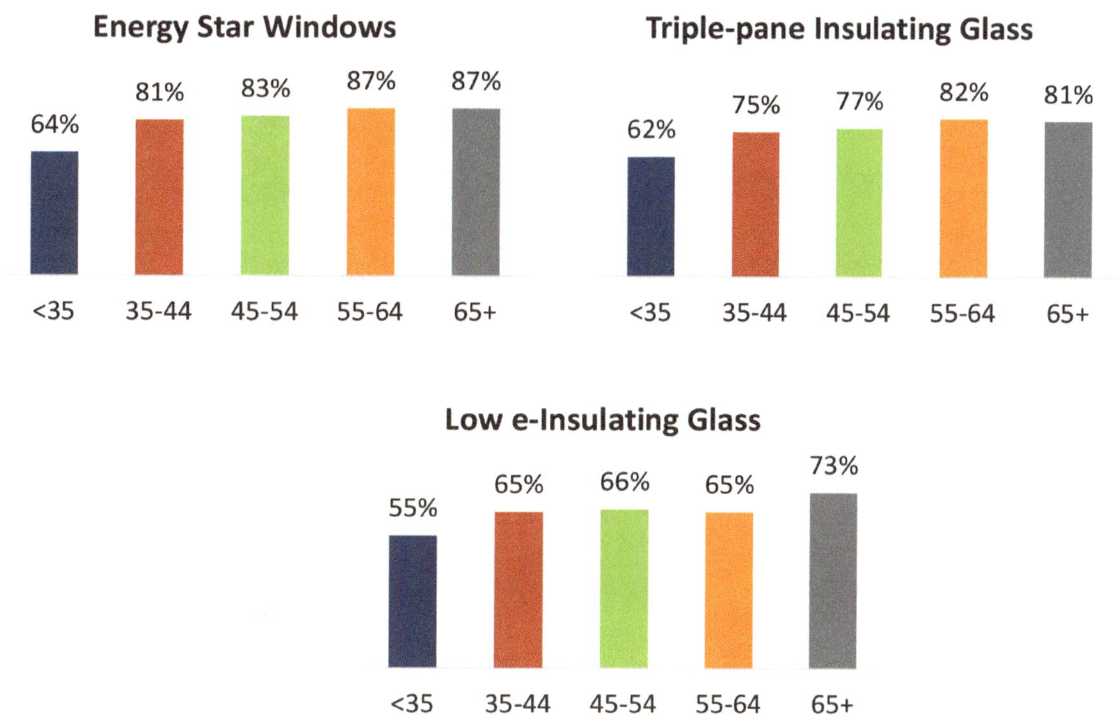

BUYERS ARE UNLIKELY TO REJECT HOMES DUE TO WINDOWS

Unlike other home features that cause a strong negative reaction from a sizable share of buyers, fewer than 25% of buyers would reject a potential home because of any particular window type or material. At most, 24% would turn down a house because of floor-to-ceiling windows, and 20% would do the same for skylights. None of the remaining windows listed would cause more than 17% of buyers to pass on a house, least of all the three most wanted, energy-efficient windows (Fig. 5-4).

Figure 5-4. Window Features NOT Wanted

(Percent of Respondents Rating 'Do Not Want')

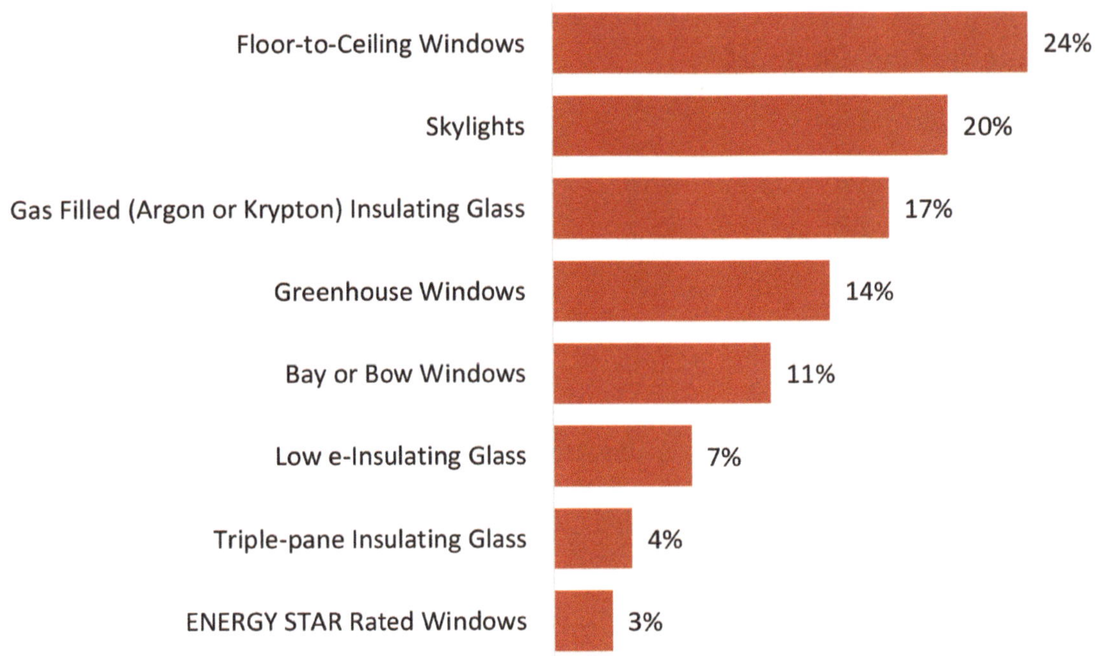

OVER HALF OF BUYERS WANT ALL FOUR EXTERIOR DOOR OPTIONS

When asked about exterior door(s) for their home, all four options were rated essential or desirable by more than 50% of home buyers, with very little difference (6 points) between the highest and lowest rated options. A similar share of 64% want sliding patio doors (20% essential; 44% desirable) and hinged/French patio doors (16% essential; 48% desirable), followed by 60% for entry door with decorative glass panels (16% essential; 44% desirable) and 58% for double main entry door (17% essential; 41% desirable) (Fig. 5-5).

Figure 5-5. Exterior Doors Rated Essential or Desirable

(Percent of Respondents)

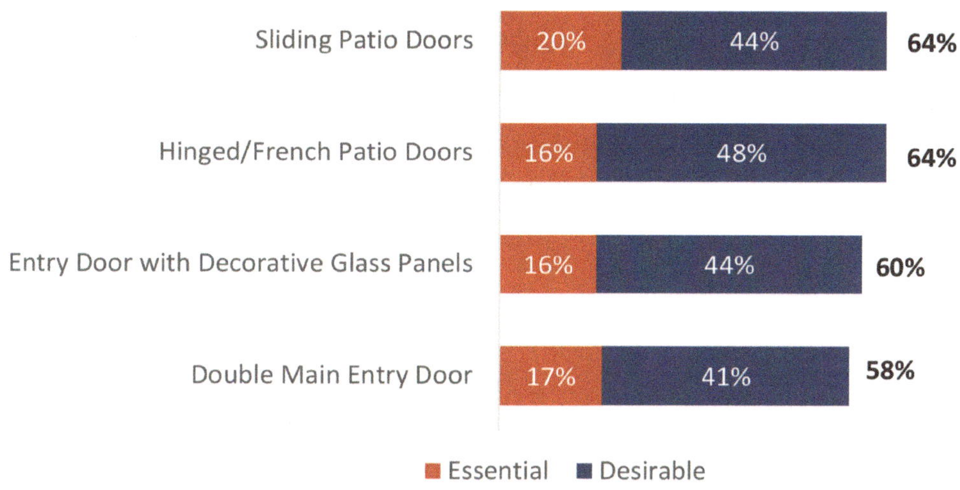

The only significant change among the exterior door options from 2020 to 2023 was for a double main entry door, with the share rating it essential/desirable increasing 10 points from 48% in 2020 to 58% in 2023. NAHB started asking about exterior doors in the 2015 NAHB survey. All four exterior door options have registered gains in popularity since 2015 (Fig. 5-6).

Figure 5-6. Exterior Doors – History

(Percent of Respondents Rating Essential or Desirable)

Sliding Patio Door	55	57	63	64
Hinged/French Patio Door	58	58	63	64
Entry Door with Decorative Glass Panels	52	53	58	60
Double Main Entry Door	44	48	48	58

POPULARITY OF FRENCH PATIO DOORS RISES WITH INCOME & PRICE POINT

Home buyer income has a statistically strong, positive effect on preferences for hinged/French patio doors. While almost three-fourths (74%) of home buyers with an income of $150,000 or more rate this feature as essential or desirable, this percentage falls to 57% of those with an income of under $50,000. The same is almost true when analyzing by the price buyers expect to pay: 73% of buyers who expect to pay at least $500,000 for their home want hinged/French patio doors, compared to 59% of buyers who expect to pay less than $250,000 (Fig. 5-7).

Figure 5-7. Hinged/French Patio Door by Income and by Price Point

(Percent of Respondents Rating Essential or Desirable)

EXTERIOR DOORS ACHIEVE LOW 'DO NOT WANT' SHARES

Exterior doors are unlikely to be why home buyers walk away from a potential new home. In fact, none of the four options listed in the survey received an 'unwanted' rating by more than 15% of buyers. Hinged/French patio doors, wanted by 64% of buyers, was rejected by the smallest share — a mere 10% (Fig. 5-8).

Figure 5-8. Exterior Doors NOT Wanted

(Percent of Respondents Rating 'Do Not Want')

HARDWOOD REMAINS THE FAVORED MAIN FLOOR OPTION

Eighty-one percent of home buyers rate hardwood as essential or desirable when asked about the type of flooring they want for the main level living space. Of those, 27% think hardwood is essential and would likely not buy a house without it. The only other flooring option rated essential/desirable by most home buyers was tile, at 68%. The next three flooring options were carpet at 48%, laminate (47%), and bamboo flooring (45%). Cork is the least favorite flooring choice, with only a third (33%) of home buyers wanting this option (Fig. 5-9).

Figure 5-9. Flooring for Main Level Rated Essential or Desirable

(Share of Respondents)

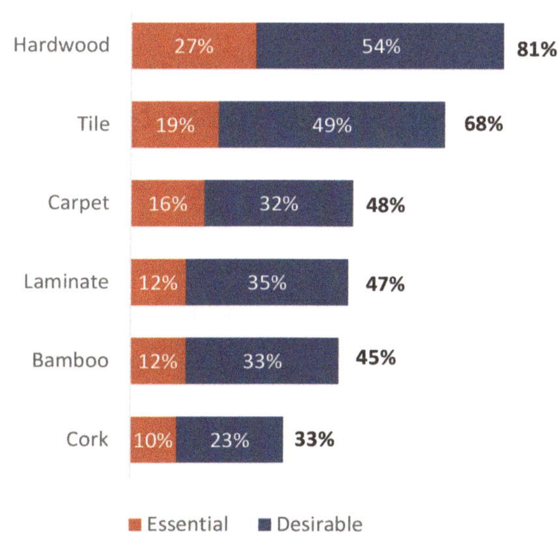

Hardwood has remained buyers' top choice for the living spaces of the main floor since adding the question to the NAHB survey in 2015. Cork, on the other hand, has remained buyers least favorable flooring option throughout this period. Curiously, the share of buyers rating cork essential/desirable rose the most from 2020 to 2023 (6 points), from 27% to 33%. In fact, the share of buyers interested in cork in 2023 (33%) is double what it was just eight years earlier in 2015 (16%) (Fig. 5-10).

Figure 5-10. Flooring for Main Level – History

(Percent of Respondents Rating Essential or Desirable)

	2015	2018	2020	2023
Hardwood	82	83	81	81
Tile	60	59	64	68
Carpet	45	42	44	48
Laminate	33	30	45	47
Bamboo	32	36	40	45
Cork	16	20	27	33

CORK FLOORING IS THE LEAST POPULAR FLOORING TYPE

Figure 5-11 exhibits the share of home buyers who do not want each flooring type for the living areas of the main level of their next home. Interestingly, cork achieved the same percentage of home buyers who do not want it (33%) as those who rated it as essential or desirable (33%). It is important to keep in mind that the survey question asks about flooring on the main floor's living spaces. Even though buyers often do not want cork for that general purpose, some may find it acceptable for a more specialized use—for example, on kitchen floors. Cork has some well-known disadvantages (being less durable and more susceptible to damage than many other types of flooring) but also some advantages—relatively low cost, for one. Some environmentalists favor cork because it is a natural material that is biodegradable and renewable.

Not all sub-populations of buyers reject cork to the same degree, especially among different racial/ethnic groups. For example, while only 13% of Hispanic buyers would reject cork, the share is a much higher (38%) among Caucasian buyers. Moreover, this difference remains statistically significant after controlling for differences in Caucasian and Hispanic buyers incomes (Appendix A, Page A6) and other characteristics. Around a quarter of buyers do not want to see carpet (27%) or bamboo (23%) on the main level living spaces of their homes (Fig. 5-11).

Figure 5-11. Flooring NOT Wanted

(Percent of Respondents Rating 'Do Not Want')

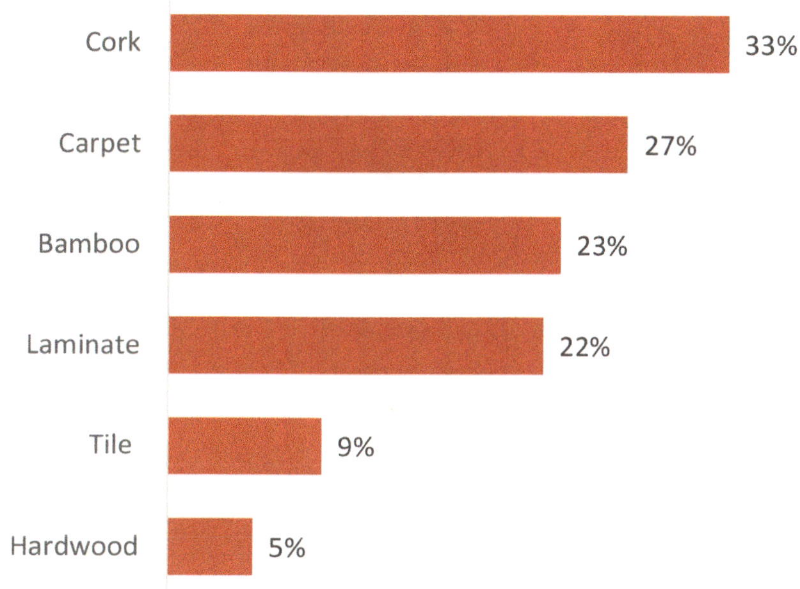

CEILING FAN WANTED BY AT LEAST FOUR OUT OF FIVE HOME BUYERS

Approximately four out of every five home buyers (81%) want a ceiling fan in the home, with 36% of them rating this feature as essential (the second highest 'essential' share among more than 200 features in the survey, as shown in Fig. 3-3). Over 50% of home buyers would also be positively influenced by built-in shelving (72%), ceiling crown molding (64%), wood burning fireplace (59%), gas fireplace (58%), built-in kitchen seating (53%), and exposed beams (51%). There are only two decorative features wanted by a minority of buyers: chair rails (46%) and tray ceiling (44%) (Fig. 5-12).

Figure 5-12. Decorative Features Rated Essential or Desirable

(Share of Respondents)

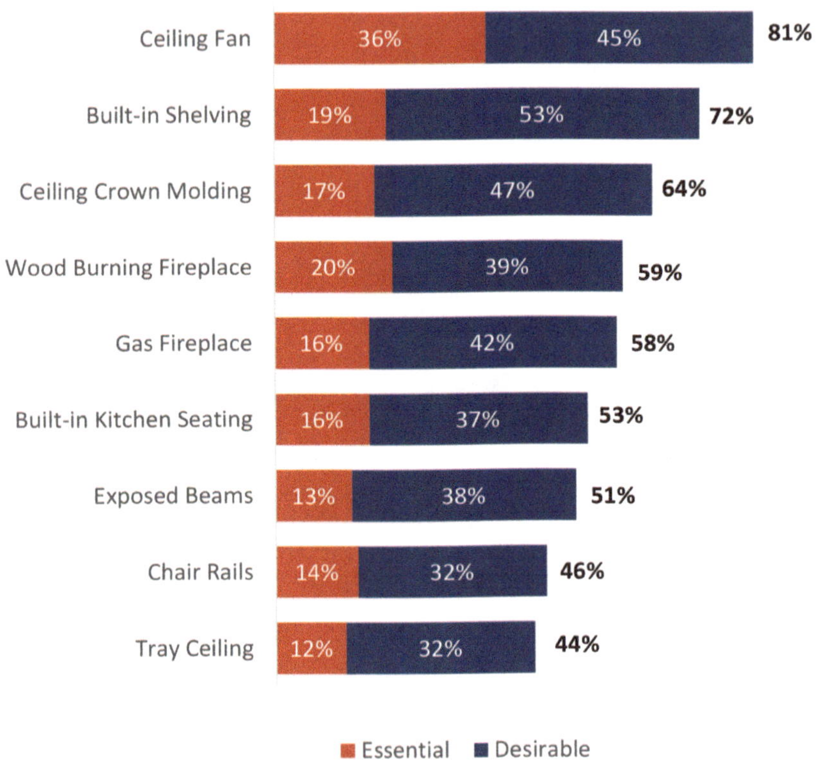

Built-in kitchen seating (+10 points, from 43% to 53%), wood burning fireplace (+8 points, 51% to 59%), and exposed beams (+7 points, 44% to 51%) had the most change in desirability from 2020 to 2023. When looking back over the last two decades, built-in kitchen seating (24% to 53%) and exposed beams (22% to 51%) have experienced the most significant growth in popularity, more than doubling the share of buyers who find them essential/desirable between 2003 and 2023 (Fig. 5-13).

Figure 5-13. Decorative Features – History

(Percent of Respondents Rating Essential or Desirable)

	2003	2007	2012	2015	2018	2020	2023
Ceiling Fan	82	85	88	86	85	83	81
Built-in Shelving	75	72	71	68	67	68	72
Ceiling Crown Molding	51	61	62	62	63	63	64
Wood Burning Fireplace	52	45	47	49	48	51	59
Gas Fireplace	44	48	49	52	55	57	58
Built-in Kitchen Seating	24	29	33	35	39	43	53
Exposed Beams	22	29	31	38	41	44	51
Chair Rails	37	39	41	40	39	42	46
Tray Ceiling	n/a	n/a	n/a	35	36	43	44

INCOME DRIVES DESIRE FOR MANY DECORATIVE FEATURES

Not surprisingly, the buyer's income has a statistically significant and positive impact on preferences for all nine of the decorative features listed in the survey, except for ceiling fans (which are popular among buyers irrespective of their incomes). The two most extreme cases, displaying a difference of more than 25 percentage points between the lowest and highest income brackets, are a gas fireplace and tray ceilings. While only 46% of buyers earning less than $50,000 want a gas fireplace, the share is 72% among those whose income tops $150,000. The shares are 34% and 60%, respectively, for a tray ceiling (Fig. 5-14). Chair rails, exposed beams, and built-in kitchen seating are other decorative features that are significantly more important to wealthier buyers (Appendix A, Pages A75-A77).

Figure 5-14. Gas Fireplace & Tray Ceiling Preferences by Buyers Income Bracket

(Percent of Respondents Rating Essential or Desirable)

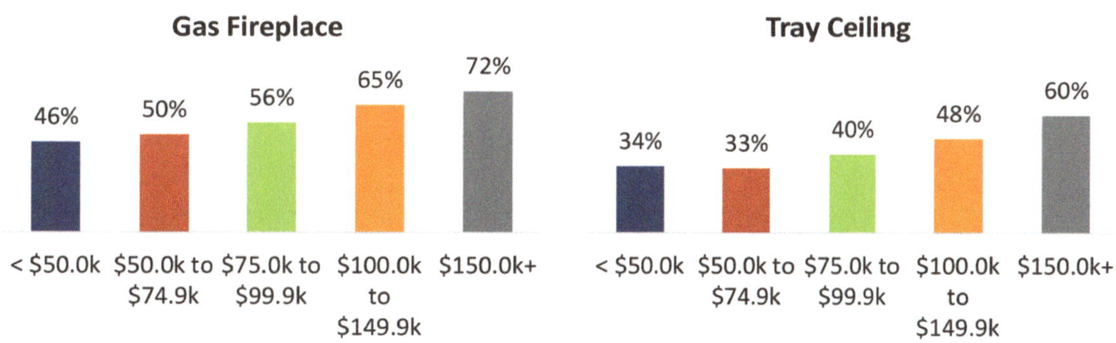

FEW BUYERS ARE AGAINST DECORATIVE FEATURES

When given the opportunity to rate decorative features as 'unwanted,' most buyers declined the chance. At worst, 20% would reject a home if it had a wood burning fireplace, while even smaller minorities would be openly against having built-in kitchen seating and a gas fireplace (both at 18%), exposed beams (17%), tray ceiling (16%), or chair rails (15%) (Fig. 5-15).

Figure 5-15. Decorative Features NOT Wanted

(Percent of Respondents Rating 'Do Not Want')

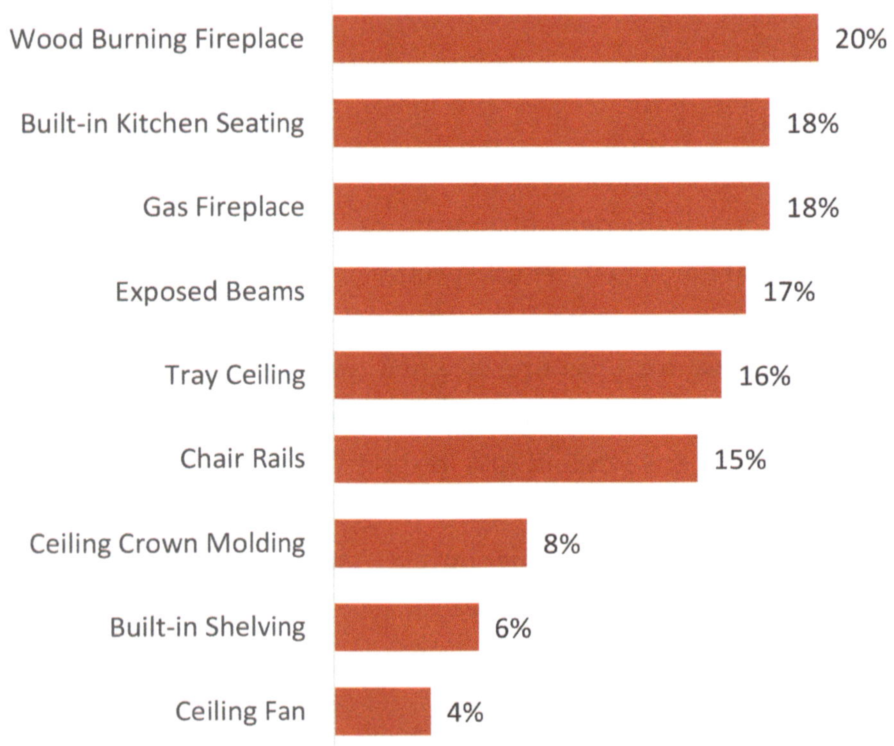

Chapter 6

Specialty Rooms & Features

LAUNDRY ROOM IS THE MOST ESSENTIAL ROOM IN THE HOUSE

The NAHB study asked recent and prospective home buyers to rate their preference for 18 specialty rooms. Their answer was unequivocal: the laundry room is the single most wanted room in the house, with 86% rating it either essential (40%) or desirable (46%). The laundry room tops the most wanted list of 200+ features, ahead of other popular features like a patio or ENERGY STAR windows (see Chapter 3). The next two most popular specialty rooms are the great room (kitchen/family room/living room), preferred by 72% of home buyers (25% essential; 47% desirable); and the dining room, preferred by 69% (24% essential; 45% desirable) (Fig. 6-1).

Figure 6-1. Specialty Rooms Rated Essential or Desirable

(Percent of Respondents)

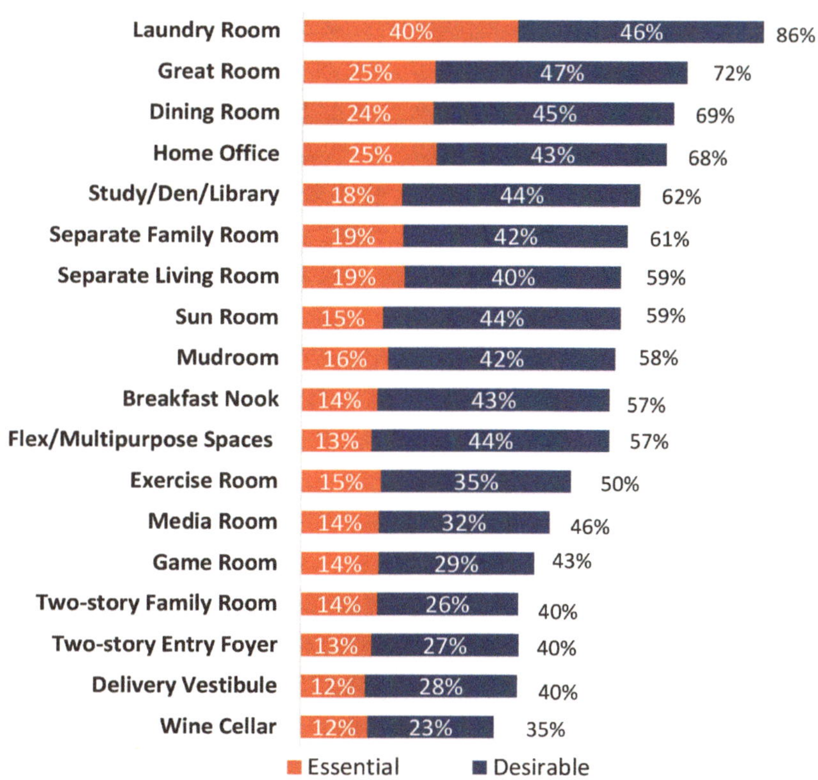

More than two-thirds of home buyers (68%) also think having a home office is essential (25%) or desirable (43%), while 62% feel the same way about a study/den/library. At least half of buyers consider another seven specialty rooms highly influential in their purchase decision: a separate family room (61%), a separate living room (59%), a sunroom (59%), a mudroom (58%), a breakfast nook (57%), flex/multipurpose spaces (57%), and an exercise room (50%).

On the other hand, fewer than half of buyers in the study find six specialty rooms essential or desirable: a media room (46%), a game room (43%), a two-story family room (40%), a two-story entry foyer (40%), a delivery vestibule (40%), and a wine cellar (35%).

Looking back between 2020 and 2023, during and in the immediate aftermath of the COVID-19 pandemic, these years had a significant impact on buyers' preferences for a number of these rooms, demonstrated by the increase in the share rating them as essential or desirable during this period (Fig. 6-2):

Figure 6-2. Specialty Rooms Rated Essential or Desirable – History
(Percent of Respondents)

	2003	2007	2012	2015	2018	2020	2023
Laundry Room	94	93	93	92	91	87	86
Great Room	n/a	n/a	67	67	65	64	72
Dining Room	79	79	76	73	71	70	69
Home Office	55	69	68	63	65	63	68
Study/Den/Library	55	63	51	52	61	52	62
Separate Family Room	n/a	n/a	n/a	n/a	57	60	61
Separate Living Room	n/a	n/a	n/a	n/a	55	62	59
Sunroom	45	56	51	51	55	54	59
Mudroom	n/a	n/a	48	46	52	50	58
Breakfast Nook	n/a	n/a	n/a	52	53	52	57
Flex/Multipurpose Spaces	n/a	n/a	n/a	n/a	n/a	56	57
Exercise Room	27	33	35	34	40	47	50
Media Room	30	39	40	38	37	40	46
Game Room	n/a	31	27	26	29	35	43
Two-story Entry Foyer	n/a	n/a	26	28	29	38	40
Two-story Family Room	n/a	n/a	23	24	24	35	40
Delivery Vestibule	n/a	n/a	n/a	n/a	n/a	n/a	40
Wine Cellar	n/a	n/a	n/a	19	21	30	35

- Study/den/library, up 10 points from 52% to 62%.
- Great room, up 8 points from 64% to 72%.
- Mudroom, up 8 points from 50% to 58%.
- Game room, up 8 points from 35% to 43%.
- Home office, up 5 points from 63% to 68%

Given the pandemic-induced trend toward spending more time at home, the increased popularity of these features is not surprising because they improve the livability of a home where multiple members need to work, study, and relax simultaneously, the efficiency and cleanliness of the entry/exit process, and the open space flexibility buyers want.

MOST BUYERS WANT A HOME OFFICE, ESPECIALLY AFFLUENT ONES

A home office is popular among most home buyers, as an overall 68% rated it essential or desirable. But, as the analysis in Chapter 12 shows, its popularity is particularly high among wealthier buyers. For example, whereas "only" 55% of buyers with household income below $50,000 want a home office, the share jumps to 80% among buyers with income of $150,000 or higher — a 25-percentage point difference. Buyers at the bottom end of the income scale face the most severe affordability challenges when buying a home, so logically, it makes sense that many would not be interested in dedicating an entire room to office space.

Given the strong correlation between income and price point (Appendix A, Page A27), it is not surprising to find a similar relationship between the preference for a home office and home price. Among buyers who expect to pay (or recently paid) less than $250,000, "only" 57% want a home office, compared to 71% of those with a price point between $250,000 and $499,999, and 82% of those paying half a million dollars or more (Fig. 6-3).

Figure 6-3. A Home Office Rated Essential or Desirable by Buyers Income & Home Price

(Percent of Respondents)

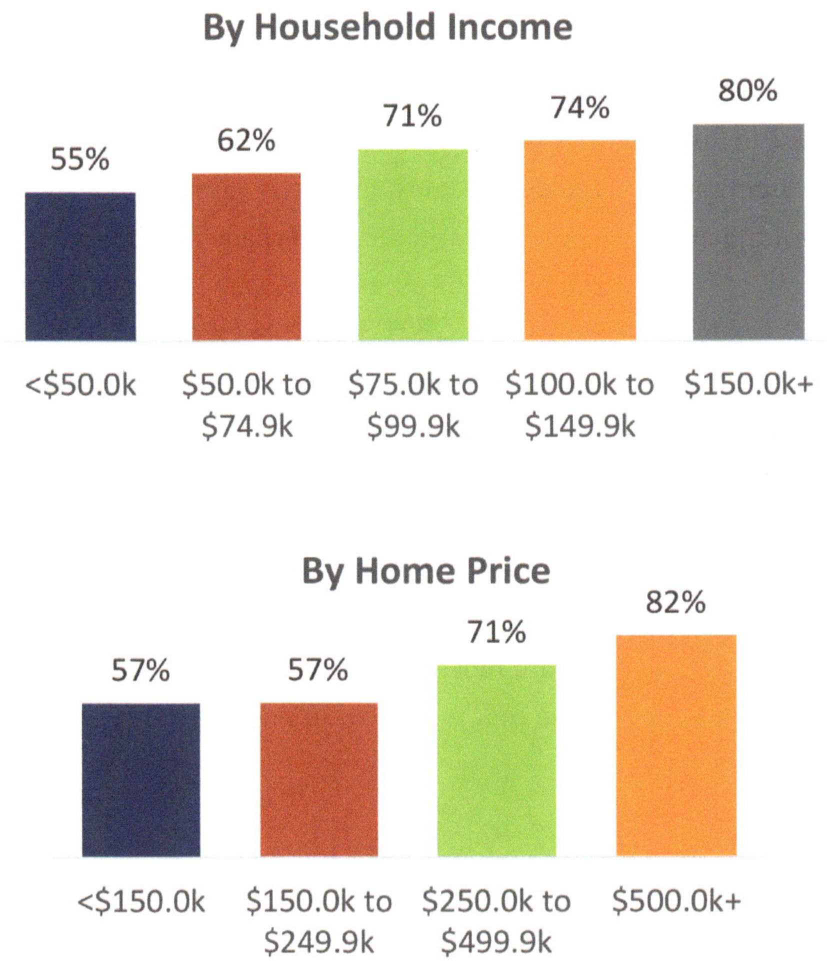

MOST HOME BUYERS WANT A MEDIUM SIZE HOME OFFICE

Fifty-nine percent of buyers who rated a home office essential or desirable agreed the home office should be of medium size between 100 and 150 square feet. A minority of 19% want a small home office, one with less than 100 square feet of space, while 22% would prefer it to be larger, with more than 150 square feet (Fig. 6-4). Combining the top two size categories yields that 81% of home buyers who want a home office prefer it to have at least 100 square feet of space.

Figure 6-4. Preference for Home Office Size

(Percent of Respondents Who Want a Home Office)

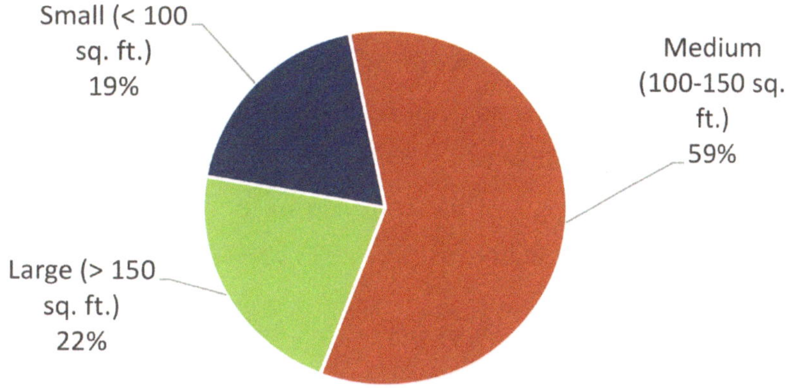

A final question on this topic asked buyers about the number of home offices or spaces dedicated to work/study from home they would prefer to have. A full two-thirds (66%) of buyers want one home office/dedicated space, 13% want at least two, and 20% want none (Fig. 6-5). Results further show that most buyers in every demographic category, regardless of age, race, income, geography, or any other factor, prefer to have one home office/dedicated space at home (Appendix A, Pages A34-A36).

Figure 6-5. Preferred Number of Home Offices/ Spaces Dedicated to Work & Study

(Percent of Respondents Who Want a Home Office)

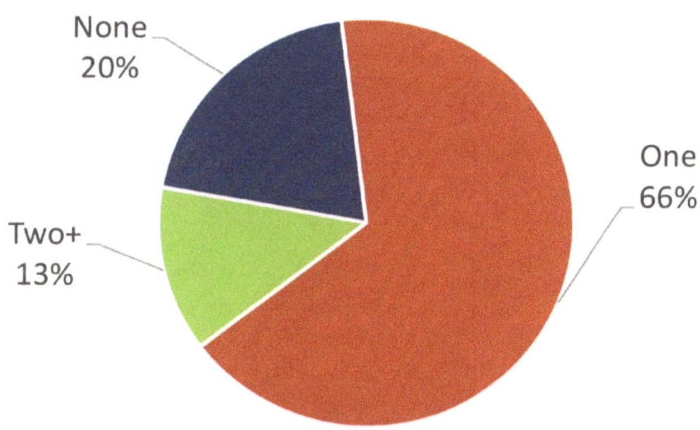

SOME BUYERS EMBRACE A DELIVERY VESTIBULE

Home deliveries already existed in early 2020. But when much of the economy was forced into lockdown by COVID-19 in March 2020, home delivery services exploded. Among thousands of other items, Americans were ordering groceries, cooked meals, coffee, and cleaning supplies online, delivered to porches, decks, driveways, and doorways. The phenomenon has continued because of its convenience, though it is less prevalent than during the pandemic. Responding to this trend, some builders began offering delivery vestibules as an option in their new homes. The 2023 NAHB study asked buyers how they felt about this new feature.

Results show delivery vestibules are more popular among younger, minority, high-income buyers with children. For example, while 55% of buyers under 35 rate it essential or desirable, the share is only 32% among those 65 or older. Across racial groups, 34% of Caucasian buyers are interested in a delivery vestibule, compared to 63% of Hispanics, 52% of Asians, and 49% of African Americans. Meanwhile, 30% of buyers with incomes below $50,000 want this feature, almost half the share (55%) among buyers earning $150,000 or more. And finally, the presence of children matters. More than half of married copies with children (52%) and a plurality of single parents (45%) want a delivery vestibule, compared to 27% of married couples without children and 28% of one-person households (Fig. 6-6). The analysis described in Chapter 12 shows that the effects of income and age on delivery vestibule are significant, that African Americans and Hispanics are statistically different from Caucasians, and that married couples with children and single parents are statistically different from other home buyers in a model that simultaneously controls for all these factors.

Figure 6-6. A Delivery Vestibule Rated Essential or Desirable by Buyer's Age, Racial Group, Income & Household Composition

(Percent of Respondents)

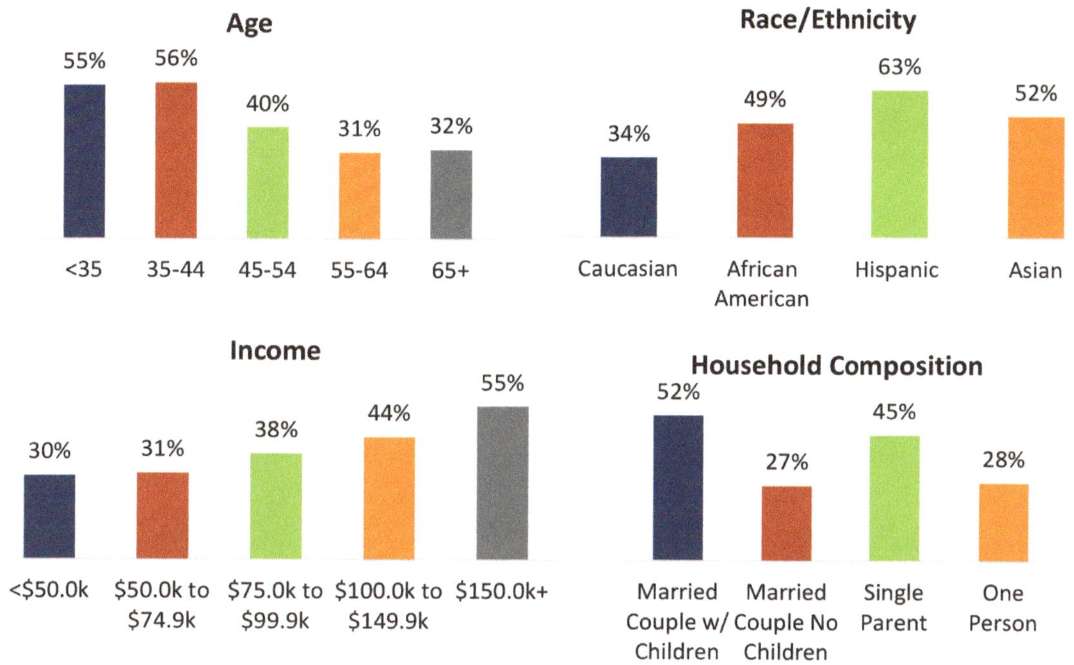

MANY BUYERS DO NOT WANT WINE CELLARS OR 2-STORY SPACES

Buyers identified the specialty rooms that would likely lead them to reject a potential home. Results show the least desired specialty room is a wine cellar, rejected by 41% of buyers, followed by a two-story family room (35%), and a two-story entry foyer (32%). More than 20% are unlikely to buy a home if it has a game room (28%), a media room (25%), a delivery vestibule (25%), and an exercise room (23%) (Fig. 6-7). Home buyers were least likely to reject a laundry room (4%), a dining room (8%), and a great room (9%), which is not surprising given that these three features are at the top of the most wanted list shown in Figure 6-1.

Figure 6-7. Specialty Rooms NOT Wanted

(Percent of Respondents)

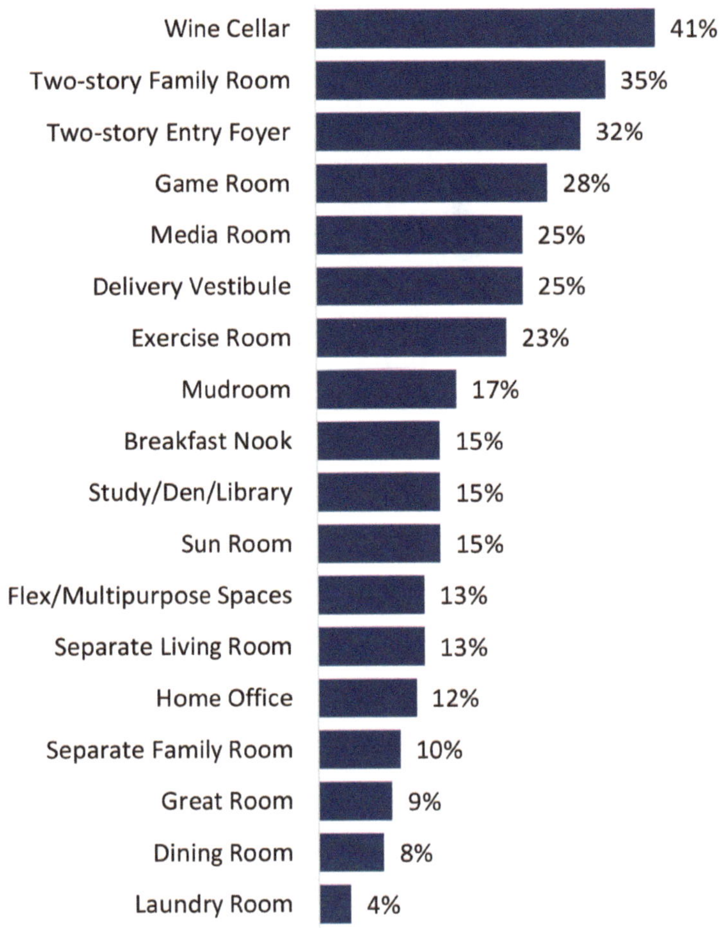

8 OF EVERY 10 BUYERS WANT GARAGE STORAGE

In addition to the 18 specialty rooms, home buyers rated 11 specialty features — miscellaneous items that do not fit naturally into a standard category. Of these, garage storage is the most critical for buyers, as 81% rated it either essential (31%) or desirable (50%). Tied in second place are soundproof walls/floors and recessed lighting throughout the house, both wanted by 66% of buyers (19% essential, 47% desirable). A drop zone (for keys, coats, etc.) is the next most wanted specialty feature by 62% of buyers (17% essential, 45% desirable). Incidentally, soundproof walls/floors and a drop zone are new features first introduced in the 2023 study to quantify preferences for features that became popular during the pandemic. The only other specialty feature rated as desirable/essential by most buyers is cathedral/vaulted ceilings (55%) (Fig. 6-8).

Figure 6-8. Specialty Features Rated Essential or Desirable

(Percent of Respondents)

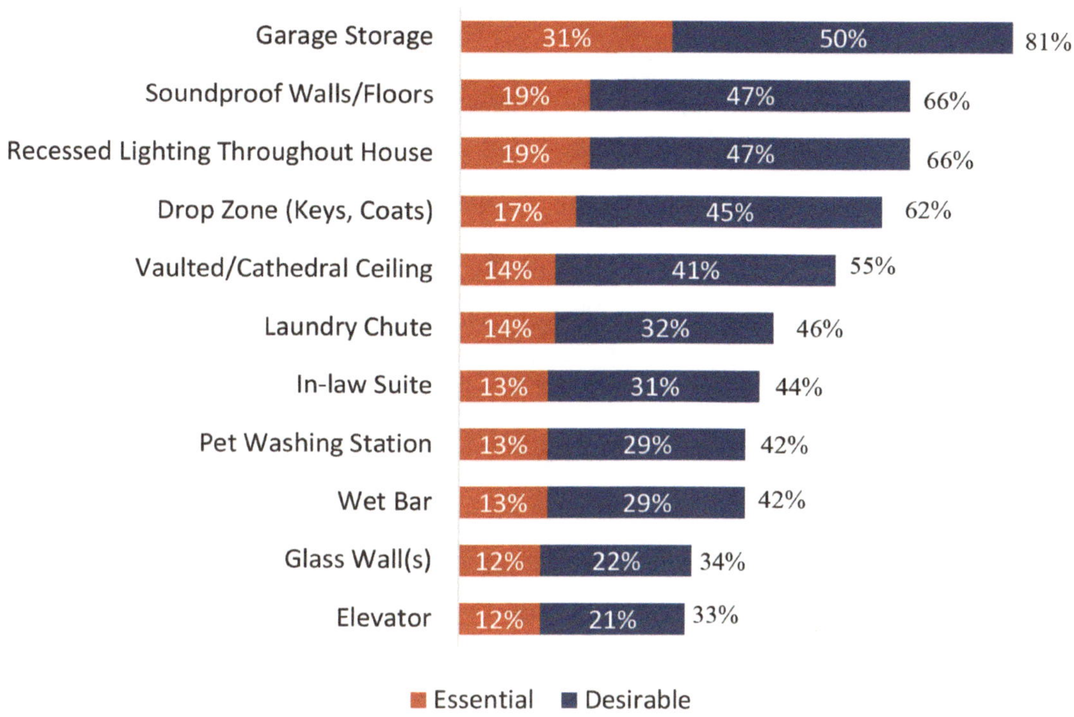

Nonetheless, the desirability of many of the features in the bottom half of Figure 6-8 rose between 2020 and 2023, demonstrated by the increase in the share rating them as essential or desirable:

- Laundry chute, up 9 points from 37% to 46%.
- In-law suite, up 7 points from 37% to 44%.
- Elevator, up 7 points from 26% to 33%.
- Glass walls, up 6 points from 28% to 34%.

In the case of the laundry chute and the elevator, the latest results show a significant increase in popularity since 2003. That year, only 31% and a mere 8% of buyers considered them essential/desirable, respectively. Historical data also show buyers who consider a pet washing station essential or desirable more than doubled between 2015 and 2023, from 20% to 42% (Fig. 6-9).

Figure 6-9. Specialty Features Rated Essential or Desirable – History

(Percent of Respondents)

	2003	2007	2012	2015	2018	2020	2023
Garage Storage	n/a	n/a	86	81	85	77	81
Soundproof Walls/Floors	n/a	n/a	n/a	n/a	n/a	n/a	66
Recessed Lighting	n/a	64	59	57	61	60	66
Drop Zone	n/a	n/a	n/a	n/a	n/a	n/a	62
Vaulted/Cathedral Ceiling	n/a	n/a	n/a	46	50	52	55
Laundry Chute	31	28	31	29	31	37	46
In-law Suite	n/a	n/a	n/a	n/a	n/a	37	44
Wet Bar	22	26	25	26	29	36	42
Pet Washing Station	n/a	n/a	n/a	20	27	33	42
Glass Wall(s)	n/a	n/a	n/a	n/a	n/a	28	34
Elevator	8	9	12	15	18	26	33

DESIRE FOR SPECIALTY FEATURES RISES WITH INCOME

As with many other goods and services in the economy, high incomes increase the likelihood a buyer will want specialty features in the home. Statistical analysis confirms that this is true for all 11 of the specialty features listed in the survey. For 6 of the 11, income has such a strong effect on preferences, that there is at least a 25-percentage point difference between the share of buyers who want them in the lowest income bracket and those in the top group. Glass walls are the most extreme case: 25% of buyers with income below $50,000 consider them essential/desirable, compared to 53% among those earning $150,000 or more. For a wet bar, the shares are 32% and 59%, respectively. For an elevator, the share of buyers who want them ranges from 26% of those in the lowest income group to 52% of those in the top income group. The other three features where income has a strong positive effect on preferences are recessed lighting, vaulted/cathedral ceilings, and an in-law suite (Fig. 6-10).

ELEVATORS & GLASS WALLS ARE THE MOST UNWANTED SPECIALTY FEATURES

An elevator and glass walls are the most unwanted specialty features, with 47% and 42% of buyers, respectively, explicitly rejecting them. More than 30% would also be unlikely

Figure 6-10. Specialty Features Rated Essential/Desirable by Buyers Income

(Percent of Respondents)

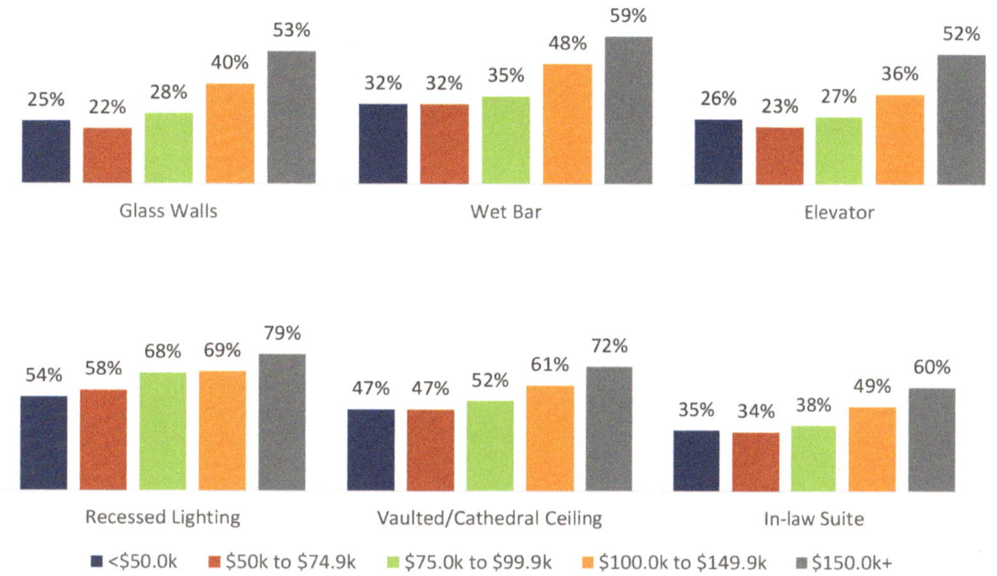

to buy a home if it had a pet washing station (34%), an in-law suite (31%), and a wet bar (31%). Meanwhile, fewer than 15% of buyers have strong negative feelings toward a drop zone, soundproof walls/floors, recessed lighting, and garage storage (Fig. 6-11).

Figure 6-11. Specialty Features NOT Wanted

(Percent of Respondents)

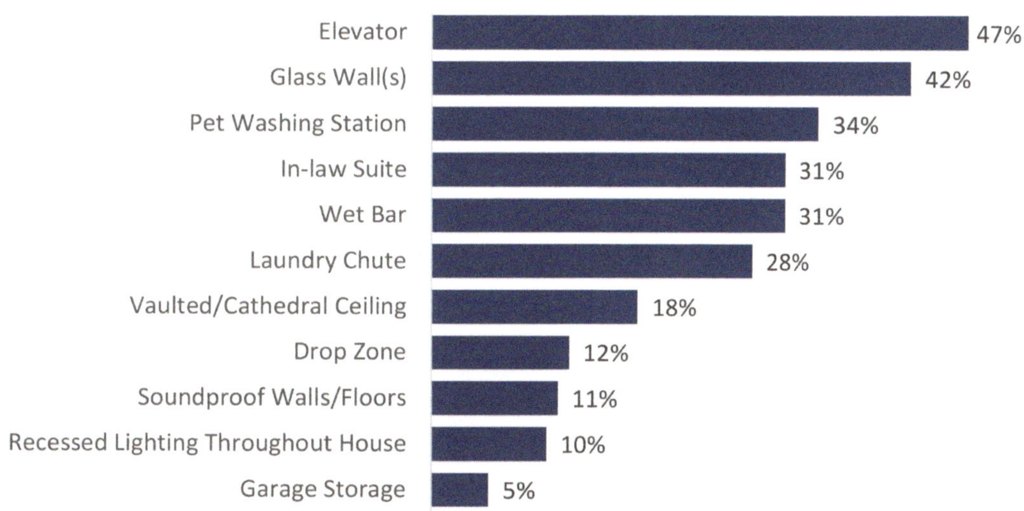

Chapter 7

Accessibility & Exterior Features

EIGHT OF EVERY 10 BUYERS WANT A FULL BATH ON THE MAIN LEVEL

In the 2023 NAHB survey, home buyers rated eight accessibility features as essential, desirable, indifferent, or unwanted. The most wanted of these features is a full bath on the main level, something eight out of every 10 buyers consider essential (33%) or desirable (47%). Non-slip floor surfaces (74%), doorways at least 3 ft. wide (73%), and hallways at least 4 ft. wide (71%) come in second, third and fourth as most popular accessibility features. Over half of buyers would also be positively influenced to buy a home with a step-less entrance (68%), bathroom aids (e.g., grab bars, shower seating) (64%), and lower kitchen cabinets (58%). Lower countertops (47%) is the only accessibility feature that less than half of buyers want. (Fig. 7-1).

Figure 7-1. Accessibility Features Rated Essential or Desirable
(Percent of Respondents)

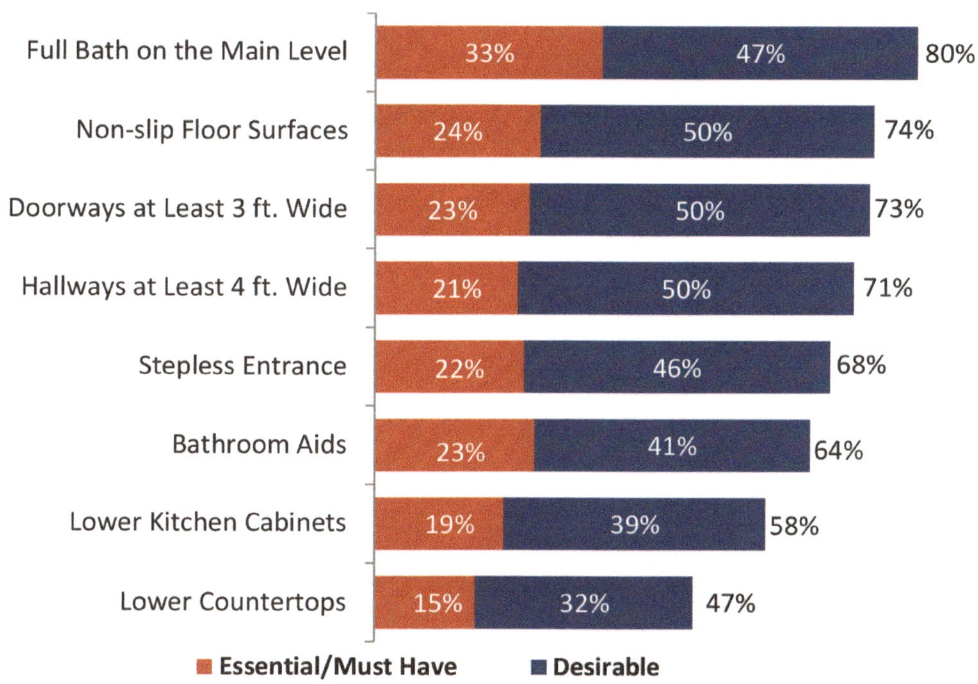

A full bath on the main level has been the most wanted accessibility feature since the 2003 NAHB survey. In 2003 and 2007, the scale asked buyers to rate these features from one to five, where one meant 'not at all important' and five 'very important.' The shares who rated each feature a four or five in both years are in Figure 7-2. Despite the differences in scale, a full bath on the main level has remained the most wanted accessibility feature throughout this period: 75% rated it important to very important in 2003, and a slightly higher share (80%) rated it essential/desirable in 2023.

Looking at changes in desirability from 2020 to 2023, only one stands out: the share of buyers interested in non-slip floor surfaces rose nine points in those three years, from 65% to 74%. Longer term, the appeal of some accessibility features has grown over time. For example, in 2003, 'only' 42% of buyers wanted a step-less entrance; by 2023, that share was up 26 points to 68%. Bathroom aids have also seen their popularity grow by more than 20 points, from 40% in 2003 to 64% in 2023.

Figure 7-2. Accessibility Features – History

(Percent of Respondents Rating Essential or Desirable in 2012 and Later, Important to Very Important in 2003 and 2007)

	2003	2007	2012	2015	2018	2020	2023
Full Bath on the Main Level	75	74	81	83	79	80	80
Non-slip Floor Surfaces	62	53	63	66	65	65	74
Doorways at Least 3' Wide	n/a	n/a	79	77	69	77	73
Hallways at Least 4' Wide	n/a	n/a	78	74	63	73	71
Stepless Entrance	42	38	50	60	60	64	68
Bathroom Aids	40	35	46	56	53	61	64
Lower Kitchen Cabinets	n/a	n/a	48	49	48	59	58
Lower Countertops	n/a	n/a	n/a	36	31	43	47

AGE USED TO DETERMINE DESIRE FOR ACCESSIBILITY FEATURES, NOT SO MUCH ANYMORE

In the 2020 survey, age was an important factor in determining if buyers had strong preferences for certain accessibility features. In 2023, those age-based differences have diminished. The most poignant example is the desirability of a step-less entrance: in 2020, 52% of the youngest cohort of buyers (under 35) wanted this feature, compared to 73% of the oldest cohort (65+) — a 21-point difference. By 2023, the difference had shrunk to only eight points: 64% of the youngest buyers now want an entrance without steps, compared to 72% among the oldest group (Fig. 7-3).

A similar trend is evident for bathroom aids and a full bath on the main level. In 2020, the difference in popularity between the youngest and oldest buyers was 16 points for bathroom aids (52% vs. 68%) and 13 points for a full bath on the main level (67% vs. 80%). By 2023, those gaps were seven points (65% vs. 72%) and nine points (76% vs. 85%), respectively. Although the positive effect of age on preferences for a step-less entrance and a full bath on the main level are still statistically significant in 2023, the effect of age on preferences for bathroom aids is not.

Figure 7-3. Accessibility Features by Age

(Percent of Respondents Rating Essential/Desirable)

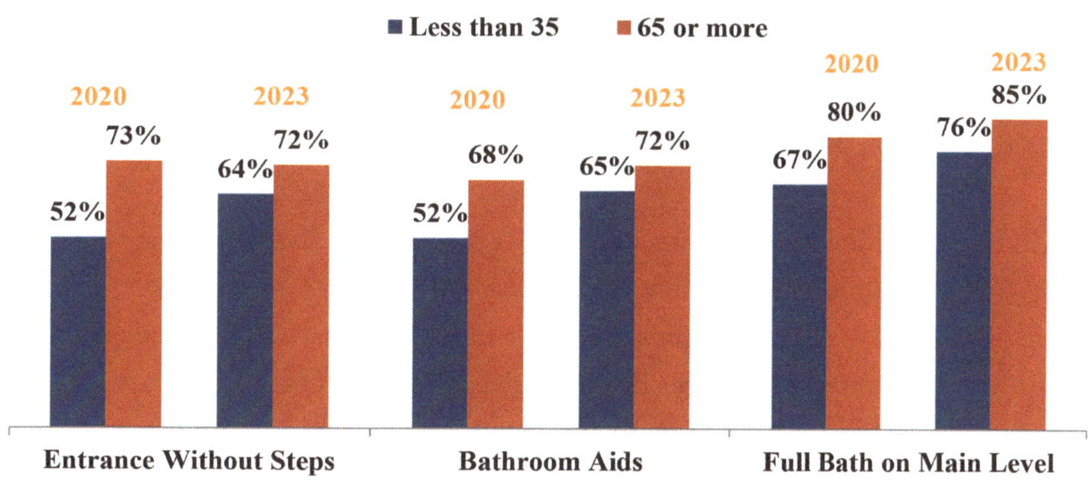

ACCESSIBILITY FEATURES DO NOT TURN BUYERS OFF

When asked to rate accessibility features, most home buyers do not say they are unwanted. As Figure 7-4 shows, accessibility features turn off fewer than 20% of home buyers. At worst, 19% dislike lower countertops, while fewer than 15% would reject a home with the remaining features on the list. An important takeaway here is that accessibility features will generally add value to a home and are not a detriment. This has not always been the case.

Figure 7-4. Accessibility Features NOT Wanted
(Percent of Respondents Rating "Do Not Want")

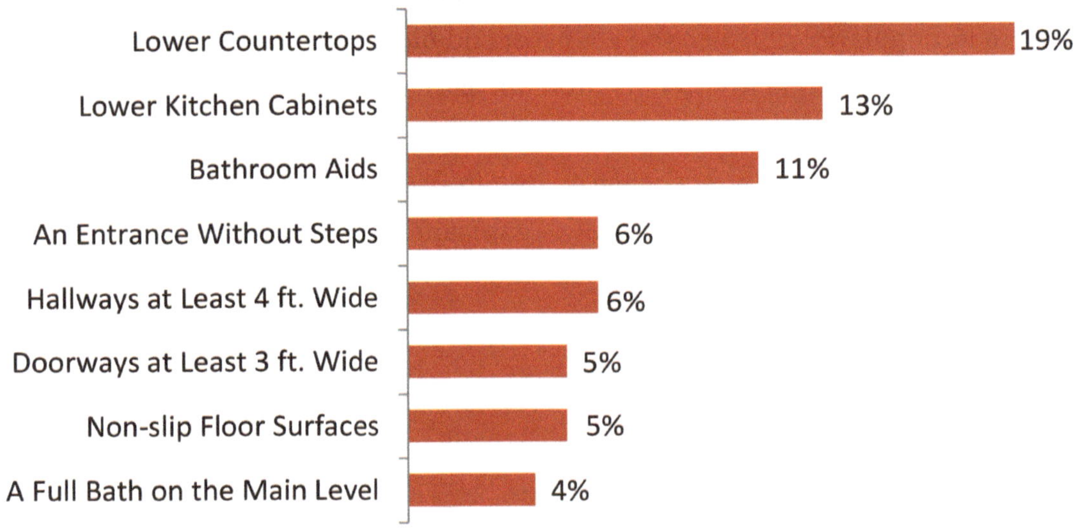

OUTDOOR FEATURES ARE IN HIGH DEMAND

The COVID-19 pandemic had short- and long-term effects on what buyers want in their homes. One of the most lasting consequences is the desire to spend more time outside in the comfort and safety of porches and back yards. Findings in this study corroborate the trend, as all 11 outdoor features listed received a rating of essential or desirable from more than 50% of buyers. At the top, the most influential of these features is a patio, with 86% of buyers rating it either essential (30%) or desirable (56%). Patios are built behind and/or beside the home and are defined by the U.S. Census Bureau as "a floored area, with or without a roof, sitting directly on the ground."[1]

---

[1] U.S. Census Bureau, Survey of Construction, Characteristics of New Housing.

After the patio, exterior lighting (wanted by 82%), a front porch (81%), and landscaping (80%) are the most popular outdoor features. A deck (79%), a rear porch (77%), and a lot with trees (74%) would influence more than 70% to buy a home. Somewhat lower shares, but still majorities, would also prefer lawn sprinklers (65%), an outdoor grill (built-in) (65%), an outdoor fireplace (59%), and an outdoor kitchen (with cooking/refrigeration/sink) (55%) (Fig. 7-5).

Figure 7-5. Outdoor Features Rated Essential or Desirable

(Percent of Respondents)

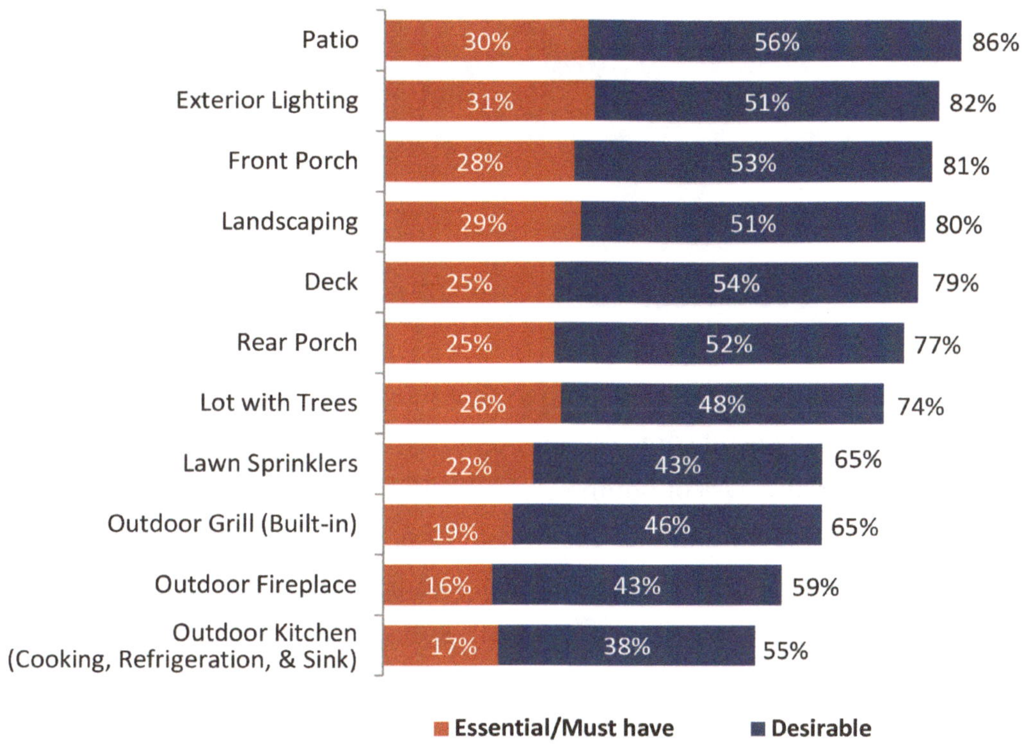

Home buyers have traditionally been fond of outdoor features throughout the two-decade period covered in this study. From 2003 to 2020, all these features were rated essential/desirable by more than 50% of buyers, except for an outdoor fireplace and an outdoor kitchen. Between 2020 and 2023, this changed when buyers influenced by an outdoor fireplace or an outdoor kitchen increased by 10 points, from 49% to 59% and from 45% to 55%, respectively (Fig. 7-6). Since every outdoor feature has become essential or desirable to most buyers, a key takeaway is that outdoor features have a strong influence on purchase decisions, so builders should enhance or add these features whenever possible. For a more architectural perspective on the type of exterior design buyers want for their homes, see Chapter 1.

Figure 7-6. Outdoor Features – History

(Percent of Respondents Rating Essential or Desirable)

	2003	2007	2012	2015	2018	2020	2023
Patio	73	81	83	84	87	82	86
Exterior Lighting	85	86	90	90	85	87	82
Front Porch	82	79	80	79	79	81	81
Landscaping	n/a	n/a	n/a	n/a	n/a	n/a	80
Deck	80	77	77	76	75	75	79
Rear Porch	n/a	n/a	72	70	71	75	77
Lot with Trees	77	76	78	75	74	71	74
Lawn Sprinklers	53	60	60	58	59	63	65
Outdoor Grill (Built-in)	n/a	n/a	62	53	55	60	65
Outdoor Fireplace	n/a	59	37	42	45	49	59
Outdoor Kitchen (Cooking, Refrigeration, Sink)	n/a	n/a	33	36	41	45	55

BOOMERS ARE LESS LIKELY TO BE FANS OF SOME OUTDOOR FEATURES

Looking at results across generations shows that Boomers are significantly less likely than younger generations to want some outdoor features in their homes. An outdoor fireplace, for instance, is a feature 49% of Boomers consider essential/desirable, compared to more than 70% of Gen Z and Millennials and 66% of Gen X buyers. A similar dichotomy exists for an outdoor kitchen (45% of Boomers want, compared to at least 63% of the younger three generations) and a built-in outdoor grill (55% of Boomers, compared to more than 70% of Gen Z, Millennial, and Gen X buyers) (Fig. 7-7). The analysis discussed in Chapter 12 shows that all three of these differences are statistically significant.

Figure 7-7. Outdoor Features Rated Essential or Desirable by Generation

(Percent of Respondents)

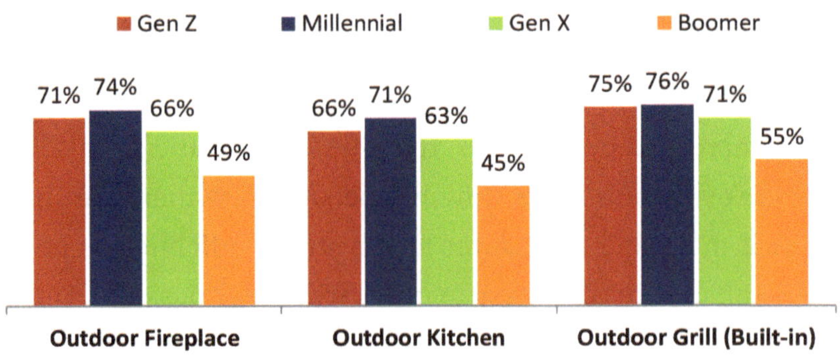

OUTDOOR FEATURES ARE UNLIKELY TO CAUSE REJECTION

Confirming that outdoor features have become increasingly popular, the survey results show that only small minorities of buyers would reject a potential home because of these features. A mere 19% and 16% of buyers, respectively, rated an outdoor kitchen and an outdoor fireplace as 'unwanted.' None of the other outdoor features listed would cause more than 15% of buyers to pass on a house because they were included (Fig. 7-8).

Figure 7-8. Outdoor Features NOT Wanted
(Percent of Respondents Rating "Do Not Want")

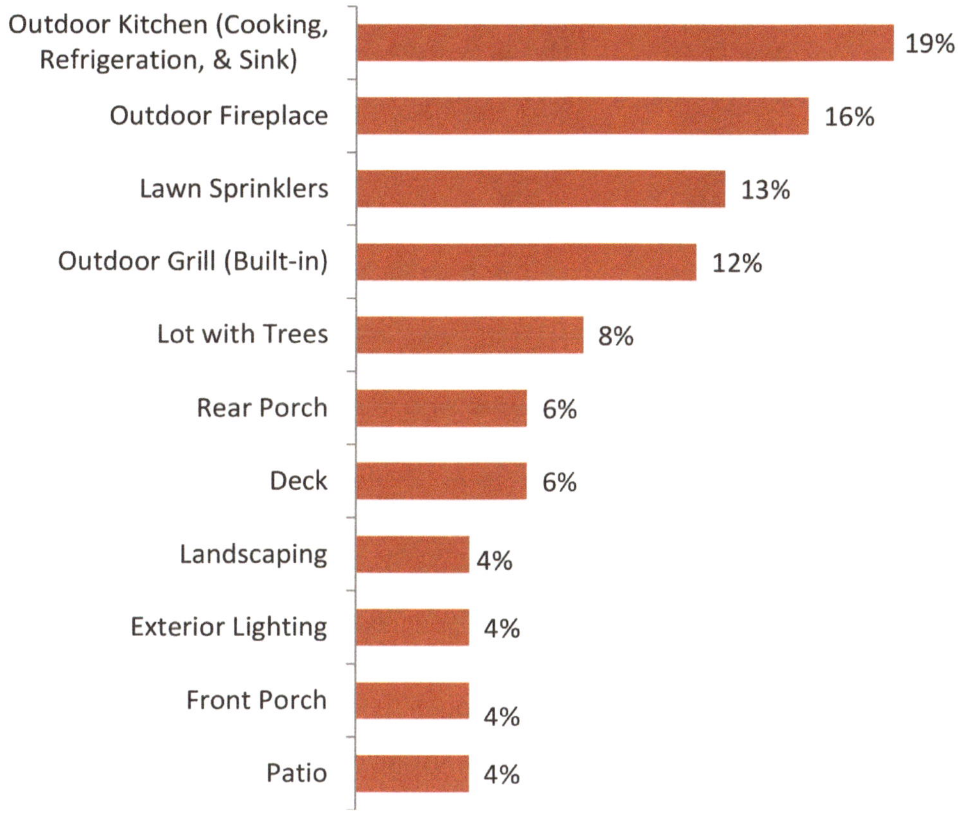

BRICK & STONE ARE FIRST CHOICES FOR THE FRONT EXTERIOR

Brick and stone are clear favorites as the siding material for the home's front exterior. At the top, 71% consider brick essential or desirable, followed closely by stone, with 70%. In third place is wood or a type of wood product, appealing to 54% of home buyers. In contrast, fewer than half of buyers favor the remaining options for their front exterior siding: vinyl/vinyl-covered aluminum (43%), stucco (42%), and fiber cement (42%) (Fig. 7-9).

Figure 7-9. Front Exterior Material Rated Essential or Desirable
(Percent of Respondents)

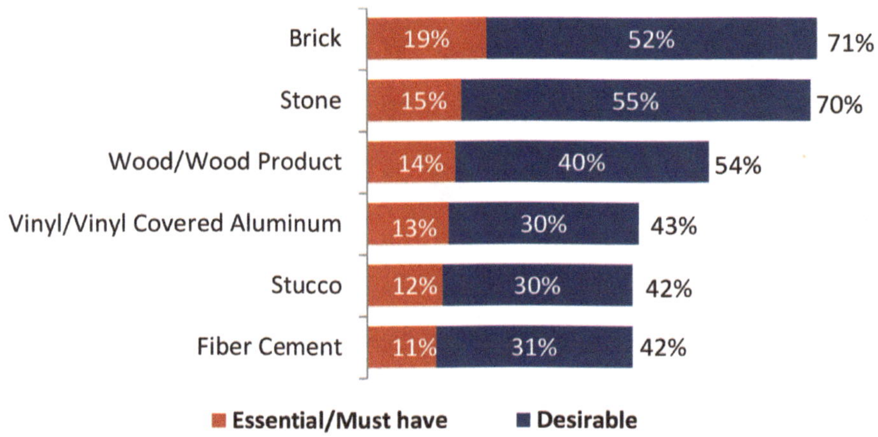

Despite these preferences, brick and stone were the principle siding material of only 18% and 1%, respectively, of single-family homes started in 2022. Cost is likely the main reason. According to the RSMeans Residential Cost book, the cost of materials and installation for common brick veneer is nearly two and a half times the equivalent cost for vinyl clapboard siding, and the cost of average rough stonework is more than five times the cost of vinyl.

Looking back at buyer preferences for the front exterior siding since 2015 (when introduced to the NAHB survey) shows that brick and stone have consistently been the top two choices for buyers over the years. The other options, although generally less popular, have gained some ground. Between 2020 and 2023, for example, the share of buyers who think wood/wood product is essential or desirable rose by 12 points, from 42% to 54%. For fiber cement, the share rose six points from 36% to 42%. Stucco, meanwhile, has seen the share of buyers who favor it rise steadily from 31% in 2015 to 42% in 2023 (Fig. 7-10).

Figure 7-10. Front Exterior Material – History

(Percent of Respondents Rating Essential or Desirable)

	2015	2018	2020	2023
Brick	70	68	68	71
Stone	69	65	69	70
Wood/Wood Product	36	35	42	54
Vinyl/Vinyl Covered Aluminum	36	33	43	43
Fiber Cement	26	28	36	42
Stucco	31	33	41	42

DESIRABILITY OF STUCCO & STONE RISES WITH HOME PRICE

The desirability of stucco and stone and the price buyers expect to pay for the home (or recently paid) are closely — and positively — linked in a statistically significant way. In other words, the pricier the home, the likelier buyers are to want these materials for the front exterior wall of their home. Stucco, for instance, is considered essential/desirable by 36% of buyers expecting to pay less than $150,000 but by nearly half (49%) of those paying $500,000 or more. Similarly, the share of buyers who would be positively influenced by stone on the front exterior wall rises from 65% of those at the lowest end of the price spectrum to 77% of those at the top end (Fig. 7-11).

Figure 7-11. Preference for Stucco & Stone on Front Exterior Wall by Home Price

(Percent of Respondents Rating Essential or Desirable)

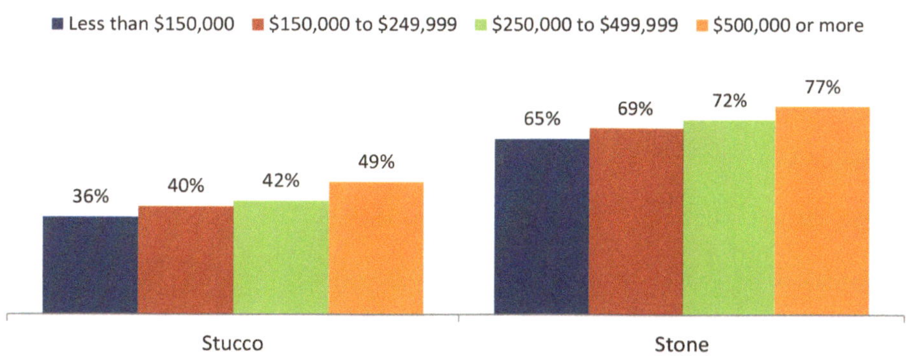

OVER 20% OF BUYERS REJECT STUCCO & VINYL ON FRONT EXTERIOR WALL

Only two materials on the front exterior wall would cause more than 20% of buyers to turn down a home: stucco (22%) and vinyl (21%). Not surprisingly, stone and brick would make only a tiny share of buyers (6% for both) walk away from a home if used as the primary material on the front exterior wall (Fig. 7-12).

Figure 7-12. Front Exterior Material NOT Wanted

(Percent of Respondents Rating "Do Not Want")

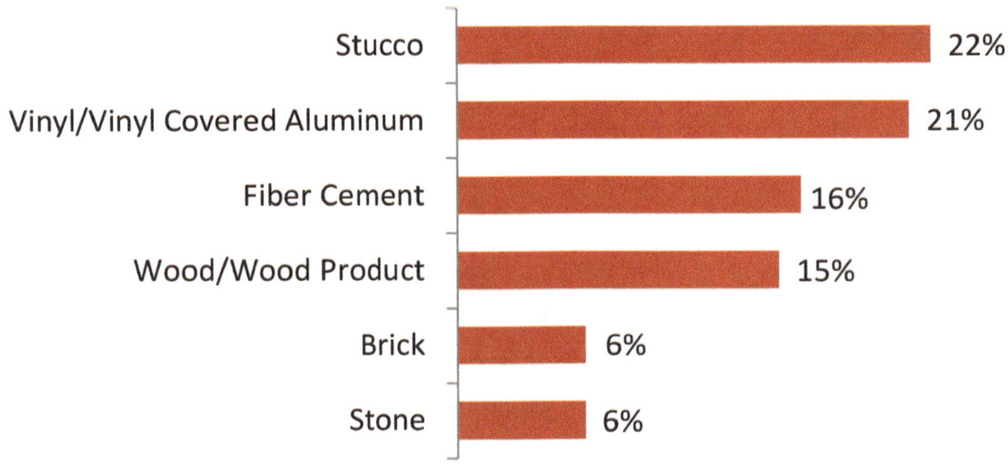

Chapter 8

Green Homes & Features

ONLY 18% WILL PAY FOR ENVIRO-FRIENDLINESS, BUT THE NUMBER IS EDGING UP

Builders, architects, product manufacturers, and other stakeholders often want to know whether home buyers are concerned about the impact of building their home on the environment and the level of their concern on willingness to pay. The answers to those questions can have practical implications on the products and techniques that go into building the home. As Figure 8-1 shows, although a large majority of home buyers are concerned about the environment, relatively few are willing to pay more for a home because of it. 30% say they want an environmentally friendly home, but don't take this into consideration when buying a home, while another 32% say they are concerned about the environment but would not pay more for it. On either side of this great divide are relatively small percentages at the extremes: 19% who are not concerned about the impact on the environment at all, and 18% who are not only concerned but would pay more for a house to reduce its environmental impact.

Figure 8-1. Buyers' Concern About Impact of Their Homes on the Environment
(Percent of Respondents)

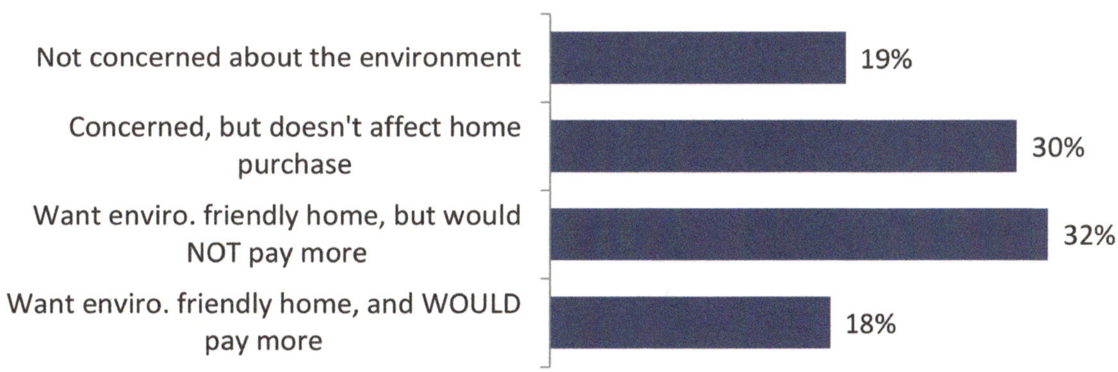

Although only 18% of home buyers are willing to pay more for an environmentally friendly home, that number increased by three percentage points from 2020 to 2023 and represents an all-time high by a single percentage point. The previous high was 17%, recorded in 2003 and 2007. The share of buyers who say they are not concerned about the environment at all, and the share who are concerned in general but not when buying a home, have remained relatively stable since 2012 (Fig. 8-2).

Figure 8-2. Concern about Impact of Home on the Environment: History

(Percent of Respondents)

	2003	2007	2012	2015	2018	2020	2023
Not Concerned About the Environment	11	13	18	18	18	22	19
Concerned About the Environment, but Not a Consideration in House Purchase	26	26	29	32	32	32	30
Want Environment Friendly Home, but Would NOT Pay More	46	44	38	36	36	31	32
WOULD Pay More for Environment Friendly Home	17	17	14	14	14	15	18

AVERAGE BUYER WILL NOW PAY $12K TO SAVE $1K A YEAR ON UTILITY BILLS

A standard feature of the NAHB home buyer survey has been a question on how much extra buyers would pay upfront for a home to save $1,000 every year in utility costs. Answers to the 2023 survey show that 20% of home buyers would pay less than $1,000 extra for a home to save $1,000 per year in utility bills, 22% would pay between $1,000 and $4,999, 19% would pay between $5,000 and $9,999, 16% would pay $10,000 to $14,999, and 23% would pay $15,000 or more (Fig. 8-3A).

An equivalent way to present the information is to turn it around and show the rate of return buyers require on the upfront investment. If a buyer is willing to pay $5,000 upfront to save $1,000 a year, this is equivalent to saying the buyer requires a 20% annual return. Analyzed this way, 39% of home buyers require less than a 10% rate of return to invest upfront in energy efficiency, 19% require somewhere between 10% and 20%, 22% require between 20% and 100%, and 20% even require more than a 100% rate of return (Fig. 8-3B).

Yet another equivalent way to present the same information is to calculate a simple payback. The simple payback is initial cost divided by annual return, or simply the price home buyers would be willing to pay upfront for $1,000 savings yearly divided by $1,000.

Figure 8-3. How Much Buyers Are Willing to Pay for Reduced Utility Bills: Three Equivalent Ways to Present the Results

(Percent of Respondents)

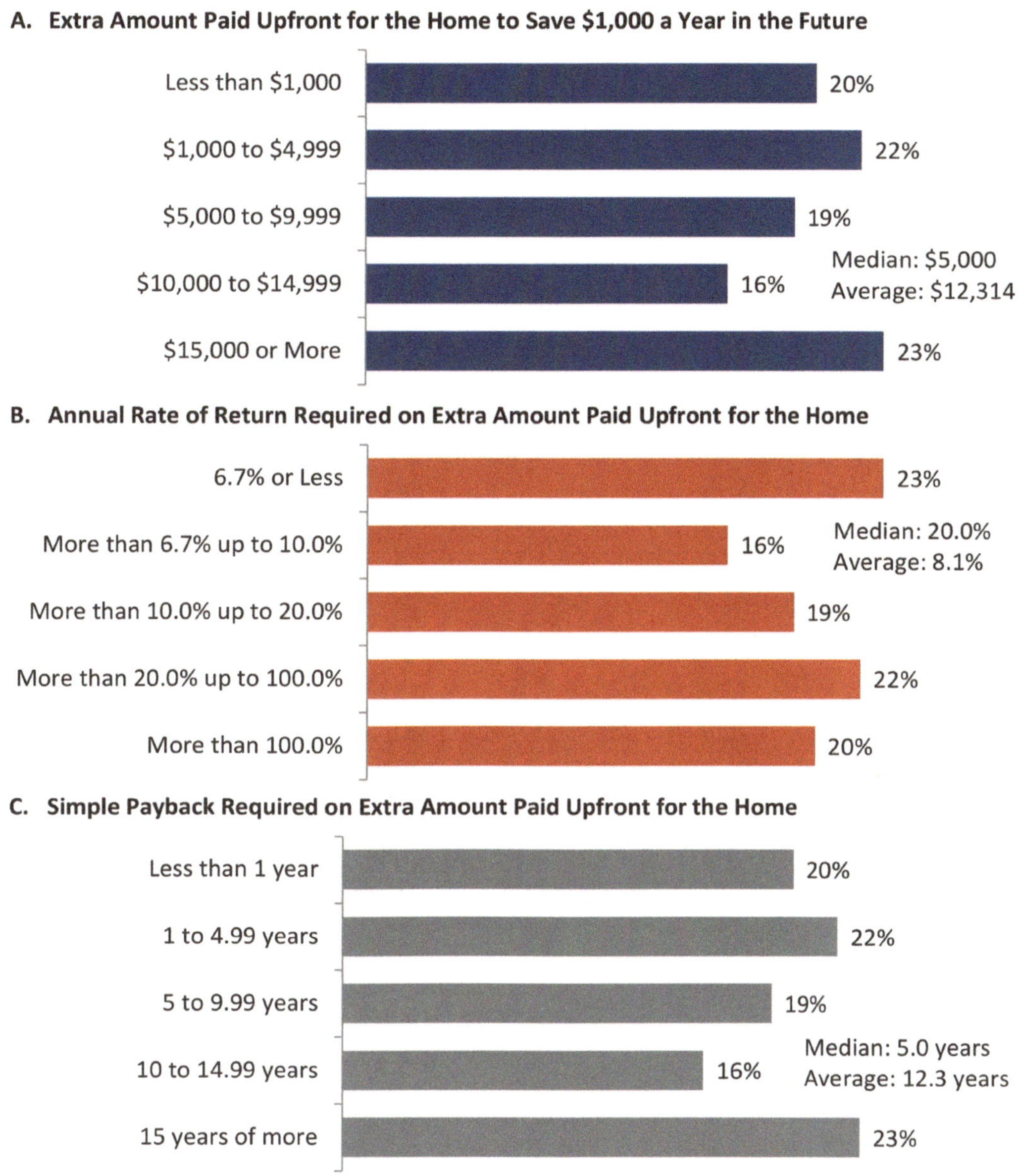

By this metric, 20% of home buyers in the 2023 survey require a payback of less than one year to invest in energy efficiency, 22% require a payback between one and five years, 19% between five and 10 years, and 39% are willing to a accept a payback of more than 10 years (Fig. 8-3C). NAHB's policy on "Cost Effective and Affordable Energy Codes and Standards" defines a cost-effective energy code provision as one with a simple payback not longer than 10 years.

The average amount home buyers are willing to pay upfront to save $1,000 a year in utility cost is $12,314 (equivalent to requiring an 8.1% annual rate of return or a 12.3-year simple payback). The median (meaning half of buyers would pay more, half would pay less) is $5,000 (20% rate of return, 5-year payback). The average is driven by a handful of buyers at the upper extreme, willing to pay quite a lot upfront — more than $50,000 in some cases — to save $1,000 a year, making the median a better measure of the typical home buyer for some purposes.

Sensitivity to extreme values also tends to make the average somewhat volatile over time. Jumps in the neighborhood of $2,000 in the average willingness to pay between iterations of the survey are not uncommon. The average amount buyers are willing to pay has generated an average payback falling short of the NAHB policy threshold of 10 years in most survey years, but longer than 10 years in 2015 and 2023. Meanwhile, the median buyers are willing to pay upfront to save $1,000 annually has remained perfectly constant, at $5,000, since 2003 (Fig. 8-4).

Figure 8-4. How Much Buyers Are Willing to Pay for Reduced Utility Bills: History

	2003	2007	2012	2015	2018	2020	2023
A. Extra Amount Paid Upfront for the Home to Save $1,000 a Year in the Future ($)							
Average	7,000	8,964	7,095	10,732	8,728	9,292	12,314
Median	5,000	5,000	5,000	5,000	5,000	5,000	5,000
B. Annual Rate of Return Required on Extra Amount Paid Upfront for the Home (%)							
Average	14.3	11.2	14.1	9.3	11.5	10.8	8.1
Median	20.0	20.0	20.0	20.0	20.0	20.0	20.0
C. Simple Payback Required on Extra Amount Paid Upfront for the Home (years)							
Average	9.0	7.1	10.7	8.7	9.3	9.3	12.3
Median	5.0	5.0	5.0	5.0	5.0	5.0	5.0

AFFORDABLE HOUSING LESS ABLE TO BEAR UPFRONT COSTS OF ENERGY SAVINGS

The latest survey results also show that the average willingness to pay for energy efficiency varies depending on the price the buyer pays, or expects to pay, for the home. Buyers are less willing (probably also less able) to cover the upfront costs of energy efficiency at the affordable end of the housing spectrum.

As shown in Figure 8-5, buyers of homes priced under $150,000 will pay an average of $9,400 to save $1,000 a year in energy costs (equivalent to 10.6% rate of return or 9.4-year simple payback) For the same annual dollar savings, buyers of homes priced $150,000 to $249,999 will pay $10,304 (9.7% return, 10.3-year payback). Buyers of homes priced $250,000 to $499,999 will pay $13,551 (7.4% return, 13.6-year payback). And buyers of homes priced $500,000 or above will pay $15,163 (6.6% return, 15.2-year payback). In short, to invest in energy efficiency, the average buyer of a home priced under $150,000 requires a rate of return 400 basis points higher than the average buyer of a $500,000+ home.

Figure 8-5. Median & Average Amount Buyers are Willing to Pay Upfront to Save $1,000 a Year in Utility Bills, by Price They Expect to Pay for the Home

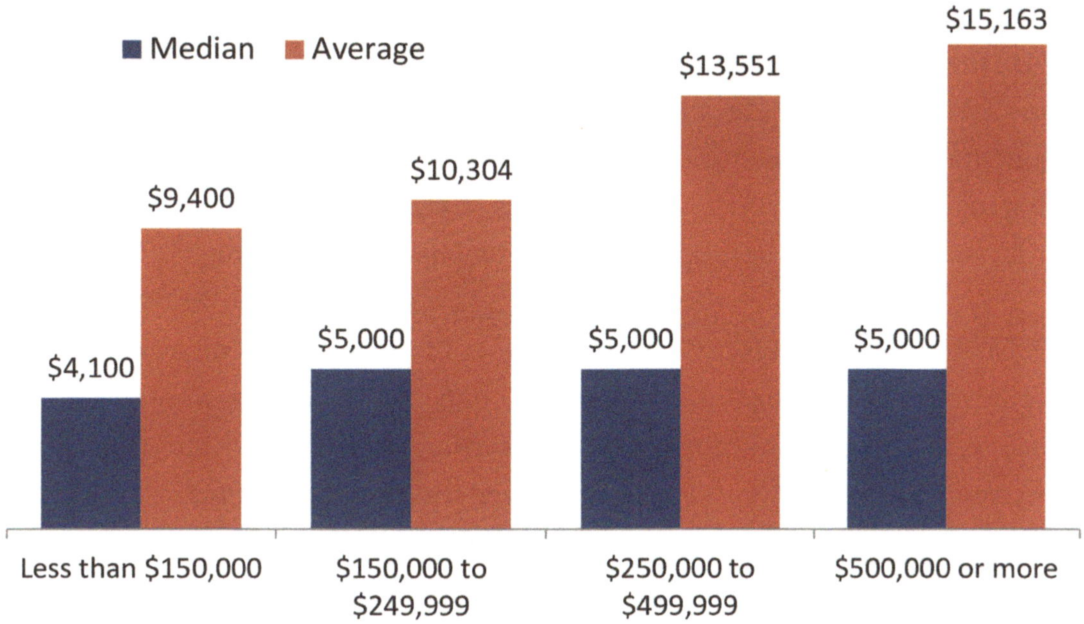

This agrees with conventional wisdom that buyers at the lower end of the market should be less willing to pay upfront for future returns. Buyers at the low end tend to be more concerned with day-to-day existence and therefore require a greater future return to persuade them to give up something today. They may also be considering somewhat different trade-offs when buying a home. Where a high-end buyer may be sacrificing hardwood trim in a secondary bedroom to cover the upfront cost of energy efficiency, a buyer at the low end may be sacrificing the entire bedroom.

As is typically the case, the medians show less variability than the averages. For four of the five price ranges in Figure 8-5, half of the buyers are unwilling to pay more than $5,000 (20.0% return, 5.0-year payback) to achieve $1,000 a year in savings. Only in the bottom tier (homes priced under $150,000) is the median somewhat lower, with half of the buyers unwilling to pay more than $4,100.

OTHER PROGRAMS GAINING GROUND, BUT ENERGY STAR STILL DOMINATES

Several programs now exist that certify if a home meets some type of green criteria. One example is a whole-home Energy Star rating, which targets a home's energy use. Another example is WaterSense, which targets its use of water. The U.S. Environmental Protection Agency manages both programs. There are also programs that take a more holistic view and certify that a home is green according to a more comprehensive set of criteria. To be certified to the National Green Building Standard® (NGBS), for instance, a home must meet separate criteria for energy efficiency, water efficiency, efficient use of resources, indoor environmental quality, homeowner education, and be on a lot designed and developed according to an additional set of green practices (conserving natural resources, managing stormwater runoff, minimizing environmental impacts during construction, etc.).

Of the various programs, ENERGY STAR remains the only one familiar to a majority of home buyers (73% in 2023). In comparison, only 36% of buyers were aware of the next most widely recognized programs: LEED for homes and HERS (the Home Energy Rating System). Between 23% and 32% recognized the other green programs on the list: WaterSense, Indoor AirPLUS, the NGBS (National Green Building Standard), ZERH (Zero Energy Ready Homes), Green Globes, the Living Building Challenge, and home certifications offered by the Passive House Institute US (PHIUS).

However, while ENERGY STAR clearly continues to dominate the public consciousness, the other green programs are just as clearly gaining ground on it. While the share of home buyers aware of ENERGY STAR declined between 2018 and 2020 and then remained stable at 73% in 2023, awareness of every other green programs in the survey increased noticeably. For example, the share of buyers aware of LEED for Homes increased from 24% in 2018 to 28% in 2020 and 36% in 2023.

That same pattern of growing public recognition prevails for every green program on the list other than ENERGY STAR. Even for PHIUS, the least well-known of the programs, the aware share increased systematically from 8% in 2018 to 15% in 2020 and then 23% in 2023 (Fig. 8-6).

Figure 8-6. Buyers Who Are Aware of Green Certification Programs for Homes

(Percent of Respondents)

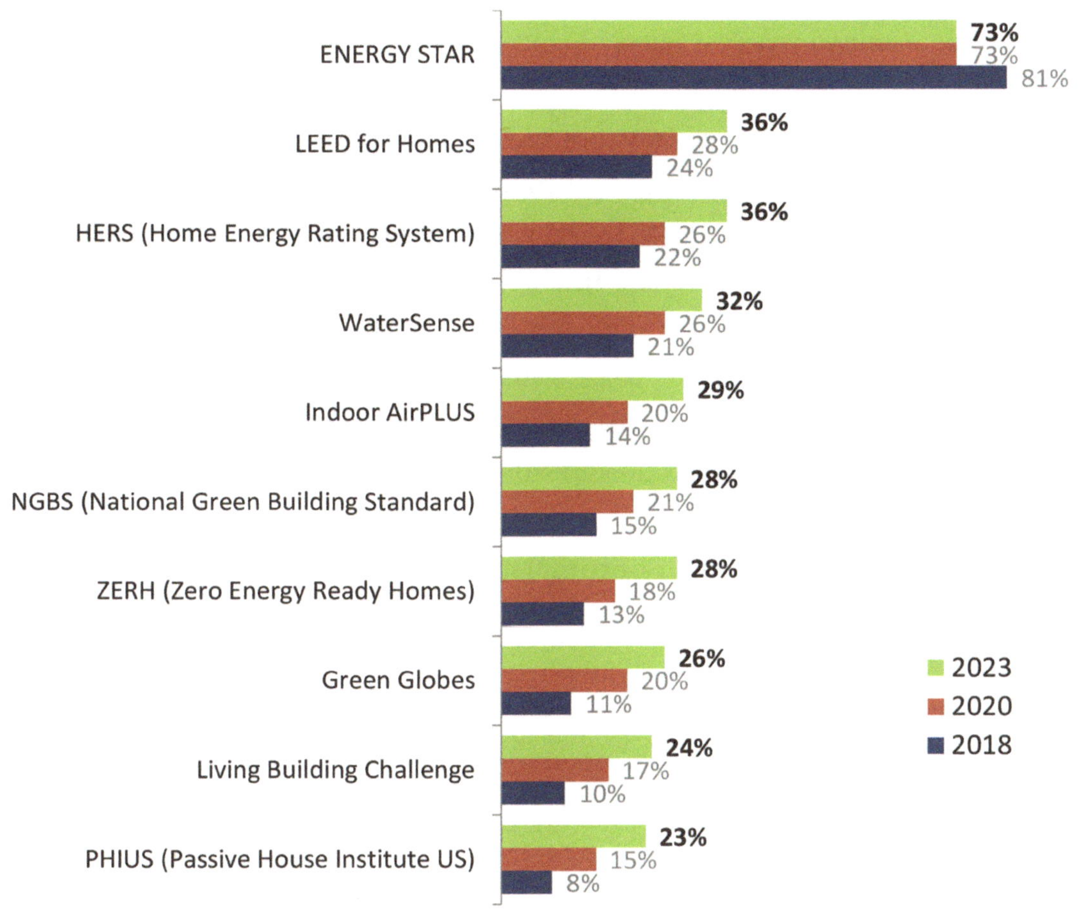

ENERGY STAR ALSO SHINES AT THE TOP OF THE MOST-WANTED GREEN LIST

The survey also captured preferences for 30 green features on the four-tier scale (essential, desirable, indifferent, or "Do Not Want") introduced in Chapter 3. As described in that chapter, the categories are defined by how they influence the home buyer's purchase decision. Figure 8-7 shows the percentages of buyers rating each of the green features essential (buyer is unlikely to purchase a home without it) or desirable (would seriously influence the buyer to purchase the home if included).

ENERGY STAR shines at the top of this chart as well. The three most popular green features all involve ENERGY STAR ratings: ENERGY STAR rated windows (considered essential or desirable by 83% of home buyers), ENERGY STAR rated appliances (80%) and an ENERGY STAR rating for the whole home (78%). The next three most wanted green features are also energy conserving: triple pane insulating glass windows (77%), efficient lighting that uses less energy than traditional bulbs (74%) and insulation higher than required by code (72%). The International Residential Code now requires efficient lighting, a change in the code NAHB determined was cost-effective and supported.

The next four most popular features on the list are various green certifications introduced into the questionnaire for the first time in 2023: certifications that the home is above health and wellness standards (rated essential or desirable by 71% of home buyers), has above-standard indoor environmental quality (70%), is above energy efficiency standards (69%) and is above water efficiency standards (68%).

At the bottom of the chart, the only green features rated essential or desirable by fewer than half of all home buyers are gas filled insulating glass windows (47%), a roof mounted electricity generating wind turbine (46%), prefabricated components such as wall panels or trusses (45%) and a roof partially or completely covered by plants (40%).

ENERGY STAR rated windows and appliances were both popular enough to make the overall list of most wanted home features discussed in Chapter 3. The four types of energy efficient windows mentioned in this chapter also appear in Chapter 5, which covers windows, doors, flooring and decorative features.

Figure 8-7. Green Features Rated Essential or Desirable

(Percent of Respondents)

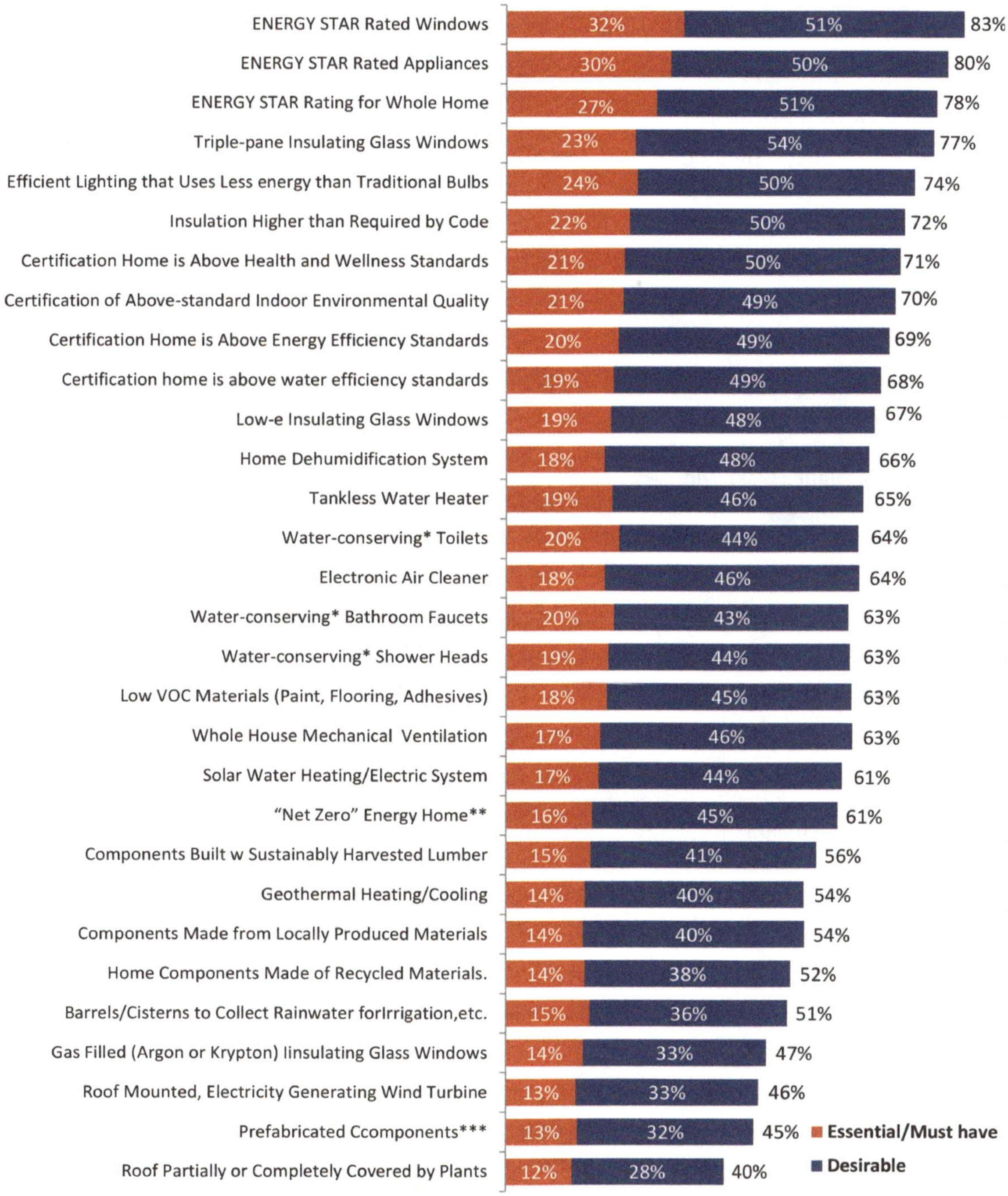

*Water-conserving is defined as below the federal conservation standard
**Net zero: produces as much energy from renewable sources as it consumes
***Components like panelized wall sections or roof & floor trusses

The green section of the NAHB home buyer survey was expanded and substantially altered in 2018. Since then, the shares of buyers who rate ENERGY STAR windows and appliances essential or desirable has actually declined, although these remain among the most highly rated of all home features in the survey. In contrast, the essential/desirable shares have increased for many of the other green features on the list. This effect is particularly noticeable at the bottom of the chart, among the least popular green features For example, prefabricated components and plant-covered roofs essential/desirable shares increased by 16 percentage points since 2018 (Fig. 8-8).

Figure 8-8. Percent of Green Features Rated Desirable or Essential: History

	2018	2020	2023
ENERGY STAR Rated Windows	89	83	83
ENERGY STAR Rated Appliances	86	81	80
ENERGY STAR Rating for Whole Home	81	79	78
Triple Pane Insulating Glass Windows	77	73	77
Efficient Lighting, Uses Less Energy than Traditional Bulbs	77	80	74
Insulation Higher than Required by Code	73	68	72
Certification Home is Above Health and Wellness Standards	na	na	71
Certification Home Has Above-Standard Indoor Environmental Quality	na	na	70
Certification Home is Above Energy Efficiency Standards	na	na	69
Certification Home Is Above Water Efficiency Standards	na	na	68
Low E-Insulating Glass Windows	62	65	67
Home Dehumidification System	58	65	66
Tankless Water Heater	61	67	65
Water-Conserving Toilets	63	59	64
Electronic Air Cleaner	57	64	64
Water-Conserving Bathroom Faucets	50	55	63
Water-Conserving Shower Heads	49	57	63
Low VOC Materials (Paint, Flooring, Adhesives)	57	62	63
Whole House Mechanical Ventilation	57	60	63
Solar Water Heating/Electric System	59	60	61
"Net Zero" Energy Home	53	57	61
Components Built w Sustainably Harvested Lumber	46	48	56
Geothermal Heating/Cooling	49	49	54
Components Made from Locally Produced Materials	45	49	54
Home Components Made of Recycled Materials	42	43	52
Barrels/Cisterns To Collect Rainwater for Irrigation, etc.	40	45	51
Gas Filled (Argon or Krypton) Insulating Glass Windows	43	44	47
Roof Mounted, Electricity Gene-Rating Wind Turbine	36	42	46
Prefabricated Components	29	38	45
Roof Partially or Completely Covered by Plants	24	32	40

FEW BUYERS ARE HOSTILE TO ANY GREEN AMENITY — IF YOU STAY OFF THEIR ROOFS

Given the increase in essential/desirable ratings for the least popular green features on the list, it should come as little surprise that few green features are explicitly rejected by large shares of home buyers. Only two green features are rated “do not want” (meaning the buyer is unlikely to purchase a home if it has this feature) by more than with one-fifth of buyers, both of them features on the home’s roof. A roof partially of completely coved by plants was rated “do not want” by 34% of buyers, and a roof mounted electricity generating wind turbine was rated “do not want” by 22%. The next highest “do not want” shares were 18% for rain-collecting barrels or cisterns and 17% for gas filled insulating glass windows (Fig. 8-9).

Figure 8-9. Green Features NOT Wanted by Home Buyers
(Percent of Respondents Rating Features “Do Not Want”)

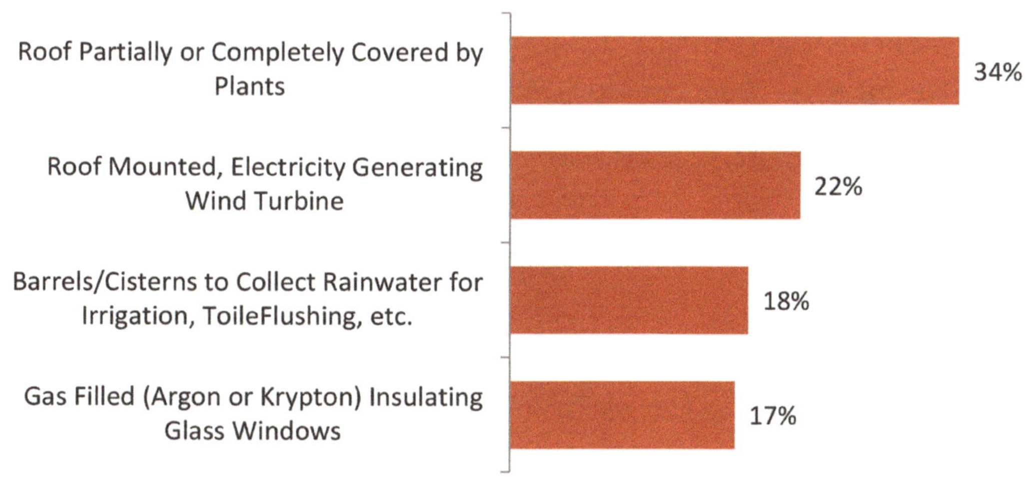

Perhaps surprisingly, prefabricated components — the second-least-wanted green feature in Figure 8-7 — are missing from the most unwanted green features shown in Figure 8-9. This is because most buyers do not have strong feelings either way about prefabricated components. Forty-two percent said they are indifferent about prefab components (Appendix A, page 133). This tied fiber cement siding for the highest indifferent percentage on any of the 200-plus features listed in the 2023 survey.

GAS STILL BEATS ELECTRICITY FOR COOKING, BUT THE GAP IS NARROWING

Most industry analysts agree that choice of fuel can have an impact on the environment, but don't always agree about which choice is the best one. Under the theory that electricity is superior to gas, for example, jurisdictions in California have adopted building codes that strongly discourage the use of natural gas. On the other hand, a 2019 National Institute of Standards and Technology study found that gas was the more environmentally friendly choice for an energy-efficient home built in Maryland.

Since 2020, NAHB's preference survey has included a question about buyers preferred energy sources. Significant differences quickly emerged with pluralities of buyers preferring electricity for space conditioning, and gas for cooking and (by a narrower margin) water heating in 2020. Since 2020, the balance has shifted noticeably in favor of electricity. For air heating and cooling systems, the share who prefer electricity increased from 52% to 59%, while the share who prefer gas declined from 33% to 28%. For water heating, the shift has been strong enough so that a plurality of 49% now prefer electricity, compared to 37% who prefer gas. For cooking, a plurality of buyers still prefer gas over electricity, but the gap has narrowed from 12 to six percentage points: 48% now prefer gas, and 42% prefer electricity (Fig. 8-10).

Figure 8-10. Energy Sources Home Buyers Prefer

(Percent of Respondents)

A. For Air Heating/Cooling System		
Gas	33	28
Electric	52	59
No Preference/Don't Know	15	13
B. For Water Heating System		
Gas	45	37
Electric	40	49
No Preference/Don't Know	15	13
C. For Cooking		
Gas	51	48
Electric	39	42
No Preference/Don't Know	9	10

There are some noticeable and statistically significant differences in cooking fuel preferences across the nine Census divisions. The share of buyers who prefer electricity for cooking is highest in the three divisions in the southern region of the country: 51% prefer electricity in the South Atlantic and adjacent East South Central divisions, and 48% prefer electricity in the West South Central. The share who prefer electricity for cooking is lowest in the Mountain (31%), Middle Atlantic (32%) and East North Central (36%) divisions (Fig. 8-11). The analysis described in Chapter 12 finds that each of the six divisions other than the East and West South Central is statistically different from the default South Atlantic in this regard.

Figure 8-11. Share of Buyers Who Prefer Electricity for Cooking by Census Division

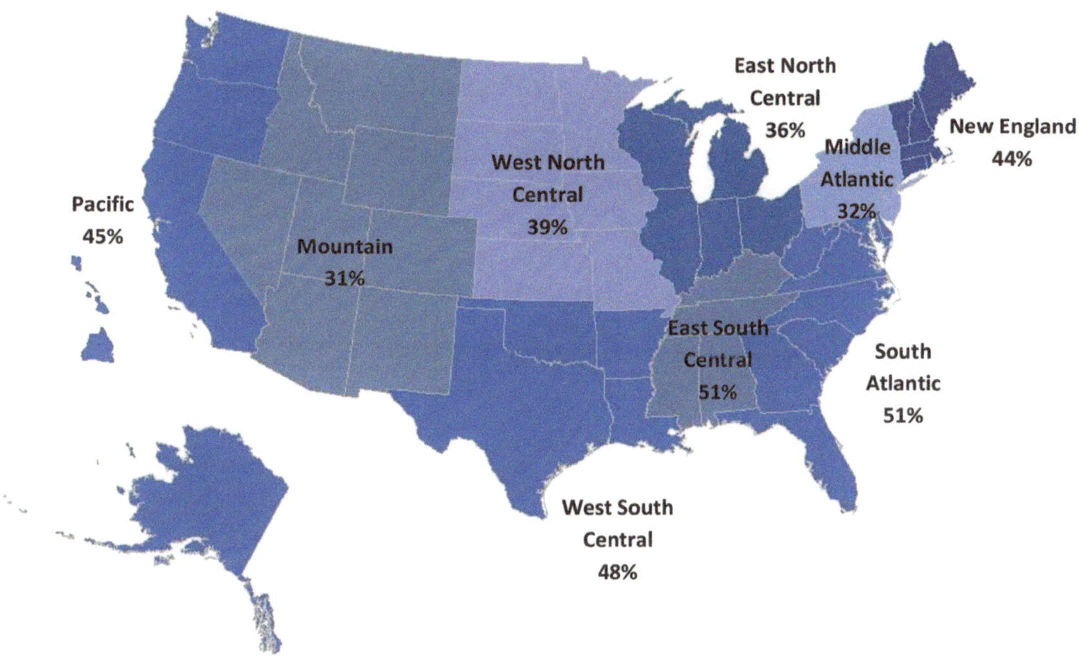

The top reasons buyers choose a particular energy source for cooking are safety, reliability and cost. Sixty percent of buyers cited safety as a reason for their choice of cooking fuel, followed at a distance by 46% who choose the fuel because it is reliable and 41% who choose it because it saves money (Fig 8-12). Smaller shares choose a cooking fuel because it improves the home's air quality (31%), is available where they want to live (29%) or lowers greenhouse gas emissions (19%).

Figure 8-12. Reasons for Choice of Energy Source for Cooking
(Percent of Respondents)

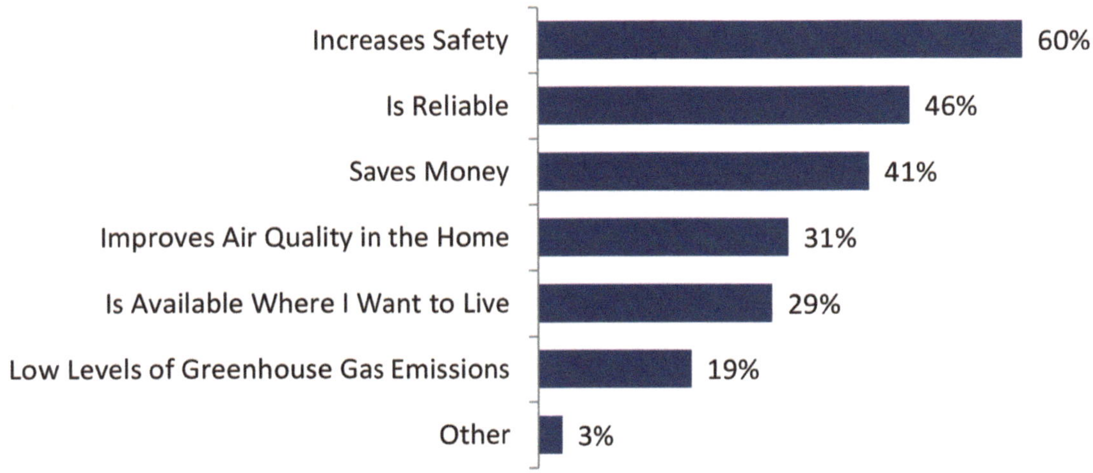

ALL-ELECTRIC HOMES GALVANIZE BUYERS IN THE SOUTH & PACIFIC DIVISIONS

For the first time the 2023 preference survey asked buyers if they would be willing to purchase an all-electric home — i.e., one not connected in any way to a gas line. Nationally, 60% said they would, in fact, be willing to buy an all-electric home; 21% said maybe; and 19% said no. A majority of buyers in seven of the nine Census divisions are open to the idea of an all-electric home. There were a few notable geographic differences, however the share who would definitely buy an all-electric home is at its highest in the Pacific (71%) and two southern divisions: the West South Central (69%) and the South Atlantic (68%). The share who would buy an all-electric home is statistically different and distinctly lower in the other six divisions: as low as under 50% in the East North Central and Middle Atlantic states (Fig. 8-13).

Figure 8-13. Would You Buy an All-Electric Home (Not Connected to Gas Lines)? by Census Division

(Percent of Respondents)

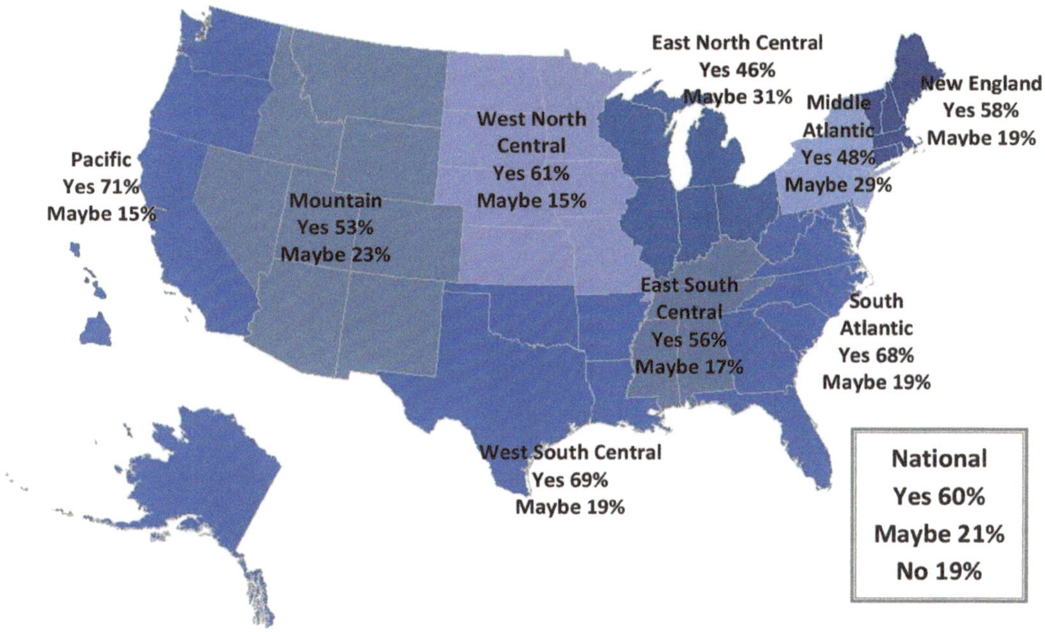

BUYERS SOMETIMES CHOOSE GREEN, BUT LIKE CUL DE SACS & UPGRADED FINISHES

In the typical case, when a buyer chooses a green option for the home, that buyer is giving up something else, an alternative option or "trade-off." If a buyer chooses an efficiently sized heating and cooling system, it means giving up a system with excess capacity. If landscaping uses native plants that require little maintenance, it means giving up traditional landscaping with a lawn and shrubs. If a home orientation uses the sun for heating and cooling, it means giving up some curb appeal. The 2023 NAHB survey included seven green trade-off questions (Fig. 8-14).

Figure 8-14. Which Alternative Would You Prefer?

(Percent of Respondents)

A heating and cooling system designed to meet your current needs efficiently	**68%**	**vs.**	A heating and cooling system larger than currently needed with some excess capacity	32%
Low maintenance landscaping with plants that grow in the local climate w minimal	**60%**	**vs.**	Conventional landscaping with a traditional lawn, trees shrubs, etc.	40%
Home oriented to make efficient use of the sun's energy for heating and cooling	**68%**	**vs.**	Home oriented to optimize the attractiveness of the home as viewed from the street	32%
Wider sidewalks and streets	**51%**	**vs.**	Narrower sidewalks and streets with more green space	49%
Features and finishes made of more expensive materials that last longer	**77%**	**vs.**	Features and finishes made of materials that cost less but need to be replaced more often	23%
Home on a Cul de sac or other street design with limited traffic flow	**69%**	**vs.**	Home on a continuous, interconnected street with more efficient traffic flow	31%
Upgraded interior finishes (e.g., flooring/counters/trim)	**54%**	**vs.**	Green features (e.g., energy/water efficiency/indoor air quality)	46%

In four of the seven cases, a majority of buyers would make the green trade-off. Three-fifths of buyers would choose low-maintenance landscaping with local plants over conventional landscaping, and 68% chose the efficiently sized heating and cooling system and a home oriented to use the sun over the less green alternatives.

However, the green alternative chosen most often by home buyers (77% of the time) is features and finishes made from more expensive but also more durable materials. Durable materials qualify as a green feature, because over time it requires fewer resources to manufacture and install the product In addition to the environmental benefits, durability offers convenience and lower maintenance and replacement costs Some buyers may deem more expensive and durable materials to have more aesthetic appeal — if they are thinking of quartz countertops, for example.

In the trade-off question that directly asks buyers to choose between aesthetic appeal and environmental benefits, aesthetic appeal wins over half the time. All else equal, 54% of buyers would choose upgraded interior finishes over green features in the home.

A slimmer majority of 51% would choose wider sidewalks and streets over narrower sidewalks and streets with more green space. Although green space is by definition a green alternative, some interest groups advocate wider streets and wider sidewalks for environmental reasons, arguing that the improved traffic flow and walkability result in reduce vehicle greenhouse gas emissions With different groups simultaneously advocating more and less concrete in subdivisions for similar environmental reasons, it is probably not surprising that developers and local jurisdictions are sometimes confused, and that home buyers are split close to 50-50 on the question.

When asked directly about living on an interconnected street with efficient traffic flow vs. a cul de sac or other street designed to limit traffic, a clear majority (69%) favor the cul de sac, making interconnected streets the green alternative least often chosen by home buyers (Fig. 8-15).

Figure 8-15. Percent of Buyers Choosing the Green Alternative

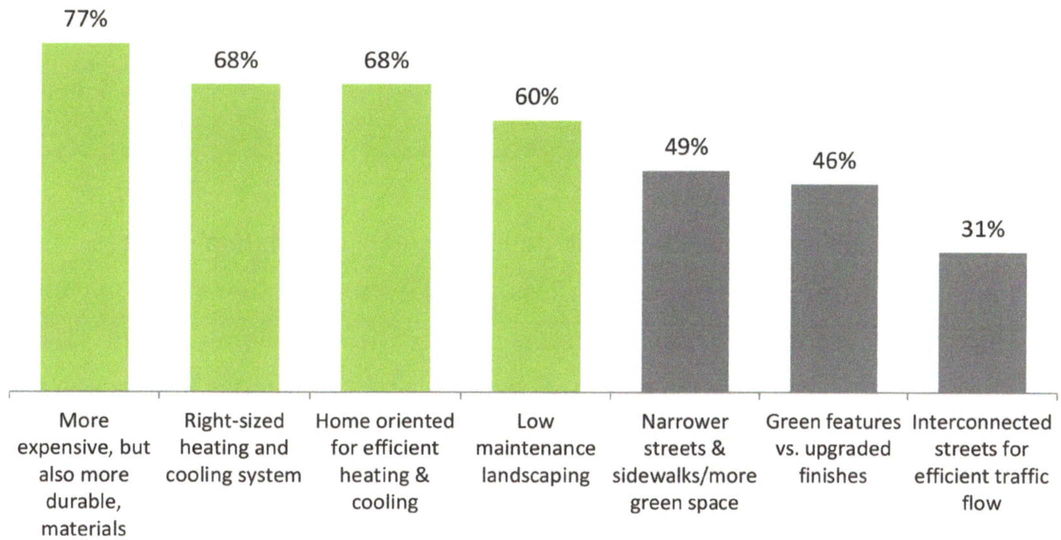

ON SEVERAL TRADE-OFFS, OLDER BUYERS ARE GREENER

The four green alternatives favored by a majority of home buyers overall, are favored even more often by older buyers. For example, 80% of Baby Boomers (born 1946 to 1964) chose the "more expensive but durable materials" option, compared to 76% of Gen X'ers (1965-1980), 72% of Millennials (1981-1996) and 65% of Gen Z'ers (1997 or later). The same regular pattern of older buyers more often favoring the green alternative is present in the preferences for a right-sized heating and cooling system, home oriented for efficient heating & cooling, and low maintenance landscaping (Fig. 8-16).

Figure 8-16. Percent of Buyers Choosing the Green Alternative by Generation

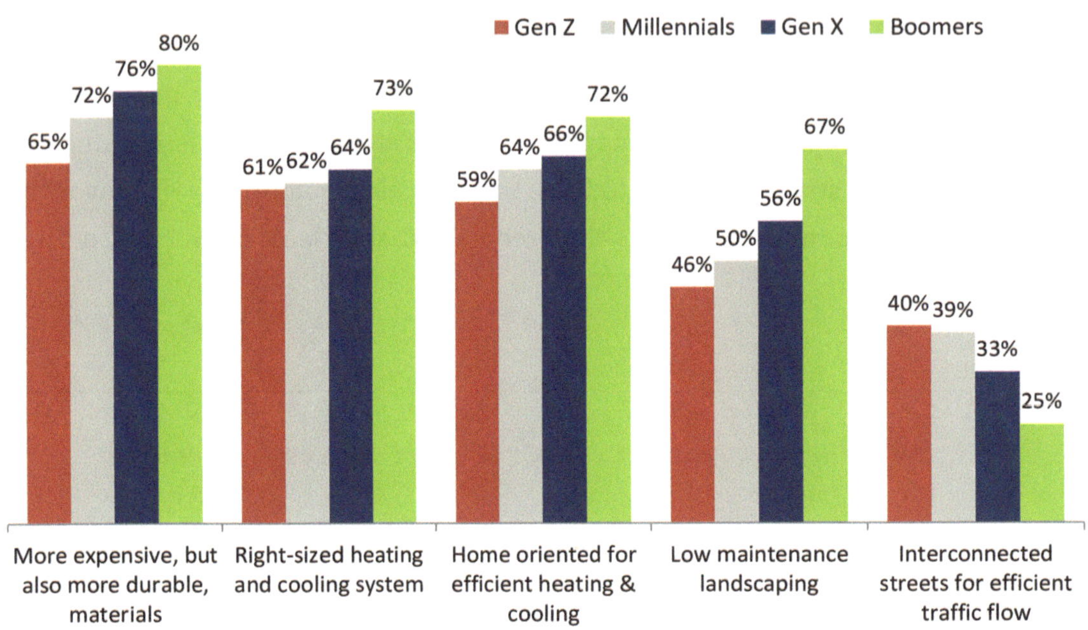

On the other side of the scale, the least popular green alternative — inter-connected streets for efficient traffic flow — is even less popular among older home buyers Only 25% of Boomers chose interconnected streets over cul de sacs, compared to 33% of Gen Xers, 39% of Millennials and 40% of Gen Z buyers The differences across generations shown in Figure 8-16 are all statistically significant according to the analyses described in Chapter 12.

GREEN SUMMARY

To summarize some of the key points in the green chapter,

- Only 18% of home buyers are willing to pay more for a home simply because it is environmentally friendly. However, the percentage is edging up slowly over time.
- Most buyers, however, will pay something for an environmentally friendly home if it reduces their future utility bills. The average amount they will pay up front to save $1,000 annually is $12,314 (equivalent to an 8.1% rate of return or 12.3-year simple payback), the highest it's been since NAHB began tracking the number in its surveys.

- The average amount, however, is driven by a relatively small number of buyers at the extreme upper end. The median amount they will pay (for some purposes, a better measure of the typical home buyer) remains stable at $5,000 (20% return, 5.0-year payback).

- Moreover, buyers at the low end of the price scale are less willing (and probably less able) to pay upfront for future savings. Buyers of homes under $150,000 will pay an average of $9,400 to save $1,000 a year, compared to $15,163 for buyers of homes priced at $500,000+.

- Equivalently, to invest in energy efficiency, the average buyer of a home priced under $150,000 requires a rate of return 400 basis points higher than the average buyer of a $500,000+ home.

- ENERGY STAR remains the only green certification program familiar to a majority of home buyers, but a large number of other green programs are making significant gains in name recognition.

- Of 30 listed green features, the six most popular specifically target energy efficiency. The three most popular are all ENERGY STAR ratings (for windows, appliances, and the entire home).

- The only green features that would prevent more than 20% of potential buyers from purchasing a particular home are a roof partially or completely covered by plants, and a roof with an electricity-generating wind turbine.

- A plurality of buyers prefer electricity for space conditioning and water heating, but gas for cooking. In all three cases, however, electricity has gained share since 2020.

- Nevertheless, 28% of buyers still want to heat their homes with gas.

- 19% of buyers would never buy an all-electric home.

- Nationally, 60% of home buyers would definitely consider purchasing an all-electric home — about 70% of buyers in the Pacific, West South Central, and South Atlantic Census divisions.

- On a series of green trade-off questions, a majority of buyers chose the green alternative in four out of seven cases. At the top, 77% chose finishes made of more expensive materials that last longer over less expensive materials that wear out more quickly. At the bottom, only 31% favored interconnected streets for efficient traffic flow over cul de sacs or other street designs with more limited traffic.

- The four green alternatives chosen by a majority of buyers (finishes made of durable materials, a right-sized heating and cooling system, home oriented to make efficient use of the sun, and low-maintenance landscaping) are all significantly more popular among older home buyers.

- Conversely, the least popular green alternative (interconnected streets) is even less popular among older buyers.

Chapter 9

Technology in the Home

TEMPERATURE CONTROL AND SECURITY TOP THE TECH WISH LIST

The ability to stay connected has become increasingly vital to our society, even when we are at home. The proliferation of technology has provided potential home buyers with numerous tools to connect their households, whether for security, energy conservation, entertainment, or simply convenience. Given all the options already available to buyers and with the anticipation of future developments, understanding which technological choices are valued the most by home buyers is imperative.

The 2023 NAHB survey asked recent and prospective home buyers to rate 19 technology features on the four-tier scale (essential, desirable, indifferent, or "do not want") first mentioned in Chapter 3. As a reminder, these categories define how features influence the home buyer's purchase decision. Figure 9-1 shows the percentages of buyers rating each technology feature as essential (i.e., buyer is unlikely to purchase a home without it) or desirable (i.e., would seriously influence the buyer to purchase the home if included).

When it comes to technology, a majority of recent and prospective buyers find nearly all features in the survey appealing. Yet the top eight features reveal that, first and foremost, buyers are turning to technology to achieve two goals: save energy by efficiently controlling the temperature of their home and increase the safety of their home. Those five most wanted tech features are a programmable thermostat (78%), security cameras (76%), a video doorbell (74%), a wireless home security system (70%), and a multi-zone HVAC system (68%).

Most of the remaining tech features, 11 out of 14, are considered essential or desirable by at least 50% of buyers, ranging from 63% for a lighting control system to 50% for a smart refrigerator. And even the relatively least influential technology features are essential/desirable to just under half of all buyers: a charging station for electric cars (49%), a smart oven (49%), and a home theater (48%).

Figure 9-1. Technology Features Rated Essential or Desirable

(Percent of Respondents)

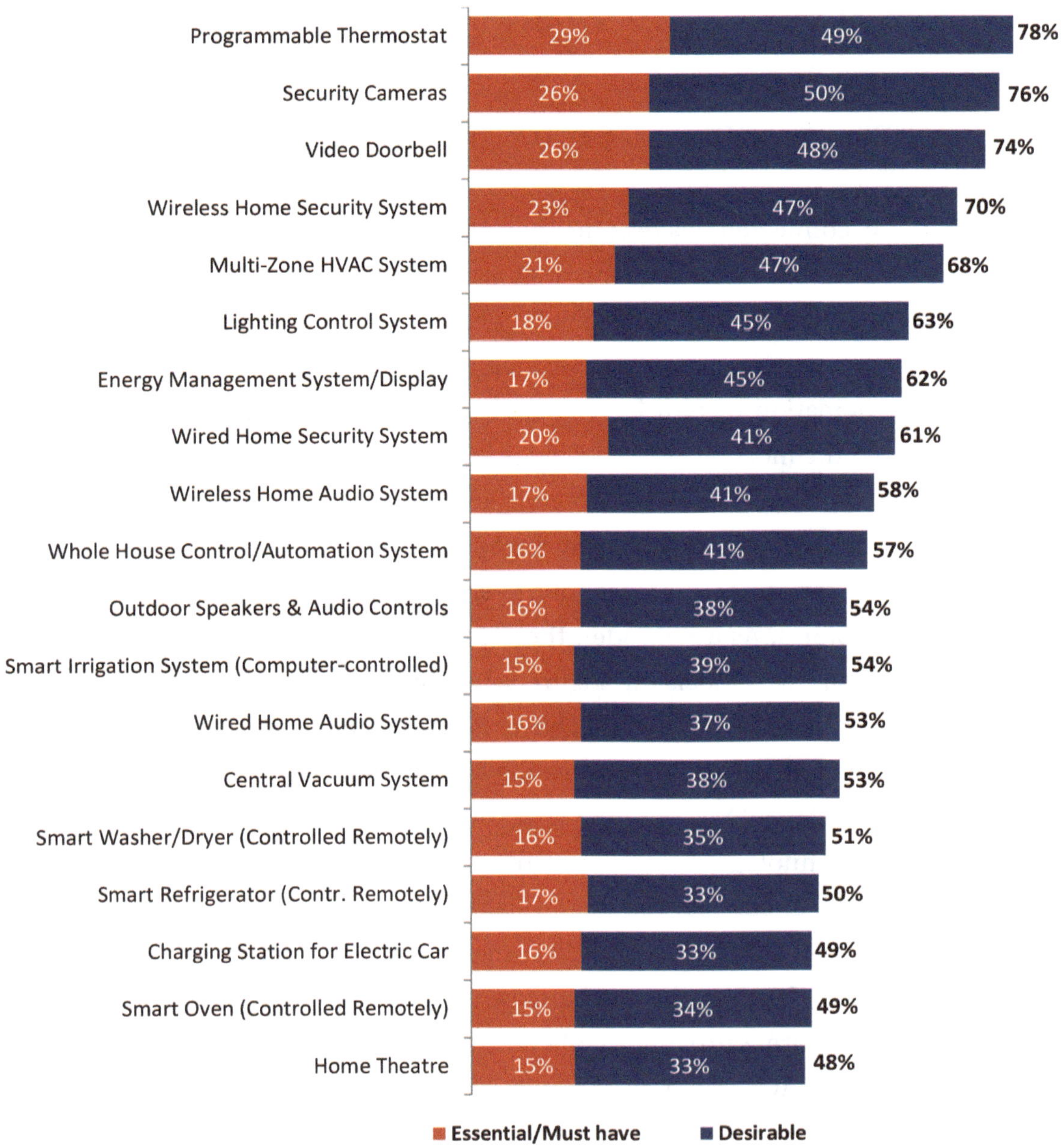

MAJORITY OF TECHNOLOGY FEATURES GROWING IN POPULARITY

Figure 9-2 details the history of the NAHB home buyer preference survey question on home technology features, but caution is advised when interpreting it. Prior to 2020, buyers were simply asked if they wanted each of the technology features or not. In 2020, the format of the question changed to shift to the essential/desirable/indifferent/unwanted scale used throughout the survey. Comparing results from 2020 and 2023 reveals that there was a significant impact on buyers' ratings of technology as essential/desirable, led by:

- Charging station for electric car, up 11 points from 38% to 49%.
- Multi-zone HVAC system, up 9 points from 59% to 68%.
- Wired home security system, up 8 points from 53% to 61%
- Smart irrigation system, up 8 points from 46% to 53%.

In fact, the popularity of 18 of the 19 technology features increased from 2020 to 2023, with the only exception being a wireless home security system, which remained unchanged at 70%.

Figure 9-2. Preferences for Technology Features: History

[Percent of Respondents who "Would Like to Have" the Feature (2007-2018) or Rate it Desirable or Essential (2020-2023)]

	2007	2012	2015	2018	2020	2023
Programmable Thermostat	n/a	47	51	44	77	78
Security Cameras	n/a	40	47	46	73	76
Video Doorbell	n/a	n/a	n/a	45	70	74
Wireless Home Security System	n/a	50	54	40	70	70
Multl-zone HVAC System	55	37	43	36	59	68
Lighting Control System	54	39	44	39	57	63
Energy Management System/Display	61	32	45	31	59	62
Wired Home Security System	n/a	26	29	31	53	61
Wireless Home Audio System	n/a	39	43	33	56	58
Whole House Control/Automation System	n/a	30	39	29	53	57
Outdoor Speakers & Audio Controls	n/a	31	37	30	49	54
Smart Irrigation System (Computer-controlled)	n/a	30	37	29	46	54
Wired Home Audio System	n/a	24	28	26	50	53
Central vacuum system	49	34	39	33	46	53
Smart Washer/Dryer (Controlled Remotely)	n/a	28	37	31	44	51
Smart Refrigerator (Controlled Remotely)	n/a	25	36	26	45	50
Charging Station for Electric Cars	n/a	23	26	21	38	49
Smart Oven (Controlled Remotely)	n/a	27	35	25	44	49
Home Theatre	54	37	39	31	45	48

DESIRABILITY FOR SOME FEATURES DIFFERS BY AGE

Age and technology do not always mix well, and in some cases desirability wanes as buyers get older. Figure 9-3 details the five technology features for which age makes the most difference. In these cases, there is at least a 30-point difference in the share rating essential/desirable between the youngest (under 35 years old) cohort and the oldest (65 years or older).

A home theatre shows the starkest discrepancy, with buyers under the age of 45-years old more than twice as likely (66%) to want this feature in their house as those 65 years or older (31%). Similarly, 69% of the youngest group wants a smart refrigerator, compared to only 37% of the oldest. For outdoor speakers/audio control, a smart oven, and a smart washer/dryer, most buyers under 55 want them, compared to at most 40% of the oldest cohort. Based on the statistical analysis performed in Chapter 12, these differences by age are highly significant.

Figure 9-3. Top Technology Features Rated Essential or Desirable Largest Margins Between Youngest and Oldest Age Groups

(Percent of Respondents Rating Features as "Essential/Must Have" or "Desirable")

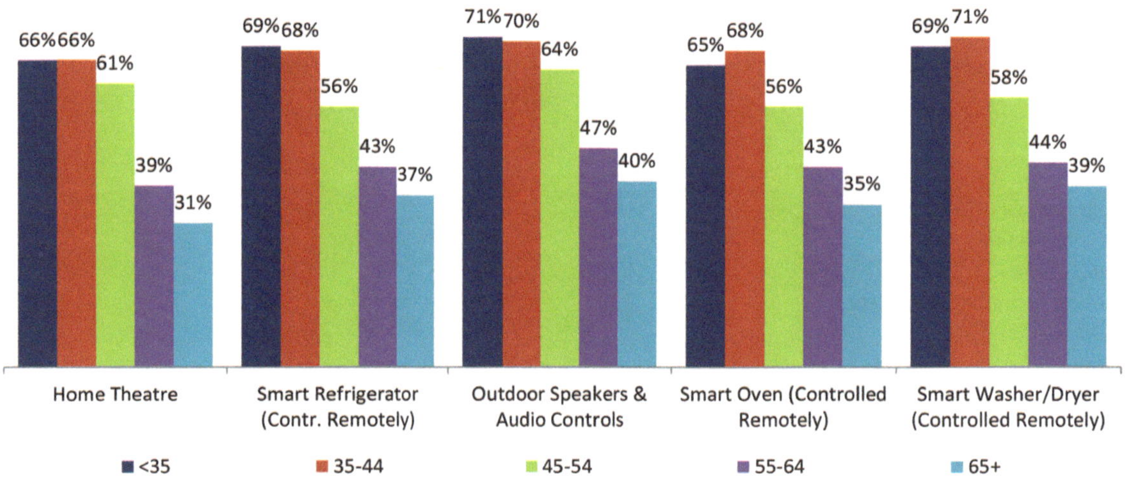

WEALTHY BUYERS WANT MORE TECHNOLOGY

As with many other goods and services in the economy, the higher the buyer income, the more likely they want technology features. In a few cases, there is at least a 25-point difference in the share of buyers in the lowest income bracket and those in the highest bracket. For example, whereas only 39% of buyers earning under $50,000 rate a charging station for an electric car as essential/desirable, the share is 68% among those earning $150,000+. While 37% of the lowest-income group want a home theater, 65% of the highest group do. A similar gap exists for a smart irrigation system, a wired home audio system, and a whole house control/automation system (Fig. 9-4). The effect of income on preferences for these technology features is statistically significant, even after controlling for age and other characteristics of the buyers, as explained in Chapter 12.

Nevertheless, the costs of new technology tend to decrease over time as its usage becomes ubiquitous and more firms enter the market as suppliers. As a result, technological features that at first are only affordable to wealthier home buyers typically become more attainable to those lower on the income spectrum. Evidence supporting this phenomenon includes the overall increase in popularity of technology features among buyers earning less than $50,000. In 2020, the average share of these buyers rating all technology features as essential or desirable was 41%. By 2023, the share had increased 10 points to 51%.

Figure 9-4. Technology Features Rated Essential or Desirable by Income, With 25+ Point Difference Between Lowest and Highest Shares

(Percent of Respondents Rating Features as "Essential/Must Have" or "Desirable")

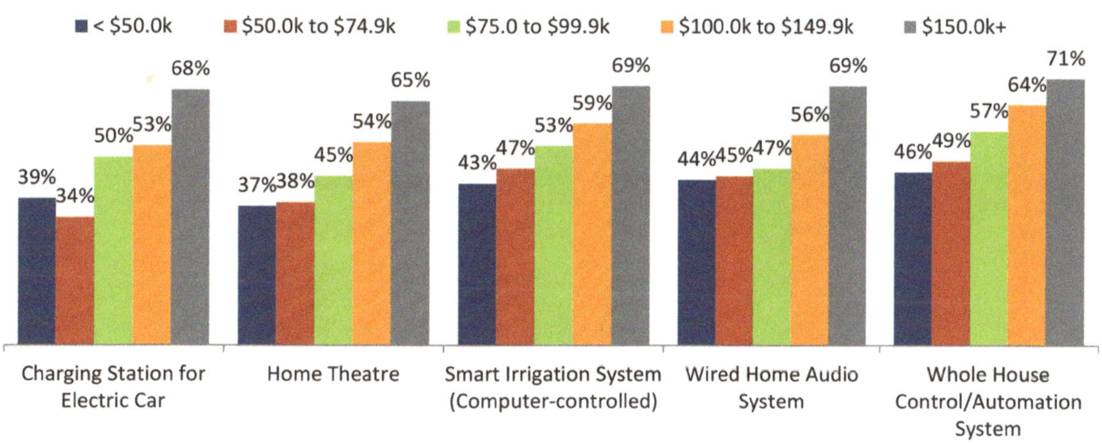

A QUARTER OF BUYERS DO NOT A WANT CHARGING STATION, HOME THEATRE

Home buyers could have also rated each technology feature as 'do not want' to indicate it would likely cause them to pass on a potential house. Of the 19 technology features listed in the survey, only two are 'unwanted' by at least a quarter of buyers: a home theater (26%) and a charging station for electric vehicles (26%). Twenty percent reject outdoor speakers/audio controls, smart refrigerator, and smart oven. Fewer than 20% of buyers reject the remaining technology features. Not surprisingly, the top ten highest rated technology features from Figure 9-1 are symmetrically the bottom ten features least likely to be 'unwanted' on Figure 9-5.

Figure 9-5. Technology Features NOT Wanted by Home Buyers

(Percent of Respondents Rating Features "Do Not Want")

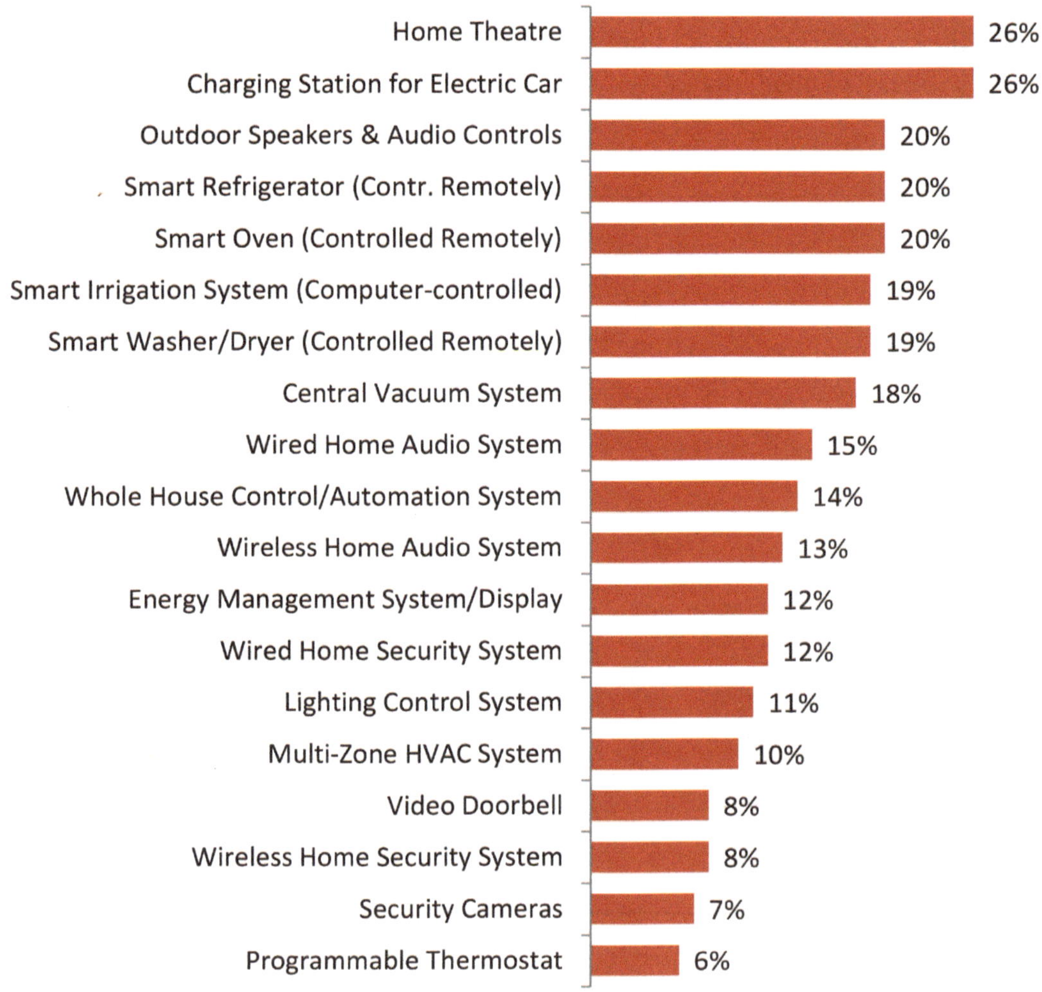

VIRTUAL HOME TOURS ARE POPULAR

When asked if they are planning to watch virtual home tours as part of the home buying process (or did watch them if they purchased a home in the last three years), 63% of buyers responded affirmatively. Of the rest, 23% said no and 14% were unsure (Fig. 9-6).

PREVALENCE OF VIRTUAL TOURS RISES WITH INCOME, PRICE POINT

With the lone exception of buyers earning less than $50,000, most buyers in each of the demographic group analyzed in Appendix A plan to watch at least one virtual home tour

Figure 9-6. Planning to Watch (or Have Already Watched) Virtual Tours During Home Purchase Process

(Percent of Respondents)

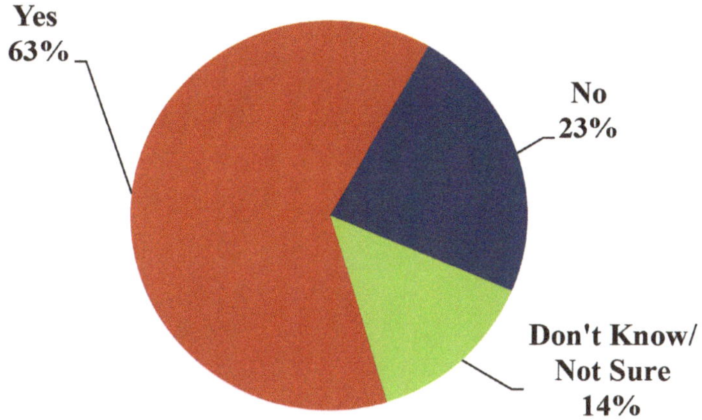

during the purchase process (or did so if already bought). Two factors, however, significantly increase the likelihood buyers will watch virtual home tours: income and price point. In the first case, only 48% of buyers with income below $50,000 plan on watching vs. 78% among those earning $150,000 or more. And across price points, the share rises from 53% of those paying less than $150,000 to 76% of those paying $500,000 or more (Fig. 9-7). The differences in plans to watch virtual tours by income, which also serves as a proxy for price of a house, are statistically significant based on the analysis outlined in Chapter 12.

Figure 9-7. Planning to Watch Virtual Tours by Income and by Price Point

(Percent of Respondents Who Indicate 'Yes')

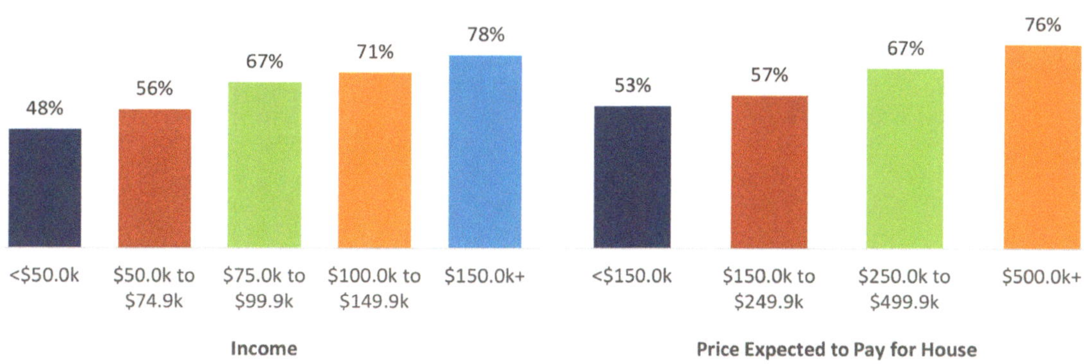

Chapter 10

Choosing a Community

BUYERS PREFER THE SUBURBS, ESPECIALLY GEN Z & BOOMERS

Often one of the first decisions buyers make when looking for a home is the overall location where they want to live. The NAHB survey asked recent and prospective buyers about their location preference, and a majority — 53% — chose the suburbs, either outlying (29%) or close-in (24%). The next largest segment of buyers would prefer a rural area (25%), and the remaining 23% would like to buy a home in the central city, either right in downtown (13%) or outside of downtown (10%) (Fig. 10-1).

Not surprisingly, location preferences are not homogeneous among buyers of different generations. A suburban location (either close-in or outlying) is significantly more important for Boomers (60%) than for Millennials (42%). The opposite is true for a central city location (either downtown or outside of it), where only 16% of the oldest group would prefer to buy a home compared to 36% of Millennial buyers. There is more of a consensus for a rural area, as the share of each generation interested in that location stays between 21% and 28%.

Figure 10-1. Location Preference by Buyer's Generation

(Percent of Respondents)

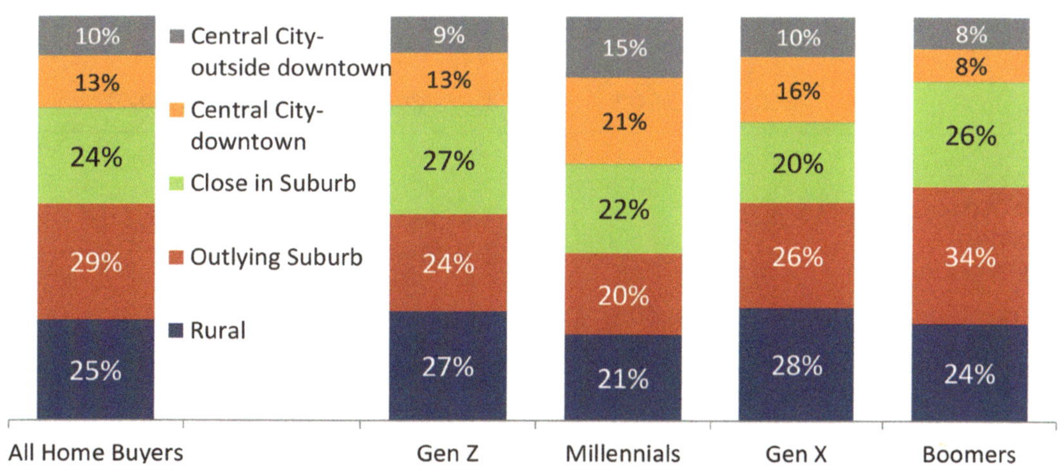

The statistical analysis described in Chapter 12 shows a significant shift away from central cities in favor of less dense outlying areas (especially outlying suburbs) as home buyers age. This shift is visually apparent in Figure 10-1 for the Millennials, Gen X'ers and Boomers. Gen Z buyers, who are relatively new to (and so far account for a relatively small share of) the home buying market, appear to be bucking the trend. The location preferences of the Gen Z'ers, in fact, resemble those of Gen X buyers or Boomers more than they do the preferences of Millennials. It will be interesting to see if this pattern persists as Gen Z ages and starts accounting for more of the market.

Before 2020, the NAHB survey used to include only one general central city option in its location question. Starting that year, however, the option was split into two in order to allow for the distinct possibility of buyers wanting to live in the central city, just not in the middle of busy downtowns. As a result, buyers now have two options: central city–downtown and central city–outside of downtown.

The change had a significant impact, as the share of buyers interested in the overall central city jumped from 11% in 2018 (before the split) to 20% and 23%, respectively, in 2020 and 2023 (after the split). In other words, roughly 10% of buyers switched to preferring a central city location, as long as it is away from downtown. The gain came at the expense of the suburbs, whose share dropped from 64% in 2018 to 53% in 2023 (Fig. 10-2). Undoubtedly, the rising weight of the Millennial generation in the housing market (along with their location preferences) is a key driver behind these changes in location preferences.

Figure 10-2. Location Preference - History

(Percent of Respondents who said 'yes')

	2003	2007	2012	2015	2018	2020	2023
Central City - Outside Downtown	} 6	6	8	8	11	9	10
Central City – Downtown						11	13
Close-in Suburb	30	27	30	30	30	28	24
Outlying Suburb	33	36	36	36	34	30	29
Rural	30	31	27	27	24	23	25

TYPICAL BUYER WILLING TO COMMUTE 11.3 MILES ONE-WAY

With more than half of home buyers reporting a desire to live in the suburbs, it is not surprising the typical one-way commute they are willing to endure is 11.3 miles. The plurality of buyers — 38% — would travel a maximum distance of 11 to 20 miles between home and work, while the next largest group — 31% — would only be willing to commute 5 to 10 miles. Sixteen percent of buyers are willing to commute less than 5 miles, and at the other extreme, 16% would accept a one-way commute of more than 20 miles (Fig. 10-3).

Figure 10-3. Farthest One-Way Distance Willing to Travel from Home to Work

(Percent of Respondents)

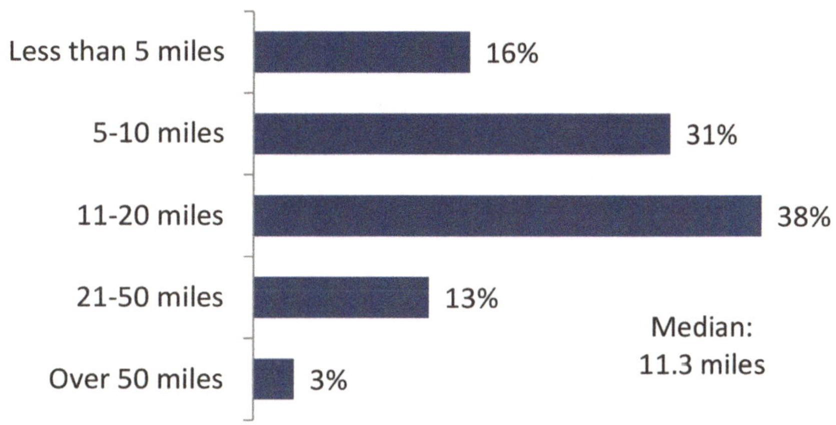

WORKING FROM HOME IS COMMON AMONG HOME BUYERS

When the COVID-19 pandemic forced mandatory lockdowns, quickly causing more than 20 million jobs to disappear from the American economy, many employers had no choice but to allow their employees to work remotely from home full-time. For a time, teachers taught virtually, doctors saw patients through a computer screen, and office workers spent entire days meeting on Zoom. But as the national health emergency began to subside and case counts plummeted, many employers summoned their workforce back to the office, at least for part of the week. This is the backdrop for a new question introduced to the 2023 NAHB survey about the ability to work from home at least two days a week.

Results show that working remotely some of the time is common among a large share of recent and prospective home buyers. To be more precise, 43% typically work from home at least 2 days a week. On the other hand, 41% do not enjoy the privilege of remote work. The remaining 15% are likely not in the workforce and therefore said the question was not applicable to them (Fig. 10-4).

Figure 10-4. Do You Typically Work from Home at Least 2 Days a Week?
(Percent of Respondents)

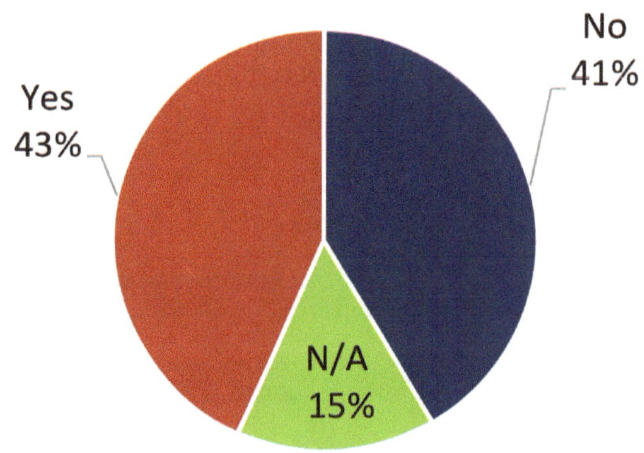

The importance of this finding is that a meaningful segment of home buyers (43%) are less tethered to their places of employment than before the pandemic, and that may have direct implications on their willingness to live farther from the office and commute longer on the day(s) they are required to be at work in-person. Across demographic breakdowns, first-time buyers (32%) are less likely than repeat buyers (45%) to work from home at least two days a week. It is the same for buyers earning less than $50,000 a year (23%), compared to those earning $150,000 or more (66%). Boomers (29%) are also significantly less likely than the younger three generations to have the ability to work from home twice a week (Gen Z, 52%; Millennials, 63%; Gen X, 53%) (Appendix A, pages A10-A12). The analysis described in Chapter 12 shows that homebuyers' income and age have independent and significant impacts on the tendency to work from home.

BUYERS WANT CONVENIENT AND WALK-FRIENDLY COMMUNITIES

The home that successfully appeals to a home buyer doesn't exist in a vacuum. It sits inside a community that buyers evaluate as thoroughly as the home itself. The onset of the COVID-19 pandemic in 2020 highlighted the importance of community features as many households shifted to working from home and started using public spaces in their neighborhoods. Three years later, as reported earlier in this chapter, a significant share of buyers continue to work remotely at least two days a week, and likely stay inside their communities several days a week. These are some of the reasons why it is paramount to understand what buyers want in a community. The 2023 NAHB survey achieves this goal by asking recent and prospective home buyers about the influence 29 community features would have on their home purchase decision, using the essential/desirable/indifferent/unwanted scale introduced in earlier chapters.

Findings show that an ideal community to most buyers is one that offers convenience, walkability, and a quintessential suburban feel. This comes from the five most essential/desirable community features. At the top, 70% want to be near retail space (e.g. grocery/drug stores). Not far behind, 66% would prefer their community to have a park, 66% want walking/jogging trails, 65% desire a walkable community (with walkways connecting homes, shopping, and public spaces/transportation), and 64% would prefer it to be a typically suburban neighborhood (all single-family detached houses) (Fig. 10-5).

In a slightly lower tier of preference, another seven community features are essential/desirable to 50% to 59% of home buyers: lake (59%), swimming pool (57%), outdoor maintenance service (55%), gated access (53%), good public schools (50%), access to public transportation (50%), and a green rating for the whole neighborhood (50%). Incidentally, the latter is a brand-new community feature added to the NAHB survey in 2023 and part of the National Green Building Standard mentioned in Chapter 8 and available from Home Innovation Research Labs.

The 10 least influential community features are all rated essential/desirable by fewer than 40%: golf course and daycare center (both 34%), pickleball court and baseball/soccer field (both 35%), tennis courts and mixed use (near office/commercial buildings) (both 36%), high density and bikeshare/carshare services (both 37%), and finally, a homeowners association (39%). Two of these features are new to the 2023 survey–pickleball court and homeowners association–and these results demonstrate most buyers do not find them appealing.

Figure 10-5. Community Features Rated Essential or Desirable

(Percent of Respondents)

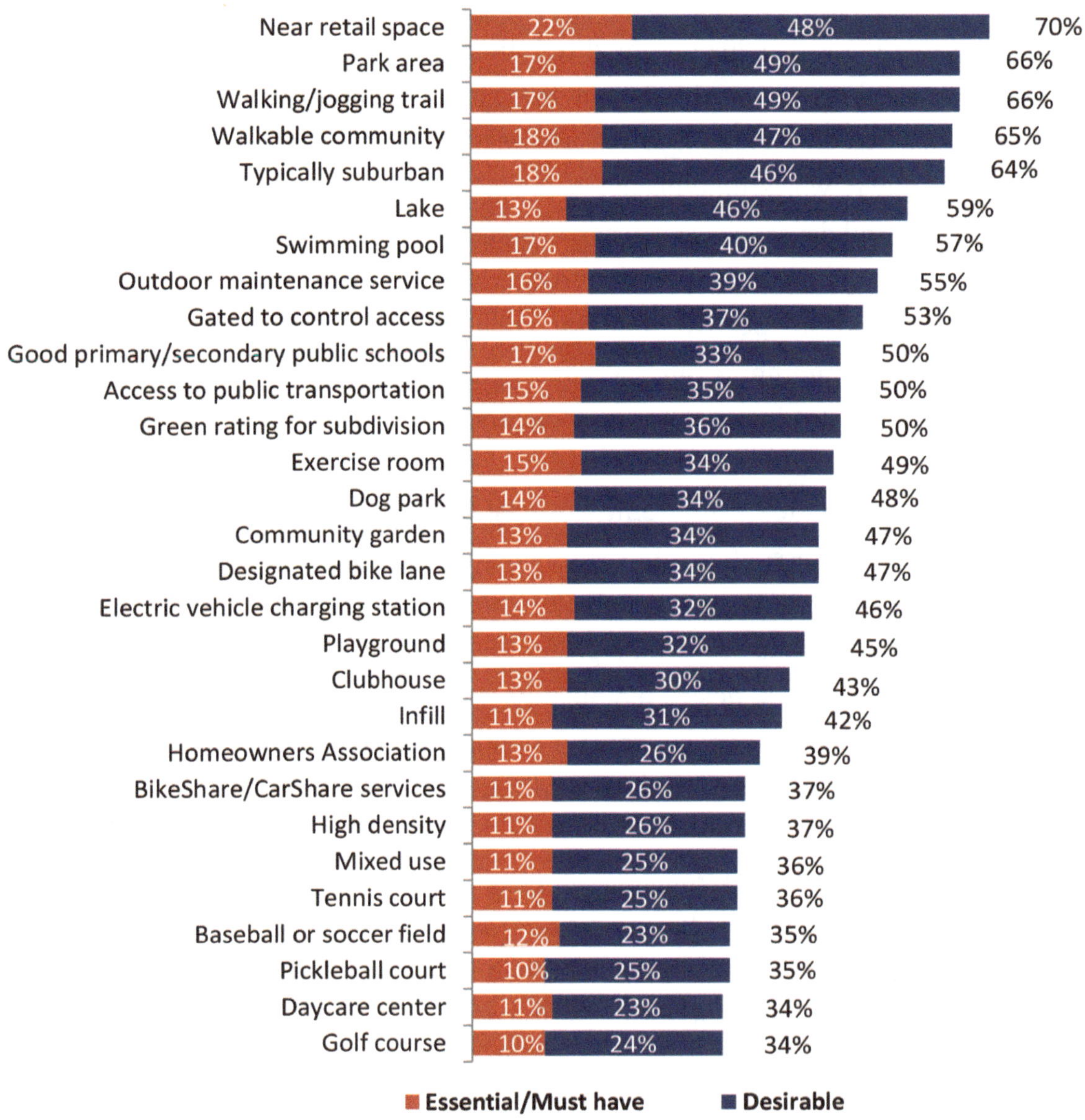

The NAHB survey has historically inquired about buyers' preferences for the community where they want to live. Before 2015, the question asked buyers to select all the community features that would seriously influence their purchase decision. In 2015, the question was redesigned, expanding the number of features covered and switching to the standard essential/desirable/indifferent/unwanted scale used throughout the survey. In 2018, 2020, and 2023, the question has been made more comprehensive by adding a few additional features each year, usually at the request of those who used the prior study.

Looking back, the years between 2020 and 2023 impacted buyers' preferences for a number of these community features, demonstrated by the 7+ point increase in the share rating them essential or desirable during this period (Fig. 10-6):

- Electric vehicle charging station, up 8 points from 38% to 46%.
- Daycare center, up 8 points from 26% to 34%.
- Community garden, up 7 points from 40% to 47%.
- Infill (in older neighborhood), up 7 points from 35% to 42%.

Figure 10-6. Community Features – History

(From 2003-2012: Percent of Respondents Seriously Influenced by Feature; 2015-2023: Percent of Respondents Rating Essential or Desirable)

	2003	2007	2012	2015	2018	2020	2023
Near retail space	n/a	n/a	n/a	64	69	64	70
Park area	52	43	54	66	62	65	66
Walking/jogging trails	51	49	60	64	66	67	66
Walkable community	n/a	n/a	n/a	n/a	61	59	65
Typically suburban	n/a	n/a	n/a	72	64	65	64
Lake	32	33	45	54	48	56	59
Swimming pool	36	36	50	48	50	54	57
Outdoor maintenance service	n/a	n/a	37	46	48	53	55
Gated to control access	n/a	n/a	n/a	41	46	49	53
Good primary/secondary public schools	n/a	n/a	n/a	n/a	n/a	53	50
Access to public transportation	34	24	29	39	44	44	50
Green rating for subdivision	n/a	n/a	n/a	n/a	n/a	n/a	50
Exercise room	30	27	39	46	43	50	49
Dog park	n/a	n/a	n/a	n/a	37	43	48
Community garden	n/a	n/a	n/a	n/a	36	40	47
Designated bike lanes	n/a	n/a	n/a	n/a	40	52	47
Electric vehicle charging station	n/a	n/a	n/a	n/a	28	38	46
Playgrounds	26	22	31	35	34	42	45
Clubhouse	21	21	26	35	33	41	43
Infill	n/a	n/a	38	28	29	35	42
Homeowners Association	n/a	n/a	n/a	n/a	n/a	n/a	39
Bike share/Car share services	n/a	n/a	n/a	n/a	25	34	37
High density	n/a	n/a	19	21	20	32	37
Mixed use	n/a	n/a	23	22	22	32	36
Tennis courts	10	10	17	24	23	36	36
Baseball or soccer fields	n/a	n/a	n/a	22	22	34	35
Pickleball court	n/a	n/a	n/a	n/a	n/a	n/a	35
Daycare center	9	8	9	15	17	26	34
Golf course	n/a	n/a	13	17	21	28	34

The latest increase in desirably for the features above is not a one-time event but rather the continuation of a longer trend of steadily rising popularity. The shares of buyers rating EV charging stations or a community garden as essential/desirable in 2018, for example, were 28% and 36%, respectively. Moreover, only 9% of buyers in 2003 wanted a daycare center in their neighborhood. Probable factors behind these trends include the growing market share of electric cars in recent years and parents working from home at least part of the week who prefer daycare to be near home and not by the office or highway.

MILLENNIALS MORE LIKELY TO WANT SOME COMMUNITY FEATURES

Although there is strong consensus on the desirability of retail space, walkability, and a suburban feel to the community across the four generations in the study, an analysis of the remaining community features shows a different pattern: Gen Z and particularly Millennials are significantly more likely to want those features than their older counterparts. In fact, the statistical analysis in Chapter 12 finds a relationship between age and preferences that is highly significant and negative (older buyers giving less favorable ratings) for 28 of the 29 community features on the list (the lone exception being "near retail space" which tends to be popular irrespective of age). Moreover, 17 of the 29 community features show at least a 20-point difference in favorability between Millennials and Boomers. The most extreme cases, with 36-point differences, are a daycare center (58% Millennials vs. 22% Boomers) and baseball/soccer fields (60% vs. 24%). Not far behind are playgrounds (69% vs. 34%), mixed use (60% vs. 26%), and good public elementary/secondary schools (71% vs. 40%) (Fig. 10-7).

Some of the additional community features Millennials find significantly more important than older buyers include high density, tennis courts, a golf course, a dog park, bikeshare/carshare services, and a pickleball court (Appendix A, pages A142-A156). It is not surprising, and in many cases it is natural, to see Millennials wanting these features more than the oldest cohort in the study. After all, Millennials are young adults between 27 and 42 years of age, who love pets and sports, grew up sharing cars and bikes, and many have (or plan to have) small children.

Figure 10-7. Community Features Rated Essential or Desirable W/ 31+ Point Difference by Generation

(Percent of Respondents)

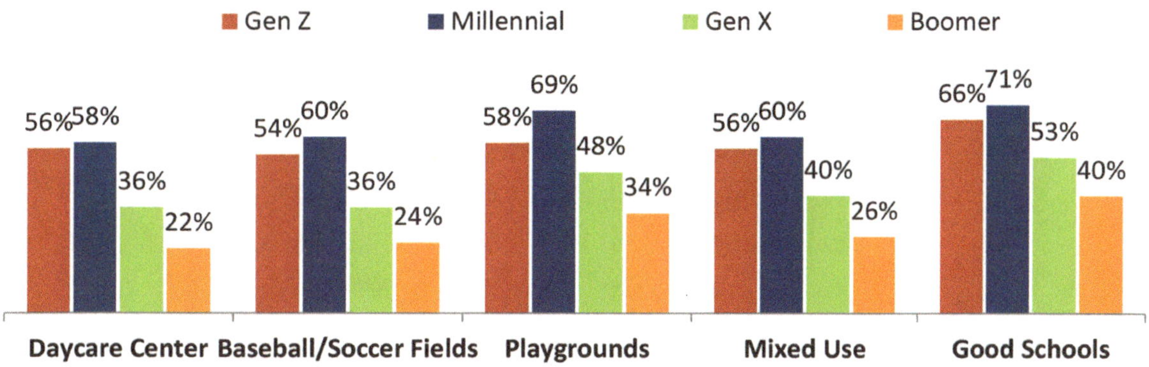

OVER ⅓ OF BUYERS REJECT A GOLF COURSE, DAYCARE CENTER & HOA

The three community features most likely to cause buyers to pass on a home are a golf course (35% of buyers rated it "do not want"), a daycare center (35%), and a homeowners association (34%). Interestingly, however, buyers are becoming less skeptical of golf courses and daycare centers, as evidenced by the much larger shares of 46% and 50%, respectively, who would not have bought homes in communities with these features in 2020.

Around one-third of buyers (32%) also strongly dislike communities with a pickleball court, high density, or baseball/soccer fields. Four more are rejected by 25% to 30%: tennis courts (30%), mixed use (29%), bikeshare/carshare services (26%), and a clubhouse (25%). The remaining features in Figure 10-8, starting with an electric vehicle charging station, are explicitly rejected by fewer than 25% of buyers. Given strong buyer preferences for being near retail space, a suburban neighborhood, or a walkable community, only around 10% of buyers reject these features.

Figure 10-8. Community Features NOT Wanted

(Percent of Respondents Rating "Do Not Want")

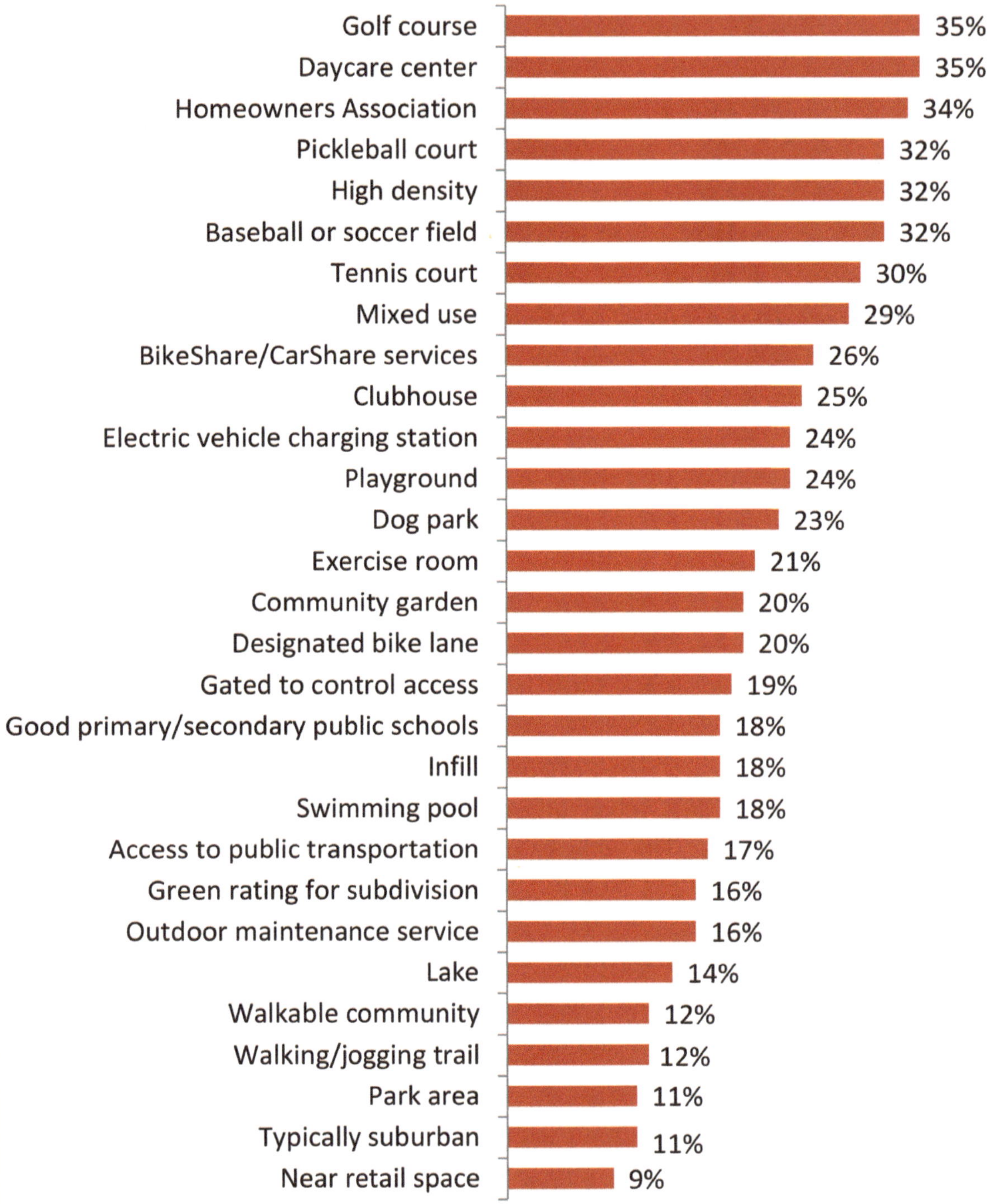

Chapter 11

Trade-Offs Buyers Are Willing to Make

BUYERS WILL ACCEPT SMALLER LOTS TO ACHIEVE AFFORDABILITY

As with any other purchase, most home buyers must eventually face the reality of having to align their wish lists to their bank accounts. In the absence of any financial constraints, it is natural for people to rate lots of home and community features as essential or desirable, but when the time comes to bid on a specific home, most buyers must scale down their desires and make trade-offs in order to achieve affordability.

One way the NAHB survey tries to understand how buyers make the affordability math work is by asking them which of 10 compromises they would be willing to accept if they were having trouble finding a home in their ideal price range. At the top, the most likely compromise buyers will make is on the land their house sits on, with 39% willing to accept a smaller lot. This emphasizes how important it is to continue reforming zoning practices and curtail restrictions like exclusionary (i.e., large lot) zoning — not only to leave more space for parks, streets and other public amenities, but also to accommodate home buyer preferences and allow them to achieve affordability in a world of rising housing costs.

Not far behind lot size, the next three most common trade-offs involve being farther from the urban core (36%), having fewer exterior amenities such as porches, decks, patios, or pools (36%), and a smaller house (35%).

The remaining compromises have fewer takers. For example, only 28% would accept a substitution of expensive materials for less expensive options, 26% would go along with more modular or prefabricated housing components, 24% would compromise by having fewer rooms, 23% would accept fewer energy efficient features (when not mandated by code), and 21% would take unfinished spaces in order to achieve affordability. At the very bottom, the most unlikely option buyers would utilize to find a home in their price range is denser development (14%) (Fig. 11-1). This is consistent with the relatively high percentage of buyers who said they do not want a high density community in Chapter 10 (Fig. 10-8).

Figure 11-1. Trade-Offs Home Buyers Are Prepared to Make for an Affordable Home

(Percent of Respondents)

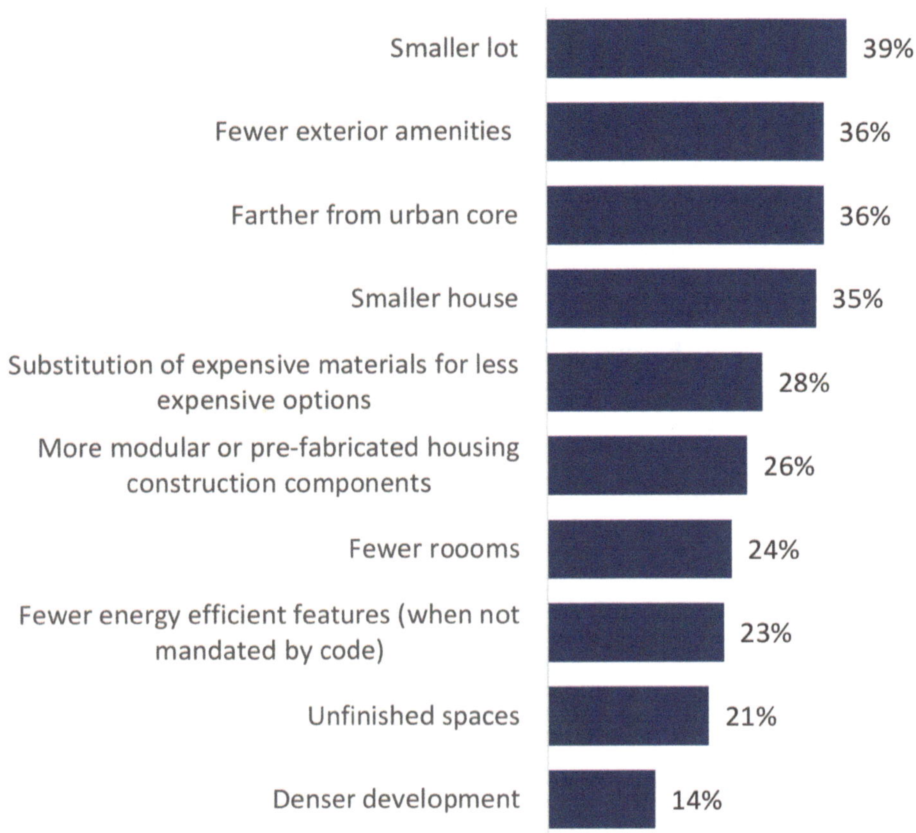

In 2023, an update was made to the affordability trade-off question to reflect options that have become popular since the pandemic. As a result, most of the compromises mentioned above are new to the survey and therefore have no historical comparison. Among the four that can be analyzed across time, Figure 11-2 reveals some interesting changes. Between 2020 and 2023, the share of buyers willing to accept the substitution of expensive materials for less expensive options jumped 12 points, from 16% to 28%. Similarly, after a one-off drop from 40% in 2018 to 32% in 2020, the share of buyers willing to accept a smaller lot in exchange for affordability rebounded in 2023 to 39%. Meanwhile, buyers are about as willing in 2023 (35%) as in 2020 (36%) to accept a smaller house as the trade-off. The one compromise buyers have become steadily more reluctant to accept in order to find a home in their desired price range is unfinished spaces. In 2012, 48% would have accepted the trade-off. By 2020, only 31% did, and in 2023, the share dropped another 10 points to 21% (Fig. 11-2).

Figure 11-2. Trade-Offs Home Buyers Are Prepared to Make for an Affordable Home – History

(Percent of Respondents)

	2003	2007	2012	2015	2018	2020	2023
Smaller lot	30	33	34	40	40	32	39
Farther from urban core	n/a	n/a	n/a	n/a	n/a	n/a	36
Fewer exterior amenities (e.g. porches/decks/patios/pools)	n/a	n/a	n/a	n/a	n/a	n/a	36
Smaller house	30	31	37	39	42	36	35
Substitution of expensive materials for less expensive options*	7	6	12	10	10	16	28
More modular/pre-fab housing construction components	n/a	n/a	n/a	n/a	n/a	n/a	26
Fewer rooms	n/a	n/a	n/a	n/a	n/a	n/a	24
Fewer energy-efficient features (when not mandated by code)	n/a	n/a	n/a	n/a	n/a	n/a	23
Unfinished spaces	41	41	48	38	36	31	21
Denser development	n/a	n/a	n/a	n/a	n/a	n/a	14

* Prior to 2020, option was 'Less expensive material.'

Despite the overall increase in buyers willing to trade-off acreage for a lower price point, some demographic groups remain more likely than others to reject that trade-off. In fact, whereas 47% of buyers 65 or older would be willing to accept a smaller lot as a compromise, the share is significantly lower among younger groups: only 27% of those under 35 and 28% among those 35 to 44. Other groups less likely to be interested in smaller plots of land are parents & Hispanic buyers. While only 33% of married couples with children and 34% of single parents would sacrifice lot size for price, the trade-off is acceptable to 46% of married couples without children and 44% of one-person households. Finally, only a quarter of Hispanic buyers find a smaller lot a compromise worth making, compared to 42% of Caucasian buyers (Fig. 11-3).

The analysis described in Chapter 12 finds strong statistical evidence that married couples with children and Hispanic households are less likely, and older households are more likely, to accept smaller lots (in a model that controls for all these characteristics, income and geography).

Figure 11-3. Home Buyers Who Will Accept a Smaller Lot to Make Home Affordable by Buyer's Age, Household Composition & Race/Ethnicity

(Percent of Respondents)

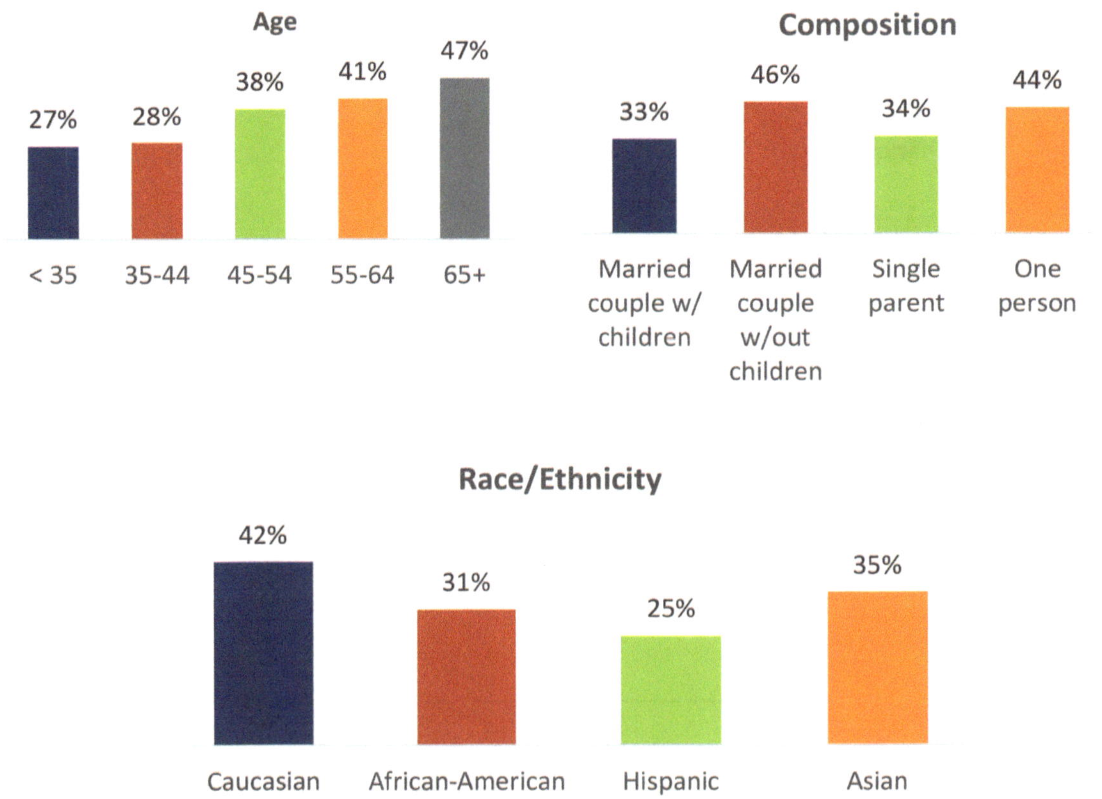

SHRINK THE HOME OFFICE, NOT THE KITCHEN

A new question introduced in the 2023 survey asked buyers willing to take a smaller home in exchange for affordability which specific areas or rooms of the house they are willing to lose square footage on in order to shrink the overall footprint of the home. Most buyers sent a clear message to builders and architects: make the home smaller by reducing the size of the home office (53%) and the dining room (52%). On the other hand, only a minority of buyers want to see the kitchen (21%), the closets (22%), or the garage and bathrooms (both 26%) lose any real estate. Between these two extremes, 30% to 39% of buyers would find it acceptable to shrink the house by losing square footage in the family room (39%), living room (35%), and bedrooms (31%) (Fig. 11-4).

Although only 22% to 26% of buyers willing to accept a smaller home in exchange for affordability would do it by reducing the size of the closets or the garage, a breakdown of

Figure 11-4. If Willing to Accept Smaller Home to Afford a Home, Which Areas Would You Be Willing to Make Smaller?

(Percent of Respondents willing to Accept Smaller Home)

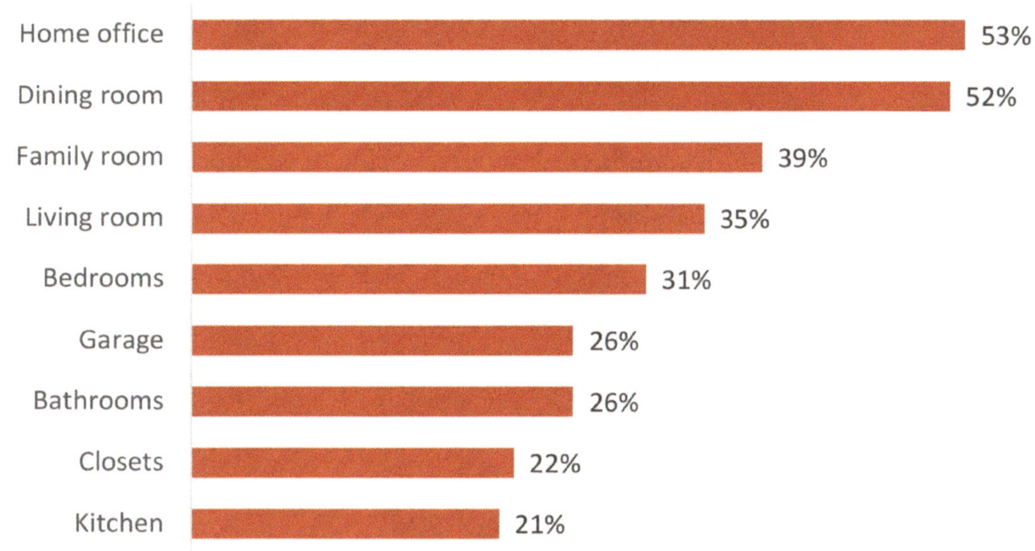

results by generation shows that younger buyers are significantly more likely than their older counterparts to make those compromises. Among Gen Z buyers willing to accept a smaller home, for example, 46% would cut down on the size of the closets and 38% on the size of the garage to reduce the home footprint. Boomers are 17% and 23%, respectively (Fig. 11-5). The statistical analysis described in the next chapter shows that the effect of age on the willingness to make these two trade-offs is highly significant.

Figure 11-5. Share Willing to Accept Smaller Closets & Garage by Generation

(Percent of Respondents)

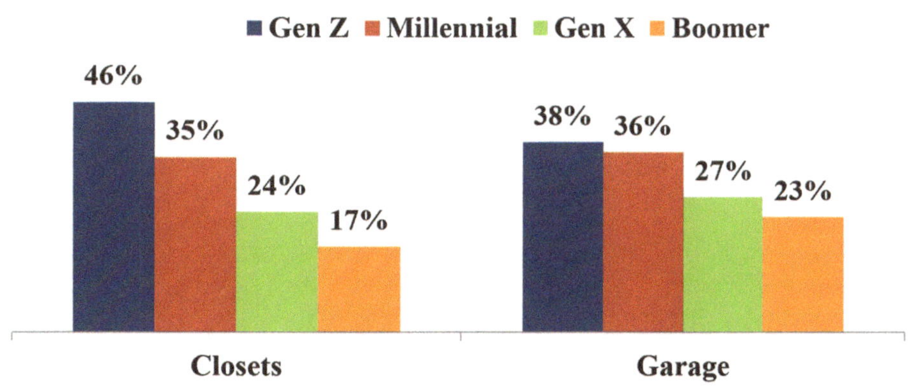

MOST HOME BUYERS WANT AMENITIES INCLUDED IN BASE PRICE

Another trade-off is how home buyers would prefer to pay for extra amenities. One pricing model is for the builder to include all the amenities and features in the price of the home, thus making the home more expensive. Another model is to offer a no-frills home and let buyers choose the extra amenities and features at an a la carte cost. Survey results show that more than two-thirds of home buyers (68%) would prefer the former model, where all features and amenities are included in the price of the home (Fig. 11-6). Most buyers across all 37 demographic breakdowns analyzed in the study would prefer this option (Appendix A, pages A58-A60).

Figure 11-6. When Purchasing a New Home, Which Would You Prefer?
(Percent of Respondents)

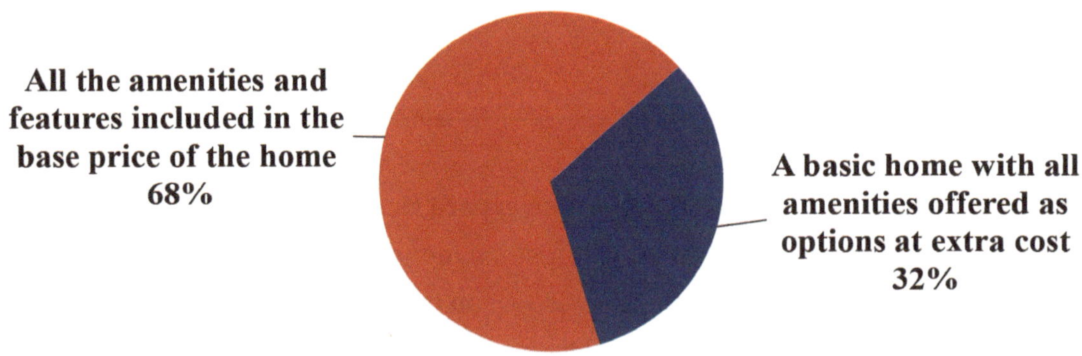

The NAHB study has presented this trade-off to home buyers since 2003. During this time, at least half of buyers have favored the alternative of all amenities included in the base price of the home. Nonetheless, this choice had lost a bit of popularity after 2015, when the share favoring it fell to 62% and 60% in 2018 and 2020, respectively. But the latest results for 2023 show the share rebounding to 68% — matching the highest point in the series set in 2015 (Fig. 11-7).

Figure 11-7. When Purchasing a Home, Which Would You Prefer? – History

	2003	2007	2012	2015	2018	2020	2023
All the amenities and features included in the base price of the home	59	64	50	68	62	60	68
A basic home with all amenities offered as options at extra cost	41	36	50	32	38	40	32

MOST BUYERS TRADE-OFF SPACE FOR AMENITIES

A final trade-off question presented buyers the option to choose between two alternatives that cost equal amounts of money, thus capturing home buyers' natural inclinations free of any financial consideration. In this scenario, 63% of buyers would prefer to buy a "smaller house with high quality products and amenities" over the 37% who would prefer a "bigger house with fewer amenities" (Fig. 11-8).

When faced with the choice between a typical kitchen or an oversized kitchen, 59% of buyers prefer the typical kitchen and living area spaces over the 41% who would rather have a larger than average kitchen and smaller living spaces. The alternative between one or two full master bedroom suites shows a slight majority of 55% would prefer two full master suites plus one standard bedroom, compared to 45% who would rather get one full master suite and three standard bedrooms. The final pair of alternatives shows an almost equal divide among buyers: 51% prefer a family room and living room about equal in size vs. 49% who would rather have a much larger family room and no living room (Fig. 11-8).

Figure 11-8. Trade-Offs Preferred

(Percent of Respondents)

A smaller house with high quality products and amenities 63%	**vs.**	**A bigger house with fewer amenities 37%**
Typical kitchen and living area spaces 59%	**vs.**	**Larger than average kitchen and smaller living area spaces 41%**
Two full master bedroom suites + one standard bedroom 55%	**vs.**	**One full master bedroom suite + three standard bedrooms 45%**
Family room and living room about equal in size 51%	**vs.**	**A much larger family room and no living room 49%**

Most home buyers have consistently preferred a smaller house with high quality products and amenities than the alternative (a bigger home with fewer amenities) since 2003, with the share ranging between 62% and 68% over the years (Fig. 11-9). In addition, although historical data show most buyers in the last two decades have preferred a typical kitchen size (instead of a larger one with smaller living area spaces), the share is lower in 2023 (59%) than it was in 2003 (70%). And finally, most buyers have consistently preferred having a living room and a family room about equal in size rather than no living room and a larger family room, with the share varying from 51% to 57% in the last 20 years.

Figure 11-9. Trade-Offs Preferred–History

(Percent of Respondents)

	2003	2007	2012	2015	2018	2020	2023
Smaller house w/ high quality products & amenities	64	65	62	68	67	64	63
Two full master bedroom suites + one standard bedroom	n/a	n/a	n/a	n/a	n/a	n/a	55
Typical kitchen and living area	70	64	65	61	62	56	59
Family and living room about equal in size	57	55	54	54	51	54	51

Cross-sectional analysis shows that at least 50% of buyers, across all 37 demographic breakdowns, prefer a smaller home with high quality products and amenities rather than the alternative, yet that preference is much stronger in some groups than in others. For example, Caucasian buyers (67%) are significantly more likely to accept a smaller house in exchange for high quality products and amenities than minorities: African-Americans (50%), Hispanics (52%), and Asians (56%) (Fig. 11-10).

Figure 11-10. Share of Buyers Who Prefer a Smaller Home with High Quality Products and Amenities by Race/Ethnicity

(Percent of Respondents)

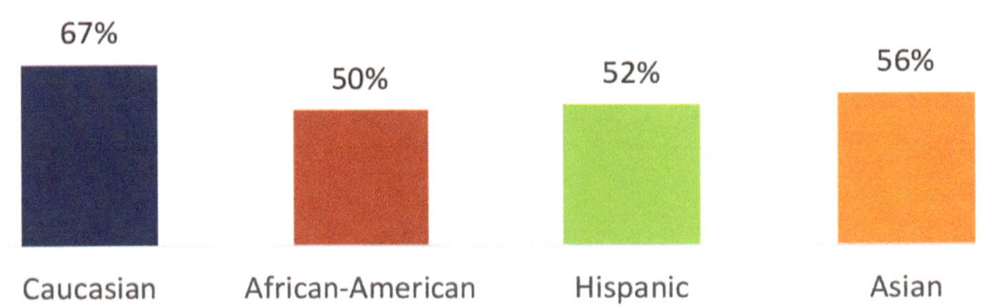

The more granular analysis also reveals that buyers expecting to pay over $500,000 for their home (or just paid if bought recently) are significantly more likely to prefer the larger than average kitchen with smaller living space alternative (51%) than those buying more modest homes: under $150,000 (36%), $150,000 to $249,999 (37%), and $250,000 to $499,999 (40%) (Fig. 11-11). Another way to describe these results is that buyers of more modest homes are less willing to sacrifice living space for kitchen size than those buying top-end homes.

Figure 11-11. Share of Buyers Who Prefer a Larger Kitchen & Smaller Living Spaces by Price Point

(Percent of Respondents)

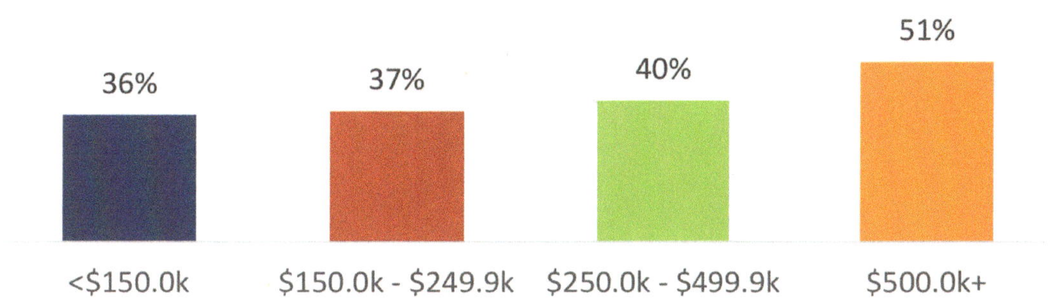

Chapter 12

Survey Methodology & Respondent Profile

SAMPLE DESIGN

The survey that collected the data for *What Home Buyers Really Want, 2024 Edition* was conducted in two phases, using an online consumer research panel maintained by Home Innovation Research Labs. Both phases were conducted electronically.

In the first phase, screener questions identified recent home buyers (households who purchased a home in the last three years) and prospective home buyers (households expecting to buy a home in the next three years). In the second phase, buyers identified in the first phase received an electronic questionnaire (Appendix B).

The design of the sample required it to be approximately proportional to percentages in the general US population across several dimensions: the four principle Census regions, six age brackets, four racial/ethnic categories crossed and five income brackets. Beyond this, to allow for detailed tabulations, NAHB required that the final sample include a minimum of 200 responses in each of the nine Census divisions.

The second phase of the survey was conducted iteratively, with the survey sent successively to selected subgroups of recent and prospective home buyers, depending on the incidence of responses received to that point, until the criteria described above were satisfied as closely as was practical.

The first phase of the data collection began in February 2023. Home Innovation completed the second iterative phase of the survey, and delivered the final data set in April 2023. The data set contained a sample of 3,008 useable observations, stratified as shown in the first two columns of Figure 12-1.

WEIGHTING

To adjust for possible oversampling of certain subgroups, bring the sample fully in line with the distribution of households who own their own homes, and allow for greater detail (e.g., stratifying the country by nine geographic divisions rather than four regions), the responses were weighted before being tabulated.

The weights were based on the percentages of homeowners in various geographic, racial, income, and age categories in the Census Bureau's most recent (2021) American Community Survey (ACS). The magnitude of the weights ranges from a low of 0.0906 (for an Asian or Pacific Islander home buyer under age 35, in the Mountain Division, with an income of less than $50,000) to a high of 3.741 (for a non-Hispanic white buyer age 65 or older in the West South Central Division, with an income of $150,000 or more). Ninety percent of the weights lie between 0.2314 and 2.2194.[1]

Figure 12-1 shows the effect of imposing this weighting scheme. In addition to the unweighted characteristics of respondents used to develop the weights, the figure shows the corresponding results after weighting and the Census Bureau's estimates from the ACS for comparison.

Outside of Figure 12-1, all *percentages* shown in this study are based on *weighted* responses. In the detailed tables, however, *numbers of responses* are always reported *unweighted,* so readers can see the actual number of cases on which a particular result is based to help them evaluate the validity of a particular result. As the figure shows, the weights were constructed so that they sum to the sample size. The primary reason for this is to eliminate any possibility of artificially inflating the significance of statistical tests, depending on how the software treats the weights (which is not completely consistent across procedures in standard statistical packages).

---

[1] In order to construct a system of weights that balanced the sample across the desired multiple characteristics in a consistent way, NAHB employed an iterative procedure sometimes called raking. This procedure was first developed by Edwards Deming in *Statistical Adjustment of Data* (1943) and translated into a FORTRAN program by MarketMath, Inc in the 1960s. The FORTRAN version was subsequently translated into a SAS program by Abt Associates, Inc. See Izrael D., Hoaglin D., and Battaglia, M. (2000). "A SAS Macro for Balancing a Weighted Sample." Proceedings from the Twenty-Fifth Annual SAS Users Group International Conference. Cary, NC: SAS Institute. NAHB used the Abt Associates version of the program to generate the weighting scheme in figure 12-1.

Figure 12-1. Respondent Characteristics Used in the Survey Design

(Unweighted and Weighted Survey Responses, and Comparison to the ACS)

	NAHB Home Buyer Survey: Unweighted		NAHB Home Buyer Survey: Weighted		Homeowners in the 2021 ACS	
	Number	Percent	Number	Percent	Number	Percent
Census Division						
New England	141	4.7	145	4.8	3,870,387	4.8
Middle Atlantic	358	11.9	369	12.3	9,858,049	12.3
East North Central	414	13.8	478	15.9	12,769,230	15.9
West North Central	236	7.9	219	7.3	5,856,727	7.3
South Atlantic	651	21.6	632	21.0	16,877,638	21.0
East South Central	224	7.5	191	6.3	5,090,529	6.3
West South Central	290	9.6	350	11.6	9,348,360	11.6
Mountain	278	9.2	230	7.7	6,147,714	7.7
Pacific	416	13.8	392	13.1	10,476,881	13.1
Race/Ethnicity						
NonHispanic White	1,997	66.4	2,258	75.1	60,280,400	75.1
NonHisp African-Amer.	390	13.0	249	8.3	6,645,211	8.3
Asian/Pacific Islander	280	9.3	154	5.1	4,115,147	5.1
Hispanic	341	11.3	347	11.5	9,254,757	11.5
Household Income						
Less than $50,000	907	30.2	834	27.7	22,271,310	27.7
$50,000-$74,999	549	18.3	499	16.6	13,323,127	16.6
$75,000-$99,999	427	14.2	418	13.9	11,153,624	13.9
$100,000-$149,999	552	18.4	575	19.1	15,361,771	19.1
$150,000+	573	19.1	681	22.7	18,185,683	22.7
Age of Household Head						
Under 35 years	934	31.1	317	10.5	8,449,425	10.5
35-44 years	610	20.3	489	16.3	13,063,136	16.3
45-54	503	16.7	553	18.4	14,767,678	18.4
55-64	436	14.5	665	22.1	17,749,169	22.1
65 and older	525	17.5	984	32.7	26,266,107	32.7
Total	**3,008**	**100.0**	**3,008**	**100.0**	**80,295,515**	**100.0**

STATISTICAL TESTS

Previous chapters of *What Home Buyers Really Want* often show housing preferences across different categories of home buyers. At times, the text mentions that the differences are significant according to a set of statistical tests. This section describes these statistical tests and explains how they were used to inform the charts and discussion in the previous chapters.

The tests analyze possible effects of a home buyer's income, age, location (in one of the nine Census divisions), race/ethnicity and household composition on housing preferences. The analysis consists of a separate regression-type model for each question, or part of a question, on the survey questionnaire (Appendix B). The specific form of the model depends on the specific form of the question. Several questions ask respondents to choose one of two options. The first question, for example, asks if the respondent currently owns his or her home. In such a two-option case, the analysis consists of a standard probit model.

Questions that give home buyers a list of items and ask them to check all that apply can also be analyzed within this two-option framework. Question 19, for example, gives buyers a list of 10 items and asks them to check all that they would accept to make a home more affordable. In this case, the buyer's two options are to check or not check each item, and a separate probit model is fit to each of the items on the list.

The most common type of question in the survey asks buyers to choose only one from a list of three or more options. If the options can be placed in a natural order, the analysis takes the form of an ordered probit model. The leading example is Question 38, which provides home buyers with a list of over 200 different home and community features and asks them to rate each one on a four-tired scale: (1) do not want, (2) indifferent, (3) desirable, (4) essential/must have. There is an obvious order to these ratings, with a higher number representing a more favorable rating.

In cases where there is no natural order to the mutually exclusive options in a particular question, the analysis consists of a multinomial logit model. An example is Question 26, which asks buyers to indicate if their preferred location for a clothes washer and dryer is the basement, garage, first floor, or on the second floor or higher. There is no natural order to these location options, so in this case a multinomial logit model is applied to the responses.

Questions that generate numbers on a continuous scale can be analyzed with an ordinary linear regression. Figure 12-2 shows the type of statistical model applied to each question.

Only one question generates a continuous variable amenable to a linear regression. NAHB tries to avoid such questions when possible, because they require respondents to write in an answer rather than simply checking a box, which tends to increase respondent burden.

Irrespective of its form, each model uses the same set of explanatory variables:

- Household income
- Age of the respondent
- Indicator variables for eight of the nine Census divisions
- Four indicator variables set to 1 if the buyer is, respectively, 1) a married couple with children, 2) a married couple without children, 3) a single parent household, 4) a one-person household.
- Three indicator variables set to 1 if the buyer is 1) Hispanic, 2) African-American, or 3) Asian.

Figure 12-2. The Statistical Models Used for Each Survey Question

Probit					
	1a	4	5	19	20
	31	35	36	37	
Ordered Probit					
	1b	1c	7	8	13
	14	15	16	17	18
	21	23	24	25	27
	28	29	30	32	33
	38	39			
Multinomial Logit					
	6	9	10	11	12
	22	26			
Linear Regression					
	34				

These variables are based on the column headings of the detailed tables in Appendix A. A few of the column headings are not used as explanatory variables due to correlations among them. Generation is not used as an explanatory variable, for example, because it is highly correlated with the continuous variable age. The home price and first-time vs. repeat buyer variables are not used because they are highly correlated with the continuous variable household income. Were all these variables included in the models, the correlations would tend to obscure significant effects. In this document, significant means a coefficient in one of the above models is statistically significant, according to a classical hypothesis test, at the .01 level.

The statistical results are used primarily as a guide for selecting appropriate graphics for the earlier chapters. When choosing a particular chart, generation may be treated as a proxy for age, and either repeat buyer status or price the buyer expects to pay for the home may be treated as a proxy for income. That is, if the effect of age (income) is significant, tabulations by generation (first-time vs. repeat buyer or price buyers expect to pay) may be illustrated instead. The decision is based on which will generate a graphic that is clear and relatively easy to interpret for the casual reader. This publication is intended for a non-technical audience and therefore does not present formal statistical results. However, anyone interested in these results can obtain them from NAHB's Economics and Housing Policy Group.

RESPONDENT PROFILE

In addition to the items used to stratify the survey sample and weight the responses (shown in Fig. 12-1), the survey collected additional demographic data on the respondents, such as their gender and household composition. In the sample overall, 56% of the respondents were female and 44% were male (Fig. 12-3).

Figure 12-3. Respondent's Gender

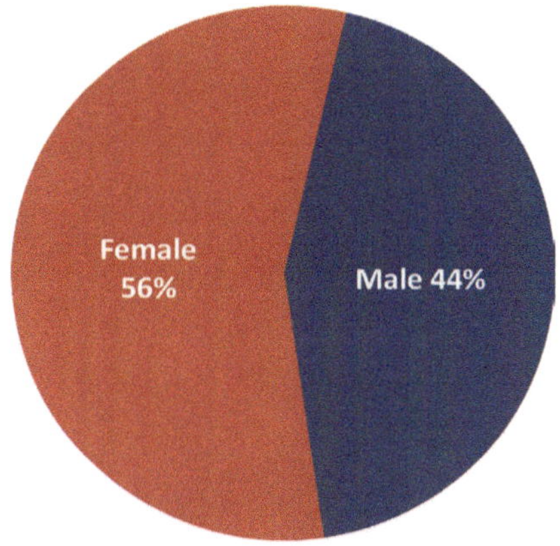

The most common household types among the respondents in the final sample are the two categories of married couples: 42% married couples with children, 23% married couples without children. Beyond that, 15% are one person households, and 10% are single parents (Fig. 12-4).

Figure 12-4. Composition of Respondent's Household

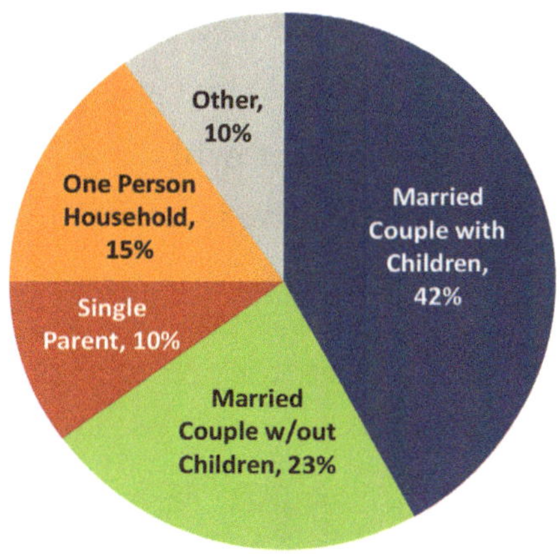

Although not used to stratify the sample, household composition is cross-tabulated against all housing preference questions in Appendix A, and appears as an explanatory variable in all the statistical tests described above. Where appropriate, the first eleven chapters call out and discuss particularly significant and interesting differences in preferences attributable to household composition. Chapter 6, for example, shows that households with children (either married couples or single parents) are much more likely than others to rate a delivery vestibule essential or desirable.

The survey also includes several questions on the respondent's housing. The most basic of these is ownership status. In the final sample, 77% of respondents currently own their own home, and the remaining 23% rent (Fig. 12-5).

Figure 12-5. Respondent's Homeownership Status

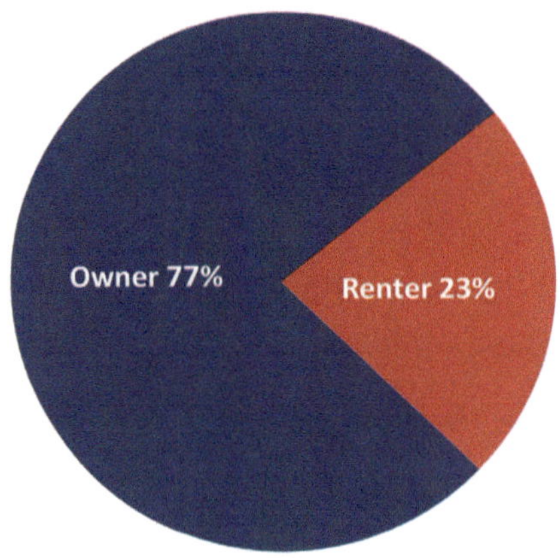

In addition to ownership status, the survey asked respondents about the type of structure they currently live in. About two-thirds (66%) live in a single-family detached home, 14% live in a multifamily building, 12% are in a townhouse/single-family attached structure, 6% live in manufactured housing, and 2% live in some "other" type of home (Fig. 12-6).

Figure 12-6. Type of Home Respondent Currently Lives In

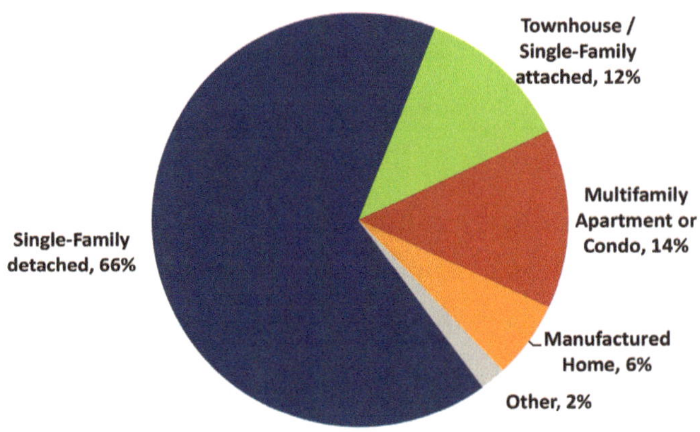

Single-family detached and multifamily homes are fairly intuitive categories, townhouse/ single-family attached probably less so. Informally, a townhouse is a group of homes arranged side-by-side, each sharing at least one wall with another. The Census Bureau has a formal definition that distinguishes between single-family attached and multifamily townhouses, based largely on how completely the vertical walls separate the units. Most home buyers, however, lacking a detailed knowledge of the Census classification scheme and x-ray vision, are unlikely to make the distinction. More likely, they simply think of any side-by-side arrangement as townhouses. A manufactured home is one built in a remote factory under a national standard managed by the Department of Housing and Urban Development, rather than a local building code. The "other" category could include boats, RVs or other types of vehicles.

The survey also asked respondents how many homes they have owned in total, including the current one, if applicable. The information was collected primarily to distinguish first-time from repeat buyers for the detailed crosstabulations in Appendix A. In the final sample, 12% of the recent and prospective home buyers have never owned a home, 39% have owned one, 21% two, 14% three, and another 14% four or more (Fig. 12-7).

Figure 12-7. Number of Homes Respondent Has Owned

(Including Present Home)

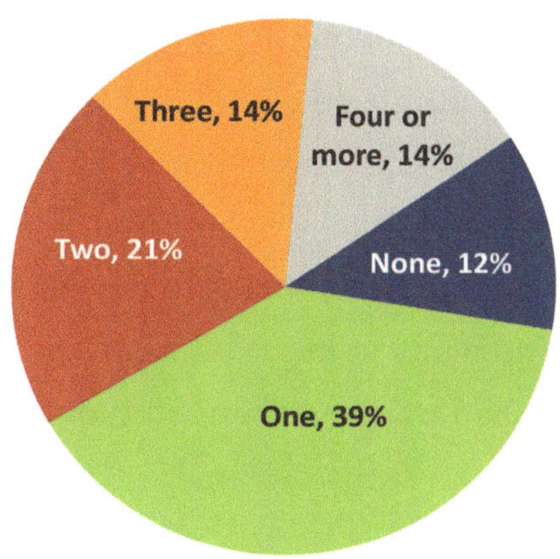

To identify recent home buyers, the survey included a question on how long owners have lived in their current homes. Tabulations of this question show that 48% have lived in their current home for less than four years, 26% have lived in their homes four to nine years, and another 26% have lived in their homes for at least 10 years (Fig. 12-8). This question was designed to help screen certain households (those who had neither bought a home in the past three years nor expected to buy one in the next three) out of the final sample.

Figure 12-8. How Long Respondent Has Lived in Current Home

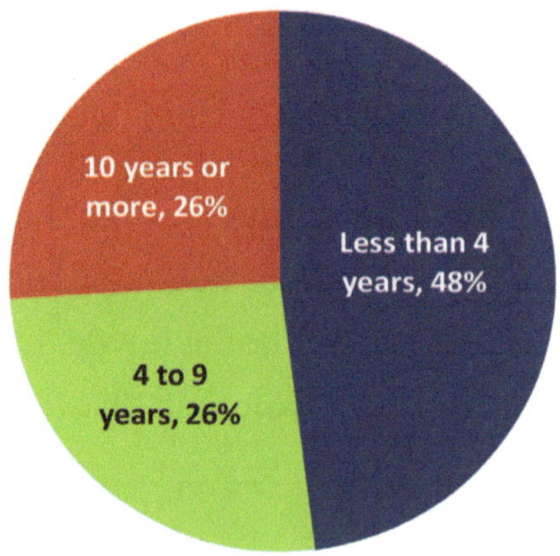

To capture prospective as well as recent buyers, another screening question asked respondents about their future plans to purchase a home. Of the households in the final sample, 25% expect to purchase a home within the next twelve months, and 47% expect to buy a home in one to three years. Another 4% planned to purchase their next homes more than three years in the future, 19% had no plans to purchase at all, and 4% were not sure (Fig. 12-9). Households with no plans to buy a home in the next three years could still be retained in the sample if they had purchased one in the past three.

Figure 12-9. Respondent Plans to Purchase a Home Within...

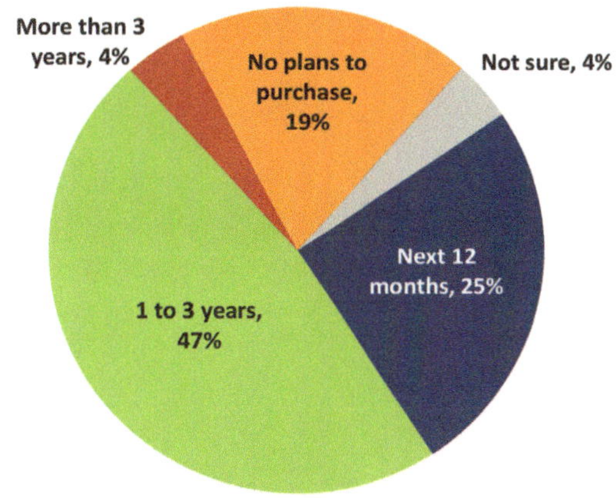

As noted above, after applying these screening questions the final sample for *What Home Buyers Really Want, 2024 Edition* consisted of 3,008 respondents who had purchased a home in the last three years and/or expect to purchase one in the next three. Because the final sample excludes households who neither purchased a home recently nor expect to purchase one in the near future, the previous two figures are not representative of U.S. households in general. In particular, Figure 12-8 does not show how long a typical U.S. household stays in a home before moving, and Figure 12-9 does not show the home buying plans of a typical U.S. household.

Appendix A

Detailed Tables

What Home Home Buyers Really Want, 2024 ed.: Detailed Tables

Q1a. Do you own or rent your current residence?
(Percent of respondents)

	All Home Buyers	Geography (Nine Census Divisions)									Buyer Type	
		New England	Middle Atlantic	East North Central	West North Central	South Atlantic	East South Central	West South Central	Mountain	Pacific	First-time	Repeat
Own	77	78	76	78	83	75	80	71	76	76		87
Rent	23	22	24	22	17	25	20	29	24	24	100	13
Responses	3,008	141	358	414	236	651	224	290	278	416	521	2,487

Q1b. How long have you lived in this home?
(Percent of respondents)

	All Home Buyers	Geography (Nine Census Divisions)									Buyer Type	
		New England	Middle Atlantic	East North Central	West North Central	South Atlantic	East South Central	West South Central	Mountain	Pacific	First-time	Repeat
Less than 4 years	48	41	37	46	44	58	51	61	50	34	52	47
4 to 9 years	26	36	28	24	40	21	13	19	30	31	33	25
10 years or more	26	23	35	30	17	21	36	20	20	35	15	28
Responses	3,008	141	358	414	236	651	224	290	278	416	521	2,487

Q1c. Do you plan to purchase a home within____?
(Percent of respondents)

	All Home Buyers	Geography (Nine Census Divisions)									Buyer Type	
		New England	Middle Atlantic	East North Central	West North Central	South Atlantic	East South Central	West South Central	Mountain	Pacific	First-time	Repeat
Next 12 months	25	27	23	26	27	22	30	23	23	33	35	24
1 to 3 years	47	52	53	47	53	43	37	46	52	49	65	45
More than 3 years	4	2	4	2	3	4	4	4	5	3		4
No plans to purchase	19	17	14	22	14	26	24	22	14	11		22
Not sure	4	2	6	4	3	4	4	5	6	4		5
Responses	3,008	141	358	414	236	651	224	290	278	416	521	2,487

Q1a. Do you own or rent your current residence?
(Percent of respondents)

	Age of Household Head					Generation (year born)				Household Composition			
	Under 35 years old	35 to 44 years old	45 to 54 years old	55 to 64 years old	65 years old or older	Gen Z (1997 or later)	Millenni-als(1981-1996)	Gen X (1965-1980)	Boomers (1946-1964)	Married couple w children	Married couple no children	Single parent	One person
Own	64	72	71	76	86	60	71	72	83	84	82	55	69
Rent	36	28	29	24	14	40	29	28	17	16	18	45	31
Responses	934	610	503	436	525	428	932	741	772	1,278	527	391	473

Q1b. How long have you lived in this home?
(Percent of respondents)

	Age of Household Head					Generation (year born)				Household Composition			
	Under 35 years old	35 to 44 years old	45 to 54 years old	55 to 64 years old	65 years old or older	Gen Z (1997 or later)	Millenni-als(1981-1996)	Gen X (1965-1980)	Boomers (1946-1964)	Married couple w children	Married couple no children	Single parent	One person
Less than 4 years	59	45	42	50	47	65	48	42	49	36	56	50	57
4 to 9 years	31	29	27	23	24	26	30	29	22	34	18	30	19
10 years or more	10	26	31	28	29	9	21	30	29	30	26	20	24
Responses	934	610	503	436	525	428	932	741	772	1,278	527	391	473

Q1c. Do you plan to purchase a home within____?
(Percent of respondents)

	Age of Household Head					Generation (year born)				Household Composition			
	Under 35 years old	35 to 44 years old	45 to 54 years old	55 to 64 years old	65 years old or older	Gen Z (1997 or later)	Millenni-als(1981-1996)	Gen X (1965-1980)	Boomers (1946-1964)	Married couple w children	Married couple no children	Single parent	One person
Next 12 months	28	28	30	21	23	26	28	29	23	32	19	26	20
1 to 3 years	52	55	47	50	41	51	53	50	43	50	42	55	44
More than 3 years	7	4	3	3	3	8	6	2	3	4	4	2	3
No plans to purchase	10	9	16	21	28	10	9	15	25	11	30	13	28
Not sure	4	4	4	5	5	5	4	4	5	2	6	4	5
Responses	934	610	503	436	525	428	932	741	772	1,278	527	391	473

Q1a. Do you own or rent your current residence?
(Percent of respondents)

	Race/Ethnicity				Home Buyers' Income Bracket					Price Expected to Pay			
	Cauca-sian	African-American	Hispanic	Asian	Under $50,000	$50,000 to $74,999	$75,000 to $99,999	$100,000 to $149,999	$150,000 or more	Less than $150,000	$150,000 to $249,999	$250,000 to $499,999	$500,000 or more
Own	79	48	78	85	63	69	74	88	90	64	72	80	86
Rent	21	52	22	15	37	31	26	12	10	36	28	20	14
Responses	1,997	390	341	280	907	549	427	552	573	718	531	1,155	530

Q1b. How long have you lived in this home?
(Percent of respondents)

	Race/Ethnicity				Home Buyers' Income Bracket					Price Expected to Pay			
	Cauca-sian	African-American	Hispanic	Asian	Under $50,000	$50,000 to $74,999	$75,000 to $99,999	$100,000 to $149,999	$150,000 or more	Less than $150,000	$150,000 to $249,999	$250,000 to $499,999	$500,000 or more
Less than 4 years	51	47	33	29	57	55	50	40	35	60	54	44	35
4 to 9 years	20	28	50	51	24	18	23	25	37	23	26	26	30
10 years or more	28	26	17	21	19	27	27	35	28	17	20	30	34
Responses	1,997	390	341	280	907	549	427	552	573	718	531	1,155	530

Q1c. Do you plan to purchase a home within____?
(Percent of respondents)

	Race/Ethnicity				Home Buyers' Income Bracket					Price Expected to Pay			
	Cauca-sian	African-American	Hispanic	Asian	Under $50,000	$50,000 to $74,999	$75,000 to $99,999	$100,000 to $149,999	$150,000 or more	Less than $150,000	$150,000 to $249,999	$250,000 to $499,999	$500,000 or more
Next 12 months	23	22	47	10	26	18	19	31	30	25	24	23	32
1 to 3 years	44	67	45	76	41	50	54	45	52	40	48	51	47
More than 3 years	4	4	3	3	2	3	5	5	3	5	3	3	3
No plans to purchase	24	6	4	9	26	24	17	17	11	24	21	19	13
Not sure	5	1	1	2	5	5	5	3	4	6	4	4	4
Responses	1,997	390	341	280	907	549	427	552	573	718	531	1,155	530

Q2a. Which of the following best represents your total annual household income?
(Percent of respondents)

	All Home Buyers	Geography (Nine Census Divisions)									Buyer Type	
		New England	Middle Atlantic	East North Central	West North Central	South Atlantic	East South Central	West South Central	Mountain	Pacific	First-time	Repeat
Under $50,000	28	25	18	32	25	30	26	30	28	29	51	25
$50,000 but less than $75,000	17	12	17	19	9	18	20	21	15	13	22	16
$75,000 but less than $100,000	14	12	14	16	17	15	10	13	13	11	14	14
$100,000 but less than $150,000	19	17	19	14	22	21	33	12	20	19	8	21
$150,000 but less than $200,000	13	25	17	11	20	8	8	15	12	16	3	15
$200,000 or more	9	8	15	7	8	8	3	8	11	12	2	10
Median	85,236	103,493	102,612	74,187	100,340	Raci	84,716	73,940	88,254	93,452	49,241	92,100
Responses	3,008	141	358	414	236	651	224	290	278	416	521	2,487

Q2b & Q2c. Racial & Ethnic background
(Percent of respondents)

	All Home Buyers	Geography (Nine Census Divisions)									Buyer Type	
		New England	Middle Atlantic	East North Central	West North Central	South Atlantic	East South Central	West South Central	Mountain	Pacific	First-time	Repeat
White (Non-Hispanic)	75	62	84	82	48	83	86	82	64	61	57	77
African-American (Non-Hispanic)	8	7	6	9	4	12	8	12	2	5	26	6
Asian/Pacific Islander	5	8	7	5	6	2	3	1	6	12	4	5
Hispanic	12	24	3	3	42	3	3	5	28	23	13	11
Responses	3,008	141	358	414	236	651	224	290	278	416	521	2,487

Q2a. Which of the following best represents your total annual household income?
(Percent of respondents)

	Age of Household Head					Generation (year born)				Household Composition			
	Under 35 years old	35 to 44 years old	45 to 54 years old	55 to 64 years old	65 years old or older	Gen Z (1997 or later)	Millenni-als(1981-1996)	Gen X (1965-1980)	Boomers (1946-1964)	Married couple w children	Married couple no children	Single parent	One person
Under $50,000	21	17	22	28	38	25	16	22	35	16	23	40	49
$50,000 but less than $75,000	22	17	14	14	18	27	17	14	17	10	21	25	22
$75,000 but less than $100,000	22	15	13	13	12	20	17	14	12	13	17	16	10
$100,000 but less than $150,000	16	24	23	18	16	15	23	22	16	25	21	11	9
$150,000 but less than $200,000	9	16	17	14	11	8	15	16	11	21	12	6	6
$200,000 or more	9	11	10	13	5	6	11	12	8	15	7	2	4
Median	82,776	102,989	102,582	90,099	66,409	73,644	99,707	99,391	71,752	121,558	84,578	60,533	51,473
Responses	934	610	503	436	525	428	932	741	772	1,278	527	391	473

Q2b & Q2c. Racial & Ethnic background
(Percent of respondents)

	Age of Household Head					Generation (year born)				Household Composition			
	Under 35 years old	35 to 44 years old	45 to 54 years old	55 to 64 years old	65 years old or older	Gen Z (1997 or later)	Millenni-als(1981-1996)	Gen X (1965-1980)	Boomers (1946-1964)	Married couple w children	Married couple no children	Single parent	One person
White (Non-Hispanic)	69	76	82	79	70	60	77	79	73	68	87	61	83
African-American (Non-Hispanic)	20	12	9	8	3	24	12	10	4	6	3	25	11
Asian/Pacific Islander	4	4	3	9	5	4	3	6	5	8	4	3	2
Hispanic	8	8	6	5	22	11	7	6	17	18	6	12	4
Responses	934	610	503	436	525	428	932	741	772	1,278	527	391	473

Q2a. Which of the following best represents your total annual household income?
(Percent of respondents)

	Race/Ethnicity				Home Buyers' Income Bracket					Price Expected to Pay			
	Cauca-sian	African-American	Hispanic	Asian	Under $50,000	$50,000 to $74,999	$75,000 to $99,999	$100,000 to $149,999	$150,000 or more	Less than $150,000	$150,000 to $249,999	$250,000 to $499,999	$500,000 or more
Under $50,000	26	38	40	12	100					63	42	13	6
$50,000 but less than $75,000	18	20	7	7		100				17	24	18	6
$75,000 but less than $100,000	14	12	13	9			100			8	15	18	10
$100,000 but less than $150,000	21	15	13	8				100		10	12	26	23
$150,000 but less than $200,000	12	7	18	29					59	2	5	17	27
$200,000 or more	8	8	8	35					41	1	2	8	28
Median	85,115	66,022	80,022	174,484	25,030	62,525	87,530	125,043	192,219	39,732	58,723	101,041	159,076
Responses	1,997	390	341	280	907	549	427	552	573	718	531	1,155	530

Q2b & Q2c. Racial & Ethnic background
(Percent of respondents)

	Race/Ethnicity				Home Buyers' Income Bracket					Price Expected to Pay			
	Cauca-sian	African-American	Hispanic	Asian	Under $50,000	$50,000 to $74,999	$75,000 to $99,999	$100,000 to $149,999	$150,000 or more	Less than $150,000	$150,000 to $249,999	$250,000 to $499,999	$500,000 or more
White (Non-Hispanic)	100				70	83	78	83	67	71	73	77	76
African-American (Non-Hispanic)		100			11	10	7	6	6	14	9	7	4
Asian/Pacific Islander				100	2	2	3	2	14	2	2	5	12
Hispanic			100		17	5	11	8	13	13	17	10	8
Responses	1,997	390	341	280	907	549	427	552	573	718	531	1,155	530

Q2d. Where is your current residence located?
(Percent of respondents)

	All Home Buyers	Geography (Nine Census Divisions)									Buyer Type	
		New England	Middle Atlantic	East North Central	West North Central	South Atlantic	East South Central	West South Central	Mountain	Pacific	First-time	Repeat
New England	5	100									5	5
Middle Atlantic	12		100								11	12
East North Central	16			100							16	16
West North Central	7				100						5	8
South Atlantic	21					100					24	21
East South Central	6						100				5	7
West South Central	12							100			13	11
Mountain	8								100		6	8
Pacific	13									100	17	13
Responses	3,008	141	358	414	236	651	224	290	278	416	521	2,487

Q2e. What is your age?
(Percent of respondents)

	All Home Buyers	Geography (Nine Census Divisions)									Buyer Type	
		New England	Middle Atlantic	East North Central	West North Central	South Atlantic	East South Central	West South Central	Mountain	Pacific	First-time	Repeat
Under 35 years	11	8	11	11	6	10	12	13	7	13	21	9
35 to 44 years	16	13	20	15	11	17	13	22	11	18	25	15
45 to 54	18	17	17	25	16	16	34	18	16	12	20	18
55 to 64	22	30	30	18	17	23	22	21	25	18	18	23
65 and older	33	33	23	31	50	34	19	26	41	39	16	35
Median	56	58	55	54	64	58	49	53	61	59	46	58
Responses	3,008	141	358	414	236	651	224	290	278	416	521	2,487

Q2f. What is your gender?
(Percent of respondents)

	All Home Buyers	Geography (Nine Census Divisions)									Buyer Type	
		New England	Middle Atlantic	East North Central	West North Central	South Atlantic	East South Central	West South Central	Mountain	Pacific	First-time	Repeat
Male	44	52	49	39	52	39	46	33	44	54	32	46
Female	56	48	51	61	48	61	54	67	56	46	68	54
Responses	3,008	141	358	414	236	651	224	290	278	416	521	2,487

Q2d. Where is your current residence located?
(Percent of respondents)

	Age of Household Head					Generation (year born)				Household Composition			
	Under 35 years old	35 to 44 years old	45 to 54 years old	55 to 64 years old	65 years old or older	Gen Z (1997 or later)	Millenni-als(1981-1996)	Gen X (1965-1980)	Boomers (1946-1964)	Married couple w children	Married couple no children	Single parent	One person
New England	3	4	4	7	5	4	4	5	5	5	6	3	4
Middle Atlantic	12	15	11	16	9	10	13	14	11	13	10	12	16
East North Central	17	15	21	13	15	19	15	20	14	13	15	25	18
West North Central	4	5	6	6	11	5	4	6	9	10	5	9	5
South Atlantic	20	21	19	22	22	19	21	18	23	16	27	20	24
East South Central	7	5	12	6	4	9	6	9	5	8	5	8	5
West South Central	15	16	11	11	9	12	17	12	10	12	11	10	11
Mountain	5	5	7	9	10	6	5	7	9	8	10	4	7
Pacific	16	14	9	11	16	15	15	9	14	16	11	9	11
Responses	934	610	503	436	525	428	932	741	772	1,278	527	391	473

Q2e. What is your age?
(Percent of respondents)

	Age of Household Head					Generation (year born)				Household Composition			
	Under 35 years old	35 to 44 years old	45 to 54 years old	55 to 64 years old	65 years old or older	Gen Z (1997 or later)	Millenni-als(1981-1996)	Gen X (1965-1980)	Boomers (1946-1964)	Married couple w children	Married couple no children	Single parent	One person
Under 35 years	100					100	30			9	6	17	13
35 to 44 years		100					70	13		24	7	26	8
45 to 54			100					69		24	12	16	14
55 to 64				100				19	34	18	29	20	26
65 and older					100				66	25	47	21	40
Median	27	38	49	59	69	22	36	49	66	49	63	48	60
Responses	934	610	503	436	525	428	932	741	772	1,278	527	391	473

Q2f. What is your gender?
(Percent of respondents)

	Age of Household Head					Generation (year born)				Household Composition			
	Under 35 years old	35 to 44 years old	45 to 54 years old	55 to 64 years old	65 years old or older	Gen Z (1997 or later)	Millenni-als(1981-1996)	Gen X (1965-1980)	Boomers (1946-1964)	Married couple w children	Married couple no children	Single parent	One person
Male	40	49	42	40	47	37	47	43	44	58	38	29	33
Female	60	51	58	60	53	63	53	57	56	42	62	71	67
Responses	934	610	503	436	525	428	932	741	772	1,278	527	391	473

Q2d. Where is your current residence located?
(Percent of respondents)

	Race/Ethnicity				Home Buyers' Income Bracket					Price Expected to Pay			
	Cauca-sian	African-American	Hispanic	Asian	Under $50,000	$50,000 to $74,999	$75,000 to $99,999	$100,000 to $149,999	$150,000 or more	Less than $150,000	$150,000 to $249,999	$250,000 to $499,999	$500,000 or more
New England	4	4	10	7	4	4	4	4	7	3	5	5	6
Middle Atlantic	14	9	3	16	8	12	12	12	17	9	10	12	18
East North Central	17	18	4	16	18	18	19	12	13	21	24	13	8
West North Central	5	4	26	8	6	4	9	8	9	9	8	8	5
South Atlantic	23	32	5	9	23	23	22	24	15	23	18	23	17
East South Central	7	6	2	3	6	8	5	11	3	7	6	6	6
West South Central	13	17	5	2	13	15	11	7	12	14	13	12	8
Mountain	6	2	19	8	8	7	7	8	8	5	7	10	6
Pacific	11	7	26	30	14	10	11	13	16	9	9	11	26
Responses	1,997	390	341	280	907	549	427	552	573	718	531	1,155	530

Q2e. What is your age?
(Percent of respondents)

	Race/Ethnicity				Home Buyers' Income Bracket					Price Expected to Pay			
	Cauca-sian	African-American	Hispanic	Asian	Under $50,000	$50,000 to $74,999	$75,000 to $99,999	$100,000 to $149,999	$150,000 or more	Less than $150,000	$150,000 to $249,999	$250,000 to $499,999	$500,000 or more
Under 35 years	10	25	7	7	8	14	16	9	9	15	10	9	9
35 to 44 years	17	23	11	13	10	17	17	21	19	17	12	17	19
45 to 54	20	20	9	11	15	15	18	23	22	19	16	19	19
55 to 64	23	20	10	37	22	19	21	21	26	20	19	23	24
65 and older	30	11	63	31	45	35	28	27	24	29	42	32	28
Median	56	46	67	58	62	56	54	52	54	54	61	56	56
Responses	1,997	390	341	280	907	549	427	552	573	718	531	1,155	530

Q2f. What is your gender?
(Percent of respondents)

	Race/Ethnicity				Home Buyers' Income Bracket					Price Expected to Pay			
	Cauca-sian	African-American	Hispanic	Asian	Under $50,000	$50,000 to $74,999	$75,000 to $99,999	$100,000 to $149,999	$150,000 or more	Less than $150,000	$150,000 to $249,999	$250,000 to $499,999	$500,000 or more
Male	41	37	60	64	34	27	42	57	59	34	40	46	56
Female	59	63	40	36	66	73	58	43	41	66	60	54	44
Responses	1,997	390	341	280	907	549	427	552	573	718	531	1,155	530

Q3. What is the composition of your household?
(Percent of respondents)

	All Home Buyers	Geography (Nine Census Divisions)									Buyer Type	
		New England	Middle Atlantic	East North Central	West North Central	South Atlantic	East South Central	West South Central	Mountain	Pacific	First-time	Repeat
Married couple with children	42	45	44	35	57	32	50	45	42	51	26	45
Married couple w/out children	23	27	18	22	16	29	19	21	31	19	16	24
Single parent	10	7	10	15	12	10	12	9	5	7	22	8
One person household	15	12	20	17	10	17	12	14	15	13	22	14
Other	10	9	9	12	6	12	7	11	7	9	14	9
Responses	3,008	141	358	414	236	651	224	290	278	416	521	2,487

Q4. Do you typically work from home at least 2 days a week?
(Percent of respondents who own their own home)

	All Home Buyers	Geography (Nine Census Divisions)									Buyer Type	
		New England	Middle Atlantic	East North Central	West North Central	South Atlantic	East South Central	West South Central	Mountain	Pacific	First-time	Repeat
Yes	43	43	53	37	42	39	39	42	42	53	32	45
No	41	47	33	46	41	42	50	43	39	36	57	39
N/A	15	10	13	17	17	19	11	15	20	11	11	16
Responses	3,008	141	358	414	236	651	224	290	278	416	521	2,487

Q5. How many homes have you owned (including your present home)'?
(Percent of respondents)

	All Home Buyers	Geography (Nine Census Divisions)									Buyer Type	
		New England	Middle Atlantic	East North Central	West North Central	South Atlantic	East South Central	West South Central	Mountain	Pacific	First-time	Repeat
None	12	11	10	11	7	13	9	13	9	15	100	
One	39	48	43	37	38	35	47	38	32	46		45
Two	21	18	21	25	30	19	17	18	23	16		23
Three	14	8	17	16	14	13	15	15	17	10		16
Four or more	14	14	9	11	10	19	12	15	19	12		16
Responses	3,008	141	358	414	236	651	224	290	278	416	521	2,487

Q3. What is the composition of your household?
(Percent of respondents)

	Age of Household Head					Generation (year born)				Household Composition			
	Under 35 years old	35 to 44 years old	45 to 54 years old	55 to 64 years old	65 years old or older	Gen Z (1997 or later)	Millennials(1981-1996)	Gen X (1965-1980)	Boomers (1946-1964)	Married couple w children	Married couple no children	Single parent	One person
Married couple with children	38	62	55	34	33	19	60	54	32	100			
Married couple w/out children	12	10	15	30	32	13	10	16	32		100		
Single parent	16	16	9	9	6	21	14	9	7			100	
One person household	19	7	11	18	18	26	9	12	19				100
Other	15	6	9	10	10	20	7	9	10				
Responses	934	610	503	436	525	428	932	741	772	1,278	527	391	473

Q4. Do you typically work from home at least 2 days a week?
(Percent of respondents who own their own home)

	Age of Household Head					Generation (year born)				Household Composition			
	Under 35 years old	35 to 44 years old	45 to 54 years old	55 to 64 years old	65 years old or older	Gen Z (1997 or later)	Millennials(1981-1996)	Gen X (1965-1980)	Boomers (1946-1964)	Married couple w children	Married couple no children	Single parent	One person
Yes	57	62	54	41	25	52	63	53	29	56	30	42	36
No	37	34	38	44	47	42	33	38	47	35	47	47	44
N/A	6	5	8	15	28	7	5	9	23	9	22	11	20
Responses	934	610	503	436	525	428	932	741	772	1,278	527	391	473

Q5. How many homes have you owned (including your present home)'?
(Percent of respondents)

	Age of Household Head					Generation (year born)				Household Composition			
	Under 35 years old	35 to 44 years old	45 to 54 years old	55 to 64 years old	65 years old or older	Gen Z (1997 or later)	Millennials(1981-1996)	Gen X (1965-1980)	Boomers (1946-1964)	Married couple w children	Married couple no children	Single parent	One person
None	23	18	13	9	6	22	19	14	7	7	8	26	17
One	52	54	45	34	28	49	55	44	30	50	27	38	31
Two	18	20	22	21	21	21	20	20	21	23	21	19	16
Three	5	5	15	19	18	6	3	15	20	12	19	11	17
Four or more	2	3	6	17	26	2	2	7	22	8	24	7	20
Responses	934	610	503	436	525	428	932	741	772	1,278	527	391	473

Q3. What is the composition of your household?
(Percent of respondents)

	Race/Ethnicity				Home Buyers' Income Bracket					Price Expected to Pay			
	Caucasian	African-American	Hispanic	Asian	Under $50,000	$50,000 to $74,999	$75,000 to $99,999	$100,000 to $149,999	$150,000 or more	Less than $150,000	$150,000 to $249,999	$250,000 to $499,999	$500,000 or more
Married couple with children	38	30	67	66	24	26	40	56	66	29	35	48	54
Married couple w/out children	26	9	13	16	19	29	28	24	19	17	25	24	24
Single parent	8	29	10	5	14	15	11	6	4	18	12	7	5
One person household	17	20	6	6	27	20	11	8	7	21	18	13	11
Other	11	11	5	7	17	10	10	6	5	14	10	8	7
Responses	1,997	390	341	280	907	549	427	552	573	718	531	1,155	530

Q4. Do you typically work from home at least 2 days a week?
(Percent of respondents who own their own home)

	Race/Ethnicity				Home Buyers' Income Bracket					Price Expected to Pay			
	Caucasian	African-American	Hispanic	Asian	Under $50,000	$50,000 to $74,999	$75,000 to $99,999	$100,000 to $149,999	$150,000 or more	Less than $150,000	$150,000 to $249,999	$250,000 to $499,999	$500,000 or more
Yes	41	50	40	71	23	34	44	54	66	33	34	46	59
No	41	44	47	23	55	47	39	34	27	51	52	38	28
N/A	17	7	13	6	22	19	17	12	7	16	14	16	13
Responses	1,997	390	341	280	907	549	427	552	573	718	531	1155	530

Q5. How many homes have you owned (including your present home)'?
(Percent of respondents)

	Race/Ethnicity				Home Buyers' Income Bracket					Price Expected to Pay			
	Caucasian	African-American	Hispanic	Asian	Under $50,000	$50,000 to $74,999	$75,000 to $99,999	$100,000 to $149,999	$150,000 or more	Less than $150,000	$150,000 to $249,999	$250,000 to $499,999	$500,000 or more
None	9	36	13	9	21	15	12	5	3	23	13	8	6
One	36	39	51	64	38	33	35	43	46	40	39	38	39
Two	20	19	27	16	16	19	23	24	25	16	22	23	20
Three	17	6	6	7	12	17	17	15	13	11	16	15	15
Four or more	18	0	2	3	14	16	13	14	14	10	10	15	20
Responses	1,997	390	341	280	907	549	427	552	573	718	531	1,155	530

Q6. Which type of home do you currently live in? What type would be your first choice if you were buying a home?
(Percent of respondents)

	All Home Buyers	Geography (Nine Census Divisions)									Buyer Type	
		New England	Middle Atlantic	East North Central	West North Central	South Atlantic	East South Central	West South Central	Mountain	Pacific	First-time	Repeat
Current Home												
Single-Family detached	66	54	63	71	65	65	77	72	69	56	38	70
Townhouse/Single-Family attached	12	25	14	8	18	9	7	6	14	16	11	12
Multifamily Apartment or Condo	14	16	18	11	10	14	8	13	11	21	41	10
Manufactured (Mobile) Home	6	3	1	7	5	10	5	8	5	5	7	6
Other	2	1	3	3	2	2	3	1	1	2	3	2
First Choice if Buying												
Single-Family detached	66	52	64	71	43	71	78	73	60	63	66	66
Townhouse/Single-Family attached	16	18	18	16	29	12	9	13	22	17	13	16
Multifamily Apartment or Condo	10	17	12	5	19	8	6	6	12	12	11	9
Manufactured (Mobile) Home	5	7	3	2	7	6	3	3	5	6	5	5
Other	4	5	3	6	2	4	4	5	1	3	5	4
Responses	3,008	141	358	414	236	651	224	290	278	416	521	2,487

Q7. If location, home size and finish quality were the same, what price discount would incentivize you to buy a townhome instead of a detached single-family home?
(Percent of respondents)

	All Home Buyers	Geography (Nine Census Divisions)									Buyer Type	
		New England	Middle Atlantic	East North Central	West North Central	South Atlantic	East South Central	West South Central	Mountain	Pacific	First-time	Repeat
5% to 10%	7	4	9	8	7	6	2	8	6	5	10	6
11% to 20%	22	32	18	22	28	20	15	22	22	24	27	21
21% to 30%	24	27	26	19	14	25	31	21	22	31	21	24
More than 30%	20	17	19	18	21	20	24	21	19	19	22	19
None (wouldn't buy a townhouse)	28	20	28	33	31	30	28	28	30	21	20	29
Median	29.7	26.0	29.3	>30.0	>30.0	>30.0	>30.0	>30.0	>30.0	27.4	26.8	30.0
Responses	1,940	82	219	281	118	437	167	198	174	264	334	1,606

Q6. Which type of home do you currently live in? What type would be your first choice if you were buying a home?
(Percent of respondents)

	Age of Household Head					Generation (year born)				Household Composition			
	Under 35 years old	35 to 44 years old	45 to 54 years old	55 to 64 years old	65 years old or older	Gen Z (1997 or later)	Millennials(1981-1996)	Gen X (1965-1980)	Boomers (1946-1964)	Married couple w children	Married couple no children	Single parent	One person
Current Home													
Single-Family detached	60	71	67	65	65	54	69	66	65	69	68	63	55
Townhouse/Single-Family attached	15	10	12	13	11	17	11	12	12	15	12	11	8
Multifamily Apartment or Condo	15	14	14	15	13	15	14	15	13	11	11	21	21
Manufactured (Mobile) Home	6	4	5	5	9	8	4	5	7	4	7	4	10
Other	4	1	2	2	3	6	2	2	2	1	2	1	6
First Choice if Buying													
Single-Family detached	61	68	71	70	61	57	67	68	65	58	74	69	69
Townhouse/Single-Family attached	20	17	13	14	18	22	18	15	16	20	14	15	12
Multifamily Apartment or Condo	10	10	10	10	9	12	10	11	9	15	5	9	6
Manufactured (Mobile) Home	5	3	4	3	6	5	4	3	5	4	5	4	6
Other	4	1	3	3	6	5	1	2	5	2	3	3	7
Responses	934	610	503	436	525	428	932	741	772	1,278	527	391	473

Q7. If location, home size and finish quality were the same, what price discount would incentivize you to buy a townhome instead of a detached single-family home?
(Percent of respondents)

	Age of Household Head					Generation (year born)				Household Composition			
	Under 35 years old	35 to 44 years old	45 to 54 years old	55 to 64 years old	65 years old or older	Gen Z (1997 or later)	Millennials(1981-1996)	Gen X (1965-1980)	Boomers (1946-1964)	Married couple w children	Married couple no children	Single parent	One person
5% to 10%	12	9	6	5	5	14	9	7	5	6	6	13	5
11% to 20%	34	28	23	17	17	38	29	21	18	24	17	26	22
21% to 30%	26	29	28	20	21	25	28	28	20	31	20	22	22
More than 30%	14	18	20	19	23	12	17	21	20	20	20	16	21
None (wouldn't buy a townhouse)	14	16	23	39	34	12	16	23	37	18	37	24	31
Median	22.2	25.1	28.1	>30.0	>30.0	20.4	24.6	28.5	>30.0	26.9	>30.0	25.9	>30.0
Responses	578	426	348	288	300	247	633	499	474	760	373	266	311

Q6. Which type of home do you currently live in? What type would be your first choice if you were buying a home?
(Percent of respondents)

	Race/Ethnicity				Home Buyers' Income Bracket					Price Expected to Pay			
	Cauca-sian	African-American	Hispanic	Asian	Under $50,000	$50,000 to $74,999	$75,000 to $99,999	$100,000 to $149,999	$150,000 or more	Less than $150,000	$150,000 to $249,999	$250,000 to $499,999	$500,000 or more
Current Home													
Single-Family detached	70	54	54	54	54	64	74	76	69	52	58	72	76
Townhouse/Single-Family attached	9	13	23	25	11	9	10	11	16	9	18	12	9
Multifamily Apartment or Condo	12	27	16	15	18	16	11	11	12	18	14	12	12
Manufactured (Mobile) Home	7	4	7	5	13	9	3	2	2	16	8	2	2
Other	2	2	1	1	4	2	2	1	1	5	3	1	1
First Choice if Buying													
Single-Family detached	73	65	31	45	63	76	73	70	55	59	66	70	66
Townhouse/Single-Family attached	13	18	32	20	13	12	15	16	23	15	15	17	16
Multifamily Apartment or Condo	6	10	25	22	9	5	6	10	17	11	10	8	13
Manufactured (Mobile) Home	4	3	10	9	8	3	2	2	4	9	6	3	3
Other	4	5	2	3	6	4	3	2	2	6	4	3	2
Responses	1,997	390	341	280	907	549	427	552	573	718	531	1,155	530

Q7. If location, home size and finish quality were the same, what price discount
would incentivize you to buy a townhome instead of a detached single-family home?
(Percent of respondents)

	Race/Ethnicity				Home Buyers' Income Bracket					Price Expected to Pay			
	Cauca-sian	African-American	Hispanic	Asian	Under $50,000	$50,000 to $74,999	$75,000 to $99,999	$100,000 to $149,999	$150,000 or more	Less than $150,000	$150,000 to $249,999	$250,000 to $499,999	$500,000 or more
5% to 10%	6	13	11	7	9	6	6	4	7	11	8	5	4
11% to 20%	20	32	34	24	17	20	27	21	27	19	27	22	20
21% to 30%	25	19	23	23	17	22	22	33	28	17	17	29	29
More than 30%	19	20	19	28	20	23	21	18	17	19	20	18	24
None (wouldn't buy a townhouse)	31	16	14	17	38	29	25	23	22	33	28	27	24
Median	>30.0	23.4	23.0	29.0	>30.0	>30.0	28.6	28.0	26.6	>30.0	29.4	28.8	29.6
Responses	1,404	243	140	153	564	405	310	376	285	425	345	774	347

Q8. What is the maximum mortgage interest rate you would accept on a loan to buy a home?
(Percent of respondents)

	All Home Buyers	Geography (Nine Census Divisions)									Buyer Type	
		New England	Middle Atlantic	East North Central	West North Central	South Atlantic	East South Central	West South Central	Mountain	Pacific	First-time	Repeat
Under 3%	14	9	12	18	15	11	11	19	19	11	21	13
3.0% to 4.9%	40	52	38	37	44	41	33	42	42	42	44	40
5.0% to 6.9%	30	25	32	30	28	29	30	27	27	34	21	31
7.0% or higher	5	1	3	5	2	5	13	3	4	6	3	5
Interest rate doesn't play a role in my decision	12	13	15	11	11	15	13	9	8	6	10	12
Median	4.46	4.29	4.57	4.44	4.31	4.53	4.93	4.24	4.26	4.66	4.07	4.52
Responses	3,008	141	358	414	236	651	224	290	278	416	521	2,487

Q9. If you were buying a home, what would your first preference be?
(Percent of respondents)

	All Home Buyers	Geography (Nine Census Divisions)									Buyer Type	
		New England	Middle Atlantic	East North Central	West North Central	South Atlantic	East South Central	West South Central	Mountain	Pacific	First-time	Repeat
A brand new home offered by a builder	40	39	45	28	45	37	47	34	42	49	35	40
An existing home	39	40	41	51	30	38	33	37	38	35	47	38
A home custom built on a lot you own	21	21	14	20	25	25	20	29	19	17	18	22
Responses	2,725	133	335	357	219	572	198	262	260	389	462	2,263
Other	2	2	3	2	2	2	2	2	1	1	1	2
Don't know/Not sure	9	5	7	16	7	12	9	7	5	5	11	9

Q8. What is the maximum mortgage interest rate you would accept on a loan to buy a home?
(Percent of respondents)

	Age of Household Head					Generation (year born)				Household Composition			
	Under 35 years old	35 to 44 years old	45 to 54 years old	55 to 64 years old	65 years old or older	Gen Z (1997 or later)	Millenni-als(1981-1996)	Gen X (1965-1980)	Boomers (1946-1964)	Married couple w children	Married couple no children	Single parent	One person
Under 3%	10	13	14	16	14	11	13	14	15	11	15	19	14
3.0% to 4.9%	41	33	38	43	43	43	35	38	44	39	40	42	41
5.0% to 6.9%	32	42	30	25	26	28	40	31	25	38	24	22	25
7.0% or higher	9	6	8	2	2	9	7	7	2	6	2	6	2
Interest rate doesn't play a role in my decision	8	6	10	13	15	9	6	9	14	5	18	11	18
Median	4.71	4.97	4.59	4.23	4.29	4.59	4.93	4.57	4.25	4.8	4.24	4.18	4.29
Responses	934	610	503	436	525	428	932	741	772	1,278	527	391	473

Q9. If you were buying a home, what would your first preference be?
(Percent of respondents)

	Age of Household Head					Generation (year born)				Household Composition			
	Under 35 years old	35 to 44 years old	45 to 54 years old	55 to 64 years old	65 years old or older	Gen Z (1997 or later)	Millenni-als(1981-1996)	Gen X (1965-1980)	Boomers (1946-1964)	Married couple w children	Married couple no children	Single parent	One person
A brand new home offered by a builder	40	50	45	31	37	29	51	43	35	53	30	34	25
An existing home	38	34	32	44	43	42	33	35	43	27	47	47	53
A home custom built on a lot you own	23	17	22	25	20	30	16	22	22	20	23	19	22
Responses	865	566	442	392	460	395	864	663	682	1,212	468	346	407
Other	2	1	2	2	2	3	1	1	2	1	2	2	2
Don't know/Not sure	5	6	10	9	12	4	6	10	11	5	10	11	16

Q8. What is the maximum mortgage interest rate you would accept on a loan to buy a home?
(Percent of respondents)

	Race/Ethnicity				Home Buyers' Income Bracket					Price Expected to Pay			
	Caucasian	African-American	Hispanic	Asian	Under $50,000	$50,000 to $74,999	$75,000 to $99,999	$100,000 to $149,999	$150,000 or more	Less than $150,000	$150,000 to $249,999	$250,000 to $499,999	$500,000 or more
Under 3%	13	21	13	10	22	16	9	7	11	24	12	12	9
3.0% to 4.9%	38	42	52	41	39	44	45	44	34	36	52	43	32
5.0% to 6.9%	29	24	29	42	19	26	30	34	41	22	24	33	38
7.0% or higher	5	4	3	2	3	4	3	8	4	6	2	3	8
Interest rate doesn't play a role in my decision	14	8	3	5	17	10	12	7	9	12	9	10	13
Median	4.51	4.15	4.34	4.82	3.96	4.29	4.49	4.78	4.98	4.07	4.25	4.54	5.09
Responses	1,997	390	341	280	907	549	427	552	573	718	531	1,155	530

Q9. If you were buying a home, what would your first preference be?
(Percent of respondents)

	Race/Ethnicity				Home Buyers' Income Bracket					Price Expected to Pay			
	Caucasian	African-American	Hispanic	Asian	Under $50,000	$50,000 to $74,999	$75,000 to $99,999	$100,000 to $149,999	$150,000 or more	Less than $150,000	$150,000 to $249,999	$250,000 to $499,999	$500,000 or more
A brand new home offered by a builder	36	38	60	44	31	26	42	49	50	31	32	44	47
An existing home	43	36	23	32	49	52	42	28	26	46	44	37	31
A home custom built on a lot you own	21	26	17	24	20	22	16	23	24	23	24	19	22
Responses	1,777	359	329	260	776	494	390	516	549	619	490	1,070	500
Other	2	1	0	1	2	1	1	2	1	4	1	1	1
Don't know/Not sure	11	7	2	4	12	11	12	7	4	11	8	9	6

Q10. If you were buying a new home, what are the top three areas you would pay more to upgrade?
(Percent of respondents)

	All Home Buyers	Geography (Nine Census Divisions)									Buyer Type	
		New England	Middle Atlantic	East North Central	West North Central	South Atlantic	East South Central	West South Central	Mountain	Pacific	First-time	Repeat
Gourmet kitchen (high end appliances, cabinets, counters)	71	69	68	70	62	71	66	74	70	78	66	71
Upgraded master bath (freestanding tub, rainfall shower)	65	60	69	61	68	67	64	68	64	61	62	65
Upgraded front exterior material	24	32	25	18	31	18	25	21	27	35	20	25
Finished basement	36	42	41	51	48	30	37	20	38	25	40	35
Hardwood floor for entire house	43	47	41	39	41	44	43	49	42	45	40	44
Outdoor features (deck, fencing, patio)	49	44	48	49	39	54	51	54	50	44	51	49
Other	4	3	5	4	6	5	7	5	2	3	5	4
None	3	0	1	3	1	4	2	3	2	3	5	2
Responses	3,008	141	358	414	236	651	224	290	278	416	521	2,487

Q11. What material would you prefer for framing the exterior walls of your home?
(Percent of respondents)

	All Home Buyers	Geography (Nine Census Divisions)									Buyer Type	
		New England	Middle Atlantic	East North Central	West North Central	South Atlantic	East South Central	West South Central	Mountain	Pacific	First-time	Repeat
Wood	37	46	34	41	34	31	39	38	38	37	41	36
Steel (additional $15,000)	23	24	26	17	29	18	31	23	23	28	18	24
Concrete (additional $35,000)	25	15	24	20	29	36	19	22	22	24	21	26
No preference	15	15	16	22	7	15	11	17	17	10	20	15
Responses	3,008	141	358	414	236	651	224	290	278	416	521	2,487

Q10. *If you were buying a new home, what are the top three areas you would pay more to upgrade?*
(Percent of respondents)

	Age of Household Head					Generation (year born)				Household Composition			
	Under 35 years old	35 to 44 years old	45 to 54 years old	55 to 64 years old	65 years old or older	Gen Z (1997 or later)	Millenni-als(1981-1996)	Gen X (1965-1980)	Boomers (1946-1964)	Married couple w children	Married couple no children	Single parent	One person
Gourmet kitchen (high end appliances, cabinets, counters)	67	72	75	72	68	64	70	73	71	73	73	72	64
Upgraded master bath (freestanding tub, rainfall shower)	63	65	67	65	65	64	64	68	64	66	65	60	67
Upgraded front exterior material	34	33	24	17	22	33	35	24	19	33	18	23	15
Finished basement	40	40	39	33	32	42	39	40	32	40	28	40	31
Hardwood floor for entire house	39	34	43	44	49	40	36	42	47	44	44	43	41
Outdoor features (deck, fencing, patio)	43	45	45	56	51	42	45	45	54	39	58	47	63
Other	4	2	3	6	5	5	2	3	6	3	5	4	7
None	4	3	1	2	3	4	3	2	3	1	3	3	5
Responses	934	610	503	436	525	428	932	741	772	1,278	527	391	473

Q11. *What material would you prefer for framing the exterior walls of your home?*
(Percent of respondents)

	Age of Household Head					Generation (year born)				Household Composition			
	Under 35 years old	35 to 44 years old	45 to 54 years old	55 to 64 years old	65 years old or older	Gen Z (1997 or later)	Millenni-als(1981-1996)	Gen X (1965-1980)	Boomers (1946-1964)	Married couple w children	Married couple no children	Single parent	One person
Wood	34	31	41	39	36	35	32	40	36	34	39	35	38
Steel (additional $15,000)	29	24	22	23	21	32	25	22	23	26	23	25	18
Concrete (additional $35,000)	27	33	20	23	26	25	31	22	25	30	21	22	23
No preference	10	13	17	15	17	9	12	16	17	10	16	17	21
Responses	934	610	503	436	525	428	932	741	772	1,278	527	391	473

Q10. If you were buying a new home, what are the top three areas you would pay more to upgrade?
(Percent of respondents)

	Race/Ethnicity				Home Buyers' Income Bracket					Price Expected to Pay			
	Cauca-sian	African-American	Hispanic	Asian	Under $50,000	$50,000 to $74,999	$75,000 to $99,999	$100,000 to $149,999	$150,000 or more	Less than $150,000	$150,000 to $249,999	$250,000 to $499,999	$500,000 or more
Gourmet kitchen (high end appliances, cabinets, counters)	73	66	64	58	66	74	71	71	73	64	70	72	76
Upgraded master bath (freestanding tub, rainfall shower)	63	70	71	66	63	62	62	67	69	66	62	65	69
Upgraded front exterior material	20	28	42	39	20	16	17	29	36	24	20	24	31
Finished basement	33	38	44	46	36	37	37	37	33	37	42	36	29
Hardwood floor for entire house	42	42	46	54	43	39	44	42	48	41	42	44	46
Outdoor features (deck, fencing, patio)	55	38	26	31	54	59	54	45	37	51	54	49	44
Other	5	4	2	1	4	7	6	4	2	5	4	5	2
None	3	5	1	2	5	2	2	1	1	4	2	2	1
Responses	1,997	390	341	280	907	549	427	552	573	718	531	1,155	530

Q11. What material would you prefer for framing the exterior walls of your home?
(Percent of respondents)

	Race/Ethnicity				Home Buyers' Income Bracket					Price Expected to Pay			
	Cauca-sian	African-American	Hispanic	Asian	Under $50,000	$50,000 to $74,999	$75,000 to $99,999	$100,000 to $149,999	$150,000 or more	Less than $150,000	$150,000 to $249,999	$250,000 to $499,999	$500,000 or more
Wood	39	30	21	41	38	39	43	34	30	43	37	35	33
Steel (additional $15,000)	21	22	34	26	19	21	23	31	24	21	24	24	23
Concrete (additional $35,000)	23	30	38	23	21	24	21	24	35	19	22	27	31
No preference	16	18	8	9	22	16	13	11	11	17	16	13	13
Responses	1,997	390	341	280	907	549	427	552	573	718	531	1,155	530

Q12. Which would you prefer for the exterior design of your new home?
(Percent of respondents) (Pictures provided)

	All Home Buyers	Geography (Nine Census Divisions)									Buyer Type	
		New England	Middle Atlantic	East North Central	West North Central	South Atlantic	East South Central	West South Central	Mountain	Pacific	First-time	Repeat
Modern	17	14	18	14	27	12	17	13	15	25	15	17
Contemporary	26	28	28	21	24	28	30	25	23	31	26	26
Traditional	34	37	37	37	30	35	39	35	33	25	34	34
Transitional	12	6	7	15	12	12	10	13	19	11	12	12
Other	3	2	2	5	6	3	1	3	4	1	2	3
No strong prefrence	8	13	8	8	2	10	4	10	7	7	11	8
Responses	3,008	141	358	414	236	651	224	290	278	416	521	2,487

Q13. In what type of area would you prefer to buy a home?
(Percent of respondents)

	All Home Buyers	Geography (Nine Census Divisions)									Buyer Type	
		New England	Middle Atlantic	East North Central	West North Central	South Atlantic	East South Central	West South Central	Mountain	Pacific	First-time	Repeat
Rural	25	26	20	32	25	22	37	29	19	16	25	25
Outlying Suburb	29	32	32	33	29	33	19	31	26	20	27	29
Close in Suburb	24	23	25	22	21	26	16	19	28	27	26	23
Central City-downtown	13	14	14	6	16	9	14	14	18	20	9	13
Central City-outside downtown	10	5	9	7	10	9	15	6	10	16	13	9
Responses	3,008	141	358	414	236	651	224	290	278	416	521	2,487

Q14. What is the farthest distance you would travel one-way between home and work?
(Percent of respondents)

	All Home Buyers	Geography (Nine Census Divisions)									Buyer Type	
		New England	Middle Atlantic	East North Central	West North Central	South Atlantic	East South Central	West South Central	Mountain	Pacific	First-time	Repeat
Less than 5 miles	16	15	16	14	16	17	19	16	16	15	22	15
5-10 miles	31	24	28	29	39	31	26	33	32	34	30	31
11-20 miles	38	41	40	39	34	36	35	38	40	36	34	38
21-50 miles	13	17	14	16	9	13	16	12	11	10	11	13
Over 50 miles	3	2	2	2	1	3	5	1	1	4	3	3
Median	11.3	13.2	12.0	12.3	9.8	11.2	12.1	10.9	11.1	10.7	10.2	11.5
Responses	3,008	141	358	414	236	651	224	290	278	416	521	2,487

Q12. Which would you prefer for the exterior design of your new home?
(Percent of respondents) (Pictures provided)

	Age of Household Head					Generation (year born)				Household Composition			
	Under 35 years old	35 to 44 years old	45 to 54 years old	55 to 64 years old	65 years old or older	Gen Z (1997 or later)	Millenni-als(1981-1996)	Gen X (1965-1980)	Boomers (1946-1964)	Married couple w children	Married couple no children	Single parent	One person
Modern	27	25	19	12	10	25	26	20	10	25	9	16	11
Contemporary	31	29	26	22	26	30	31	25	25	32	22	24	20
Traditional	25	30	33	41	35	26	28	34	37	28	39	35	38
Transitional	12	11	12	11	13	14	11	11	13	10	15	15	12
Other	2	1	4	3	4	2	1	3	4	2	5	1	6
No strong prefrence	2	4	5	10	12	2	3	7	11	4	10	9	13
Responses	934	610	503	436	525	428	932	741	772	1,278	527	391	473

Q13. In what type of area would you prefer to buy a home?
(Percent of respondents)

	Age of Household Head					Generation (year born)				Household Composition			
	Under 35 years old	35 to 44 years old	45 to 54 years old	55 to 64 years old	65 years old or older	Gen Z (1997 or later)	Millenni-als(1981-1996)	Gen X (1965-1980)	Boomers (1946-1964)	Married couple w children	Married couple no children	Single parent	One person
Rural	25	22	28	30	20	27	21	28	24	21	26	28	27
Outlying Suburb	23	20	24	33	36	24	20	26	34	24	37	28	32
Close in Suburb	23	23	19	25	26	27	22	20	26	20	24	28	26
Central City-downtown	17	21	17	7	10	13	21	16	8	23	5	7	6
Central City-outside downtown	12	14	12	6	8	9	15	10	8	12	6	9	9
Responses	934	610	503	436	525	428	932	741	772	1,278	527	391	473

Q14. What is the farthest distance you would travel one-way between home and work?
(Percent of respondents)

	Age of Household Head					Generation (year born)				Household Composition			
	Under 35 years old	35 to 44 years old	45 to 54 years old	55 to 64 years old	65 years old or older	Gen Z (1997 or later)	Millenni-als(1981-1996)	Gen X (1965-1980)	Boomers (1946-1964)	Married couple w children	Married couple no children	Single parent	One person
Less than 5 miles	13	12	13	13	23	12	12	12	20	13	17	19	21
5-10 miles	35	34	29	23	34	38	33	30	31	30	29	35	33
11-20 miles	38	38	38	42	34	36	39	39	35	40	40	34	30
21-50 miles	12	14	17	18	7	12	14	16	11	14	12	11	13
Over 50 miles	2	3	3	4	2	2	3	3	2	3	2	2	3
Median	11.2	11.7	12.8	13.7	9.3	10.7	11.8	12.7	10.2	12.2	11.4	10.0	9.8
Responses	934	610	503	436	525	428	932	741	772	1,278	527	391	473

Q12. Which would you prefer for the exterior design of your new home?
(Percent of respondents) (Pictures provided)

	Race/Ethnicity				Home Buyers' Income Bracket					Price Expected to Pay			
	Cauca-sian	African-American	Hispanic	Asian	Under $50,000	$50,000 to $74,999	$75,000 to $99,999	$100,000 to $149,999	$150,000 or more	Less than $150,000	$150,000 to $249,999	$250,000 to $499,999	$500,000 or more
Modern	14	20	28	21	10	7	15	24	26	15	11	15	24
Contemporary	24	31	34	36	22	25	25	31	28	22	26	27	31
Traditional	38	28	20	19	41	40	36	29	26	37	39	35	26
Transitional	11	12	12	18	10	14	12	11	14	11	13	12	13
Other	4	0	1	2	6	4	3	2	1	5	4	3	1
No strong prefrence	9	9	5	5	11	10	10	4	5	10	7	8	5
Responses	1,997	390	341	280	907	549	427	552	573	718	531	1,155	530

Q13. In what type of area would you prefer to buy a home?
(Percent of respondents)

	Race/Ethnicity				Home Buyers' Income Bracket					Price Expected to Pay			
	Cauca-sian	African-American	Hispanic	Asian	Under $50,000	$50,000 to $74,999	$75,000 to $99,999	$100,000 to $149,999	$150,000 or more	Less than $150,000	$150,000 to $249,999	$250,000 to $499,999	$500,000 or more
Rural	27	19	11	26	31	31	22	18	18	37	29	21	16
Outlying Suburb	30	32	22	26	26	34	39	28	25	27	33	32	25
Close in Suburb	22	25	27	32	24	23	26	22	23	18	20	25	27
Central City-downtown	11	12	28	11	10	5	8	19	20	10	11	15	14
Central City-outside downtown	9	12	13	5	9	6	5	13	13	8	7	8	17
Responses	1,997	390	341	280	907	549	427	552	573	718	531	1,155	530

Q14. What is the farthest distance you would travel one-way between home and work?
(Percent of respondents)

	Race/Ethnicity				Home Buyers' Income Bracket					Price Expected to Pay			
	Cauca-sian	African-American	Hispanic	Asian	Under $50,000	$50,000 to $74,999	$75,000 to $99,999	$100,000 to $149,999	$150,000 or more	Less than $150,000	$150,000 to $249,999	$250,000 to $499,999	$500,000 or more
Less than 5 miles	16	15	20	11	25	15	14	13	10	23	17	12	14
5-10 miles	29	34	42	27	32	32	24	30	33	33	35	27	33
11-20 miles	38	38	31	46	30	36	45	43	39	29	37	44	35
21-50 miles	14	10	5	14	10	14	16	12	15	12	9	14	15
Over 50 miles	3	3	2	2	3	3	2	2	2	2	2	3	2
Median	11.8	10.9	9.0	13.3	9.3	11.4	13.3	12.2	12.2	9.5	10.2	13.0	11.2
Responses	1,997	390	341	280	907	549	427	552	573	718	531	1,155	530

Q15. Are you planning on watching virtual home tours during the home purchase process
(Percent of respondents)

	All Home Buyers	Geography (Nine Census Divisions)									Buyer Type	
		New England	Middle Atlantic	East North Central	West North Central	South Atlantic	East South Central	West South Central	Mountain	Pacific	First-time	Repeat
Yes	63	74	63	58	71	60	58	57	63	72	56	64
No	23	14	19	24	18	24	28	26	26	19	23	23
Don't know/Not sure	14	12	17	18	12	16	14	17	11	8	22	14
Responses	3,008	141	358	414	236	651	224	290	278	416	521	2,487

Q16. What price would you expect to pay (or did you pay if you bought a home in the last three years)?
(Percent of respondents)

	All Home Buyers	Geography (Nine Census Divisions)									Buyer Type	
		New England	Middle Atlantic	East North Central	West North Central	South Atlantic	East South Central	West South Central	Mountain	Pacific	First-time	Repeat
Less than $100,000	8	3	5	11	10	9	10	10	7	5	20	7
$100,000-$149,999	11	11	9	15	13	13	11	13	6	9	20	10
$150,000-$249,999	19	19	16	29	20	16	19	21	16	12	22	18
$250,000-$349,999	21	17	17	19	26	23	21	25	26	12	19	21
$350,000-$499,999	21	26	24	16	18	23	19	17	30	22	9	23
$500,000-$999,999	16	22	22	6	12	13	20	10	14	29	8	17
$1 million and over	4	3	7	4	1	3	1	4	1	11	2	5
Median	307,061	355,089	367,466	233,088	279,333	303,275	298,836	276,897	331,967	432,956	199,154	321,033
Responses	2,934	134	349	404	233	635	218	282	275	404	503	2,431

Q15. Are you planning on watching virtual home tours during the home purchase process
(Percent of respondents)

	Age of Household Head					Generation (year born)				Household Composition			
	Under 35 years old	35 to 44 years old	45 to 54 years old	55 to 64 years old	65 years old or older	Gen Z (1997 or later)	Millenni-als(1981-1996)	Gen X (1965-1980)	Boomers (1946-1964)	Married couple w children	Married couple no children	Single parent	One person
Yes	67	73	65	57	59	61	74	65	59	75	57	57	53
No	22	16	20	22	27	26	17	20	26	16	27	26	28
Don't know/Not sure	11	11	14	20	13	13	10	16	15	9	16	17	19
Responses	934	610	503	436	525	428	932	741	772	1,278	527	391	473

Q16. What price would you expect to pay (or did you pay if you bought a home in the last three years)?
(Percent of respondents)

	Age of Household Head					Generation (year born)				Household Composition			
	Under 35 years old	35 to 44 years old	45 to 54 years old	55 to 64 years old	65 years old or older	Gen Z (1997 or later)	Millenni-als(1981-1996)	Gen X (1965-1980)	Boomers (1946-1964)	Married couple w children	Married couple no children	Single parent	One person
Less than $100,000	13	9	8	9	6	16	9	8	7	4	6	15	13
$100,000-$149,999	15	12	12	9	12	21	11	11	11	9	9	20	15
$150,000-$249,999	19	14	17	16	24	20	15	17	22	15	20	24	22
$250,000-$349,999	22	19	20	24	19	20	21	20	19	21	21	20	20
$350,000-$499,999	14	24	23	21	21	12	21	23	21	25	23	11	15
$500,000-$999,999	13	17	15	18	14	8	18	15	16	19	17	7	10
$1 million and over	4	6	6	4	3	3	5	6	3	6	4	3	4
Median	264,655	332,669	320,100	319,993	292,262	217,046	324,166	316,537	299,882	352,704	323,357	213,159	248,243
Responses	914	597	494	422	507	419	912	725	747	1,262	518	381	454

Q15. Are you planning on watching virtual home tours during the home purchase process
(Percent of respondents)

	Race/Ethnicity				Home Buyers' Income Bracket					Price Expected to Pay			
	Cauca-sian	African-American	Hispanic	Asian	Under $50,000	$50,000 to $74,999	$75,000 to $99,999	$100,000 to $149,999	$150,000 or more	Less than $150,000	$150,000 to $249,999	$250,000 to $499,999	$500,000 or more
Yes	60	66	75	80	48	56	67	71	78	53	57	67	76
No	24	20	20	12	33	22	17	22	15	30	27	20	17
Don't know/Not sure	16	14	5	8	20	22	17	8	7	17	17	14	7
Responses	1,997	390	341	280	907	549	427	552	573	718	531	1155	530

Q16. What price would you expect to pay (or did you pay if you bought a home in the last three years)?
(Percent of respondents)

	Race/Ethnicity				Home Buyers' Income Bracket					Price Expected to Pay			
	Cauca-sian	African-American	Hispanic	Asian	Under $50,000	$50,000 to $74,999	$75,000 to $99,999	$100,000 to $149,999	$150,000 or more	Less than $150,000	$150,000 to $249,999	$250,000 to $499,999	$500,000 or more
Less than $100,000	8	16	7	3	25	6	1	1	0	42			
$100,000-$149,999	11	17	15	4	21	14	10	9	2	58			
$150,000-$249,999	18	20	27	6	29	27	20	11	6		100		
$250,000-$349,999	21	25	20	12	13	27	29	24	17			49	
$350,000-$499,999	22	12	17	30	8	18	25	32	27			51	
$500,000-$999,999	16	5	12	34	3	7	14	21	32				78
$1 million and over	4	4	2	11	1	0	1	3	16				22
Median	314,390	233,106	254,465	476,566	164,471	261,827	314,720	376,231	486,257	107,224	200,091	352,098	821,885
Responses	1,950	375	337	272	860	535	421	549	569	718	531	1,155	530

Q17. What is the finished area of your present home, and how many would you like to have in your new home?
(Percent of respondents who own their home)

	All Home Buyers	Geography (Nine Census Divisions)									Buyer Type	
		New England	Middle Atlantic	East North Central	West North Central	South Atlantic	East South Central	West South Central	Mountain	Pacific	First-time	Repeat
Present Home												
Less than 1,200 sqft	15	14	13	19	25	15	9	7	23	14		15
1,200-1,599 sqft	25	24	20	29	31	23	21	27	28	24		25
1,600-1,999 sqft	19	20	21	17	22	19	19	21	16	16		19
2,000-2,499 sqft	20	29	19	19	11	19	26	20	17	22		20
2,500-2,999 sqft	12	3	17	9	8	13	8	14	11	14		12
3,000-3,999 sqft	7	6	7	6	3	8	5	7	4	8		7
4,000 sqft or more	3	4	3	2	1	3	13	4	1	1		3
Median (Square Feet)	1,802	1839	1924	1654	1531	1846	2033	1912	1596	1895		1,802
Would Like to Have												
Less than 1,200 sqft	8	10	7	8	8	8	5	9	8	8		8
1,200-1,599 sqft	18	25	17	24	21	19	15	10	19	14		18
1,600-1,999 sqft	21	20	22	22	22	20	19	14	29	19		21
2,000-2,499 sqft	22	20	18	18	25	21	26	34	22	20		22
2,500-2,999 sqft	16	15	19	17	13	17	14	16	12	20		16
3,000-3,999 sqft	8	4	10	7	7	9	4	10	8	11		8
4,000 sqft or more	6	6	7	3	4	5	18	6	4	7		6
Median (Square Feet)	2,067	1,923	2,109	1,915	1,987	2,055	2,222	2,234	1,927	2,210		2,067
Responses	2,106	105	251	289	177	442	159	194	193	296		2,106

Q18. What is your preference for lot size?
(Percent of respondents)

	All Home Buyers	Geography (Nine Census Divisions)									Buyer Type	
		New England	Middle Atlantic	East North Central	West North Central	South Atlantic	East South Central	West South Central	Mountain	Pacific	First-time	Repeat
2+ acres	18	15	13	20	18	20	24	22	10	14	23	17
1 acre	23	23	26	23	16	24	30	26	18	17	26	22
1/2 acre	21	32	17	17	21	23	17	18	21	24	17	21
1/4 acre	17	16	18	14	16	13	17	19	23	20	10	18
1/8 acre	9	5	10	10	11	9	8	6	12	12	6	10
No preference	13	9	16	16	17	12	5	9	16	13	17	13
Responses	3,008	141	358	414	236	651	224	290	278	416	521	2,487

Q17. What is the finished area of your present home, and how many would you like to have in your new home?
(Percent of respondents who own their home)

	Age of Household Head					Generation (year born)				Household Composition			
	Under 35 years old	35 to 44 years old	45 to 54 years old	55 to 64 years old	65 years old or older	Gen Z (1997 or later)	Millenni-als(1981-1996)	Gen X (1965-1980)	Boomers (1946-1964)	Married couple w children	Married couple no children	Single parent	One person
Present Home													
Less than 1,200 sqft	13	10	13	13	21	8	11	13	19	12	14	21	28
1,200-1,599 sqft	21	16	21	27	30	23	17	24	29	22	25	23	33
1,600-1,999 sqft	24	22	14	21	17	23	23	16	17	17	25	18	12
2,000-2,499 sqft	19	28	24	19	14	22	26	21	18	22	18	23	13
2,500-2,999 sqft	11	15	13	10	10	12	14	12	10	15	10	6	5
3,000-3,999 sqft	6	6	7	7	6	7	5	8	6	8	6	4	6
4,000 sqft or more	5	3	8	3	0	6	3	7	1	4	3	3	3
Median (Square Feet)	1868	2037	2036	1799	1583	1,940	1,966	1936	1649	1,963	1793	1719	1467
Would Like to Have													
Less than 1,200 sqft	5	4	7	8	11	3	4	6	11	4	7	8	18
1,200-1,599 sqft	12	9	14	18	26	15	9	14	24	14	18	24	30
1,600-1,999 sqft	20	15	16	25	23	22	16	18	24	18	27	23	18
2,000-2,499 sqft	22	25	27	21	19	21	25	24	21	24	24	21	15
2,500-2,999 sqft	19	24	17	14	14	18	24	17	13	22	13	12	8
3,000-3,999 sqft	10	13	10	9	5	8	12	11	6	11	7	7	4
4,000 sqft or more	11	10	10	5	2	12	10	10	2	7	4	5	6
Median (Square Feet)	2,288	2,437	2,257	1,981	1,829	2,244	2,408	2,247	1,869	2,290	1,969	1,918	1,642
Responses	568	411	351	329	447	247	616	517	633	1,041	402	189	282

Q18. What is your preference for lot size?
(Percent of respondents)

	Age of Household Head					Generation (year born)				Household Composition			
	Under 35 years old	35 to 44 years old	45 to 54 years old	55 to 64 years old	65 years old or older	Gen Z (1997 or later)	Millenni-als(1981-1996)	Gen X (1965-1980)	Boomers (1946-1964)	Married couple w children	Married couple no children	Single parent	One person
2+ acres	24	22	22	20	10	25	22	22	13	16	18	16	21
1 acre	28	24	28	25	16	26	25	27	19	22	23	27	20
1/2 acre	18	23	18	18	23	17	23	18	22	26	15	21	16
1/4 acre	13	18	13	13	22	14	16	13	19	19	18	10	15
1/8 acre	7	6	6	9	14	7	5	7	13	8	12	11	9
No preference	9	8	13	15	16	11	8	13	15	9	14	15	20
Responses	934	610	503	436	525	428	932	741	772	1,278	527	391	473

Q17. What is the finished area of your present home, and how many would you like to have in your new home?
(Percent of respondents who own their home)

	Race/Ethnicity				Home Buyers' Income Bracket					Price Expected to Pay			
	Cauca-sian	African-American	Hispanic	Asian	Under $50,000	$50,000 to $74,999	$75,000 to $99,999	$100,000 to $149,999	$150,000 or more	Less than $150,000	$150,000 to $249,999	$250,000 to $499,999	$500,000 or more
Present Home													
Less than 1,200 sqft	13	10	33	11	29	14	11	10	11	35	20	9	8
1,200-1,599 sqft	24	23	26	37	35	34	22	18	19	35	37	22	16
1,600-1,999 sqft	19	17	17	23	13	24	24	21	17	13	21	23	14
2,000-2,499 sqft	21	24	15	8	13	15	24	26	19	11	16	24	20
2,500-2,999 sqft	13	12	5	11	6	9	10	12	18	4	5	13	21
3,000-3,999 sqft	7	8	3	9	2	3	8	7	10	1	2	6	16
4,000 sqft or more	3	7	1	1	1	1	1	5	6	1	1	4	6
Median (Square Feet)	1,865	2023	1457	1632	1440	1642	1893	2021	2076	1377	1532	1935	2308
Would Like to Have													
Less than 1,200 sqft	8	11	5	6	21	5	6	5	2	22	11	4	2
1,200-1,599 sqft	18	10	23	16	25	26	21	15	10	28	28	15	10
1,600-1,999 sqft	21	20	26	7	23	30	25	18	14	22	25	23	12
2,000-2,499 sqft	22	16	25	26	16	19	26	28	22	17	16	27	22
2,500-2,999 sqft	16	17	14	23	9	13	12	17	26	7	13	17	25
3,000-3,999 sqft	8	11	3	18	3	5	7	9	15	2	4	8	18
4,000 sqft or more	6	16	4	5	4	2	4	7	10	2	3	6	12
Median (Square Feet)	2,051	2,305	1,942	2,409	1,679	1,856	1,980	2,211	2,534	1,617	1,775	2,149	2,581
Responses	1,469	181	241	215	489	335	295	473	514	406	343	869	442

Q18. What is your preference for lot size?
(Percent of respondents)

	Race/Ethnicity				Home Buyers' Income Bracket					Price Expected to Pay			
	Cauca-sian	African-American	Hispanic	Asian	Under $50,000	$50,000 to $74,999	$75,000 to $99,999	$100,000 to $149,999	$150,000 or more	Less than $150,000	$150,000 to $249,999	$250,000 to $499,999	$500,000 or more
2+ acres	20	22	8	4	22	22	16	15	13	27	19	15	13
1 acre	24	25	15	22	22	25	22	21	24	24	23	22	23
1/2 acre	18	20	28	37	17	19	21	24	23	18	20	22	22
1/4 acre	16	14	20	19	12	13	17	22	20	10	13	21	18
1/8 acre	9	9	11	8	10	9	9	9	8	9	10	9	10
No preference	13	11	18	11	16	11	16	9	12	13	15	10	13
Responses	1,997	390	341	280	907	549	427	552	573	718	531	1,155	530

Q19. If you were having trouble finding a home in your ideal price range, which of the following potential compromises would you be willing to accept in order to be able to afford it? (Check all that apply) (Percent of respondents)

	All Home Buyers	Geography (Nine Census Divisions)									Buyer Type	
		New England	Middle Atlantic	East North Central	West North Central	South Atlantic	East South Central	West South Central	Mountain	Pacific	First-time	Repeat
Smaller house	35	38	33	36	39	39	32	29	40	33	34	36
Smaller lot	39	43	39	38	29	42	36	40	42	36	37	39
Unfinished spaces	21	29	20	28	28	19	22	15	19	19	20	22
Fewer roooms	24	29	21	23	30	22	21	22	28	24	20	24
Fewer energy efficient features (when not mandated by code)	23	30	22	17	25	18	28	23	27	28	22	23
Farther from urban core	36	35	33	39	35	37	30	36	37	38	29	37
Substitution of expensive materials for less expensive options	28	32	26	30	32	26	18	26	30	31	34	27
Fewer exterior amenities (e.g. porches, decks, patios, pools, etc.)	36	36	32	38	38	34	32	40	38	38	39	36
More modular or pre-fabricated housing construction components	26	30	26	25	31	22	23	23	25	34	23	26
Denser development	14	20	14	10	19	12	12	12	16	22	12	15
Other	3	2	3	3	2	4	4	4	0	3	4	3
Responses	3,008	141	358	414	236	651	224	290	278	416	521	2,487

Q20. What areas would you be wiloling to make smaller? (Check all that apply) (Percent of respondents who are willing to accept a smaller home)

	All Home Buyers	Geography (Nine Census Divisions)									Buyer Type	
		New England	Middle Atlantic	East North Central	West North Central	South Atlantic	East South Central	West South Central	Mountain	Pacific	First-time	Repeat
Kitchen	21	29	21	18	27	18	14	18	19	33	22	21
Bedrooms	31	31	36	32	36	25	22	31	30	43	25	32
Bathrooms	26	20	17	29	32	23	19	24	30	35	20	26
Closets	22	18	20	25	24	22	21	20	26	18	30	21
Family room	39	49	37	37	47	42	26	29	37	42	41	39
Living room	35	45	22	40	42	39	29	28	34	35	30	36
Dining room	52	53	45	46	55	56	46	62	58	49	50	52
Home office	53	44	51	50	52	56	44	61	58	56	56	53
Garage	26	26	32	22	18	31	19	29	21	26	33	25
Other	4	4	9	3	3	4	5	2	0	3	6	4
Responses	974	54	104	137	87	222	63	75	104	128	172	802

Q19. If you were having trouble finding a home in your ideal price range, which of the following potential compromises would you be willing to accept in order to be able to afford it? (Check all that apply) (Percent of respondents)

	Age of Household Head					Generation (year born)				Household Composition			
	Under 35 years old	35 to 44 years old	45 to 54 years old	55 to 64 years old	65 years old or older	Gen Z (1997 or later)	Millenni-als(1981-1996)	Gen X (1965-1980)	Boomers (1946-1964)	Married couple w children	Married couple no children	Single parent	One person
Smaller house	25	24	34	42	41	25	23	36	41	27	42	36	48
Smaller lot	27	28	38	41	47	28	26	37	46	33	46	34	44
Unfinished spaces	23	23	25	21	18	23	23	24	19	23	20	20	21
Fewer roooms	22	20	20	25	28	20	21	22	27	22	26	21	31
Fewer energy efficient features (when not mandated by code)	27	27	23	16	23	25	27	24	20	28	16	24	17
Farther from urban core	27	32	37	35	42	26	31	34	40	35	41	35	37
Substitution of expensive materials for less expensive options	31	37	28	23	25	31	34	29	24	32	21	26	24
Fewer exterior amenities (e.g. porches, decks, patios, pools, etc.)	36	41	34	33	37	36	40	34	35	38	33	34	35
More modular or pre-fabricated housing construction components	26	32	25	23	25	24	31	26	25	33	22	24	17
Denser development	16	19	13	11	15	14	18	14	13	19	11	13	11
Other	4	4	4	4	1	6	3	3	3	2	3	3	5
Responses	934	610	503	436	525	428	932	741	772	1,278	527	391	473

Q20. What areas would you be wiloling to make smaller? (Check all that apply) (Percent of respondents who are willing to accept a smaller home)

	Age of Household Head					Generation (year born)				Household Composition			
	Under 35 years old	35 to 44 years old	45 to 54 years old	55 to 64 years old	65 years old or older	Gen Z (1997 or later)	Millenni-als(1981-1996)	Gen X (1965-1980)	Boomers (1946-1964)	Married couple w children	Married couple no children	Single parent	One person
Kitchen	25	27	21	17	22	15	27	22	20	27	15	21	25
Bedrooms	28	32	31	26	35	27	29	32	32	39	28	25	31
Bathrooms	28	38	26	16	28	30	33	25	26	37	21	24	20
Closets	40	32	26	19	15	46	35	24	17	24	17	32	18
Family room	30	40	34	39	43	27	37	35	42	36	37	38	46
Living room	23	35	39	29	40	25	32	35	36	35	34	32	39
Dining room	46	51	52	52	54	46	48	50	54	50	59	45	51
Home office	51	50	51	54	55	49	50	51	56	51	53	53	57
Garage	32	38	26	26	22	38	36	27	23	20	23	37	33
Other	3	4	3	7	2	3	3	3	4	1	5	4	5
Responses	247	155	174	184	214	113	235	261	314	320	197	127	205

Q19. If you were having trouble finding a home in your ideal price range, which of the following potential compromises would you be willing to accept in order to be able to afford it? (Check all that apply) (Percent of respondents)

	Race/Ethnicity				Home Buyers' Income Bracket					Price Expected to Pay			
	Caucasian	African-American	Hispanic	Asian	Under $50,000	$50,000 to $74,999	$75,000 to $99,999	$100,000 to $149,999	$150,000 or more	Less than $150,000	$150,000 to $249,999	$250,000 to $499,999	$500,000 or more
Smaller house	38	25	27	33	42	39	39	32	27	40	39	34	31
Smaller lot	42	31	25	35	41	43	39	39	32	35	40	40	39
Unfinished spaces	21	15	24	27	19	20	25	21	24	20	20	22	23
Fewer roooms	24	20	27	27	24	23	24	23	25	24	24	24	23
Fewer energy efficient features (when not mandated by code)	20	27	37	28	21	17	22	25	27	22	24	23	21
Farther from urban core	38	27	35	26	36	37	39	38	34	31	36	39	35
Substitution of expensive materials for less expensive options	26	28	37	31	30	22	28	29	29	27	29	30	23
Fewer exterior amenities (e.g. porches, decks, patios, pools, etc.)	36	35	40	38	36	37	41	36	33	37	38	37	32
More modular or pre-fabricated housing construction components	24	22	41	30	24	23	22	29	31	27	30	24	26
Denser development	13	11	26	20	11	9	14	18	20	14	11	14	20
Other	3	5	1	2	4	4	2	3	2	5	3	2	3
Responses	1,997	390	341	280	907	549	427	552	573	718	531	1,155	530

Q20. What areas would you be wiloling to make smaller? (Check all that apply) (Percent of respondents who are willing to accept a smaller home)

	Race/Ethnicity				Home Buyers' Income Bracket					Price Expected to Pay			
	Caucasian	African-American	Hispanic	Asian	Under $50,000	$50,000 to $74,999	$75,000 to $99,999	$100,000 to $149,999	$150,000 or more	Less than $150,000	$150,000 to $249,999	$250,000 to $499,999	$500,000 or more
Kitchen	18	31	36	33	25	12	21	24	22	25	23	19	19
Bedrooms	29	36	49	41	31	27	26	33	39	31	33	30	36
Bathrooms	21	29	56	38	26	17	25	27	34	24	23	26	29
Closets	21	26	24	22	22	23	25	22	18	30	21	19	19
Family room	38	52	44	37	48	37	34	34	33	48	48	32	31
Living room	34	27	49	40	33	31	37	39	37	36	32	37	33
Dining room	53	40	53	45	47	58	52	51	56	45	50	57	53
Home office	55	44	48	46	54	56	61	49	47	53	54	54	50
Garage	27	32	15	24	28	32	25	26	17	33	29	22	22
Other	4	7	3	1	3	3	8	3	4	3	5	5	3
Responses	693	86	98	97	350	184	146	159	135	256	180	362	152

Q21. How many home offices (or spaces dedicated to work/study from home) would you prefer to have?
(Percent of respondents)

	All Home Buyers	Geography (Nine Census Divisions)									Buyer Type	
		New England	Middle Atlantic	East North Central	West North Central	South Atlantic	East South Central	West South Central	Mountain	Pacific	First-time	Repeat
None	20	19	15	27	14	20	28	19	16	19	27	19
One	66	71	69	61	72	67	61	67	69	65	62	67
Two	12	9	15	11	13	12	11	14	13	14	10	13
More than two	1	1	2	1	1	1	1	1	2	2	1	1
Responses	3,008	141	358	414	236	651	224	290	278	416	521	2,487

Q22a. Which of the following kitchen-dining room arrangements do you prefer?
(Percent of respondents)

	All Home Buyers	Geography (Nine Census Divisions)									Buyer Type	
		New England	Middle Atlantic	East North Central	West North Central	South Atlantic	East South Central	West South Central	Mountain	Pacific	First-time	Repeat
Completely open	46	47	48	43	34	46	55	49	47	48	41	47
In separate areas of the house	15	22	15	14	24	10	10	9	19	18	17	14
Partially open (separated by half wall, arch, counter etc.)	30	20	30	33	31	34	26	30	25	26	34	29
Side-by-side separate rooms	7	8	5	6	10	7	7	8	7	5	6	7
Home without a dining room	3	3	2	5	1	2	1	4	1	1	2	3
Responses	3,008	141	358	414	236	651	224	290	278	416	521	2,487

Q22b. Which of the following kitchen-family room arrangements do you prefer?
(Percent of respondents)

	All Home Buyers	Geography (Nine Census Divisions)									Buyer Type	
		New England	Middle Atlantic	East North Central	West North Central	South Atlantic	East South Central	West South Central	Mountain	Pacific	First-time	Repeat
Completely open	41	38	42	40	32	42	48	48	40	40	32	43
In separate areas of the house	19	25	22	20	33	15	16	12	17	24	23	19
Partially open (separated by half wall, arch, counter etc.)	31	32	30	33	25	32	27	33	33	29	34	31
Side-by-side separate rooms	7	4	5	6	8	8	7	5	9	7	7	7
Home without a family room	2	1	2	2	2	3	2	2	2	0	3	1
Responses	3,008	141	358	414	236	651	224	290	278	416	521	2,487

Q21. How many home offices (or spaces dedicated to work/study from home) would you prefer to have?
(Percent of respondents)

	Age of Household Head					Generation (year born)				Household Composition			
	Under 35 years old	35 to 44 years old	45 to 54 years old	55 to 64 years old	65 years old or older	Gen Z (1997 or later)	Millenni-als(1981-1996)	Gen X (1965-1980)	Boomers (1946-1964)	Married couple w children	Married couple no children	Single parent	One person
None	9	12	20	22	26	10	10	20	25	14	21	23	28
One	67	67	64	68	66	67	68	65	66	68	68	63	64
Two	20	19	15	9	7	19	20	14	8	16	10	12	7
More than two	4	2	2	1	1	4	2	1	1	2	0	2	1
Responses	934	610	503	436	525	428	932	741	772	1,278	527	391	473

Q22a. Which of the following <u>kitchen-dining room</u> arrangements do you prefer?
(Percent of respondents)

	Age of Household Head					Generation (year born)				Household Composition			
	Under 35 years old	35 to 44 years old	45 to 54 years old	55 to 64 years old	65 years old or older	Gen Z (1997 or later)	Millenni-als(1981-1996)	Gen X (1965-1980)	Boomers (1946-1964)	Married couple w children	Married couple no children	Single parent	One person
Completely open	44	46	55	50	40	37	47	50	44	47	46	46	46
In separate areas of the house	16	16	13	11	17	20	15	14	15	21	10	15	8
Partially open (separated by half wall, arch, counter etc.)	32	33	25	28	32	33	33	27	30	25	34	28	35
Side-by-side separate rooms	6	4	6	7	8	7	4	6	7	6	7	9	6
Home without a dining room	2	1	1	4	4	2	1	2	3	1	3	2	5
Responses	934	610	503	436	525	428	932	741	772	1,278	527	391	473

Q22b. Which of the following <u>kitchen-family room</u> arrangements do you prefer?
(Percent of respondents)

	Age of Household Head					Generation (year born)				Household Composition			
	Under 35 years old	35 to 44 years old	45 to 54 years old	55 to 64 years old	65 years old or older	Gen Z (1997 or later)	Millenni-als(1981-1996)	Gen X (1965-1980)	Boomers (1946-1964)	Married couple w children	Married couple no children	Single parent	One person
Completely open	38	41	50	46	35	31	41	47	39	41	44	36	41
In separate areas of the house	19	21	18	14	23	21	21	18	20	25	15	18	12
Partially open (separated by half wall, arch, counter etc.)	33	30	27	33	32	38	30	29	31	26	34	36	36
Side-by-side separate rooms	8	7	5	5	8	9	7	5	7	7	6	9	7
Home without a family room	2	0	0	2	3	2	1	1	2	1	1	1	4
Responses	934	610	503	436	525	428	932	741	772	1,278	527	391	473

Q21. How many home offices (or spaces dedicated to work/study from home) would you prefer to have?
(Percent of respondents)

	Race/Ethnicity				Home Buyers' Income Bracket					Price Expected to Pay			
	Cauca-sian	African-American	Hispanic	Asian	Under $50,000	$50,000 to $74,999	$75,000 to $99,999	$100,000 to $149,999	$150,000 or more	Less than $150,000	$150,000 to $249,999	$250,000 to $499,999	$500,000 or more
None	21	13	19	11	34	20	15	16	9	31	25	17	7
One	65	68	66	79	57	70	72	67	71	58	62	71	71
Two	12	16	14	9	7	9	13	16	18	9	11	11	19
More than two	1	3	2	1	1	1	1	1	3	1	1	1	3
Responses	1,997	390	341	280	907	549	427	552	573	718	531	1,155	530

Q22a. Which of the following <u>kitchen-dining room</u> arrangements do you prefer?
(Percent of respondents)

	Race/Ethnicity				Home Buyers' Income Bracket					Price Expected to Pay			
	Cauca-sian	African-American	Hispanic	Asian	Under $50,000	$50,000 to $74,999	$75,000 to $99,999	$100,000 to $149,999	$150,000 or more	Less than $150,000	$150,000 to $249,999	$250,000 to $499,999	$500,000 or more
Completely open	50	41	32	34	43	47	45	55	43	44	41	48	50
In separate areas of the house	9	19	43	30	16	9	11	15	20	18	17	13	15
Partially open (separated by half wall, arch, counter etc.)	31	33	18	29	30	35	35	25	26	29	32	30	28
Side-by-side separate rooms	7	5	6	6	7	6	4	5	9	5	9	6	6
Home without a dining room	3	3	1	1	3	3	4	1	2	4	2	2	2
Responses	1,997	390	341	280	907	549	427	552	573	718	531	1,155	530

Q22b. Which of the following <u>kitchen-family room</u> arrangements do you prefer?
(Percent of respondents)

	Race/Ethnicity				Home Buyers' Income Bracket					Price Expected to Pay			
	Cauca-sian	African-American	Hispanic	Asian	Under $50,000	$50,000 to $74,999	$75,000 to $99,999	$100,000 to $149,999	$150,000 or more	Less than $150,000	$150,000 to $249,999	$250,000 to $499,999	$500,000 or more
Completely open	44	39	27	36	36	42	41	46	44	38	36	43	48
In separate areas of the house	15	25	44	26	21	13	18	19	23	20	24	19	16
Partially open (separated by half wall, arch, counter etc.)	33	28	19	28	32	38	33	29	25	33	32	30	30
Side-by-side separate rooms	6	5	10	9	7	6	5	6	8	7	7	7	5
Home without a family room	2	3	0	1	3	0	2	1	1	2	1	2	1
Responses	1,997	390	341	280	907	549	427	552	573	718	531	1,155	530

Q22c. Which of the following dining room-family room arrangements do you prefer?
(Percent of respondents)

	All Home Buyers	Geography (Nine Census Divisions)									Buyer Type	
		New England	Middle Atlantic	East North Central	West North Central	South Atlantic	East South Central	West South Central	Mountain	Pacific	First-time	Repeat
Completely open	37	33	37	36	30	39	45	41	35	35	30	38
In separate areas of the house	22	29	20	23	29	19	16	17	24	25	26	21
Partially open (separated by half wall, arch, counter etc.)	28	26	30	27	29	29	25	30	24	30	31	28
Side-by-side separate rooms	8	8	8	8	10	7	8	8	13	8	8	8
N/A, don't want one or both of the rooms	4	4	5	6	2	6	6	4	4	1	5	4
Responses	3,008	141	358	414	236	651	224	290	278	416	521	2,487

Q23. Excluding any basement, which of these floor plan types would you prefer, assuming each plan had the same amount of floor space/living area?
(Percent of respondents)

	All Home Buyers	Geography (Nine Census Divisions)									Buyer Type	
		New England	Middle Atlantic	East North Central	West North Central	South Atlantic	East South Central	West South Central	Mountain	Pacific	First-time	Repeat
Single-story	54	44	40	58	47	60	56	62	57	47	44	55
Two-story	38	48	47	35	46	31	38	31	37	46	45	37
Three-story	6	7	9	5	5	5	4	4	6	5	6	6
Split-level	2	1	3	2	1	3	2	3	1	2	5	2
Responses	3,008	141	358	414	236	651	224	290	278	416	521	2,487

Q24. What type of basement would you prefer?
(Percent of respondents)

	All Home Buyers	Geography (Nine Census Divisions)									Buyer Type	
		New England	Middle Atlantic	East North Central	West North Central	South Atlantic	East South Central	West South Central	Mountain	Pacific	First-time	Repeat
No basement	34	10	19	24	17	45	32	56	39	37	37	33
Half basement (add $22,500)	32	41	36	29	44	27	33	29	33	34	27	33
A full basement (add $45,000)	34	49	45	47	38	28	35	15	29	29	35	34
Responses	3,008	141	358	414	236	651	224	290	278	416	521	2,487

Q22c. Which of the following <u>dining room-family room</u> arrangements do you prefer?
(Percent of respondents)

	Age of Household Head					Generation (year born)				Household Composition			
	Under 35 years old	35 to 44 years old	45 to 54 years old	55 to 64 years old	65 years old or older	Gen Z (1997 or later)	Millenni-als(1981-1996)	Gen X (1965-1980)	Boomers (1946-1964)	Married couple w children	Married couple no children	Single parent	One person
Completely open	37	38	48	37	31	29	39	44	33	37	39	30	41
In separate areas of the house	23	23	20	17	24	24	22	21	22	26	18	25	16
Partially open (separated by half wall, arch, counter etc.)	27	27	23	30	32	33	27	25	31	27	29	30	26
Side-by-side separate rooms	10	9	7	8	8	12	9	7	8	8	7	10	8
N/A, don't want one or both of the rooms	3	2	2	8	5	3	2	4	6	1	7	5	8
Responses	934	610	503	436	525	428	932	741	772	1,278	527	391	473

Q23. Excluding any basement, which of these floor plan types would you prefer, assuming each plan had the same amount of floor space/living area?
(Percent of respondents)

	Age of Household Head					Generation (year born)				Household Composition			
	Under 35 years old	35 to 44 years old	45 to 54 years old	55 to 64 years old	65 years old or older	Gen Z (1997 or later)	Millenni-als(1981-1996)	Gen X (1965-1980)	Boomers (1946-1964)	Married couple w children	Married couple no children	Single parent	One person
Single-story	29	33	44	62	71	27	32	44	69	39	70	49	69
Two-story	55	55	46	31	26	57	55	45	27	51	25	39	25
Three-story	14	9	6	4	2	16	10	6	2	8	3	8	4
Split-level	2	3	4	2	1	1	3	4	1	2	2	4	3
Responses	934	610	503	436	525	428	932	741	772	1,278	527	391	473

Q24. What type of basement would you prefer?
(Percent of respondents)

	Age of Household Head					Generation (year born)				Household Composition			
	Under 35 years old	35 to 44 years old	45 to 54 years old	55 to 64 years old	65 years old or older	Gen Z (1997 or later)	Millenni-als(1981-1996)	Gen X (1965-1980)	Boomers (1946-1964)	Married couple w children	Married couple no children	Single parent	One person
No basement	20	20	27	41	44	22	18	28	45	24	41	33	45
Half basement (add $22,500)	40	38	33	23	33	43	39	33	29	40	28	33	23
A full basement (add $45,000)	40	42	40	36	23	36	43	39	26	36	31	34	32
Responses	934	610	503	436	525	428	932	741	772	1,278	527	391	473

Q22c. Which of the following dining room-family room arrangements do you prefer?
(Percent of respondents)

	Race/Ethnicity				Home Buyers' Income Bracket					Price Expected to Pay			
	Cauca-sian	African-American	Hispanic	Asian	Under $50,000	$50,000 to $74,999	$75,000 to $99,999	$100,000 to $149,999	$150,000 or more	Less than $150,000	$150,000 to $249,999	$250,000 to $499,999	$500,000 or more
Completely open	40	38	21	26	36	38	35	41	37	34	35	37	41
In separate areas of the house	18	27	41	30	22	20	19	21	25	23	24	21	20
Partially open (separated by half wall, arch, counter etc.)	29	23	26	32	27	31	34	26	27	29	27	29	28
Side-by-side separate rooms	8	9	10	10	10	8	5	8	9	8	9	9	8
N/A, don't want one or both of the rooms	5	2	1	1	6	3	7	3	3	6	4	5	3
Responses	1,997	390	341	280	907	549	427	552	573	718	531	1,155	530

Q23. Excluding any basement, which of these floor plan types would you prefer, assuming each plan had the same amount of floor space/living area?
(Percent of respondents)

	Race/Ethnicity				Home Buyers' Income Bracket					Price Expected to Pay			
	Cauca-sian	African-American	Hispanic	Asian	Under $50,000	$50,000 to $74,999	$75,000 to $99,999	$100,000 to $149,999	$150,000 or more	Less than $150,000	$150,000 to $249,999	$250,000 to $499,999	$500,000 or more
Single-story	60	39	31	40	63	63	58	47	38	60	59	53	43
Two-story	33	45	62	51	31	30	37	45	49	33	36	40	44
Three-story	5	11	6	7	3	4	3	6	11	4	3	5	10
Split-level	2	5	1	2	3	3	2	1	2	2	2	2	2
Responses	1,997	390	341	280	907	549	427	552	573	718	531	1,155	530

Q24. What type of basement would you prefer?
(Percent of respondents)

	Race/Ethnicity				Home Buyers' Income Bracket					Price Expected to Pay			
	Cauca-sian	African-American	Hispanic	Asian	Under $50,000	$50,000 to $74,999	$75,000 to $99,999	$100,000 to $149,999	$150,000 or more	Less than $150,000	$150,000 to $249,999	$250,000 to $499,999	$500,000 or more
No basement	36	32	23	33	45	36	31	30	24	39	37	31	30
Half basement (add $22,500)	29	29	55	42	26	26	33	39	38	33	31	34	32
A full basement (add $45,000)	36	39	23	25	29	38	36	31	38	29	32	35	38
Responses	1,997	390	341	280	907	549	427	552	573	718	531	1,155	530

Q25. How many bedrooms would you like to have in a new home?
(Percent of respondents)

	All Home Buyers	Geography (Nine Census Divisions)									Buyer Type	
		New England	Middle Atlantic	East North Central	West North Central	South Atlantic	East South Central	West South Central	Mountain	Pacific	First-time	Repeat
One	4	3	5	4	6	2	4	2	4	4	2	4
Two	22	30	23	23	34	19	14	17	27	19	24	21
Three	45	45	40	46	35	49	49	50	49	40	43	46
Four	23	20	25	22	18	24	19	27	14	24	24	22
Five or more	7	2	7	5	7	5	15	5	6	13	6	7
Mean	3.1	2.9	3.1	3.0	2.9	3.1	3.3	3.2	2.9	3.2	3.1	3.1
Median	3.0	3.0	3.0	3.0	3.0	3.0	3.0	3.0	3.0	3.0	3.0	3.0
Responses	3,008	141	358	414	236	651	224	290	278	416	521	2,487

Q26. Where would you like to have your clothes washer and dryer in a new home?
(Percent of respondents)

	All Home Buyers	Geography (Nine Census Divisions)									Buyer Type	
		New England	Middle Atlantic	East North Central	West North Central	South Atlantic	East South Central	West South Central	Mountain	Pacific	First-time	Repeat
Basement	17	24	25	19	16	12	21	7	11	23	21	16
Garage	15	12	7	8	21	15	22	15	22	18	17	14
On the first floor	60	59	57	66	57	65	47	70	60	51	55	61
On the second or higher floor	7	6	10	7	4	7	6	6	6	8	5	7
Other	1		1	1	1	2	5	2	1	0	2	1
Responses	3,008	141	358	414	236	651	224	290	278	416	521	2,487

Q25. How many bedrooms would you like to have in a new home?
(Percent of respondents)

	Age of Household Head					Generation (year born)				Household Composition			
	Under 35 years old	35 to 44 years old	45 to 54 years old	55 to 64 years old	65 years old or older	Gen Z (1997 or later)	Millenni-als(1981-1996)	Gen X (1965-1980)	Boomers (1946-1964)	Married couple w children	Married couple no children	Single parent	One person
One	7	2	3	3	4	4	4	3	4	4	2	4	5
Two	17	12	13	24	31	19	13	16	28	18	22	17	36
Three	36	37	49	51	47	42	34	48	49	38	59	47	43
Four	29	35	28	18	15	25	34	27	16	30	15	24	11
Five or more	12	14	7	4	4	10	14	7	3	10	3	7	4
Mean	3.2	3.5	3.2	3.0	2.8	3.2	3.4	3.2	2.9	3.2	2.9	3.1	2.7
Median	3.0	3.0	3.0	3.0	3.0	3.0	3.0	3.0	3.0	3.0	3.0	3.0	3.0
Responses	934	610	503	436	525	428	932	741	772	1,278	527	391	473

Q26. Where would you like to have your clothes washer and dryer in a new home?
(Percent of respondents)

	Age of Household Head					Generation (year born)				Household Composition			
	Under 35 years old	35 to 44 years old	45 to 54 years old	55 to 64 years old	65 years old or older	Gen Z (1997 or later)	Millenni-als(1981-1996)	Gen X (1965-1980)	Boomers (1946-1964)	Married couple w children	Married couple no children	Single parent	One person
Basement	24	26	18	13	13	22	26	17	13	21	12	20	14
Garage	20	18	16	10	13	18	18	16	12	17	10	19	12
On the first floor	47	47	56	67	69	51	46	56	68	52	72	53	67
On the second or higher floor	8	7	8	9	4	8	8	8	6	9	5	5	5
Other	1	2	2	1	1	1	1	2	1	1	1	2	2
Responses	934	610	503	436	525	428	932	741	772	1,278	527	391	473

Q25. How many bedrooms would you like to have in a new home?
(Percent of respondents)

	Race/Ethnicity				Home Buyers' Income Bracket					Price Expected to Pay			
	Cauca-sian	African-American	Hispanic	Asian	Under $50,000	$50,000 to $74,999	$75,000 to $99,999	$100,000 to $149,999	$150,000 or more	Less than $150,000	$150,000 to $249,999	$250,000 to $499,999	$500,000 or more
One	3	3	5	14	4	2	3	3	5	6	3	3	4
Two	21	14	30	32	28	22	21	17	18	31	26	18	15
Three	49	36	36	30	48	49	49	46	36	41	47	49	41
Four	22	35	20	18	16	22	23	24	30	17	20	24	28
Five or more	6	12	10	7	5	4	3	10	11	5	4	6	12
Mean	3.1	3.4	3.0	2.7	2.9	3.0	3.0	3.2	3.2	2.8	3.0	3.1	3.3
Median	3.0	3.0	3.0	3.0	3.0	3.0	3.0	3.0	3.0	3.0	3.0	3.0	3.0
Responses	1,997	390	341	280	907	549	427	552	573	718	531	1,155	530

Q26. Where would you like to have your clothes washer and dryer in a new home?
(Percent of respondents)

	Race/Ethnicity				Home Buyers' Income Bracket					Price Expected to Pay			
	Cauca-sian	African-American	Hispanic	Asian	Under $50,000	$50,000 to $74,999	$75,000 to $99,999	$100,000 to $149,999	$150,000 or more	Less than $150,000	$150,000 to $249,999	$250,000 to $499,999	$500,000 or more
Basement	14	32	22	20	17	15	16	20	16	20	21	15	16
Garage	12	18	29	22	13	13	13	17	17	16	14	13	18
On the first floor	66	45	40	50	63	66	64	54	56	60	60	64	53
On the second or higher floor	7	4	9	8	5	4	6	8	10	3	5	7	13
Other	1	2	0	1	2	2	1	1	0	2	1	1	1
Responses	1,997	390	341	280	907	549	427	552	573	718	531	1,155	530

Q27. Please indicate the number of bathrooms you prefer, assuming an additional cost of $25,000 for each full bathroom
(Percent of respondents)

	All Home Buyers	Geography (Nine Census Divisions)									Buyer Type	
		New England	Middle Atlantic	East North Central	West North Central	South Atlantic	East South Central	West South Central	Mountain	Pacific	First-time	Repeat
1	5	1	3	4	12	4	5	2	9	4	5	5
1 1/2	11	28	16	16	7	8	11	6	6	11	13	11
2	39	34	36	42	48	40	30	37	45	35	41	39
2 1/2	24	18	21	26	16	26	25	30	25	20	22	24
3	12	7	15	7	10	13	15	14	11	17	11	13
3 1/2	6	5	5	2	4	6	9	7	3	8	4	6
4 or more	3	5	4	3	3	3	5	3	2	5	5	3
Mean	2.3	2.2	2.3	2.2	2.1	2.3	2.4	2.4	2.2	2.4	2.3	2.3
Median	2.0	2.0	2.0	2.0	2.0	2.0	2.5	2.5	2.0	2.0	2.0	2.0
Responses	3,008	141	358	414	236	651	224	290	278	416	521	2,487

Q28. Which type of parking facility would you prefer with your new home, taking into account the probable differences in cost?
(Percent of respondents)

	All Home Buyers	Geography (Nine Census Divisions)									Buyer Type	
		New England	Middle Atlantic	East North Central	West North Central	South Atlantic	East South Central	West South Central	Mountain	Pacific	First-time	Repeat
1 carport (add $10,000)	13	11	12	11	12	14	13	12	14	15	19	12
2 carport (add $18,000)	20	19	21	15	33	21	14	19	19	20	29	19
1 car garage (add $30,000)	16	23	21	16	12	13	19	12	15	18	13	16
2 car garage (add $50,000)	35	41	30	42	27	38	33	36	32	29	25	36
3+ car garage (add $70,000)	12	4	8	12	14	9	16	17	16	15	6	13
None	5	2	7	4	2	6	5	4	3	3	9	4
Responses	3,008	141	358	414	236	651	224	290	278	416	521	2,487

Q29. Would you prefer to purchase a home designed to house multiple generations?
(Percent of respondents)

	All Home Buyers	Geography (Nine Census Divisions)									Buyer Type	
		New England	Middle Atlantic	East North Central	West North Central	South Atlantic	East South Central	West South Central	Mountain	Pacific	First-time	Repeat
Yes	45	49	42	45	62	36	41	46	39	56	48	45
No	36	39	36	33	29	42	38	36	43	30	30	37
Don't know/Not sure	19	13	21	23	9	22	21	18	18	14	22	18
Responses	3,008	141	358	414	236	651	224	290	278	416	521	2,487

Q27. Please indicate the number of bathrooms you prefer, assuming an additional cost of $25,000 for each full bathroom (Percent of respondents)

	Age of Household Head					Generation (year born)				Household Composition			
	Under 35 years old	35 to 44 years old	45 to 54 years old	55 to 64 years old	65 years old or older	Gen Z (1997 or later)	Millenni-als(1981-1996)	Gen X (1965-1980)	Boomers (1946-1964)	Married couple w children	Married couple no children	Single parent	One person
1	4	4	5	4	5	3	4	6	4	5	3	5	7
1 1/2	10	7	9	11	15	11	8	8	15	8	11	13	21
2	32	39	33	37	46	31	38	34	43	38	42	37	37
2 1/2	24	23	28	28	19	26	23	27	23	24	28	22	21
3	17	16	12	12	10	16	17	12	10	14	12	13	8
3 1/2	7	6	8	6	3	7	6	7	4	7	3	6	4
4 or more	5	6	5	2	1	5	5	5	2	4	2	5	2
Mean	2.4	2.4	2.4	2.3	2.1	2.4	2.4	2.4	2.2	2.4	2.3	2.3	2.1
Median	2.5	2.5	2.5	2.0	2.0	2.5	2.5	2.5	2.0	2.0	2.0	2.0	2.0
Responses	934	610	503	436	525	428	932	741	772	1,278	527	391	473

Q28. Which type of parking facility would you prefer with your new home, taking into account the probable differences in cost? (Percent of respondents)

	Age of Household Head					Generation (year born)				Household Composition			
	Under 35 years old	35 to 44 years old	45 to 54 years old	55 to 64 years old	65 years old or older	Gen Z (1997 or later)	Millenni-als(1981-1996)	Gen X (1965-1980)	Boomers (1946-1964)	Married couple w children	Married couple no children	Single parent	One person
1 carport (add $10,000)	13	12	9	9	17	14	12	10	14	12	10	16	16
2 carport (add $18,000)	25	23	22	16	18	26	23	21	17	21	17	23	16
1 car garage (add $30,000)	19	20	15	18	13	17	22	16	14	21	10	16	16
2 car garage (add $50,000)	29	30	35	36	39	27	30	33	38	29	45	32	37
3+ car garage (add $70,000)	12	10	15	15	10	13	9	14	12	13	15	7	10
None	3	4	5	6	4	4	4	6	4	4	3	7	5
Responses	934	610	503	436	525	428	932	741	772	1,278	527	391	473

Q29. Would you prefer to purchase a home designed to house multiple generations? (Percent of respondents)

	Age of Household Head					Generation (year born)				Household Composition			
	Under 35 years old	35 to 44 years old	45 to 54 years old	55 to 64 years old	65 years old or older	Gen Z (1997 or later)	Millenni-als(1981-1996)	Gen X (1965-1980)	Boomers (1946-1964)	Married ccuple w children	Married couple no children	Single parent	One person
Yes	62	65	49	38	32	56	68	50	33	63	23	55	25
No	23	20	31	41	48	29	19	30	46	24	55	27	50
Don't know/Not sure	14	15	20	22	20	15	13	20	21	13	22	18	25
Responses	934	610	503	436	525	428	932	741	772	1,278	527	391	473

Q27. Please indicate the number of bathrooms you prefer, assuming an additional cost of $25,000 for each full bathroom
(Percent of respondents)

	Race/Ethnicity				Home Buyers' Income Bracket					Price Expected to Pay			
	Cauca-sian	African-American	Hispanic	Asian	Under $50,000	$50,000 to $74,999	$75,000 to $99,999	$100,000 to $149,999	$150,000 or more	Less than $150,000	$150,000 to $249,999	$250,000 to $499,999	$500,000 or more
1	4	4	10	6	6	2	3	4	6	7	6	4	3
1 1/2	12	9	11	7	21	11	9	7	4	19	20	8	2
2	38	33	43	45	47	43	39	29	34	51	41	37	29
2 1/2	26	25	13	17	14	29	29	33	21	12	23	31	24
3	12	14	14	12	8	9	13	15	18	6	7	13	21
3 1/2	6	8	3	7	2	3	6	7	10	3	2	5	12
4 or more	3	6	5	6	2	2	1	4	7	2	2	2	8
Mean	2.3	2.4	2.2	2.3	2.1	2.2	2.3	2.4	2.5	2.0	2.1	2.3	2.6
Median	2.0	2.5	2.0	2.0	2.0	2.0	2.0	2.5	2.5	2.0	2.0	2.5	2.5
Responses	1,997	390	341	280	907	549	427	552	573	718	531	1,155	530

Q28. Which type of parking facility would you prefer with your new home, taking into account the probable differences in cost?
(Percent of respondents)

	Race/Ethnicity				Home Buyers' Income Bracket					Price Expected to Pay			
	Cauca-sian	African-American	Hispanic	Asian	Under $50,000	$50,000 to $74,999	$75,000 to $99,999	$100,000 to $149,999	$150,000 or more	Less than $150,000	$150,000 to $249,999	$250,000 to $499,999	$500,000 or more
1 carport (add $10,000)	10	16	23	20	22	12	9	8	9	27	16	8	6
2 carport (add $18,000)	16	27	38	16	21	23	18	20	17	26	22	19	14
1 car garage (add $30,000)	16	12	16	29	15	11	13	18	21	14	15	17	17
2 car garage (add $50,000)	39	29	13	28	27	42	47	37	29	21	35	41	36
3+ car garage (add $70,000)	13	12	6	7	6	8	10	14	22	5	5	13	25
None	5	4	5	1	9	3	4	2	3	8	6	3	2
Responses	1,997	390	341	280	907	549	427	552	573	718	531	1,155	530

Q29. Would you prefer to purchase a home designed to house multiple generations?
(Percent of respondents)

	Race/Ethnicity				Home Buyers' Income Bracket					Price Expected to Pay			
	Cauca-sian	African-American	Hispanic	Asian	Under $50,000	$50,000 to $74,999	$75,000 to $99,999	$100,000 to $149,999	$150,000 or more	Less than $150,000	$150,000 to $249,999	$250,000 to $499,999	$500,000 or more
Yes	37	61	72	71	38	38	43	45	60	46	42	45	52
No	41	24	23	18	40	39	32	40	29	34	37	38	35
Don't know/Not sure	22	15	6	11	22	23	25	14	11	20	21	18	13
Responses	1,997	390	341	280	907	549	427	552	573	718	531	1,155	530

Q30. Which energy source do you prefer for the following systems?
1. Air Heating/Cooling system
(Percent of respondents)

	All Home Buyers	Geography (Nine Census Divisions)									Buyer Type	
		New England	Middle Atlantic	East North Central	West North Central	South Atlantic	East South Central	West South Central	Mountain	Pacific	First-time	Repeat
Gas	28	35	44	35	23	20	28	22	29	25	19	30
Electric	59	54	43	48	65	69	58	66	58	63	66	58
Have no preference/Don't know	13	11	13	17	11	12	13	12	13	12	14	13
Responses	3,008	141	358	414	236	651	224	290	278	416	521	2,487

Q30. Which energy source do you prefer for the following systems?
2. Water heating system
(Percent of respondents)

	All Home Buyers	Geography (Nine Census Divisions)									Buyer Type	
		New England	Middle Atlantic	East North Central	West North Central	South Atlantic	East South Central	West South Central	Mountain	Pacific	First-time	Repeat
Gas	37	33	48	45	29	29	37	39	38	35	32	38
Electric	49	54	38	38	57	58	51	51	49	53	53	49
Have no preference/Don't know	13	13	14	16	13	13	12	10	13	12	15	13
Responses	3,008	141	358	414	236	651	224	290	278	416	521	2,487

Q30. Which energy source do you prefer for the following systems?
3. Cooking
(Percent of respondents)

	All Home Buyers	Geography (Nine Census Divisions)									Buyer Type	
		New England	Middle Atlantic	East North Central	West North Central	South Atlantic	East South Central	West South Central	Mountain	Pacific	First-time	Repeat
Gas	48	48	59	56	52	38	37	43	59	47	44	49
Electric	42	44	32	36	39	51	51	48	31	45	47	42
Have no preference/Don't know	10	8	9	8	10	11	12	9	10	7	9	10
Responses	3,008	141	358	414	236	651	224	290	278	416	521	2,487

Q30. Which energy source do you prefer for the following systems?
1. Air Heating/Cooling system
(Percent of respondents)

	Age of Household Head					Generation (year born)				Household Composition			
	Under 35 years old	35 to 44 years old	45 to 54 years old	55 to 64 years old	65 years old or older	Gen Z (1997 or later)	Millenni-als(1981-1996)	Gen X (1965-1980)	Boomers (1946-1964)	Married couple w children	Married couple no children	Single parent	One person
Gas	23	24	30	29	31	18	25	29	30	29	32	24	28
Electric	67	63	56	58	57	71	63	58	57	61	55	64	54
Have no preference/Don't know	11	13	14	13	12	11	12	14	13	10	12	13	17
Responses	934	610	503	436	525	428	932	741	772	1,278	527	391	473

Q30. Which energy source do you prefer for the following systems?
2. Water heating system
(Percent of respondents)

	Age of Household Head					Generation (year born)				Household Composition			
	Under 35 years old	35 to 44 years old	45 to 54 years old	55 to 64 years old	65 years old or older	Gen Z (1997 or later)	Millenni-als(1981-1996)	Gen X (1965-1980)	Boomers (1946-1964)	Married couple w children	Married couple no children	Single parent	One person
Gas	28	32	38	42	40	24	31	38	40	35	43	32	38
Electric	58	56	46	46	47	61	57	48	47	55	42	54	47
Have no preference/Don't know	14	12	16	13	13	15	12	14	13	10	15	14	15
Responses	934	610	503	436	525	428	932	741	772	1,278	527	391	473

Q30. Which energy source do you prefer for the following systems?
3. Cooking
(Percent of respondents)

	Age of Household Head					Generation (year born)				Household Composition			
	Under 35 years old	35 to 44 years old	45 to 54 years old	55 to 64 years old	65 years old or older	Gen Z (1997 or later)	Millenni-als(1981-1996)	Gen X (1965-1980)	Boomers (1946-1964)	Married couple w children	Married couple no children	Single parent	One person
Gas	36	43	50	49	52	32	41	50	52	49	51	41	46
Electric	53	47	38	42	39	58	49	39	40	41	39	50	44
Have no preference/Don't know	10	10	12	9	8	10	10	11	8	10	10	9	10
Responses	934	610	503	436	525	428	932	741	772	1,278	527	391	473

Q30. Which energy source do you prefer for the following systems?
1. Air Heating/Cooling system
(Percent of respondents)

	Race/Ethnicity				Home Buyers' Income Bracket					Price Expected to Pay			
	Cauca-sian	African-American	Hispanic	Asian	Under $50,000	$50,000 to $74,999	$75,000 to $99,999	$100,000 to $149,999	$150,000 or more	Less than $150,000	$150,000 to $249,999	$250,000 to $499,999	$500,000 or more
Gas	30	22	23	21	21	28	31	32	32	22	27	31	31
Electric	55	65	71	72	65	56	58	56	57	66	61	56	55
Have no preference/Don't know	14	13	6	7	14	16	12	12	10	12	11	12	13
Responses	1,997	390	341	280	907	549	427	552	573	718	531	1,155	530

Q30. Which energy source do you prefer for the following systems?
2. Water heating system
(Percent of respondents)

	Race/Ethnicity				Home Buyers' Income Bracket					Price Expected to Pay			
	Cauca-sian	African-American	Hispanic	Asian	Under $50,000	$50,000 to $74,999	$75,000 to $99,999	$100,000 to $149,999	$150,000 or more	Less than $150,000	$150,000 to $249,999	$250,000 to $499,999	$500,000 or more
Gas	40	34	26	28	31	40	44	41	37	30	37	41	39
Electric	46	53	65	65	54	46	43	46	53	58	50	47	47
Have no preference/Don't know	14	13	9	8	15	14	13	13	10	12	13	12	14
Responses	1,997	390	341	280	907	549	427	552	573	718	531	1,155	530

Q30. Which energy source do you prefer for the following systems?
3. Cooking
(Percent of respondents)

	Race/Ethnicity				Home Buyers' Income Bracket					Price Expected to Pay			
	Cauca-sian	African-American	Hispanic	Asian	Under $50,000	$50,000 to $74,999	$75,000 to $99,999	$100,000 to $149,999	$150,000 or more	Less than $150,000	$150,000 to $249,999	$250,000 to $499,999	$500,000 or more
Gas	47	40	54	62	38	48	49	51	58	37	49	51	52
Electric	43	50	38	32	52	43	41	40	32	55	44	39	36
Have no preference/Don't know	10	10	8	6	10	9	10	9	10	8	7	10	12
Responses	1,997	390	341	280	907	549	427	552	573	718	531	1,155	530

Q31. Please indicate the reasons for your preference of energy source for cooking
(Percent of respondents)

	All Home Buyers	Geography (Nine Census Divisions)									Buyer Type	
		New England	Middle Atlantic	East North Central	West North Central	South Atlantic	East South Central	West South Central	Mountain	Pacific	First-time	Repeat
Saves money	41	39	47	42	37	37	38	46	36	41	48	40
Increases safety	60	57	68	64	59	58	55	56	61	58	58	60
Improves air quality in the home	31	36	28	26	44	24	24	30	39	42	26	32
Is reliable	46	50	55	45	46	46	42	43	46	44	44	47
Is available where I want to live	29	28	30	29	38	25	23	27	32	34	23	30
Produces low levels of greenhouse gas emissions to operate	19	30	18	16	15	20	19	22	17	24	21	19
Other	3	4	1	3	3	3	3	3	2	3	2	3
Responses	3,008	141	358	414	236	651	224	290	278	416	521	2,487

Q32. Would you consider buying an all-electric home (i.e., not connected to gas lines)?
(Percent of respondents)

	All Home Buyers	Geography (Nine Census Divisions)									Buyer Type	
		New England	Middle Atlantic	East North Central	West North Central	South Atlantic	East South Central	West South Central	Mountain	Pacific	First-time	Repeat
Yes	60	58	48	46	61	68	56	69	53	71	60	60
No	19	23	23	23	23	13	26	12	24	14	17	19
Maybe/Not sure	21	19	29	31	15	19	17	19	23	15	23	21
Responses	3,008	141	358	414	236	651	224	290	278	416	521	2,487

Q33. How concerned are you about the impact of building your home on the environment?
(Percent of respondents)

	All Home Buyers	Geography (Nine Census Divisions)									Buyer Type	
		New England	Middle Atlantic	East North Central	West North Central	South Atlantic	East South Central	West South Central	Mountain	Pacific	First-time	Repeat
Not concerned	19	11	21	22	9	23	28	21	16	11	22	18
Concerned about environment, but not a consideration in house purchase	30	36	30	32	32	29	28	32	31	28	29	31
Want environment friendly home, but would not pay more	32	27	28	30	40	35	29	27	36	36	38	32
Would pay more for environment friendly home	18	26	22	15	19	14	15	20	16	25	11	19
Responses	3,008	141	358	414	236	651	224	290	278	416	521	2,487

Q31. Please indicate the reasons for your preference of energy source for cooking
(Percent of respondents)

	Age of Household Head					Generation (year born)				Household Composition			
	Under 35 years old	35 to 44 years old	45 to 54 years old	55 to 64 years old	65 years old or older	Gen Z (1997 or later)	Millenni-als(1981-1996)	Gen X (1965-1980)	Boomers (1946-1964)	Married couple w children	Married couple no children	Single parent	One person
Saves money	46	45	40	38	39	47	45	41	38	42	38	46	39
Increases safety	49	52	60	65	65	47	52	60	65	57	63	55	62
Improves air quality in the home	35	35	25	24	35	35	37	27	31	41	23	33	24
Is reliable	42	45	41	48	51	44	45	42	49	47	48	48	43
Is available where I want to live	22	30	27	25	35	25	27	27	31	32	29	31	25
Produces low levels of greenhouse gas emissions to operate	17	18	17	21	21	19	18	17	22	17	20	22	24
Other	1	0	3	4	3	1	1	3	3	1	4	2	5
Responses	934	610	503	436	525	428	932	741	772	1,278	527	391	473

Q32. Would you consider buying an all-electric home (i.e., not connected to gas lines)?
(Percent of respondents)

	Age of Household Head					Generation (year born)				Household Composition			
	Under 35 years old	35 to 44 years old	45 to 54 years old	55 to 64 years old	65 years old or older	Gen Z (1997 or later)	Millenni-als(1981-1996)	Gen X (1965-1980)	Boomers (1946-1964)	Married couple w children	Married couple no children	Single parent	One person
Yes	67	72	59	56	54	62	74	60	55	67	54	61	56
No	17	12	21	16	23	20	12	20	20	17	21	23	19
Maybe/Not sure	16	16	20	28	22	17	14	21	25	17	25	16	25
Responses	934	610	503	436	525	428	932	741	772	1,278	527	391	473

Q33. How concerned are you about the impact of building your home on the environment?
(Percent of respondents)

	Age of Household Head					Generation (year born)				Household Composition			
	Under 35 years old	35 to 44 years old	45 to 54 years old	55 to 64 years old	65 years old or older	Gen Z (1997 or later)	Millenni-als(1981-1996)	Gen X (1965-1980)	Boomers (1946-1964)	Married couple w children	Married couple no children	Single parent	One person
Not concerned	15	15	23	20	19	13	14	22	20	14	23	21	22
Concerned about environment, but not a consideration in house purchase	37	31	28	28	31	41	32	27	29	33	27	33	26
Want environment friendly home, but would not pay more	30	26	27	38	35	36	26	30	36	28	34	30	38
Would pay more for environment friendly home	18	28	22	14	15	11	28	20	15	25	15	16	14
Responses	934	610	503	436	525	428	932	741	772	1,278	527	391	473

Q31. Please indicate the reasons for your preference of energy source for cooking
(Percent of respondents)

	Race/Ethnicity				Home Buyers' Income Bracket					Price Expected to Pay			
	Cauca-sian	African-American	Hispanic	Asian	Under $50,000	$50,000 to $74,999	$75,000 to $99,999	$100,000 to $149,999	$150,000 or more	Less than $150,000	$150,000 to $249,999	$250,000 to $499,999	$500,000 or more
Saves money	40	46	43	32	40	42	43	40	39	45	45	40	35
Increases safety	60	55	64	64	62	62	62	57	58	59	66	61	55
Improves air quality in the home	26	29	60	42	29	23	29	31	40	27	33	31	34
Is reliable	46	47	44	54	43	47	52	45	49	41	43	50	48
Is available where I want to live	26	24	44	45	28	29	24	26	36	26	33	28	32
Produces low levels of greenhouse gas emissions to operate	21	23	10	18	20	19	18	20	20	16	21	18	22
Other	3	2	1	2	3	3	3	2	1	3	2	2	2
Responses	1,997	390	341	280	907	549	427	552	573	718	531	1,155	530

Q32. Would you consider buying an all-electric home (i.e., not connected to gas lines)?
(Percent of respondents)

	Race/Ethnicity				Home Buyers' Income Bracket					Price Expected to Pay			
	Cauca-sian	African-American	Hispanic	Asian	Under $50,000	$50,000 to $74,999	$75,000 to $99,999	$100,000 to $149,999	$150,000 or more	Less than $150,000	$150,000 to $249,999	$250,000 to $499,999	$500,000 or more
Yes	57	62	68	75	60	57	54	61	64	65	58	58	62
No	19	18	25	11	19	18	19	19	19	19	18	19	19
Maybe/Not sure	24	19	7	14	21	26	27	20	17	16	24	23	18
Responses	1,997	390	341	280	907	549	427	552	573	718	531	1,155	530

Q33. How concerned are you about the impact of building your home on the environment?
(Percent of respondents)

	Race/Ethnicity				Home Buyers' Income Bracket					Price Expected to Pay			
	Cauca-sian	African-American	Hispanic	Asian	Under $50,000	$50,000 to $74,999	$75,000 to $99,999	$100,000 to $149,999	$150,000 or more	Less than $150,000	$150,000 to $249,999	$250,000 to $499,999	$500,000 or more
Not concerned	21	19	8	9	26	22	16	17	12	24	23	16	14
Concerned about environment, but not a consideration in house purchase	28	33	34	48	29	31	33	30	30	33	35	29	27
Want environment friendly home, but would not pay more	31	34	37	34	35	33	36	30	28	32	32	34	29
Would pay more for environment friendly home	19	14	21	9	11	14	15	23	30	10	10	21	30
Responses	1,997	390	341	280	907	549	427	552	573	718	531	1,155	530

Q34. How much extra would you pay up front, in the purchase price for your next home, if it would save $1,000 every year in utility costs?
(Percent of respondents)

	All Home Buyers	Geography (Nine Census Divisions)									Buyer Type	
		New England	Middle Atlantic	East North Central	West North Central	South Atlantic	East South Central	West South Central	Mountain	Pacific	First-time	Repeat
Less than $1,000	20	11	21	22	8	22	29	26	18	16	22	20
$1,000 to $4,999	22	28	24	24	15	22	27	18	15	22	21	22
$5,000 to $9,999	19	14	19	19	19	22	12	20	18	21	19	19
$10,000 to $14,999	16	11	15	19	12	17	15	19	14	14	15	16
$15,000 or more	23	36	21	17	46	18	17	18	35	27	23	23
Mean	12,314	15,262	11,441	10,382	24,082	9,915	8,981	10,029	18,067	12,345	11,487	12,423
Median	5,000	5,000	5,000	5,000	10,000	5,000	3,000	5,000	7,000	5,000	5,000	5,000
Responses	2,963	139	356	408	228	645	224	283	270	410	515	2,448

Q34. How much extra would you pay up front, in the purchase price for your next home, if it would save $1,000 every year in utility costs?
(Percent of respondents)

	Age of Household Head					Generation (year born)				Household Composition			
	Under 35 years old	35 to 44 years old	45 to 54 years old	55 to 64 years old	65 years old or older	Gen Z (1997 or later)	Millenni-als(1981-1996)	Gen X (1965-1980)	Boomers (1946-1964)	Married couple w children	Married couple no children	Single parent	One person
Less than $1,000	27	23	26	17	15	28	22	25	16	18	20	27	22
$1,000 to $4,999	27	22	20	20	21	30	22	21	21	25	19	24	18
$5,000 to $9,999	16	19	18	23	19	16	19	18	21	16	23	13	22
$10,000 to $14,999	13	12	15	15	19	9	13	15	17	14	20	10	17
$15,000 or more	18	24	21	25	26	17	24	21	26	28	19	25	22
Mean	9,905	11,864	12,156	12,048	13,569	8,962	12,352	11,737	13,093	14,906	10,451	10,351	10,786
Median	3,000	5,000	5,000	5,000	5,000	2,300	5,000	5,000	5,000	5,000	5,000	4,000	5,000
Responses	915	601	500	429	518	416	920	733	760	1,246	523	388	470

Q34. How much extra would you pay up front, in the purchase price for your next home, if it would save $1,000 every year in utility costs?
(Percent of respondents)

	Race/Ethnicity				Home Buyers' Income Bracket					Price Expected to Pay			
	Cauca-sian	African-American	Hispanic	Asian	Under $50,000	$50,000 to $74,999	$75,000 to $99,999	$100,000 to $149,999	$150,000 or more	Less than $150,000	$150,000 to $249,999	$250,000 to $499,999	$500,000 or more
Less than $1,000	21	30	8	15	25	21	16	20	16	26	17	17	21
$1,000 to $4,999	20	25	21	40	22	22	20	22	22	24	24	20	21
$5,000 to $9,999	21	18	11	13	20	20	18	19	18	17	23	20	15
$10,000 to $14,999	18	8	5	11	15	19	18	16	12	14	15	17	15
$15,000 or more	19	18	56	21	18	18	28	23	32	19	21	25	28
Mean	10,236	10,036	27,653	13,528	9,561	9,742	13,494	11,609	17,595	9,400	10,304	13,551	15,163
Median	5,000	3,000	18,000	4,500	5,000	5,000	5,000	5,000	5,000	4,100	5,000	5,000	5,000
Responses	1,974	386	325	278	897	546	420	546	554	710	525	1,139	516

Q35. Are you aware of any of the following specific green certification programs for homes?
(Percent of respondents)

	All Home Buyers	Geography (Nine Census Divisions)									Buyer Type	
		New England	Middle Atlantic	East North Central	West North Central	South Atlantic	East South Central	West South Central	Mountain	Pacific	First-time	Repeat
ENERGY STAR												
Yes	73	72	80	73	70	75	66	73	72	74	63	75
No	27	28	20	27	30	25	34	27	28	26	37	25
Green Globes												
Yes	26	28	30	20	37	19	24	22	32	34	22	26
No	74	72	70	80	63	81	76	78	68	66	78	74
HERS (Home Energy Rating System)												
Yes	36	35	39	28	40	35	35	33	39	47	29	37
No	64	65	61	72	60	65	65	67	61	53	71	63
Indoor AirPLUS												
Yes	29	29	32	22	38	25	28	23	29	41	28	29
No	71	71	68	78	62	75	72	77	71	59	72	71
LEED for Homes												
Yes	36	43	35	29	43	33	27	33	40	45	28	37
No	64	57	65	71	57	67	73	67	60	55	72	63
Living Building Challenge												
Yes	24	31	29	14	39	19	22	19	25	35	21	25
No	76	69	71	86	61	81	78	81	75	65	79	75
NGBS (National Green Building Standard												
Yes	28	31	32	23	37	22	21	25	35	38	23	29
No	72	69	68	77	63	78	79	75	65	62	77	71
PHIUS (Passive House Institute US)												
Yes	23	28	26	18	31	16	21	21	24	34	20	23
No	77	72	74	82	69	84	79	79	76	66	80	77
WaterSense												
Yes	32	38	34	24	38	28	25	32	37	40	30	32
No	68	62	66	76	62	72	75	68	63	60	70	68
ZERH (Zero Energy Ready Homes)												
Yes	28	32	30	20	39	22	24	23	32	40	27	28
No	72	68	70	80	61	78	76	77	68	60	73	72
Responses	3,008	141	358	414	236	651	224	290	278	416	521	2,487

Q35. Are you aware of any of the following specific green certification programs for homes?
(Percent of respondents)

	Age of Household Head					Generation (year born)				Household Composition			
	Under 35 years old	35 to 44 years old	45 to 54 years old	55 to 64 years old	65 years old or older	Gen Z (1997 or later)	Millenni-als(1981-1996)	Gen X (1965-1980)	Boomers (1946-1964)	Married couple w children	Married couple no children	Single parent	One person
ENERGY STAR													
Yes	61	74	74	78	74	57	72	74	76	72	76	75	75
No	39	26	26	22	26	43	28	26	24	28	24	25	25
Green Globes													
Yes	42	44	28	16	17	43	45	30	16	41	13	29	10
No	58	56	72	84	83	57	55	70	84	59	87	71	90
HERS (Home Energy Rating System)													
Yes	46	52	36	28	32	44	51	37	31	49	25	37	23
No	54	48	64	72	68	56	49	63	69	51	75	63	77
Indoor AirPLUS													
Yes	45	46	30	17	23	46	45	31	20	44	15	32	14
No	55	54	70	83	77	54	55	69	80	56	85	68	86
LEED for Homes													
Yes	44	48	38	30	29	42	47	40	28	49	26	31	25
No	56	52	62	70	71	58	53	60	72	51	74	69	75
Living Building Challenge													
Yes	45	40	25	15	16	48	41	26	15	39	11	25	11
No	55	60	75	85	84	52	59	74	85	61	89	75	89
NGBS (National Green Building Standard													
Yes	41	44	27	18	24	41	44	28	21	42	18	29	14
No	59	56	73	82	76	59	56	72	79	58	82	71	86
PHIUS (Passive House Institute US)													
Yes	40	38	21	13	18	41	38	25	15	36	11	24	12
No	60	62	79	87	82	59	62	75	85	64	89	76	88
WaterSense													
Yes	49	49	34	24	23	51	49	35	23	45	19	39	17
No	51	51	66	76	77	49	51	65	77	55	81	61	83
ZERH (Zero Energy Ready Homes)													
Yes	39	43	31	17	22	36	42	31	21	42	15	29	14
No	61	57	69	83	78	64	58	69	79	58	85	71	86
Responses	934	610	503	436	525	428	932	741	772	1,278	527	391	473

Q35. Are you aware of any of the following specific green certification programs for homes?
(Percent of respondents)

	Race/Ethnicity				Home Buyers' Income Bracket					Price Expected to Pay			
	Cauca-sian	African-American	Hispanic	Asian	Under $50,000	$50,000 to $74,999	$75,000 to $99,999	$100,000 to $149,999	$150,000 or more	Less than $150,000	$150,000 to $249,999	$250,000 to $499,999	$500,000 or more
ENERGY STAR													
Yes	76	74	57	74	66	77	77	76	76	66	72	76	78
No	24	26	43	26	34	23	23	24	24	34	28	24	22
Green Globes													
Yes	21	32	48	43	17	14	23	30	44	27	21	26	32
No	79	68	52	57	83	86	77	70	56	73	79	74	68
HERS (Home Energy Rating System)													
Yes	32	43	54	45	27	30	33	42	50	31	37	36	45
No	68	57	46	55	73	70	67	58	50	69	63	64	55
Indoor AirPLUS													
Yes	23	37	54	44	20	18	27	33	45	29	25	28	37
No	77	63	46	56	80	82	73	67	55	71	75	72	63
LEED for Homes													
Yes	32	41	48	51	24	20	33	44	57	32	28	36	49
No	68	59	52	49	76	80	67	56	43	68	72	64	51
Living Building Challenge													
Yes	19	32	47	43	16	13	21	30	40	26	21	23	32
No	81	68	53	57	84	87	79	70	60	74	79	77	68
NGBS (National Green Building Standard													
Yes	24	31	50	45	20	18	25	33	43	28	24	27	37
No	76	69	50	55	80	82	75	67	57	72	76	73	63
PHIUS (Passive House Institute US)													
Yes	18	28	48	40	17	11	21	28	37	25	18	22	30
No	82	72	52	60	83	89	79	72	63	75	82	78	70
WaterSense													
Yes	27	42	49	47	23	21	30	35	49	31	27	32	40
No	73	58	51	53	77	79	70	65	51	69	73	68	60
ZERH (Zero Energy Ready Homes)													
Yes	22	31	55	47	20	16	27	33	43	28	23	27	36
No	78	69	45	53	80	84	73	67	57	72	77	73	64
Responses	1,997	390	341	280	907	549	427	552	573	718	531	1,155	530

Q36. When purchasing a new home, which would you prefer?
(Percent of respondents)

	All Home Buyers	Geography (Nine Census Divisions)									Buyer Type	
		New England	Middle Atlantic	East North Central	West North Central	South Atlantic	East South Central	West South Central	Mountain	Pacific	First-time	Repeat
All amenities & features included in the base price of the home	68	67	65	68	59	70	66	73	67	66	70	67
A basic home with all amenities offered as options at extra cost	32	33	35	32	41	30	34	27	33	34	30	33
Home on a cul de sac or other street design with limited traffic flow	69	69	69	71	62	73	68	75	67	64	69	69
Home on a continuous, interconnected street with more efficient traffic flow	31	31	31	29	38	27	32	25	33	36	31	31
Wider sidewalks and streets	51	53	53	49	45	52	49	51	51	52	56	50
Narrower sidewalks and streets with more green space	49	47	47	51	55	48	51	49	49	48	44	50
Home oriented to make efficient use of the sun's energy	68	69	69	68	58	72	59	71	65	70	69	68
Home oriented to optimize the attractiveness of the home as viewed from the street	32	31	31	32	42	28	41	29	35	30	31	32
A heating and cooling system designed to meet your current needs efficiently	68	65	72	72	57	72	61	66	65	67	73	67
A heating and cooling system larger than currently needed with some excess capacity for future needs	32	35	28	28	43	28	39	34	35	33	27	33
Conventional landscaping with a traditional lawn, trees shrubs, etc.	40	32	46	42	37	38	42	38	38	42	49	39
Low maintenance landscaping with plants that grow in the local climate with minimal watering, etc.	60	68	54	58	63	62	58	62	62	58	51	61
Features and finishes made of more expensive materials that last longer	77	73	79	78	69	81	72	78	73	76	72	78
Features and finishes made of materials that cost less but need to be replaced more often	23	27	21	22	31	19	28	22	27	24	28	22
Upgraded interior finishes (e.g., flooring/counters/trim)	54	53	58	52	46	54	61	57	51	53	57	53
Green features (e.g., energy/water efficiency/indoor air quality)	46	47	42	48	54	46	39	43	49	47	43	47
Responses	3,008	141	358	414	236	651	224	290	278	416	521	2,487

Q36. When purchasing a new home, which would you prefer?
(Percent of respondents)

	Age of Household Head					Generation (year born)				Household Composition			
	Under 35 years old	35 to 44 years old	45 to 54 years old	55 to 64 years old	65 years old or older	Gen Z (1997 or later)	Millenni-als(1981-1996)	Gen X (1965-1980)	Boomers (1946-1964)	Married couple w children	Married couple no children	Single parent	One person
All amenities & features included in the base price of the home	60	63	68	71	69	59	61	68	71	62	71	70	71
A basic home with all amenities offered as options at extra cost	40	37	32	29	31	41	39	32	29	38	29	30	29
Home on a cul de sac or other street design with limited traffic flow	59	61	68	75	74	60	61	67	75	62	77	69	75
Home on a continuous, interconnected street with more efficient traffic flow	41	39	32	25	26	40	39	33	25	38	23	31	25
Wider sidewalks and streets	52	54	49	50	50	50	53	49	51	52	51	52	47
Narrower sidewalks and streets with more green space	48	46	51	50	50	50	47	51	49	48	49	48	53
Home oriented to make efficient use of the sun's energy	61	65	65	76	68	59	64	66	72	61	75	70	74
Home oriented to optimize the attractiveness of the home as viewed from the street	39	35	35	24	32	41	36	34	28	39	25	30	26
A heating and cooling system designed to meet your current needs efficiently	63	62	61	73	73	61	62	64	73	61	72	69	78
A heating and cooling system larger than currently needed with some excess capacity for future needs	37	38	39	27	27	39	38	36	27	39	28	31	22
Conventional landscaping with a traditional lawn, trees shrubs, etc.	52	50	43	35	33	54	50	44	33	46	32	46	35
Low maintenance landscaping with plants that grow in the local climate with minimal watering, etc.	48	50	57	65	67	46	50	56	67	54	68	54	65
Features and finishes made of more expensive materials that last longer	68	73	76	80	80	65	72	76	80	71	84	76	81
Features and finishes made of materials that cost less but need to be replaced more often	32	27	24	20	20	35	28	24	20	29	16	24	19
Upgraded interior finishes (e.g., flooring/counters/trim)	54	57	58	51	52	58	54	57	51	54	60	56	48
Green features (e.g., energy/water efficiency/indoor air quality)	46	43	42	49	48	42	46	43	49	46	40	44	52
Responses	934	610	503	436	525	428	932	741	772	1,278	527	391	473

Q36. When purchasing a new home, which would you prefer?
(Percent of respondents)

	Race/Ethnicity				Home Buyers' Income Bracket					Price Expected to Pay			
	Cauca-sian	African-American	Hispanic	Asian	Under $50,000	$50,000 to $74,999	$75,000 to $99,999	$100,000 to $149,999	$150,000 or more	Less than $150,000	$150,000 to $249,999	$250,000 to $499,999	$500,000 or more
All amenities & features included in the base price of the home	69	69	58	59	71	73	70	63	61	68	71	66	65
A basic home with all amenities offered as options at extra cost	31	31	42	41	29	27	30	37	39	32	29	34	35
Home on a cul de sac or other street design with limited traffic flow	72	64	56	65	70	76	74	70	61	65	72	70	68
Home on a continuous, interconnected street with more efficient traffic flow	28	36	44	35	30	24	26	30	39	35	28	30	32
Wider sidewalks and streets	49	59	50	57	45	53	51	50	57	47	51	50	55
Narrower sidewalks and streets with more green space	51	41	50	43	55	47	49	50	43	53	49	50	45
Home oriented to make efficient use of the sun's energy	71	65	55	67	70	73	70	67	62	65	71	69	65
Home oriented to optimize the attractiveness of the home as viewed from the street	29	35	45	33	30	27	30	33	38	35	29	31	35
A heating and cooling system designed to meet your current needs efficiently	71	63	52	61	74	72	70	65	59	69	75	66	62
A heating and cooling system larger than currently needed with some excess capacity for future needs	29	37	48	39	26	28	30	35	41	31	25	34	38
Conventional landscaping with a traditional lawn, trees shrubs, etc.	38	47	48	41	38	38	38	40	46	40	43	37	44
Low maintenance landscaping with plants that grow in the local climate with minimal watering, etc.	62	53	52	59	62	62	62	60	54	60	57	63	56
Features and finishes made of more expensive materials that last longer	81	67	60	65	75	83	79	76	75	70	75	78	83
Features and finishes made of materials that cost less but need to be replaced more often	19	33	40	35	25	17	21	24	25	30	25	22	17
Upgraded interior finishes (e.g., flooring/counters/trim)	55	52	49	49	52	54	57	55	53	51	54	53	59
Green features (e.g., energy/water efficiency/indoor air quality)	45	48	51	51	48	46	43	45	47	49	46	47	41
Responses	1,997	390	341	280	907	549	427	552	573	718	531	1,155	530

Q37. For the same amount of money, which of the following would you choose?
(Percent of respondents)

	All Home Buyers	Geography (Nine Census Divisions)									Buyer Type	
		New England	Middle Atlantic	East North Central	West North Central	South Atlantic	East South Central	West South Central	Mountain	Pacific	First-time	Repeat
A bigger house with fewer amenities	37	26	36	36	40	36	45	39	35	36	43	36
A smaller house with high quality products and amenities	63	74	64	64	60	64	55	61	65	64	57	64
A much larger family room and no living room	49	48	43	47	52	52	45	50	53	48	39	50
Family room and living room about equal in size	51	52	57	53	48	48	55	50	47	52	61	50
Larger than average kitchen and smaller living area spaces	41	40	46	39	39	40	42	38	42	43	44	41
Typical kitchen and living area spaces	59	60	54	61	61	60	58	62	58	57	56	59
Two full master bedroom suites plus one standard bedroom	55	51	58	57	54	55	51	61	49	54	56	55
One full master bedroom suite plus three standard bedrooms	45	49	42	43	46	45	49	39	51	46	44	45
Responses	3,008	141	358	414	236	651	224	290	278	416	521	2,487

Q38. How would the following various designs and features influence your purchase decision?
(Percent of respondents)

	All Home Buyers	Geography (Nine Census Divisions)									Buyer Type	
		New England	Middle Atlantic	East North Central	West North Central	South Atlantic	East South Central	West South Central	Mountain	Pacific	First-time	Repeat
WINDOWS												
Low e- insulating glass												
Do not want	7	5	8	9	3	9	8	7	5	4	10	6
Indifferent	26	24	30	26	21	31	29	25	22	21	39	25
Desirable	48	48	48	47	53	46	48	52	46	47	38	49
Essential/Must Have	19	22	14	18	22	15	15	16	26	27	13	20
Gas filled (Argon or Krypton) insulating glass												
Do not want	17	18	14	16	8	23	24	19	9	14	25	16
Indifferent	36	28	39	40	33	40	34	35	39	26	43	35
Desirable	33	42	34	29	40	26	30	34	36	42	25	35
Essential/Must Have	14	12	13	14	19	11	12	12	17	19	7	15

Q37. For the same amount of money, which of the following would you choose?
(Percent of respondents)

	Age of Household Head					Generation (year born)				Household Composition			
	Under 35 years old	35 to 44 years old	45 to 54 years old	55 to 64 years old	65 years old or older	Gen Z (1997 or later)	Millenni-als(1981-1996)	Gen X (1965-1980)	Boomers (1946-1964)	Married couple w children	Married couple no children	Single parent	One person
A bigger house with fewer amenities	48	49	37	32	30	47	48	39	30	42	28	49	24
A smaller house with high quality products and amenities	52	51	63	68	70	53	52	61	70	58	72	51	76
A much larger family room and no living room	44	42	49	53	52	43	43	48	52	47	55	44	51
Family room and living room about equal in size	56	58	51	47	48	57	57	52	48	53	45	56	49
Larger than average kitchen and smaller living area spaces	43	44	46	42	35	47	41	46	38	47	39	42	31
Typical kitchen and living area spaces	57	56	54	58	65	53	59	54	62	53	61	58	69
Two full master bedroom suites plus one standard bedroom	59	56	55	58	53	59	58	54	55	55	58	56	55
One full master bedroom suite plus three standard bedrooms	41	44	45	42	47	41	42	46	45	45	42	44	45
Responses	934	610	503	436	525	428	932	741	772	1,278	527	391	473

Q38. How would the following various designs and features influence your purchase decision?
(Percent of respondents)

	Age of Household Head					Generation (year born)				Household Composition			
	Under 35 years old	35 to 44 years old	45 to 54 years old	55 to 64 years old	65 years old or older	Gen Z (1997 or later)	Millenni-als(1981-1996)	Gen X (1965-1980)	Boomers (1946-1964)	Married couple w children	Married couple no children	Single parent	One person
WINDOWS													
Low e- insulating glass													
Do not want	10	9	7	6	5	13	8	8	5	7	5	9	6
Indifferent	35	26	28	28	22	40	27	28	23	23	25	31	31
Desirable	38	45	49	47	52	33	46	46	52	50	48	44	47
Essential/Must Have	17	20	17	18	21	15	19	18	20	20	21	16	16
Gas filled (Argon or Krypton) insulating glass													
Do not want	18	15	17	20	15	21	16	17	17	12	15	27	20
Indifferent	36	35	38	36	35	38	33	38	35	30	41	37	38
Desirable	30	30	32	32	38	29	31	31	36	39	34	25	31
Essential/Must Have	16	19	13	11	13	13	20	14	13	20	11	11	10

Q37. For the same amount of money, which of the following would you choose?
(Percent of respondents)

	Race/Ethnicity				Home Buyers' Income Bracket					Price Expected to Pay			
	Cauca-sian	African-American	Hispanic	Asian	Under $50,000	$50,000 to $74,999	$75,000 to $99,999	$100,000 to $149,999	$150,000 or more	Less than $150,000	$150,000 to $249,999	$250,000 to $499,999	$500,000 or more
A bigger house with fewer amenities	33	50	48	44	35	34	38	40	37	38	40	35	35
A smaller house with high quality products and amenities	67	50	52	56	65	66	62	60	63	62	60	65	65
A much larger family room and no living room	50	42	48	42	46	44	51	53	52	46	45	52	52
Family room and living room about equal in size	50	58	52	58	54	56	49	47	48	54	55	48	48
Larger than average kitchen and smaller living area spaces	39	45	45	48	33	38	45	43	49	36	37	40	51
Typical kitchen and living area spaces	61	55	55	52	67	62	55	57	51	64	63	60	49
Two full master bedroom suites plus one standard bedroom	56	54	50	58	54	57	56	55	56	52	57	52	63
One full master bedroom suite plus three standard bedrooms	44	46	50	42	46	43	44	45	44	48	43	48	37
Responses	1,997	390	341	280	907	549	427	552	573	718	531	1,155	530

Q38. How would the following various designs and features influence your purchase decision?
(Percent of respondents)

	Race/Ethnicity				Home Buyers' Income Bracket					Price Expected to Pay			
	Cauca-sian	African-American	Hispanic	Asian	Under $50,000	$50,000 to $74,999	$75,000 to $99,999	$100,000 to $149,999	$150,000 or more	Less than $150,000	$150,000 to $249,999	$250,000 to $499,999	$500,000 or more
WINDOWS													
Low e- insulating glass													
Do not want	7	9	4	7	8	7	7	7	6	10	9	5	7
Indifferent	27	27	20	25	32	31	25	24	19	30	28	26	20
Desirable	48	45	47	49	43	48	54	46	52	45	45	50	49
Essential/Must Have	17	19	29	19	17	14	14	24	24	15	18	19	25
Gas filled (Argon or Krypton) insulating glass													
Do not want	18	24	8	10	23	20	20	12	9	23	17	15	12
Indifferent	38	32	26	32	36	41	42	36	27	35	38	37	30
Desirable	32	28	44	44	30	32	31	32	42	30	31	34	40
Essential/Must Have	13	16	22	15	11	7	7	20	22	11	14	14	18

Q38. How would the following various designs and features influence your purchase decision?
(Percent of respondents)

	All Home Buyers	Geography (Nine Census Divisions)									Buyer Type	
		New England	Middle Atlantic	East North Central	West North Central	South Atlantic	East South Central	West South Central	Mountain	Pacific	First-time	Repeat
WINDOWS												
Triple-pane insulating glass												
Do not want	4	0	4	5	4	5	7	3	2	5	7	4
Indifferent	18	20	18	17	14	22	18	20	14	17	25	17
Desirable	54	59	57	55	56	52	51	51	58	54	51	55
Essential/Must Have	23	20	21	23	26	21	24	26	27	24	17	24
ENERGY STAR® rated Windows												
Do not want	3	4	2	3	5	4	6	2	3	2	5	3
Indifferent	14	12	15	12	20	12	18	14	13	13	19	13
Desirable	51	44	54	48	45	53	54	57	49	47	49	51
Essential/Must Have	32	40	29	37	30	31	23	27	35	37	26	33
Bay or bow Windows												
Do not want	11	5	10	15	12	14	13	8	8	8	11	11
Indifferent	29	26	27	32	25	30	33	34	31	25	28	30
Desirable	45	51	48	39	41	47	41	47	40	49	47	45
Essential/Must Have	14	18	15	14	22	8	14	11	21	18	14	15
Greenhouse Windows												
Do not want	14	9	14	17	7	20	15	12	8	8	17	13
Indifferent	34	27	30	38	35	35	42	38	36	27	32	35
Desirable	38	50	41	33	40	35	29	38	41	41	39	38
Essential/Must Have	14	14	14	12	17	9	14	11	15	24	13	14
Skylights												
Do not want	20	14	17	25	15	27	25	19	18	11	13	21
Indifferent	24	23	25	22	24	28	24	26	20	20	26	24
Desirable	40	49	41	37	44	36	36	39	46	46	45	40
Essential/Must Have	15	13	16	16	16	9	15	16	16	23	16	15
Floor-to-ceiling windows												
Do not want	24	25	19	36	14	28	27	22	21	18	23	25
Indifferent	25	22	28	24	24	29	23	25	27	20	30	25
Desirable	37	42	37	30	45	34	35	43	35	40	34	37
Essential/Must Have	14	11	16	10	17	10	15	10	17	22	13	14

Q38. How would the following various designs and features influence your purchase decision?
(Percent of respondents)

	Age of Household Head					Generation (year born)				Household Composition			
	Under 35 years old	35 to 44 years old	45 to 54 years old	55 to 64 years old	65 years old or older	Gen Z (1997 or later)	Millenni-als(1981-1996)	Gen X (1965-1980)	Boomers (1946-1964)	Married couple w children	Married couple no children	Single parent	One person
WINDOWS													
Triple-pane insulating glass													
Do not want	9	4	5	3	3	11	5	5	3	5	2	7	5
Indifferent	28	20	18	16	16	32	21	18	16	18	15	24	18
Desirable	43	48	54	60	57	40	49	52	58	51	61	48	55
Essential/Must Have	19	27	23	22	24	17	25	25	23	26	22	22	22
ENERGY STAR® rated Windows													
Do not want	8	4	3	2	2	11	4	3	2	3	2	5	2
Indifferent	28	15	14	11	11	36	17	14	10	16	10	17	13
Desirable	44	51	48	56	51	38	50	50	53	47	54	48	55
Essential/Must Have	20	30	35	31	36	15	29	34	35	34	34	30	30
Bay or bow Windows													
Do not want	10	6	9	15	13	15	6	9	14	9	11	15	13
Indifferent	28	25	30	30	31	32	26	28	30	26	33	26	35
Desirable	45	47	46	45	44	40	48	45	45	46	45	41	46
Essential/Must Have	17	23	16	10	12	14	21	18	11	20	10	18	7
Greenhouse Windows													
Do not want	12	11	13	16	15	14	10	13	15	10	14	18	20
Indifferent	31	26	36	37	38	34	26	34	37	29	44	33	35
Desirable	39	41	36	38	36	34	43	37	38	41	32	36	37
Essential/Must Have	18	22	15	9	11	17	21	16	11	20	10	13	9
Skylights													
Do not want	11	11	16	27	26	12	11	16	26	14	26	16	30
Indifferent	23	23	25	23	26	23	23	24	24	22	26	28	22
Desirable	46	42	44	40	36	45	43	43	38	42	38	41	40
Essential/Must Have	21	24	16	9	12	19	23	17	11	22	10	15	8
Floor-to-ceiling windows													
Do not want	14	13	21	31	30	16	13	21	31	16	31	22	33
Indifferent	25	24	23	25	27	29	23	23	27	23	25	25	26
Desirable	41	41	39	35	33	34	43	40	33	41	36	36	33
Essential/Must Have	20	21	16	9	10	20	21	16	9	19	8	17	9

Q38. How would the following various designs and features influence your purchase decision?
(Percent of respondents)

	Race/Ethnicity				Home Buyers' Income Bracket					Price Expected to Pay			
	Cauca-sian	African-American	Hispanic	Asian	Under $50,000	$50,000 to $74,999	$75,000 to $99,999	$100,000 to $149,999	$150,000 or more	Less than $150,000	$150,000 to $249,999	$250,000 to $499,999	$500,000 or more
WINDOWS													
Triple-pane insulating glass													
Do not want	4	6	5	8	5	4	4	5	3	6	4	4	3
Indifferent	17	22	21	20	20	21	18	17	14	23	17	17	14
Desirable	56	47	45	50	55	55	56	54	51	49	56	56	55
Essential/Must Have	22	25	29	21	19	19	22	24	32	22	23	23	28
ENERGY STAR® rated Windows													
Do not want	2	5	6	4	4	3	2	3	3	4	4	3	2
Indifferent	12	16	21	18	16	13	12	13	13	20	14	12	13
Desirable	53	46	38	53	53	54	52	49	46	53	54	49	49
Essential/Must Have	32	33	35	25	26	30	33	35	38	23	28	37	36
Bay or bow Windows													
Do not want	12	10	7	14	14	12	15	8	8	13	13	9	12
Indifferent	31	28	18	30	27	30	29	32	30	26	30	30	30
Desirable	45	46	46	40	47	47	46	43	42	49	43	47	41
Essential/Must Have	12	17	29	16	12	11	10	17	20	13	14	14	18
Greenhouse Windows													
Do not want	15	16	6	10	17	15	12	13	11	18	13	13	12
Indifferent	38	26	21	26	35	41	36	33	30	29	39	37	31
Desirable	35	44	47	49	38	34	40	37	39	39	37	37	38
Essential/Must Have	12	15	27	15	11	9	12	17	21	14	11	14	19
Skylights													
Do not want	23	16	6	11	24	24	19	19	14	21	21	21	16
Indifferent	25	23	19	23	25	28	25	28	17	23	25	25	21
Desirable	39	44	46	48	40	37	42	35	47	42	41	39	43
Essential/Must Have	13	17	29	18	11	11	14	17	22	14	13	15	20
Floor-to-ceiling windows													
Do not want	28	22	8	13	37	29	22	19	12	29	30	23	14
Indifferent	26	27	23	25	24	28	30	28	20	26	25	29	18
Desirable	35	37	42	49	28	34	39	36	49	32	33	37	47
Essential/Must Have	11	14	28	14	11	9	9	17	19	13	12	12	20

Q38. How would the following various designs and features influence your purchase decision?
(Percent of respondents)

	All Home Buyers	Geography (Nine Census Divisions)									Buyer Type	
		New England	Middle Atlantic	East North Central	West North Central	South Atlantic	East South Central	West South Central	Mountain	Pacific	First-time	Repeat
EXTERIOR DOORS												
Double main entry door												
Do not want	15	16	10	21	12	18	11	11	20	9	12	15
Indifferent	27	30	29	30	24	28	31	26	24	25	23	28
Desirable	41	34	43	36	41	42	38	50	37	44	50	40
Essential/Must Have	17	20	19	14	23	12	20	13	18	22	14	17
Entry door with decorative glass panels												
Do not want	12	8	12	13	10	15	9	14	14	11	14	12
Indifferent	27	31	26	31	30	27	27	21	31	22	34	26
Desirable	44	48	45	42	41	45	46	49	39	44	40	45
Essential/Must Have	16	12	17	15	19	13	18	16	16	23	12	17
Sliding patio door												
Do not want	12	5	7	15	11	15	19	19	11	5	6	13
Indifferent	23	28	21	25	19	22	27	26	23	20	22	23
Desirable	44	50	49	42	51	45	39	40	44	45	48	44
Essential/Must Have	20	17	23	18	19	18	15	15	22	30	24	20
Hinged/French patio door												
Do not want	10	12	10	9	11	11	12	12	10	9	7	11
Indifferent	25	20	28	29	24	27	21	24	22	24	31	25
Desirable	48	52	45	49	50	46	50	50	47	48	48	48
Essential/Must Have	16	16	17	13	15	16	17	14	21	20	14	17
FRONT EXTERIOR SIDING												
Vinyl/Vinyl covered aluminum												
Do not want	21	17	17	21	12	25	25	23	26	21	20	22
Indifferent	35	31	34	37	28	41	34	41	31	28	43	34
Desirable	30	42	35	32	37	24	28	26	24	34	30	30
Essential/Must Have	13	10	15	11	23	9	13	11	18	17	8	14
Wood/Wood product												
Do not want	15	9	16	17	8	18	20	10	19	11	11	15
Indifferent	32	29	33	34	26	37	26	34	28	27	35	31
Desirable	40	49	41	36	46	37	40	42	37	41	43	39
Essential/Must Have	14	13	10	13	21	8	14	14	16	21	12	14
Fiber Cement												
Do not want	16	21	16	20	9	16	20	12	12	13	16	16
Indifferent	42	31	41	48	37	46	39	50	42	34	47	42
Desirable	31	32	33	24	40	30	29	28	37	32	29	31
Essential/Must Have	11	16	10	8	14	8	12	10	9	22	8	12

Q38. How would the following various designs and features influence your purchase decision?
(Percent of respondents)

	Age of Household Head					Generation (year born)				Household Composition			
	Under 35 years old	35 to 44 years old	45 to 54 years old	55 to 64 years old	65 years old or older	Gen Z (1997 or later)	Millenni-als(1981-1996)	Gen X (1965-1980)	Boomers (1946-1964)	Married couple w children	Married couple no children	Single parent	One person
EXTERIOR DOORS													
Double main entry door													
Do not want	10	6	12	17	21	11	7	12	19	9	21	14	19
Indifferent	23	22	23	30	32	27	22	24	31	21	33	21	33
Desirable	45	46	50	42	32	39	47	48	36	47	34	45	38
Essential/Must Have	22	26	15	12	14	22	25	16	13	23	12	20	10
Entry door with decorative glass panels													
Do not want	12	9	11	15	13	13	11	12	14	8	15	13	18
Indifferent	25	22	27	28	29	32	20	26	29	22	29	26	31
Desirable	41	44	44	46	45	36	44	44	45	46	45	43	42
Essential/Must Have	22	25	18	10	13	20	25	18	12	23	11	18	9
Sliding patio door													
Do not want	7	5	11	14	17	6	6	11	16	9	17	10	15
Indifferent	19	21	23	23	25	24	19	22	25	21	27	24	24
Desirable	47	49	44	49	39	45	50	45	41	46	41	40	45
Essential/Must Have	27	24	22	14	19	25	24	21	18	24	16	25	16
Hinged/French patio door													
Do not want	8	5	9	11	14	10	6	9	14	7	14	9	13
Indifferent	23	22	22	30	26	24	22	24	26	22	27	24	27
Desirable	47	50	54	47	45	47	49	52	46	49	46	51	49
Essential/Must Have	22	23	15	12	15	19	23	15	14	21	14	16	12
FRONT EXTERIOR SIDING													
Vinyl/Vinyl covered aluminum													
Do not want	14	13	17	27	27	16	13	17	27	15	29	17	29
Indifferent	34	30	38	38	34	38	31	37	35	29	37	37	40
Desirable	34	36	32	26	28	31	36	32	27	36	27	32	23
Essential/Must Have	18	21	13	9	11	15	20	14	10	20	7	14	7
Wood/Wood product													
Do not want	9	6	13	15	22	11	6	12	20	10	19	16	23
Indifferent	26	27	29	38	33	27	26	30	35	25	39	27	36
Desirable	45	45	43	38	35	44	45	41	36	44	33	43	36
Essential/Must Have	20	23	15	8	10	18	23	16	9	21	9	15	5
Fiber Cement													
Do not want	12	8	17	19	17	16	9	16	18	10	21	15	20
Indifferent	37	35	43	43	46	36	35	41	46	34	47	41	51
Desirable	36	38	29	30	27	34	38	30	28	37	26	34	25
Essential/Must Have	15	18	11	7	10	14	17	13	8	19	7	11	4

Q38. How would the following various designs and features influence your purchase decision?
(Percent of respondents)

	Race/Ethnicity				Home Buyers' Income Bracket					Price Expected to Pay			
	Cauca-sian	African-American	Hispanic	Asian	Under $50,000	$50,000 to $74,999	$75,000 to $99,999	$100,000 to $149,999	$150,000 or more	Less than $150,000	$150,000 to $249,999	$250,000 to $499,999	$500,000 or more
EXTERIOR DOORS													
Double main entry door													
Do not want	17	8	5	10	18	18	16	15	7	16	18	14	10
Indifferent	30	22	15	30	29	30	33	25	22	28	30	29	22
Desirable	39	50	44	46	39	40	38	39	48	40	39	41	46
Essential/Must Have	14	19	36	14	14	12	13	21	22	16	13	16	22
Entry door with decorative glass panels													
Do not want	13	13	6	11	15	15	15	11	8	12	15	12	9
Indifferent	27	28	24	28	28	35	29	25	20	30	24	26	27
Desirable	45	42	45	44	47	40	40	45	47	40	49	47	40
Essential/Must Have	15	16	26	16	10	10	16	19	26	17	12	15	24
Sliding patio door													
Do not want	13	14	7	10	14	13	12	10	11	11	13	13	12
Indifferent	24	21	19	21	23	27	24	22	21	26	26	23	18
Desirable	45	44	42	51	45	42	43	46	45	46	44	43	45
Essential/Must Have	18	21	32	18	17	18	21	22	23	17	17	21	25
Hinged/French patio door													
Do not want	12	7	6	7	15	12	12	9	4	13	13	10	6
Indifferent	26	24	20	26	27	27	27	23	22	28	28	24	21
Desirable	48	51	47	52	44	49	47	50	51	45	45	49	53
Essential/Must Have	15	17	26	15	13	11	14	18	23	14	14	17	20
FRONT EXTERIOR SIDING													
Vinyl/Vinyl covered aluminum													
Do not want	24	19	9	15	22	22	21	22	21	18	18	22	27
Indifferent	38	34	23	29	37	45	41	31	25	35	39	37	27
Desirable	28	33	38	44	29	28	27	30	35	33	32	28	31
Essential/Must Have	11	14	30	12	12	5	11	16	19	14	11	13	14
Wood/Wood product													
Do not want	16	15	8	8	17	16	13	15	12	14	16	14	15
Indifferent	34	30	18	30	34	35	33	30	28	29	33	34	28
Desirable	38	41	48	45	38	43	41	36	41	43	39	37	43
Essential/Must Have	12	14	26	16	10	6	13	19	19	14	13	14	14
Fiber Cement													
Do not want	18	13	5	13	18	18	16	15	11	16	17	15	14
Indifferent	46	38	24	35	46	53	49	38	29	41	47	45	32
Desirable	27	40	46	37	27	24	29	31	41	30	26	30	38
Essential/Must Have	9	10	25	15	9	6	6	16	18	12	10	10	16

Q38. How would the following various designs and features influence your purchase decision?
(Percent of respondents)

	All Home Buyers	Geography (Nine Census Divisions)									Buyer Type	
		New England	Middle Atlantic	East North Central	West North Central	South Atlantic	East South Central	West South Central	Mountain	Pacific	First-time	Repeat
FRONT EXTERIOR SIDING												
Stucco												
Do not want	22	27	21	33	17	22	30	21	15	13	19	23
Indifferent	36	35	37	36	35	38	34	44	33	32	50	35
Desirable	30	26	32	22	32	32	26	25	36	36	23	31
Essential/Must Have	12	12	10	10	16	8	10	10	16	19	8	12
Brick												
Do not want	6	14	5	8	4	6	5	5	4	6	8	6
Indifferent	23	25	25	20	26	24	22	17	25	25	26	22
Desirable	52	45	54	54	52	53	48	55	54	44	48	52
Essential/Must Have	19	15	15	18	18	17	25	23	17	25	18	19
Stone												
Do not want	6	9	5	7	5	5	10	4	2	6	6	6
Indifferent	24	27	26	27	20	24	23	20	28	23	26	24
Desirable	55	47	54	53	55	60	50	59	57	50	54	55
Essential/Must Have	15	17	15	13	19	11	17	16	13	21	14	16
FLOORING FOR LIVING SPACES ON MAIN FLOOR												
Bamboo												
Do not want	23	21	25	27	13	28	24	25	21	14	26	23
Indifferent	32	30	33	31	31	35	27	34	30	27	34	31
Desirable	33	37	30	33	38	30	35	31	34	38	30	33
Essential/Must Have	12	13	12	9	17	7	14	10	14	21	10	12
Carpet												
Do not want	27	34	23	24	13	35	28	33	27	20	24	27
Indifferent	25	22	26	30	23	24	27	26	22	23	24	25
Desirable	32	26	34	32	41	28	29	29	32	37	37	31
Essential/Must Have	16	18	17	13	23	13	16	13	19	20	15	16
Cork												
Do not want	33	27	34	42	21	38	33	37	32	22	33	33
Indifferent	34	33	35	32	30	39	29	33	30	34	41	33
Desirable	23	23	23	18	34	16	29	22	27	26	19	23
Essential/Must Have	10	18	8	8	16	7	9	8	11	17	7	11
Hardwood												
Do not want	5	3	3	5	6	7	3	3	8	5	4	5
Indifferent	14	9	10	13	17	12	16	18	18	15	13	14
Desirable	54	49	56	55	54	58	50	53	52	53	57	54
Essential/Must Have	27	39	31	27	23	23	31	26	23	27	25	27

Q38. How would the following various designs and features influence your purchase decision?
(Percent of respondents)

	Age of Household Head					Generation (year born)				Household Composition			
	Under 35 years old	35 to 44 years old	45 to 54 years old	55 to 64 years old	65 years old or older	Gen Z (1997 or later)	Millenni-als(1981-1996)	Gen X (1965-1980)	Boomers (1946-1964)	Married couple w children	Married couple no children	Single parent	One person
FRONT EXTERIOR SIDING													
Stucco													
Do not want	16	13	26	26	24	18	14	23	24	16	28	24	28
Indifferent	36	34	32	42	36	41	32	35	39	31	40	38	39
Desirable	31	33	31	25	30	27	35	29	29	34	25	30	29
Essential/Must Have	16	20	11	6	10	13	19	13	8	19	7	9	5
Brick													
Do not want	9	5	5	6	7	11	6	5	7	5	6	9	7
Indifferent	24	23	21	26	22	26	22	23	23	20	27	21	23
Desirable	48	47	54	52	54	44	49	49	55	50	52	50	55
Essential/Must Have	19	25	21	16	17	18	24	22	16	25	15	20	15
Stone													
Do not want	7	4	5	7	6	8	5	5	7	4	7	6	7
Indifferent	22	21	20	27	26	23	20	21	27	21	29	20	26
Desirable	50	53	58	56	54	50	53	56	55	54	53	56	59
Essential/Must Have	21	22	16	10	14	19	21	18	11	21	12	18	9
FLOORING FOR LIVING SPACES ON MAIN FLOOR													
Bamboo													
Do not want	14	15	21	28	28	15	15	21	28	17	28	25	27
Indifferent	32	28	31	34	32	34	28	30	33	25	37	32	37
Desirable	35	38	37	32	28	34	39	38	28	39	28	31	31
Essential/Must Have	18	19	11	6	12	17	19	11	10	19	6	13	5
Carpet													
Do not want	16	16	23	34	32	20	15	23	33	18	36	25	35
Indifferent	28	19	25	29	25	27	21	24	27	23	27	24	29
Desirable	36	38	36	27	30	35	37	35	28	38	26	33	26
Essential/Must Have	20	27	16	10	13	19	26	17	12	22	12	18	11
Cork													
Do not want	23	18	34	40	39	26	18	32	40	23	43	30	42
Indifferent	33	33	32	35	34	32	33	33	34	28	38	37	38
Desirable	28	32	23	19	19	26	32	24	19	31	16	23	15
Essential/Must Have	16	17	10	5	8	16	17	11	7	18	3	10	4
Hardwood													
Do not want	6	4	5	3	6	9	4	5	5	4	5	5	5
Indifferent	18	14	11	10	17	19	15	12	14	13	13	14	15
Desirable	47	49	55	64	53	47	48	54	57	52	57	54	57
Essential/Must Have	28	33	29	22	25	25	33	29	23	30	25	27	23

Q38. How would the following various designs and features influence your purchase decision?
(Percent of respondents)

	Race/Ethnicity				Home Buyers' Income Bracket					Price Expected to Pay			
	Cauca-sian	African-American	Hispanic	Asian	Under $50,000	$50,000 to $74,999	$75,000 to $99,999	$100,000 to $149,999	$150,000 or more	Less than $150,000	$150,000 to $249,999	$250,000 to $499,999	$500,000 or more
FRONT EXTERIOR SIDING													
Stucco													
Do not want	26	18	7	10	26	22	23	21	17	26	21	22	19
Indifferent	38	40	25	35	38	45	42	33	28	37	40	36	31
Desirable	28	29	42	36	27	28	27	32	35	25	30	31	33
Essential/Must Have	9	13	26	19	9	5	9	14	20	11	10	11	16
Brick													
Do not want	7	4	3	11	7	6	7	5	6	8	6	5	8
Indifferent	24	17	16	25	23	30	22	25	17	24	24	22	21
Desirable	52	57	49	49	54	52	56	47	50	49	54	54	50
Essential/Must Have	17	22	32	15	16	12	16	23	26	18	17	20	22
Stone													
Do not want	6	6	2	4	9	5	7	4	3	9	5	4	5
Indifferent	24	30	20	24	27	28	25	23	18	26	27	24	18
Desirable	56	46	51	56	54	56	54	55	55	51	54	56	59
Essential/Must Have	13	19	28	16	11	10	14	17	24	14	15	16	18
FLOORING FOR LIVING SPACES ON MAIN FLOOR													
Bamboo													
Do not want	26	20	11	14	28	27	27	20	15	23	27	23	18
Indifferent	33	33	23	27	34	36	34	28	27	32	33	31	31
Desirable	32	34	35	44	28	31	31	36	40	33	30	35	35
Essential/Must Have	9	13	32	15	10	7	8	16	18	12	10	12	16
Carpet													
Do not want	30	23	10	19	30	32	27	24	22	24	27	27	27
Indifferent	27	17	16	27	26	27	24	28	21	24	26	26	23
Desirable	29	38	45	37	31	30	35	29	35	34	33	31	33
Essential/Must Have	13	21	30	17	13	11	14	19	22	17	15	16	17
Cork													
Do not want	38	29	13	21	41	41	32	29	22	35	38	33	26
Indifferent	36	36	22	29	34	37	40	31	29	32	36	34	33
Desirable	19	25	37	37	17	18	19	26	32	23	17	23	30
Essential/Must Have	7	10	28	13	7	4	9	13	16	11	9	11	11
Hardwood													
Do not want	5	5	6	5	6	5	4	4	5	6	5	5	4
Indifferent	14	10	17	19	13	17	13	14	13	15	17	13	11
Desirable	55	56	47	52	58	56	58	51	49	57	57	53	51
Essential/Must Have	26	30	30	24	23	21	25	31	33	22	21	29	33

Q38. How would the following various designs and features influence your purchase decision?
(Percent of respondents)

	All Home Buyers	Geography (Nine Census Divisions)									Buyer Type	
		New England	Middle Atlantic	East North Central	West North Central	South Atlantic	East South Central	West South Central	Mountain	Pacific	First-time	Repeat
FLOORING FOR LIVING SPACES ON MAIN FLOOR												
Laminate												
Do not want	22	26	24	23	13	23	20	22	24	20	20	22
Indifferent	31	27	30	37	33	32	30	34	24	28	36	31
Desirable	35	37	33	33	32	36	37	33	39	34	34	35
Essential/Must Have	12	10	13	8	22	9	13	11	13	18	9	13
Tile												
Do not want	9	4	7	10	11	12	8	4	8	9	8	9
Indifferent	24	24	23	30	22	22	24	25	22	20	27	23
Desirable	49	49	50	42	48	51	49	53	50	47	49	49
Essential/Must Have	19	23	20	18	19	16	19	18	20	23	15	19
DECORATIVE AND OTHER FEATURES												
Ceiling crown molding												
Do not want	8	7	8	9	7	8	6	9	7	7	10	7
Indifferent	28	28	25	36	35	25	24	21	34	28	32	28
Desirable	47	57	49	39	42	52	49	52	43	41	44	47
Essential/Must Have	17	7	18	16	15	15	20	18	16	24	14	18
Tray ceiling												
Do not want	16	18	18	19	11	17	13	14	12	13	17	15
Indifferent	41	39	39	44	34	41	35	48	46	39	47	40
Desirable	32	33	33	28	39	32	38	28	29	30	26	32
Essential/Must Have	12	10	10	8	15	10	13	11	14	18	10	12
Chair rails												
Do not want	15	9	15	18	13	15	13	16	19	14	16	15
Indifferent	39	34	36	45	35	41	35	43	40	37	42	39
Desirable	32	42	32	27	37	33	39	27	28	30	33	32
Essential/Must Have	14	15	17	11	15	11	12	14	12	19	9	14
Built-in shelving												
Do not want	6	5	7	7	7	7	5	3	10	5	7	6
Indifferent	22	21	24	26	22	20	22	21	19	19	20	22
Desirable	53	48	52	51	50	58	52	55	50	53	51	53
Essential/Must Have	19	26	18	16	21	15	22	22	21	23	22	19
Built-in kitchen seating												
Do not want	18	17	19	20	16	21	15	15	20	15	14	19
Indifferent	29	28	25	29	24	33	32	32	28	26	28	29
Desirable	37	38	41	39	36	36	36	39	34	37	42	37
Essential/Must Have	16	18	14	12	25	11	17	14	17	22	16	15

Q38. How would the following various designs and features influence your purchase decision?
(Percent of respondents)

	Age of Household Head					Generation (year born)				Household Composition			
	Under 35 years old	35 to 44 years old	45 to 54 years old	55 to 64 years old	65 years old or older	Gen Z (1997 or later)	Millennials(1981-1996)	Gen X (1965-1980)	Boomers (1946-1964)	Married couple w children	Married couple no children	Single parent	One person
FLOORING FOR LIVING SPACES ON MAIN FLOOR													
Laminate													
Do not want	17	14	22	27	24	17	15	21	24	14	30	22	27
Indifferent	30	29	33	34	31	34	28	31	32	27	33	31	36
Desirable	36	39	33	32	35	35	39	35	34	40	30	32	31
Essential/Must Have	16	18	13	7	11	14	18	14	9	19	7	14	6
Tile													
Do not want	8	6	7	9	11	8	6	8	10	6	10	9	11
Indifferent	22	23	24	27	23	24	22	23	24	23	25	20	26
Desirable	45	47	50	50	48	45	47	50	49	48	49	53	50
Essential/Must Have	25	24	18	14	18	24	25	19	17	24	16	18	13
DECORATIVE AND OTHER FEATURES													
Ceiling crown molding													
Do not want	9	6	5	9	9	11	6	6	8	6	6	8	11
Indifferent	30	23	30	34	26	34	24	30	28	26	30	25	30
Desirable	40	47	47	45	51	34	46	44	50	47	47	45	49
Essential/Must Have	21	25	19	13	15	20	24	19	13	22	16	22	10
Tray ceiling													
Do not want	12	11	13	18	19	15	10	13	19	10	18	17	23
Indifferent	36	33	40	48	42	38	33	39	44	33	48	36	49
Desirable	35	37	36	27	29	30	38	35	28	38	28	34	23
Essential/Must Have	17	20	11	7	10	17	19	13	9	19	6	13	5
Chair rails													
Do not want	11	9	14	20	18	12	9	14	19	10	19	14	22
Indifferent	31	31	38	43	45	34	30	37	44	33	44	38	46
Desirable	39	37	35	29	27	37	38	34	27	35	29	34	27
Essential/Must Have	19	24	14	9	10	17	23	15	9	21	8	14	6
Built-in shelving													
Do not want	7	4	7	5	7	8	5	6	7	6	6	7	7
Indifferent	20	15	23	25	22	20	15	23	23	20	22	23	23
Desirable	48	51	51	54	56	48	52	51	55	51	56	48	58
Essential/Must Have	25	30	19	15	15	24	28	21	15	24	16	23	12
Built-in kitchen seating													
Do not want	10	8	13	22	26	10	9	13	25	10	25	17	26
Indifferent	25	21	27	35	31	29	20	26	34	24	34	26	37
Desirable	41	46	42	35	31	37	46	42	31	43	32	38	31
Essential/Must Have	24	25	18	8	11	24	25	19	10	23	9	19	6

Q38. *How would the following various designs and features influence your purchase decision?*
(Percent of respondents)

	Race/Ethnicity				Home Buyers' Income Bracket					Price Expected to Pay			
	Caucasian	African-American	Hispanic	Asian	Under $50,000	$50,000 to $74,999	$75,000 to $99,999	$100,000 to $149,999	$150,000 or more	Less than $150,000	$150,000 to $249,999	$250,000 to $499,999	$500,000 or more
FLOORING FOR LIVING SPACES ON MAIN FLOOR													
Laminate													
Do not want	24	23	9	19	24	19	22	20	22	18	18	22	27
Indifferent	34	26	18	28	34	40	35	29	22	33	36	33	22
Desirable	33	39	42	39	33	35	33	35	37	37	34	33	36
Essential/Must Have	9	13	31	13	9	7	9	16	18	12	12	12	15
Tile													
Do not want	10	8	4	7	11	7	11	7	7	12	10	6	9
Indifferent	25	24	19	21	25	27	25	26	18	26	27	24	18
Desirable	49	48	47	50	48	52	49	44	50	48	45	50	51
Essential/Must Have	17	19	29	21	16	15	15	22	25	14	19	20	22
DECORATIVE AND OTHER FEATURES													
Ceiling crown molding													
Do not want	9	5	6	4	13	4	9	7	4	12	9	5	6
Indifferent	29	24	23	29	31	32	25	28	24	31	30	29	22
Desirable	47	51	44	51	44	49	52	45	46	41	46	49	50
Essential/Must Have	15	20	27	16	12	14	14	20	25	16	15	17	22
Tray ceiling													
Do not want	18	17	5	8	22	17	16	13	8	20	16	14	11
Indifferent	44	37	27	35	44	50	44	38	32	41	44	41	37
Desirable	29	34	41	40	26	27	30	34	40	29	29	33	36
Essential/Must Have	9	13	27	17	8	6	10	14	20	10	11	12	15
Chair rails													
Do not want	17	13	6	13	21	16	13	13	11	17	17	14	14
Indifferent	42	33	28	33	40	49	43	40	28	39	45	39	35
Desirable	29	39	39	42	29	27	31	31	38	33	27	33	34
Essential/Must Have	12	15	26	12	9	8	14	16	22	10	11	15	18
Built-in shelving													
Do not want	6	5	6	11	7	4	8	4	7	7	5	5	8
Indifferent	22	17	21	20	20	28	21	26	15	21	25	22	16
Desirable	55	51	47	51	56	51	56	48	53	54	51	54	53
Essential/Must Have	17	27	27	18	16	17	15	22	25	18	19	18	23
Built-in kitchen seating													
Do not want	21	11	7	12	23	22	17	17	11	17	18	18	17
Indifferent	31	26	18	29	31	31	30	30	24	31	31	28	27
Desirable	35	46	43	42	34	38	40	34	42	37	36	38	38
Essential/Must Have	13	18	32	17	12	9	12	19	23	15	15	15	18

Q38. How would the following various designs and features influence your purchase decision?
(Percent of respondents)

	All Home Buyers	Geography (Nine Census Divisions)									Buyer Type	
		New England	Middle Atlantic	East North Central	West North Central	South Atlantic	East South Central	West South Central	Mountain	Pacific	First-time	Repeat
DECORATIVE AND OTHER FEATURES												
Exposed beams												
Do not want	17	13	20	18	15	20	18	14	13	12	17	16
Indifferent	32	28	34	35	27	35	26	34	31	30	37	32
Desirable	38	38	32	35	37	36	40	39	45	42	36	38
Essential/Must Have	13	21	14	12	21	8	16	14	11	17	10	14
Wood burning fireplace												
Do not want	20	12	19	22	19	25	14	19	21	21	11	22
Indifferent	21	21	19	24	18	23	23	18	21	16	22	20
Desirable	39	39	42	37	42	38	42	40	38	40	45	39
Essential/Must Have	20	29	21	17	22	15	22	23	20	22	21	20
Gas fireplace												
Do not want	18	12	15	17	10	24	18	19	17	17	20	18
Indifferent	24	22	25	29	17	26	25	25	21	22	31	24
Desirable	42	48	43	41	50	38	39	42	44	40	36	42
Essential/Must Have	16	17	16	14	23	12	18	14	18	21	13	17
Ceiling fan												
Do not want	4	5	7	4	6	3	4	2	3	5	4	4
Indifferent	14	21	15	14	14	11	17	11	16	18	17	14
Desirable	45	53	47	43	44	46	47	47	44	43	49	45
Essential/Must Have	36	22	31	40	36	40	33	41	37	34	30	37
KITCHEN FEATURES												
Glass front on at least one cabinet												
Do not want	22	19	18	25	21	27	22	19	25	14	18	22
Indifferent	29	28	31	31	24	27	33	31	27	26	31	28
Desirable	36	37	36	33	36	35	33	41	35	39	39	36
Essential/Must Have	13	16	15	11	19	10	12	8	14	21	12	13
Central island												
Do not want	7	4	5	10	7	8	8	7	5	5	7	7
Indifferent	19	22	20	20	16	17	20	15	19	26	24	19
Desirable	52	48	49	51	49	54	55	57	53	47	51	52
Essential/Must Have	22	26	26	20	28	21	17	21	23	22	18	23
Central island with range												
Do not want	16	19	18	18	15	16	15	14	20	12	11	17
Indifferent	28	30	25	28	26	29	26	29	27	29	27	28
Desirable	41	42	39	40	39	42	44	42	38	42	49	40
Essential/Must Have	15	9	18	14	20	13	15	15	15	18	14	15

Q38. How would the following various designs and features influence your purchase decision?
(Percent of respondents)

	Age of Household Head					Generation (year born)				Household Composition			
	Under 35 years old	35 to 44 years old	45 to 54 years old	55 to 64 years old	65 years old or older	Gen Z (1997 or later)	Millenni-als(1981-1996)	Gen X (1965-1980)	Boomers (1946-1964)	Married couple w children	Married couple no children	Single parent	One person
DECORATIVE AND OTHER FEATURES													
Exposed beams													
Do not want	13	9	12	17	23	15	10	13	21	11	20	14	23
Indifferent	28	28	30	38	34	31	27	29	35	27	36	35	36
Desirable	40	41	42	36	34	37	42	40	36	42	35	38	33
Essential/Must Have	19	22	16	10	8	17	21	17	8	20	9	13	8
Wood burning fireplace													
Do not want	10	7	14	23	33	12	7	14	30	13	33	16	25
Indifferent	20	18	19	22	22	23	17	21	21	20	19	19	24
Desirable	46	48	44	38	32	41	49	42	34	42	33	43	37
Essential/Must Have	24	28	23	17	14	24	27	23	15	25	15	22	14
Gas fireplace													
Do not want	14	11	14	22	22	17	12	14	22	10	22	21	26
Indifferent	27	22	26	26	23	29	22	26	23	22	23	28	28
Desirable	39	43	44	41	40	35	44	43	42	45	42	35	39
Essential/Must Have	20	24	16	10	15	19	23	17	12	22	13	15	8
Ceiling fan													
Do not want	6	4	3	5	4	6	5	3	4	3	4	5	6
Indifferent	17	14	15	12	14	20	14	13	14	16	11	13	16
Desirable	45	47	45	48	44	40	47	46	44	44	44	44	47
Essential/Must Have	32	36	37	35	38	33	34	37	38	37	41	38	30
KITCHEN FEATURES													
Glass front on at least one cabinet													
Do not want	13	12	20	27	27	16	12	19	27	14	29	21	28
Indifferent	25	25	30	31	30	25	24	29	30	25	34	24	31
Desirable	39	41	38	34	33	37	41	38	33	41	29	38	34
Essential/Must Have	22	22	13	8	10	23	23	13	10	19	8	17	7
Central island													
Do not want	9	5	6	6	9	10	6	6	8	5	8	7	9
Indifferent	22	17	16	22	20	26	17	18	21	18	20	19	24
Desirable	45	50	53	53	53	40	50	51	54	50	53	48	52
Essential/Must Have	25	28	25	20	18	24	28	25	18	27	20	26	14
Central island with range													
Do not want	9	8	13	21	21	12	8	13	21	12	21	12	21
Indifferent	23	23	22	32	32	29	22	24	33	24	33	25	32
Desirable	45	46	47	37	36	40	48	43	37	43	36	46	37
Essential/Must Have	22	23	18	10	11	19	23	20	9	21	10	17	10

Q38. How would the following various designs and features influence your purchase decision?
(Percent of respondents)

	Race/Ethnicity				Home Buyers' Income Bracket					Price Expected to Pay			
	Cauca-sian	African-American	Hispanic	Asian	Under $50,000	$50,000 to $74,999	$75,000 to $99,999	$100,000 to $149,999	$150,000 or more	Less than $150,000	$150,000 to $249,999	$250,000 to $499,999	$500,000 or more
DECORATIVE AND OTHER FEATURES													
Exposed beams													
Do not want	18	20	7	16	23	17	19	14	10	16	22	14	15
Indifferent	35	28	21	30	34	37	31	33	27	33	32	35	26
Desirable	36	39	48	36	34	38	38	37	42	37	37	37	41
Essential/Must Have	12	14	24	17	9	8	12	17	21	13	10	14	18
Wood burning fireplace													
Do not want	24	10	6	21	24	23	22	20	15	19	19	21	21
Indifferent	21	19	18	21	20	22	21	22	19	20	21	21	20
Desirable	38	46	45	39	41	40	38	36	41	42	45	36	38
Essential/Must Have	18	25	31	19	16	15	20	23	25	18	15	22	21
Gas fireplace													
Do not want	20	19	6	12	25	23	20	12	9	22	19	17	12
Indifferent	25	29	19	27	28	27	24	23	19	25	28	25	19
Desirable	42	35	45	45	35	41	40	44	49	37	41	41	50
Essential/Must Have	14	17	29	15	11	9	16	21	23	16	12	17	20
Ceiling fan													
Do not want	4	2	3	7	4	4	5	5	3	4	3	4	5
Indifferent	13	15	21	19	13	13	12	17	15	16	12	13	17
Desirable	45	49	43	50	49	47	45	38	46	49	47	43	45
Essential/Must Have	38	33	34	24	34	36	38	39	36	31	38	40	33
KITCHEN FEATURES													
Glass front on at least one cabinet													
Do not want	26	13	7	10	28	27	24	18	13	25	24	23	12
Indifferent	30	26	22	29	29	33	31	31	23	27	32	31	24
Desirable	33	43	46	42	34	31	34	35	44	36	32	34	45
Essential/Must Have	11	18	25	19	9	9	11	16	20	12	12	12	19
Central island													
Do not want	7	10	5	7	11	6	6	5	4	14	7	4	5
Indifferent	18	21	24	27	23	21	19	18	15	22	25	18	15
Desirable	54	47	42	50	49	58	53	49	50	47	49	55	51
Essential/Must Have	21	22	30	17	16	15	22	27	31	17	19	23	29
Central island with range													
Do not want	18	12	6	15	22	16	15	14	12	19	16	14	15
Indifferent	29	22	27	21	29	29	29	30	23	28	32	28	24
Desirable	39	48	45	48	37	44	44	39	42	40	37	42	43
Essential/Must Have	14	18	22	17	12	10	13	17	23	13	14	16	17

Q38. How would the following various designs and features influence your purchase decision?
(Percent of respondents)

	All Home Buyers	Geography (Nine Census Divisions)									Buyer Type	
		New England	Middle Atlantic	East North Central	West North Central	South Atlantic	East South Central	West South Central	Mountain	Pacific	First-time	Repeat
KITCHEN FEATURES												
Double island												
Do not want	20	24	17	26	16	20	17	18	21	15	16	20
Indifferent	34	36	37	33	34	34	35	33	27	33	32	34
Desirable	33	27	30	29	33	36	36	36	36	35	40	32
Essential/Must Have	14	13	15	13	17	10	13	14	15	17	12	14
Induction cooktop												
Do not want	13	15	19	20	6	11	12	9	13	10	13	13
Indifferent	33	24	32	35	29	36	41	40	30	25	32	33
Desirable	39	43	33	33	50	43	34	38	43	42	41	39
Essential/Must Have	14	18	16	11	16	9	13	13	14	23	14	14
Steam oven												
Do not want	23	26	25	28	16	26	24	18	22	14	16	24
Indifferent	35	30	31	39	33	37	32	36	36	37	34	35
Desirable	28	29	29	22	32	26	29	34	28	31	37	27
Essential/Must Have	14	15	15	11	18	11	15	12	14	19	12	14
Walk-in pantry												
Do not want	5	11	6	3	5	3	7	3	5	5	4	5
Indifferent	15	13	16	17	22	14	15	8	12	15	17	14
Desirable	51	50	51	51	47	54	52	53	54	49	53	51
Essential/Must Have	29	26	27	28	27	29	26	36	29	31	26	30
Butler's pantry												
Do not want	12	9	13	15	12	12	13	11	12	8	12	12
Indifferent	26	28	23	29	21	28	26	23	27	24	31	25
Desirable	44	46	45	43	40	47	40	49	41	44	39	45
Essential/Must Have	18	17	19	14	27	14	20	17	20	24	17	18
Double sink (side-by-side)												
Do not want	7	9	10	8	3	6	6	6	11	5	6	7
Indifferent	15	14	19	14	18	13	16	12	14	18	15	15
Desirable	46	48	46	45	46	48	46	48	37	42	44	46
Essential/Must Have	32	29	25	33	32	33	31	33	38	35	35	32
Recessed lighting												
Do not want	6	3	5	7	9	6	10	4	4	4	7	6
Indifferent	25	22	23	25	22	26	23	28	25	24	33	24
Desirable	49	49	50	48	47	52	47	51	52	47	44	50
Essential/Must Have	20	26	22	19	22	16	19	17	19	25	15	21

Q38. How would the following various designs and features influence your purchase decision?
(Percent of respondents)

	Age of Household Head					Generation (year born)				Household Composition			
	Under 35 years old	35 to 44 years old	45 to 54 years old	55 to 64 years old	65 years old or older	Gen Z (1997 or later)	Millenni-als(1981-1996)	Gen X (1965-1980)	Boomers (1946-1964)	Married couple w children	Married couple no children	Single parent	One person
KITCHEN FEATURES													
Double island													
Do not want	9	10	16	20	30	9	9	15	27	12	28	19	27
Indifferent	29	27	30	39	36	34	26	32	37	27	42	31	37
Desirable	41	40	39	33	24	37	43	38	27	41	24	35	26
Essential/Must Have	21	22	15	8	10	20	23	15	9	19	7	15	9
Induction cooktop													
Do not want	10	7	11	15	17	11	7	11	16	8	16	12	19
Indifferent	29	26	33	36	37	31	25	32	37	28	41	32	38
Desirable	41	43	42	40	35	37	45	41	38	44	35	40	34
Essential/Must Have	21	24	15	9	10	21	23	16	9	21	7	16	9
Steam oven													
Do not want	12	9	17	27	33	15	10	17	31	13	34	19	32
Indifferent	29	30	35	39	38	29	28	35	39	30	38	30	41
Desirable	38	38	31	28	19	37	39	30	22	35	21	37	21
Essential/Must Have	21	23	18	7	9	20	23	18	8	22	8	13	7
Walk-in pantry													
Do not want	7	4	3	5	5	8	4	4	5	4	4	5	5
Indifferent	15	15	12	13	17	18	14	13	16	14	14	15	16
Desirable	48	51	53	55	49	43	52	53	51	49	52	49	58
Essential/Must Have	30	31	32	27	28	30	29	31	28	32	30	31	21
Butler's pantry													
Do not want	10	6	9	13	16	15	7	9	15	10	11	13	17
Indifferent	27	24	27	26	25	29	24	26	25	22	29	27	26
Desirable	41	44	44	50	43	37	45	44	45	45	45	42	43
Essential/Must Have	22	26	21	12	16	18	24	21	15	23	15	19	13
Double sink (side-by-side)													
Do not want	8	4	7	8	7	10	5	7	8	5	9	7	8
Indifferent	17	14	17	13	15	22	14	16	15	17	15	13	13
Desirable	44	50	42	50	43	38	49	44	45	46	42	46	46
Essential/Must Have	31	32	34	29	35	30	32	33	32	32	34	33	32
Recessed lighting													
Do not want	9	6	5	5	6	11	6	5	6	5	5	7	7
Indifferent	26	22	23	25	26	28	22	24	26	20	25	29	29
Desirable	43	46	49	56	49	39	46	49	52	48	53	44	56
Essential/Must Have	22	27	23	14	18	21	26	22	17	27	17	20	8

Q38. How would the following various designs and features influence your purchase decision?
(Percent of respondents)

	Race/Ethnicity				Home Buyers' Income Bracket					Price Expected to Pay			
	Cauca-sian	African-American	Hispanic	Asian	Under $50,000	$50,000 to $74,999	$75,000 to $99,999	$100,000 to $149,999	$150,000 or more	Less than $150,000	$150,000 to $249,999	$250,000 to $499,999	$500,000 or more
KITCHEN FEATURES													
Double island													
Do not want	22	13	8	17	27	21	22	16	10	26	22	17	15
Indifferent	35	30	26	30	32	40	36	36	28	31	34	36	32
Desirable	31	39	40	42	31	30	29	32	43	30	30	35	37
Essential/Must Have	11	18	26	12	10	10	12	16	19	13	14	13	16
Induction cooktop													
Do not want	15	8	6	11	18	13	15	10	9	16	14	12	11
Indifferent	36	26	23	21	35	41	36	33	24	33	38	36	24
Desirable	37	47	47	51	36	36	36	43	45	37	37	39	45
Essential/Must Have	12	19	23	18	11	10	13	14	22	14	12	13	20
Steam oven													
Do not want	27	10	8	15	28	25	27	20	14	27	24	22	17
Indifferent	38	31	27	30	37	40	37	35	29	33	39	36	33
Desirable	25	42	38	39	25	30	28	27	33	27	26	28	33
Essential/Must Have	11	17	28	16	10	6	9	18	24	14	11	14	17
Walk-in pantry													
Do not want	4	6	6	6	7	2	3	5	4	7	5	3	4
Indifferent	13	13	21	22	16	14	16	15	13	17	17	13	13
Desirable	53	50	41	49	52	52	54	46	53	50	52	52	51
Essential/Must Have	29	31	31	23	24	32	28	34	31	25	26	31	32
Butler's pantry													
Do not want	12	12	6	14	15	16	11	9	7	16	14	10	8
Indifferent	27	25	21	24	26	31	26	28	19	23	31	24	25
Desirable	45	45	40	44	45	39	43	43	50	44	40	47	45
Essential/Must Have	16	18	33	18	13	15	19	20	24	16	15	18	22
Double sink (side-by-side)													
Do not want	8	3	3	10	6	6	10	6	7	8	4	7	8
Indifferent	14	12	22	18	15	15	14	15	17	15	16	14	16
Desirable	46	50	38	48	45	49	47	46	42	48	47	45	44
Essential/Must Have	32	35	38	25	34	31	29	33	34	29	33	34	32
Recessed lighting													
Do not want	5	8	5	9	9	5	5	4	5	8	7	5	3
Indifferent	26	23	23	18	29	29	26	24	17	30	27	25	17
Desirable	50	51	43	54	49	54	47	46	52	45	50	51	53
Essential/Must Have	19	18	28	18	13	13	23	26	26	17	17	20	27

Q38. How would the following various designs and features influence your purchase decision?
(Percent of respondents)

	All Home Buyers	Geography (Nine Census Divisions)									Buyer Type	
		New England	Middle Atlantic	East North Central	West North Central	South Atlantic	East South Central	West South Central	Mountain	Pacific	First-time	Repeat
KITCHEN FEATURES												
Instant hot water dispenser												
Do not want	11	12	11	13	8	12	7	11	11	10	8	11
Indifferent	29	29	29	34	30	28	32	33	25	25	31	29
Desirable	42	44	44	38	42	44	44	38	45	41	43	42
Essential/Must Have	18	15	16	15	20	16	16	17	19	24	18	18
Drinking water filtration												
Do not want	6	3	4	7	4	7	7	6	5	6	6	6
Indifferent	19	17	17	21	16	17	26	23	16	18	16	19
Desirable	49	50	51	50	48	50	45	50	49	45	51	49
Essential/Must Have	26	30	28	23	31	26	23	21	30	31	27	26
Trash compactor												
Do not want	19	20	17	26	19	20	19	17	20	15	11	21
Indifferent	29	27	27	28	25	31	34	31	32	26	31	29
Desirable	35	38	39	32	35	34	33	36	32	38	41	34
Essential/Must Have	16	16	17	13	20	15	14	16	16	22	17	16
Table space for eating												
Do not want	4	3	3	6	3	3	3	5	5	5	4	4
Indifferent	16	12	13	18	14	15	17	16	19	18	14	16
Desirable	51	51	50	50	58	57	50	45	48	50	52	51
Essential/Must Have	29	33	34	27	25	26	30	33	28	26	30	28
Breakfast bar												
Do not want	11	7	12	14	7	12	9	11	12	10	8	12
Indifferent	28	34	28	34	27	26	26	30	31	23	30	28
Desirable	44	39	41	38	44	49	51	46	42	44	46	44
Essential/Must Have	16	20	19	14	22	13	14	14	16	23	16	17
Warming drawer												
Do not want	19	16	20	22	15	20	17	18	18	14	14	19
Indifferent	35	37	32	39	30	36	36	38	30	33	42	34
Desirable	34	34	33	31	37	33	35	32	34	37	33	34
Essential/Must Have	13	14	15	9	18	10	12	13	17	16	11	13
Pull-out shelves												
Do not want	5	5	6	5	6	5	11	3	3	4	5	5
Indifferent	21	20	21	23	21	18	20	23	21	20	26	20
Desirable	52	54	52	51	53	56	47	51	52	50	48	53
Essential/Must Have	22	21	21	20	20	21	21	23	24	26	21	22

Q38. How would the following various designs and features influence your purchase decision?
(Percent of respondents)

	Age of Household Head					Generation (year born)				Household Composition			
	Under 35 years old	35 to 44 years old	45 to 54 years old	55 to 64 years old	65 years old or older	Gen Z (1997 or later)	Millenni-als(1981-1996)	Gen X (1965-1980)	Boomers (1946-1964)	Married couple w children	Married couple no children	Single parent	One person
KITCHEN FEATURES													
Instant hot water dispenser													
Do not want	8	6	9	13	15	10	6	9	15	8	13	9	15
Indifferent	25	20	29	32	34	27	21	28	32	25	32	31	32
Desirable	43	46	41	45	38	40	47	42	41	43	41	39	42
Essential/Must Have	24	27	21	10	14	22	26	22	12	24	13	20	10
Drinking water filtration													
Do not want	7	5	5	6	6	7	5	5	7	5	6	10	6
Indifferent	18	16	17	19	21	22	16	18	20	18	21	16	21
Desirable	45	46	48	55	48	40	46	47	51	46	50	48	52
Essential/Must Have	30	33	30	20	24	31	33	30	22	31	22	26	21
Trash compactor													
Do not want	10	9	14	23	28	12	9	14	27	13	26	17	30
Indifferent	27	26	30	32	29	29	25	31	30	24	36	28	30
Desirable	42	39	38	33	31	39	41	36	32	40	28	36	30
Essential/Must Have	22	26	19	11	12	21	26	20	11	23	10	19	9
Table space for eating													
Do not want	5	2	4	2	6	7	3	3	5	5	4	3	4
Indifferent	16	17	16	16	15	17	15	17	16	15	18	15	17
Desirable	44	47	48	57	54	41	47	48	55	48	51	53	54
Essential/Must Have	35	34	32	24	25	35	34	32	24	32	26	30	24
Breakfast bar													
Do not want	10	6	8	14	14	13	6	8	15	7	12	12	17
Indifferent	23	22	27	30	33	25	21	27	32	22	38	27	32
Desirable	42	46	45	46	42	38	46	46	43	47	41	42	42
Essential/Must Have	25	26	19	9	12	24	26	19	11	24	10	19	10
Warming drawer													
Do not want	13	11	15	22	23	15	11	15	24	12	22	17	28
Indifferent	29	25	35	38	39	32	25	34	39	29	40	38	38
Desirable	37	37	36	33	30	34	38	35	31	38	32	33	29
Essential/Must Have	21	27	14	6	8	19	25	15	6	21	6	11	5
Pull-out shelves													
Do not want	7	5	5	5	5	9	5	6	5	5	3	9	6
Indifferent	23	21	21	21	20	24	20	22	20	20	20	20	22
Desirable	46	48	50	55	55	43	49	50	55	51	56	48	54
Essential/Must Have	24	26	24	19	21	24	26	23	20	25	22	24	18

Q38. How would the following various designs and features influence your purchase decision?
(Percent of respondents)

	Race/Ethnicity				Home Buyers' Income Bracket					Price Expected to Pay			
	Cauca-sian	African-American	Hispanic	Asian	Under $50,000	$50,000 to $74,999	$75,000 to $99,999	$100,000 to $149,999	$150,000 or more	Less than $150,000	$150,000 to $249,999	$250,000 to $499,999	$500,000 or more
KITCHEN FEATURES													
Instant hot water dispenser													
Do not want	12	9	5	9	14	9	14	10	8	11	11	11	10
Indifferent	32	21	23	24	32	36	34	29	20	30	36	30	21
Desirable	40	51	43	46	40	45	36	41	46	42	37	43	45
Essential/Must Have	15	20	29	20	14	11	16	20	26	16	17	16	24
Drinking water filtration													
Do not want	6	7	3	9	8	4	5	6	5	9	3	5	6
Indifferent	19	15	19	21	20	21	20	18	17	20	23	17	17
Desirable	50	46	42	49	49	52	50	47	48	47	47	51	50
Essential/Must Have	25	32	36	21	23	23	25	29	31	24	27	27	27
Trash compactor													
Do not want	23	10	8	15	25	18	21	18	14	20	23	18	18
Indifferent	32	23	21	22	29	38	31	27	24	27	32	31	25
Desirable	33	42	42	44	32	34	34	35	41	37	33	34	39
Essential/Must Have	13	25	29	20	14	11	14	20	21	16	13	17	19
Table space for eating													
Do not want	4	3	5	8	6	4	3	2	4	4	5	3	4
Indifferent	16	13	18	18	17	17	17	14	15	19	19	15	12
Desirable	53	48	46	50	53	53	51	52	48	53	50	51	52
Essential/Must Have	28	36	31	23	24	25	29	31	34	24	26	30	32
Breakfast bar													
Do not want	12	8	5	10	16	12	9	9	7	15	11	10	9
Indifferent	30	22	23	29	29	32	29	29	23	29	27	30	25
Desirable	44	48	43	39	41	46	49	43	44	40	47	44	46
Essential/Must Have	14	22	29	22	14	10	13	18	25	16	14	16	21
Warming drawer													
Do not want	21	14	8	18	26	20	20	15	11	24	22	18	11
Indifferent	37	33	26	34	36	44	35	33	29	33	37	35	33
Desirable	32	38	40	34	30	29	35	35	39	32	31	34	38
Essential/Must Have	10	15	26	15	8	7	10	17	21	12	10	13	17
Pull-out shelves													
Do not want	5	7	5	4	7	5	5	4	4	9	3	4	4
Indifferent	21	19	21	16	24	25	20	18	16	23	25	21	13
Desirable	53	46	48	56	52	52	56	53	50	48	53	55	51
Essential/Must Have	21	27	26	24	17	18	19	24	31	20	18	20	31

Q38. How would the following various designs and features influence your purchase decision?
(Percent of respondents)

	All Home Buyers	Geography (Nine Census Divisions)									Buyer Type	
		New England	Middle Atlantic	East North Central	West North Central	South Atlantic	East South Central	West South Central	Mountain	Pacific	First-time	Repeat
KITCHEN FEATURES												
Wine cooler												
Do not want	31	29	30	39	27	33	29	31	26	23	26	31
Indifferent	27	28	20	30	24	28	26	26	28	27	32	26
Desirable	30	32	38	21	35	28	30	33	31	32	31	30
Essential/Must Have	12	11	12	10	14	11	14	10	15	17	11	13
Special use storage (wine rack, spice drawer, pots & pans cabinet)												
Do not want	10	6	12	13	9	11	9	10	7	11	8	11
Indifferent	23	24	25	26	22	23	27	25	21	19	26	23
Desirable	47	43	44	46	44	51	45	46	53	48	45	48
Essential/Must Have	19	28	20	15	24	16	18	19	19	23	20	19
Recycling center												
Do not want	14	10	12	18	11	13	17	17	13	9	13	14
Indifferent	32	33	29	34	28	35	33	33	33	26	34	31
Desirable	40	43	42	37	46	39	39	38	40	42	40	40
Essential/Must Have	15	14	17	11	15	13	11	11	15	24	13	15
Sensor-operated faucets												
Do not want	16	12	16	18	17	19	15	19	13	13	16	17
Indifferent	30	38	29	33	19	32	36	28	32	29	29	31
Desirable	39	32	38	39	46	38	36	41	38	38	38	39
Essential/Must Have	14	19	16	10	18	11	13	13	17	20	17	14
Desk/Computer area												
Do not want	15	15	14	16	11	15	15	16	17	13	12	15
Indifferent	25	22	20	26	22	25	26	26	30	24	24	25
Desirable	40	41	42	41	38	42	35	39	33	41	41	40
Essential/Must Have	21	21	24	17	29	17	25	20	20	22	23	21
Solid surface countertop (Corian etc.)												
Do not want	11	8	11	15	5	9	14	14	12	7	10	11
Indifferent	29	30	26	31	26	31	32	28	28	24	33	28
Desirable	45	48	48	41	52	45	42	44	40	46	42	45
Essential/Must Have	16	14	16	13	17	15	12	14	20	23	14	16
Ceramic tile countertop												
Do not want	25	25	25	29	20	28	24	24	29	20	13	27
Indifferent	28	29	27	29	26	30	30	26	26	26	34	27
Desirable	34	34	33	32	36	33	34	38	29	35	41	33
Essential/Must Have	13	12	15	10	18	10	12	12	16	19	11	14

Q38. How would the following various designs and features influence your purchase decision?
(Percent of respondents)

	Age of Household Head					Generation (year born)				Household Composition			
	Under 35 years old	35 to 44 years old	45 to 54 years old	55 to 64 years old	65 years old or older	Gen Z (1997 or later)	Millenni-als(1981-1996)	Gen X (1965-1980)	Boomers (1946-1964)	Married couple w children	Married couple no children	Single parent	One person
KITCHEN FEATURES													
Wine cooler													
Do not want	14	16	27	36	42	16	15	26	41	19	41	28	45
Indifferent	25	25	28	27	27	28	23	28	26	23	30	28	26
Desirable	36	38	31	33	22	31	39	31	27	39	23	29	23
Essential/Must Have	25	21	15	5	8	26	22	15	6	19	6	14	6
Special use storage (wine rack, spice drawer, pots & pans cabinet)													
Do not want	8	6	9	8	16	9	6	8	14	8	11	8	16
Indifferent	21	22	22	27	23	23	20	24	25	19	28	25	28
Desirable	46	43	48	50	47	41	46	47	48	49	48	43	44
Essential/Must Have	26	28	21	15	14	26	28	21	14	24	14	24	12
Recycling center													
Do not want	11	8	13	17	15	13	8	13	16	11	16	13	17
Indifferent	26	25	31	36	34	26	25	31	34	25	36	35	39
Desirable	42	42	41	37	39	37	44	41	39	44	38	35	35
Essential/Must Have	21	24	15	10	11	23	22	16	11	20	9	17	8
Sensor-operated faucets													
Do not want	13	9	12	19	22	16	9	13	21	11	21	12	24
Indifferent	26	25	30	32	34	29	24	29	33	23	40	29	36
Desirable	39	42	41	39	35	34	42	41	37	43	32	45	32
Essential/Must Have	22	25	16	10	9	21	25	17	9	23	7	13	8
Desk/Computer area													
Do not want	9	9	16	18	16	10	9	14	18	10	18	14	22
Indifferent	21	19	24	26	27	23	19	24	28	21	31	24	25
Desirable	43	43	36	40	39	43	43	38	39	42	37	38	37
Essential/Must Have	27	29	24	15	17	25	29	24	16	27	15	24	16
Solid surface countertop (Corian etc.)													
Do not want	10	5	11	12	12	11	6	10	12	8	13	12	12
Indifferent	27	26	27	34	28	31	25	28	30	25	35	28	29
Desirable	42	40	46	45	47	37	43	43	47	44	43	42	48
Essential/Must Have	22	28	16	10	13	21	26	18	12	24	9	17	12
Ceramic tile countertop													
Do not want	12	11	21	30	35	13	10	20	35	17	36	19	33
Indifferent	27	25	29	30	27	30	25	31	26	24	32	28	28
Desirable	41	42	36	33	27	37	43	35	30	39	24	37	33
Essential/Must Have	20	22	14	7	11	20	22	15	9	20	8	17	6

Q38. How would the following various designs and features influence your purchase decision?
(Percent of respondents)

	Race/Ethnicity				Home Buyers' Income Bracket					Price Expected to Pay			
	Cauca-sian	African-American	Hispanic	Asian	Under $50,000	$50,000 to $74,999	$75,000 to $99,999	$100,000 to $149,999	$150,000 or more	Less than $150,000	$150,000 to $249,999	$250,000 to $499,999	$500,000 or more
KITCHEN FEATURES													
Wine cooler													
Do not want	36	16	10	18	43	39	34	25	12	37	36	30	18
Indifferent	26	27	28	24	25	32	30	25	24	26	28	27	26
Desirable	27	38	41	36	24	23	29	32	43	27	27	29	41
Essential/Must Have	10	19	22	22	9	6	8	17	21	10	9	14	16
Special use storage (wine rack, spice drawer, pots & pans cabinet)													
Do not want	11	6	6	9	15	10	10	10	5	14	12	9	7
Indifferent	24	24	16	24	22	29	28	22	18	23	24	26	18
Desirable	47	42	48	50	48	45	43	46	53	45	47	47	50
Essential/Must Have	17	28	30	18	15	17	19	22	24	18	16	18	25
Recycling center													
Do not want	15	12	7	10	20	13	12	12	9	19	14	12	9
Indifferent	33	34	21	25	33	42	33	29	24	29	36	34	25
Desirable	39	37	47	47	35	37	43	40	47	38	36	40	49
Essential/Must Have	13	16	25	18	12	9	13	18	20	14	13	14	17
Sensor-operated faucets													
Do not want	19	10	7	14	22	15	19	12	13	19	19	16	12
Indifferent	34	22	16	26	32	39	31	35	19	29	35	32	26
Desirable	36	48	47	44	35	39	39	37	45	38	35	39	42
Essential/Must Have	11	21	29	16	11	7	12	16	24	15	11	14	19
Desk/Computer area													
Do not want	17	8	4	11	18	16	13	13	13	15	13	15	14
Indifferent	26	19	22	22	25	30	25	27	17	26	28	25	20
Desirable	38	45	44	46	43	37	42	38	38	41	44	38	39
Essential/Must Have	19	28	30	22	14	18	20	21	32	18	15	22	26
Solid surface countertop (Corian etc.)													
Do not want	11	10	5	11	13	8	9	9	12	10	12	9	13
Indifferent	28	32	26	28	31	34	31	28	20	31	28	30	23
Desirable	45	41	43	47	43	49	44	43	45	44	48	45	43
Essential/Must Have	15	17	25	14	12	10	16	20	23	15	12	16	21
Ceramic tile countertop													
Do not want	30	14	7	15	26	26	23	26	24	20	22	27	30
Indifferent	29	27	21	26	31	30	33	26	20	30	30	27	22
Desirable	31	39	43	39	33	37	34	33	33	36	36	33	31
Essential/Must Have	10	20	28	21	10	8	10	15	23	15	12	12	17

Q38. How would the following various designs and features influence your purchase decision?
(Percent of respondents)

	All Home Buyers	Geography (Nine Census Divisions)									Buyer Type	
		New England	Middle Atlantic	East North Central	West North Central	South Atlantic	East South Central	West South Central	Mountain	Pacific	First-time	Repeat
KITCHEN FEATURES												
Granite/Natural stone countertop												
Do not want	7	5	9	10	11	5	9	6	10	5	7	7
Indifferent	19	19	19	19	19	19	22	18	19	20	21	19
Desirable	51	51	49	51	48	52	48	54	54	51	52	51
Essential/Must Have	22	25	23	19	22	24	21	21	17	24	19	22
Laminate countertop												
Do not want	32	29	30	34	23	37	29	35	34	26	21	33
Indifferent	29	25	28	30	21	31	32	31	27	27	37	28
Desirable	27	32	31	25	34	25	26	24	24	29	30	27
Essential/Must Have	13	14	12	10	22	8	13	10	16	18	12	13
Quartz/Engineered stone countertop												
Do not want	9	11	13	14	9	7	10	8	6	6	9	9
Indifferent	24	20	22	21	26	27	29	24	16	24	34	22
Desirable	49	49	49	48	44	49	43	52	58	48	43	50
Essential/Must Have	18	21	17	17	21	16	18	17	21	22	15	19
Customized backsplash												
Do not want	6	6	7	7	4	7	7	5	6	5	8	6
Indifferent	26	24	28	28	27	26	26	24	27	21	31	25
Desirable	48	49	44	44	50	47	49	55	45	51	44	48
Essential/Must Have	20	21	20	21	19	20	19	17	22	23	17	21
BATH FEATURES												
Both shower stall & tub in primary bath												
Do not want	6	4	6	7	3	7	10	4	5	5	4	6
Indifferent	16	10	17	18	20	14	15	14	12	22	17	16
Desirable	48	55	48	48	46	48	47	50	55	43	48	48
Essential/Must Have	30	31	30	27	31	31	28	33	28	31	31	30
Only a shower stall in primary bath												
Do not want	23	30	21	24	12	26	27	26	21	19	24	23
Indifferent	31	26	29	36	24	30	29	36	33	30	33	31
Desirable	28	26	31	26	43	25	31	21	27	30	26	28
Essential/Must Have	18	18	20	14	20	19	13	16	19	20	16	18
Whirlpool tub in primary bath												
Do not want	19	20	20	23	16	21	13	18	19	14	10	20
Indifferent	22	25	22	25	19	21	21	18	21	25	22	22
Desirable	41	37	38	38	42	43	46	44	40	41	51	40
Essential/Must Have	18	19	19	14	24	15	20	21	20	20	18	18

Q38. How would the following various designs and features influence your purchase decision?
(Percent of respondents)

	Age of Household Head					Generation (year born)				Household Composition			
	Under 35 years old	35 to 44 years old	45 to 54 years old	55 to 64 years old	65 years old or older	Gen Z (1997 or later)	Millenni-als(1981-1996)	Gen X (1965-1980)	Boomers (1946-1964)	Married couple w children	Married couple no children	Single parent	One person
KITCHEN FEATURES													
Granite/Natural stone countertop													
Do not want	8	4	4	8	11	10	4	5	9	6	10	7	10
Indifferent	20	20	18	20	19	24	20	18	19	17	19	23	20
Desirable	48	50	52	55	50	44	49	53	52	52	48	44	56
Essential/Must Have	25	26	26	17	20	23	27	24	19	25	23	27	14
Laminate countertop													
Do not want	15	17	30	41	39	14	16	29	40	21	47	28	40
Indifferent	30	26	29	30	28	33	26	30	29	27	29	28	32
Desirable	35	36	28	22	23	33	37	27	23	33	18	29	23
Essential/Must Have	20	21	13	7	10	20	20	14	8	20	6	15	5
Quartz/Engineered stone countertop													
Do not want	10	6	7	9	11	12	6	8	10	7	10	11	11
Indifferent	27	23	23	26	21	28	23	24	22	20	24	25	27
Desirable	42	46	49	51	51	38	46	48	52	49	51	41	50
Essential/Must Have	22	25	20	14	16	22	24	20	15	23	14	23	12
Customized backsplash													
Do not want	9	6	5	5	6	11	6	5	6	5	4	8	7
Indifferent	26	22	25	27	28	30	22	23	28	22	29	24	30
Desirable	43	48	48	52	47	39	47	50	48	48	49	46	49
Essential/Must Have	22	25	23	16	19	20	24	22	18	25	18	22	14
BATH FEATURES													
Both shower stall & tub in primary bath													
Do not want	6	3	6	6	7	7	3	6	7	6	6	3	7
Indifferent	16	16	16	15	17	20	15	15	17	16	16	19	15
Desirable	46	49	46	51	47	42	49	48	48	47	49	45	53
Essential/Must Have	32	32	32	28	29	32	33	31	28	32	29	33	25
Only a shower stall in primary bath													
Do not want	15	16	24	29	25	15	16	23	26	17	26	20	30
Indifferent	29	29	34	32	30	34	27	34	31	27	34	32	34
Desirable	34	35	26	25	26	31	36	26	26	34	24	30	22
Essential/Must Have	22	20	17	14	19	21	21	17	17	22	17	18	13
Whirlpool tub in primary bath													
Do not want	9	7	12	23	29	13	7	13	27	12	26	13	31
Indifferent	21	20	18	22	25	22	19	20	24	22	27	18	18
Desirable	45	46	46	42	34	42	47	45	37	43	35	46	40
Essential/Must Have	24	27	24	13	12	23	27	22	12	24	12	24	11

Q38. How would the following various designs and features influence your purchase decision?
(Percent of respondents)

	Race/Ethnicity				Home Buyers' Income Bracket					Price Expected to Pay			
	Cauca-sian	African-American	Hispanic	Asian	Under $50,000	$50,000 to $74,999	$75,000 to $99,999	$100,000 to $149,999	$150,000 or more	Less than $150,000	$150,000 to $249,999	$250,000 to $499,999	$500,000 or more
KITCHEN FEATURES													
Granite/Natural stone countertop													
Do not want	8	7	5	6	11	7	7	7	4	10	9	6	5
Indifferent	19	24	19	19	23	22	19	19	14	25	22	18	13
Desirable	52	41	50	56	50	56	49	49	52	47	50	53	55
Essential/Must Have	21	28	26	19	17	15	24	25	30	18	19	23	27
Laminate countertop													
Do not want	37	20	9	23	29	35	35	33	30	24	27	36	37
Indifferent	31	23	23	23	34	36	32	25	17	32	34	28	21
Desirable	23	38	38	39	27	24	22	26	33	32	28	24	28
Essential/Must Have	9	19	29	15	9	6	11	16	20	12	10	13	15
Quartz/Engineered stone countertop													
Do not want	9	8	6	14	14	8	9	6	7	11	11	7	7
Indifferent	24	25	19	23	25	31	25	23	16	26	27	22	19
Desirable	50	45	49	43	47	51	52	47	50	46	48	52	51
Essential/Must Have	17	22	26	21	14	10	14	24	28	17	14	19	23
Customized backsplash													
Do not want	6	10	5	7	10	3	6	5	3	11	9	3	4
Indifferent	27	23	21	26	28	34	27	25	18	28	26	27	20
Desirable	49	44	46	46	47	44	49	46	53	46	45	47	54
Essential/Must Have	19	23	28	21	14	19	19	24	26	15	20	23	22
BATH FEATURES													
Both shower stall & tub in primary bath													
Do not want	6	3	4	5	7	5	6	6	5	6	6	5	7
Indifferent	16	14	19	19	17	15	19	15	15	19	19	14	15
Desirable	48	49	44	51	50	49	47	47	45	48	49	49	44
Essential/Must Have	30	34	32	25	26	30	28	32	35	27	26	31	35
Only a shower stall in primary bath													
Do not want	26	21	8	17	28	28	26	17	16	28	21	22	22
Indifferent	33	23	26	29	32	34	32	33	25	30	36	31	26
Desirable	25	32	39	36	25	26	26	30	34	27	28	29	28
Essential/Must Have	16	23	27	18	15	13	16	20	24	15	15	18	24
Whirlpool tub in primary bath													
Do not want	22	11	7	11	23	20	16	18	15	17	20	18	21
Indifferent	22	16	22	24	19	27	25	20	21	19	23	23	19
Desirable	40	47	43	45	42	41	44	41	39	44	40	42	38
Essential/Must Have	16	26	28	19	15	13	15	21	25	19	17	17	22

Q38. How would the following various designs and features influence your purchase decision?
(Percent of respondents)

	All Home Buyers	Geography (Nine Census Divisions)									Buyer Type	
		New England	Middle Atlantic	East North Central	West North Central	South Atlantic	East South Central	West South Central	Mountain	Pacific	First-time	Repeat
BATH FEATURES												
Private toilet compartment in primary bath												
Do not want	8	7	9	13	8	8	9	4	5	5	6	8
Indifferent	23	28	26	25	27	20	21	15	24	25	24	23
Desirable	46	43	44	41	44	51	46	53	49	39	47	46
Essential/Must Have	24	22	21	20	21	22	23	28	22	32	23	24
Multiple shower heads in prim. bath												
Do not want	10	11	8	13	7	10	13	6	9	10	9	10
Indifferent	27	30	28	27	31	27	26	24	28	25	26	27
Desirable	45	45	45	42	44	43	47	52	45	45	48	45
Essential/Must Have	18	14	19	18	19	19	15	18	18	20	18	18
Body spray panel (shower head(s) plus spray massage jets)												
Do not want	12	18	12	14	10	14	12	8	10	10	9	12
Indifferent	28	27	25	32	27	26	26	30	26	29	28	28
Desirable	44	41	44	41	48	43	43	46	48	42	45	43
Essential/Must Have	16	14	18	13	15	17	19	17	16	19	18	16
Skylight in primary bath												
Do not want	22	21	21	26	19	25	23	21	18	15	14	23
Indifferent	27	27	27	30	16	29	30	28	24	27	28	27
Desirable	36	38	36	32	42	34	32	35	39	41	42	35
Essential/Must Have	15	13	16	12	23	13	15	16	18	17	16	15
Linen closet in primary bath												
Do not want	5	5	5	4	4	5	5	2	5	8	6	5
Indifferent	19	17	20	24	19	16	18	16	20	22	22	19
Desirable	51	46	48	48	52	55	53	53	56	48	49	52
Essential/Must Have	25	31	27	24	24	24	24	28	19	22	23	25
Dual toilets in primary bath												
Do not want	33	36	31	41	27	37	32	29	35	26	25	34
Indifferent	29	27	28	29	25	28	32	31	27	29	34	28
Desirable	25	24	26	22	30	24	26	27	21	27	28	25
Essential/Must Have	13	14	15	9	19	10	10	12	16	18	13	13
Double vanity in primary bath												
Do not want	11	12	14	13	9	10	10	10	10	10	13	11
Indifferent	22	15	25	23	27	19	25	23	20	20	29	21
Desirable	43	50	40	42	41	44	45	40	42	44	41	43
Essential/Must Have	24	23	21	22	22	26	20	28	28	25	17	25

Q38. How would the following various designs and features influence your purchase decision?
(Percent of respondents)

	Age of Household Head					Generation (year born)				Household Composition			
	Under 35 years old	35 to 44 years old	45 to 54 years old	55 to 64 years old	65 years old or older	Gen Z (1997 or later)	Millenni-als(1981-1996)	Gen X (1965-1980)	Boomers (1946-1964)	Married couple w children	Married couple no children	Single parent	One person
BATH FEATURES													
Private toilet compartment in primary bath													
Do not want	7	6	7	8	9	8	6	7	9	6	8	10	10
Indifferent	23	18	20	24	26	26	18	20	25	19	24	21	28
Desirable	44	47	47	48	44	39	47	47	46	46	47	46	45
Essential/Must Have	26	30	26	20	21	26	29	26	21	29	21	23	16
Multiple shower heads in prim. bath													
Do not want	9	6	8	10	13	12	6	8	12	6	12	9	15
Indifferent	20	20	22	29	34	22	20	22	32	22	31	26	32
Desirable	44	49	47	46	41	41	47	48	43	49	44	41	41
Essential/Must Have	27	24	22	15	12	25	26	22	13	23	13	24	11
Body spray panel (shower head(s) plus spray massage jets)													
Do not want	8	6	9	14	17	9	6	8	17	8	13	13	19
Indifferent	24	24	26	29	32	27	23	27	30	25	32	25	27
Desirable	45	46	46	44	40	40	48	46	41	45	45	40	43
Essential/Must Have	23	24	19	13	11	24	24	19	12	22	10	22	11
Skylight in primary bath													
Do not want	10	9	16	28	31	11	10	16	30	14	27	17	34
Indifferent	24	25	27	28	28	30	23	26	30	24	31	28	26
Desirable	42	42	39	34	30	35	45	40	31	39	33	40	32
Essential/Must Have	23	23	18	10	11	25	23	18	10	22	10	15	8
Linen closet in primary bath													
Do not want	7	4	5	4	5	8	4	5	6	4	4	4	8
Indifferent	21	21	18	18	20	24	20	19	18	20	17	20	19
Desirable	44	47	50	57	52	40	48	50	55	48	55	50	54
Essential/Must Have	28	29	27	21	23	28	28	27	22	28	24	26	19
Dual toilets in primary bath													
Do not want	15	15	28	44	44	17	14	28	45	19	46	31	50
Indifferent	24	27	30	27	31	26	25	29	29	27	33	25	27
Desirable	37	33	29	22	18	33	37	29	18	35	15	27	16
Essential/Must Have	24	25	12	7	8	24	25	13	8	19	6	17	7
Double vanity in primary bath													
Do not want	9	6	8	14	14	10	6	9	14	7	10	11	23
Indifferent	22	22	20	20	23	26	21	20	22	18	21	21	25
Desirable	43	43	45	47	38	39	45	45	41	46	40	46	38
Essential/Must Have	27	29	27	19	24	26	28	25	23	29	28	21	15

Q38. How would the following various designs and features influence your purchase decision?
(Percent of respondents)

	Race/Ethnicity				Home Buyers' Income Bracket					Price Expected to Pay			
	Cauca-sian	African-American	Hispanic	Asian	Under $50,000	$50,000 to $74,999	$75,000 to $99,999	$100,000 to $149,999	$150,000 or more	Less than $150,000	$150,000 to $249,999	$250,000 to $499,999	$500,000 or more
BATH FEATURES													
Private toilet compartment in primary bath													
Do not want	9	3	5	7	12	7	8	6	5	10	9	6	6
Indifferent	24	18	20	22	25	31	27	19	15	28	24	23	17
Desirable	45	47	48	48	47	44	45	46	46	44	50	46	44
Essential/Must Have	22	32	27	23	16	18	21	28	34	18	18	26	32
Multiple shower heads in prim. bath													
Do not want	11	8	4	9	15	9	9	8	6	12	10	9	8
Indifferent	28	18	24	28	30	31	31	26	18	29	30	27	21
Desirable	44	51	46	44	41	46	43	44	52	42	43	47	48
Essential/Must Have	17	23	25	20	14	14	18	22	23	18	17	17	22
Body spray panel (shower head(s) plus spray massage jets)													
Do not want	14	7	5	10	17	11	11	10	8	14	12	11	10
Indifferent	29	26	24	22	27	33	31	30	22	26	31	29	25
Desirable	43	44	49	46	43	42	44	43	46	45	44	44	43
Essential/Must Have	14	23	22	22	13	14	13	18	24	15	13	16	22
Skylight in primary bath													
Do not want	25	13	7	15	27	25	20	18	16	24	22	21	18
Indifferent	28	28	22	23	26	34	27	30	22	26	29	28	24
Desirable	34	41	43	43	35	31	40	35	39	36	35	35	40
Essential/Must Have	13	18	28	19	12	10	14	17	23	15	14	15	19
Linen closet in primary bath													
Do not want	5	6	5	7	8	2	4	4	4	7	5	3	4
Indifferent	19	17	23	21	19	18	21	23	16	21	20	19	16
Desirable	52	53	45	53	54	56	52	45	50	50	54	51	52
Essential/Must Have	25	25	27	19	19	24	23	28	30	22	21	26	28
Dual toilets in primary bath													
Do not want	40	18	8	16	40	43	34	32	19	33	35	35	27
Indifferent	29	27	28	32	30	30	29	27	27	28	32	27	29
Desirable	21	36	40	34	21	20	24	26	34	27	23	24	28
Essential/Must Have	10	19	25	17	10	7	13	15	20	12	10	13	17
Double vanity in primary bath													
Do not want	12	9	6	12	17	12	9	6	8	15	14	9	7
Indifferent	22	18	23	23	26	24	25	19	16	27	24	20	17
Desirable	43	44	43	41	42	45	43	44	42	41	43	44	44
Essential/Must Have	23	29	28	24	15	19	23	31	34	17	19	27	33

Q38. How would the following various designs and features influence your purchase decision?
(Percent of respondents)

	All Home Buyers	Geography (Nine Census Divisions)									Buyer Type	
		New England	Middle Atlantic	East North Central	West North Central	South Atlantic	East South Central	West South Central	Mountain	Pacific	First-time	Repeat
BATH FEATURES												
Granite vanity												
Do not want	10	13	12	14	11	7	13	7	10	8	9	10
Indifferent	26	22	25	32	23	25	26	25	29	22	30	25
Desirable	48	51	47	43	50	51	45	48	43	51	48	48
Essential/Must Have	16	14	17	11	16	17	16	20	18	18	14	17
Cultured marble vanity												
Do not want	12	18	13	13	13	12	17	10	12	9	12	12
Indifferent	30	25	27	35	29	29	30	31	37	27	32	30
Desirable	43	43	45	41	40	47	40	46	35	46	43	43
Essential/Must Have	14	15	16	12	18	12	13	13	16	18	14	14
Dressing/make-up area												
Do not want	14	15	15	22	11	13	13	13	14	12	12	15
Indifferent	28	30	34	29	26	30	26	25	27	24	25	29
Desirable	40	39	36	36	47	40	49	44	40	40	44	40
Essential/Must Have	17	16	15	13	16	17	12	18	19	24	19	17
His & Her baths												
Do not want	24	29	27	27	18	27	20	18	26	20	15	25
Indifferent	29	25	29	36	25	28	28	29	26	26	29	29
Desirable	32	31	27	23	37	34	34	37	32	35	39	31
Essential/Must Have	16	16	17	14	19	12	17	16	15	19	17	15
Toilet, tub and sink - white												
Do not want	6	3	4	8	4	8	10	8	4	5	7	6
Indifferent	26	27	27	33	20	29	23	21	26	24	25	26
Desirable	43	48	46	38	45	39	42	51	46	45	42	44
Essential/Must Have	24	23	24	21	31	25	25	20	24	26	26	24
Toilet, tub and sink - color												
Do not want	13	13	12	13	19	14	11	17	11	8	8	14
Indifferent	29	29	27	31	23	29	30	29	33	27	29	29
Desirable	39	38	44	38	40	41	38	32	40	38	42	39
Essential/Must Have	19	20	18	18	18	16	20	22	16	26	22	19
Ceramic tile walls												
Do not want	10	9	7	13	8	10	9	7	11	12	10	10
Indifferent	25	26	25	29	20	26	25	25	24	22	31	24
Desirable	48	54	49	47	52	47	48	53	43	46	45	49
Essential/Must Have	17	11	20	11	20	17	18	15	23	19	14	17

Q38. How would the following various designs and features influence your purchase decision?
(Percent of respondents)

	Age of Household Head					Generation (year born)				Household Composition			
	Under 35 years old	35 to 44 years old	45 to 54 years old	55 to 64 years old	65 years old or older	Gen Z (1997 or later)	Millenni-als(1981-1996)	Gen X (1965-1980)	Boomers (1946-1964)	Married couple w children	Married couple no children	Single parent	One person
BATH FEATURES													
Granite vanity													
Do not want	8	6	6	13	14	8	6	7	14	7	14	13	11
Indifferent	25	21	25	27	28	30	21	24	27	23	25	23	31
Desirable	44	48	52	49	46	40	47	51	47	50	47	45	47
Essential/Must Have	22	26	17	12	12	21	26	17	12	20	14	19	10
Cultured marble vanity													
Do not want	8	5	9	14	18	10	5	10	17	8	16	11	18
Indifferent	24	28	29	34	32	24	26	30	32	23	36	30	36
Desirable	45	43	47	43	41	41	45	45	42	48	40	42	39
Essential/Must Have	23	24	15	9	10	25	24	16	9	20	9	17	8
Dressing/make-up area													
Do not want	8	8	13	18	18	8	7	12	19	9	17	15	22
Indifferent	22	22	25	35	31	24	21	25	34	23	33	27	31
Desirable	44	46	43	36	39	41	46	44	37	45	38	39	37
Essential/Must Have	26	25	19	11	12	27	25	19	11	23	11	19	10
His & Her baths													
Do not want	11	8	19	31	33	12	8	19	33	15	29	21	41
Indifferent	23	23	26	32	33	25	22	26	33	25	34	25	31
Desirable	40	42	36	28	25	37	43	35	26	37	29	34	21
Essential/Must Have	26	26	19	9	9	26	27	19	8	24	8	20	7
Toilet, tub and sink - white													
Do not want	6	4	6	7	7	8	5	6	7	5	7	7	10
Indifferent	21	19	25	31	29	21	20	26	29	23	34	25	27
Desirable	42	43	47	44	41	40	43	46	42	45	38	40	44
Essential/Must Have	32	34	21	18	22	31	33	22	22	27	21	28	19
Toilet, tub and sink - color													
Do not want	9	6	12	13	18	11	6	12	17	11	15	8	21
Indifferent	23	22	28	34	31	24	22	28	32	26	33	25	31
Desirable	43	41	38	41	36	38	44	39	38	39	38	41	36
Essential/Must Have	25	30	22	12	16	28	28	21	14	24	14	25	12
Ceramic tile walls													
Do not want	9	7	9	12	11	10	7	8	12	8	12	9	12
Indifferent	24	24	28	27	23	26	23	27	24	20	25	29	32
Desirable	42	44	48	50	51	39	46	47	50	49	52	43	44
Essential/Must Have	24	25	15	11	15	24	25	17	14	22	12	19	11

Q38. How would the following various designs and features influence your purchase decision?
(Percent of respondents)

	Race/Ethnicity				Home Buyers' Income Bracket					Price Expected to Pay			
	Cauca-sian	African-American	Hispanic	Asian	Under $50,000	$50,000 to $74,999	$75,000 to $99,999	$100,000 to $149,999	$150,000 or more	Less than $150,000	$150,000 to $249,999	$250,000 to $499,999	$500,000 or more
BATH FEATURES													
Granite vanity													
Do not want	11	8	8	10	13	9	13	8	7	12	12	8	9
Indifferent	27	21	22	25	30	27	27	26	18	30	29	26	18
Desirable	47	54	49	50	45	51	46	45	52	44	47	49	52
Essential/Must Have	15	18	21	15	11	12	14	20	24	15	13	17	21
Cultured marble vanity													
Do not want	14	8	6	8	17	13	10	10	9	13	16	11	11
Indifferent	32	30	23	25	32	36	33	29	22	34	30	31	24
Desirable	43	44	42	51	40	42	43	45	47	39	42	45	47
Essential/Must Have	12	18	29	16	10	9	14	16	21	14	12	14	18
Dressing/make-up area													
Do not want	17	9	5	9	21	14	11	13	10	18	16	12	12
Indifferent	30	24	23	19	30	34	30	26	22	29	30	30	24
Desirable	39	44	44	49	35	40	43	43	43	36	40	41	43
Essential/Must Have	14	23	29	23	13	12	16	18	25	16	13	17	22
His & Her baths													
Do not want	28	9	9	14	32	27	20	21	16	24	27	22	22
Indifferent	30	22	24	29	28	38	29	27	25	28	31	30	25
Desirable	29	45	39	40	29	28	36	32	36	31	32	32	34
Essential/Must Have	13	23	27	18	11	8	15	20	23	17	10	16	19
Toilet, tub and sink - white													
Do not want	7	6	4	8	7	7	7	5	5	8	6	5	6
Indifferent	29	17	19	24	27	30	29	28	20	28	25	27	23
Desirable	43	47	44	50	45	43	43	41	44	43	44	44	44
Essential/Must Have	22	30	33	18	21	20	20	26	31	22	25	23	27
Toilet, tub and sink - color													
Do not want	15	8	6	10	13	11	15	12	14	11	14	12	15
Indifferent	31	22	21	27	32	36	27	29	21	30	32	30	22
Desirable	38	43	40	43	38	39	40	38	40	42	36	38	41
Essential/Must Have	16	27	33	20	17	14	18	22	25	17	18	20	22
Ceramic tile walls													
Do not want	11	9	5	9	12	9	10	10	8	10	13	9	9
Indifferent	26	26	16	27	27	28	32	23	19	28	26	24	22
Desirable	48	46	51	49	47	54	42	47	50	46	48	49	49
Essential/Must Have	15	19	28	15	14	10	16	20	23	16	13	18	20

Q38. How would the following various designs and features influence your purchase decision?
(Percent of respondents)

	All Home Buyers	Geography (Nine Census Divisions)									Buyer Type	
		New England	Middle Atlantic	East North Central	West North Central	South Atlantic	East South Central	West South Central	Mountain	Pacific	First-time	Repeat
BATH FEATURES												
Bidet												
Do not want	27	30	26	33	20	31	25	28	23	22	23	28
Indifferent	29	27	29	30	27	28	32	32	30	29	36	28
Desirable	30	26	30	26	37	31	30	27	34	33	30	30
Essential/Must Have	13	18	14	11	16	10	14	13	14	16	11	13
SPECIALTY ROOMS OR FEATURES												
Delivery vestibule												
Do not want	25	27	22	30	22	28	28	22	23	19	22	25
Indifferent	36	35	31	36	35	36	35	45	37	33	36	36
Desirable	28	25	33	25	33	26	27	23	27	31	31	27
Essential/Must Have	12	13	15	9	10	10	10	10	13	17	11	12
Great room (kitchen/family room/living room combined)												
Do not want	9	13	8	9	11	8	11	9	7	7	7	9
Indifferent	20	23	23	19	20	22	21	17	17	18	24	20
Desirable	47	41	43	49	48	48	39	46	53	47	44	47
Essential/Must Have	25	24	26	22	21	22	29	28	22	28	25	25
Laundry room												
Do not want	4	4	3	5	4	2	6	2	3	6	3	4
Indifferent	11	10	11	10	16	9	10	7	15	12	12	10
Desirable	46	50	48	45	44	46	41	48	43	48	47	46
Essential/Must Have	40	36	37	40	36	44	43	43	39	35	38	40
Dining room												
Do not want	8	11	7	12	7	7	11	6	9	5	6	9
Indifferent	23	17	20	26	26	22	20	23	27	22	18	23
Desirable	45	48	46	41	43	48	44	47	42	43	51	44
Essential/Must Have	24	23	27	21	23	23	25	24	21	30	25	24
Separate living room												
Do not want	13	13	12	14	11	15	15	13	13	9	8	14
Indifferent	28	29	27	32	27	28	21	30	32	25	25	29
Desirable	40	37	41	37	46	39	41	42	34	42	46	39
Essential/Must Have	19	21	20	16	17	18	23	15	21	23	22	18
Separate family room												
Do not want	10	8	9	12	7	11	11	11	9	10	9	11
Indifferent	29	36	30	33	27	29	19	34	31	24	27	30
Desirable	42	36	43	38	48	41	48	40	41	42	44	41
Essential/Must Have	19	20	17	18	18	18	22	14	20	23	20	19

Q38. How would the following various designs and features influence your purchase decision?
(Percent of respondents)

	Age of Household Head					Generation (year born)				Household Composition			
	Under 35 years old	35 to 44 years old	45 to 54 years old	55 to 64 years old	65 years old or older	Gen Z (1997 or later)	Millennials(1981-1996)	Gen X (1965-1980)	Boomers (1946-1964)	Married couple w children	Married couple no children	Single parent	One person
BATH FEATURES													
Bidet													
Do not want	14	15	24	35	35	13	15	24	36	19	34	24	39
Indifferent	26	28	31	30	29	29	26	30	29	26	34	30	29
Desirable	39	35	30	28	26	37	37	31	27	36	26	32	25
Essential/Must Have	21	22	15	7	10	21	23	15	8	20	7	14	7
SPECIALTY ROOMS OR FEATURES													
Delivery vestibule													
Do not want	14	14	23	31	31	17	13	22	32	17	32	23	35
Indifferent	31	30	37	39	37	34	29	37	37	31	41	32	37
Desirable	35	34	29	24	24	29	36	29	24	33	22	33	23
Essential/Must Have	20	22	11	7	8	20	22	12	8	19	5	12	5
Great room (kitchen/family room/living room combined)													
Do not want	8	5	7	8	12	9	5	7	10	7	9	10	12
Indifferent	20	17	16	21	23	22	17	19	22	16	22	15	26
Desirable	42	48	52	48	44	38	48	48	46	49	46	42	42
Essential/Must Have	30	29	25	23	21	31	29	26	22	28	23	33	19
Laundry room													
Do not want	7	3	3	2	4	10	4	3	3	5	2	4	4
Indifferent	14	13	10	8	10	19	12	11	9	13	9	12	8
Desirable	43	46	44	50	45	39	46	46	46	44	46	45	46
Essential/Must Have	35	38	42	40	40	32	38	40	41	39	43	40	42
Dining room													
Do not want	6	5	7	9	11	8	5	7	10	6	10	8	12
Indifferent	17	16	20	24	29	20	16	20	27	19	28	17	29
Desirable	44	46	44	49	42	40	46	44	45	45	45	47	40
Essential/Must Have	33	34	29	18	18	32	33	28	19	31	17	27	18
Separate living room													
Do not want	8	7	11	16	17	11	7	11	17	9	18	12	17
Indifferent	24	21	23	33	33	27	21	25	31	22	34	23	35
Desirable	39	48	45	37	36	35	46	43	38	45	34	43	34
Essential/Must Have	29	25	21	14	14	27	27	21	14	23	13	22	15
Separate family room													
Do not want	7	5	9	12	14	10	5	9	13	7	11	12	17
Indifferent	25	22	25	36	33	27	22	25	34	22	38	25	38
Desirable	40	45	43	41	40	37	45	44	39	48	37	41	33
Essential/Must Have	27	29	23	11	14	26	28	21	13	24	14	22	12

Q38. How would the following various designs and features influence your purchase decision?
(Percent of respondents)

	Race/Ethnicity				Home Buyers' Income Bracket					Price Expected to Pay			
	Cauca-sian	African-American	Hispanic	Asian	Under $50,000	$50,000 to $74,999	$75,000 to $99,999	$100,000 to $149,999	$150,000 or more	Less than $150,000	$150,000 to $249,999	$250,000 to $499,999	$500,000 or more
BATH FEATURES													
Bidet													
Do not want	32	22	9	16	35	32	27	25	18	29	32	26	23
Indifferent	30	30	25	30	32	35	30	29	22	30	32	29	25
Desirable	27	34	42	38	25	25	33	30	39	29	26	32	34
Essential/Must Have	11	15	24	16	9	7	11	16	22	11	10	14	17
SPECIALTY ROOMS OR FEATURES													
Delivery vestibule													
Do not want	28	22	9	17	34	27	22	23	15	30	25	23	19
Indifferent	38	30	28	31	36	42	39	34	30	35	39	37	31
Desirable	25	33	39	38	22	24	28	29	36	24	24	28	37
Essential/Must Have	9	16	24	14	8	7	10	15	19	11	12	12	14
Great room (kitchen/family room/living room combined)													
Do not want	9	6	7	7	14	7	7	7	5	11	10	6	8
Indifferent	19	21	24	21	23	23	18	20	15	24	21	19	17
Desirable	48	43	40	49	43	48	49	47	50	45	48	49	47
Essential/Must Have	23	30	29	23	19	22	26	27	30	21	21	26	28
Laundry room													
Do not want	3	2	6	8	4	2	3	3	4	5	4	2	4
Indifferent	8	14	23	17	10	10	9	12	11	13	14	10	8
Desirable	47	41	40	53	53	46	45	41	43	51	44	44	46
Essential/Must Have	42	42	32	22	33	42	43	44	41	31	37	44	42
Dining room													
Do not want	9	4	5	7	12	8	8	7	5	13	9	7	6
Indifferent	24	13	24	17	24	27	25	22	19	20	28	24	18
Desirable	44	48	42	54	45	44	46	43	46	45	41	46	46
Essential/Must Have	22	35	29	22	19	22	22	29	30	22	21	24	29
Separate living room													
Do not want	15	7	5	10	15	12	17	12	11	14	14	13	13
Indifferent	30	20	23	23	28	33	28	29	24	25	30	30	25
Desirable	38	47	45	45	40	42	39	37	41	44	41	38	40
Essential/Must Have	16	25	27	23	17	13	16	23	24	18	16	19	22
Separate family room													
Do not want	12	8	4	8	16	11	7	7	7	15	14	7	8
Indifferent	32	18	22	27	31	32	34	28	24	27	32	31	27
Desirable	39	43	51	51	37	42	44	42	45	39	38	45	42
Essential/Must Have	17	31	24	14	16	15	15	23	24	18	17	17	23

Q38. How would the following various designs and features influence your purchase decision?
(Percent of respondents)

	All Home Buyers	Geography (Nine Census Divisions)									Buyer Type	
		New England	Middle Atlantic	East North Central	West North Central	South Atlantic	East South Central	West South Central	Mountain	Pacific	First-time	Repeat
SPECIALTY ROOMS OR FEATURES												
Two story entry foyer												
Do not want	32	26	31	37	19	38	28	36	34	26	27	33
Indifferent	27	26	27	30	27	24	34	32	25	24	30	27
Desirable	27	36	27	20	33	28	24	23	27	32	32	26
Essential/Must Have	13	12	15	13	20	9	14	10	13	18	11	13
Two story family room												
Do not want	35	33	34	41	20	44	33	37	34	26	26	36
Indifferent	25	24	20	25	30	21	29	29	26	24	28	24
Desirable	26	30	30	24	27	23	22	24	25	31	32	25
Essential/Must Have	14	12	16	10	22	12	16	11	14	19	14	14
Flex/multipurpose spaces												
Do not want	13	15	13	19	10	13	13	12	11	10	16	13
Indifferent	29	31	30	28	29	32	34	29	28	23	27	29
Desirable	44	39	43	43	41	45	39	48	46	49	43	45
Essential/Must Have	13	15	14	10	20	10	14	12	15	18	15	13
Sun room												
Do not want	15	10	14	16	11	19	16	17	15	13	17	15
Indifferent	25	22	26	24	25	22	23	30	30	27	27	25
Desirable	44	52	42	46	46	47	49	41	40	38	40	45
Essential/Must Have	15	15	18	14	18	12	11	12	14	22	16	15
Media room												
Do not want	25	22	27	32	18	29	21	27	21	15	21	25
Indifferent	29	35	25	27	20	30	34	31	34	29	29	29
Desirable	32	33	32	29	45	30	29	29	30	34	37	31
Essential/Must Have	14	10	16	12	17	11	16	13	15	22	13	15
Exercise room												
Do not want	23	22	21	26	24	27	23	24	24	12	18	23
Indifferent	27	26	27	28	23	27	27	29	29	29	26	28
Desirable	35	40	34	34	37	34	42	31	31	40	42	34
Essential/Must Have	15	13	18	12	16	12	9	16	16	19	14	15
Game room												
Do not want	28	28	29	35	23	32	24	26	25	21	20	29
Indifferent	29	32	27	28	30	30	30	28	31	28	27	29
Desirable	29	27	25	24	30	27	32	34	29	33	40	27
Essential/Must Have	14	13	19	14	17	11	14	12	15	18	14	14

Q38. How would the following various designs and features influence your purchase decision?
(Percent of respondents)

	Age of Household Head					Generation (year born)				Household Composition			
	Under 35 years old	35 to 44 years old	45 to 54 years old	55 to 64 years old	65 years old or older	Gen Z (1997 or later)	Millennials(1981-1996)	Gen X (1965-1980)	Boomers (1946-1964)	Married couple w children	Married couple no children	Single parent	One person
SPECIALTY ROOMS OR FEATURES													
Two story entry foyer													
Do not want	14	14	25	43	45	16	13	26	45	20	44	29	49
Indifferent	26	27	30	28	26	28	26	29	27	25	30	25	30
Desirable	38	38	31	23	19	34	39	30	21	36	20	29	14
Essential/Must Have	22	22	14	7	10	23	22	15	8	20	6	16	7
Two story family room													
Do not want	14	13	25	46	51	16	13	26	50	19	51	29	54
Indifferent	24	25	27	25	23	27	24	26	23	23	25	23	26
Desirable	37	37	32	21	17	33	38	32	18	35	18	30	13
Essential/Must Have	25	24	16	8	9	25	26	16	8	23	5	17	6
Flex/multipurpose spaces													
Do not want	10	7	10	15	18	12	6	11	17	8	12	18	22
Indifferent	23	24	29	33	31	27	22	28	32	26	34	28	31
Desirable	42	48	47	44	42	36	49	46	42	46	47	39	39
Essential/Must Have	25	22	14	8	9	25	23	15	8	20	7	15	8
Sun room													
Do not want	9	9	14	17	20	10	8	13	19	11	17	17	21
Indifferent	26	24	22	28	26	28	23	24	26	22	29	29	26
Desirable	40	43	48	46	42	37	44	48	43	46	44	40	43
Essential/Must Have	25	24	15	9	11	24	25	16	11	21	11	15	10
Media room													
Do not want	10	11	17	30	37	12	10	18	35	14	33	24	36
Indifferent	23	26	27	33	31	26	24	27	33	25	36	25	34
Desirable	41	43	37	28	23	37	43	37	24	40	23	34	21
Essential/Must Have	26	20	19	9	9	25	22	18	8	21	7	17	8
Exercise room													
Do not want	10	9	15	27	35	12	8	16	33	13	33	19	35
Indifferent	23	23	28	31	28	26	21	28	29	23	31	26	31
Desirable	42	45	38	32	28	36	47	37	30	42	28	38	27
Essential/Must Have	25	23	19	10	8	26	24	18	8	22	8	17	8
Game room													
Do not want	9	11	21	35	41	11	10	21	39	16	39	24	46
Indifferent	23	22	28	33	33	27	20	28	33	27	33	28	25
Desirable	42	42	35	25	17	33	46	33	19	36	20	32	20
Essential/Must Have	26	25	17	7	9	30	24	17	8	21	7	17	8

Q38. How would the following various designs and features influence your purchase decision?
(Percent of respondents)

	Race/Ethnicity				Home Buyers' Income Bracket					Price Expected to Pay			
	Caucasian	African-American	Hispanic	Asian	Under $50,000	$50,000 to $74,999	$75,000 to $99,999	$100,000 to $149,999	$150,000 or more	Less than $150,000	$150,000 to $249,999	$250,000 to $499,999	$500,000 or more
SPECIALTY ROOMS OR FEATURES													
Two story entry foyer													
Do not want	38	22	8	18	44	39	32	27	19	38	37	30	25
Indifferent	29	25	21	24	27	32	33	27	22	25	28	29	24
Desirable	23	34	45	37	21	20	27	30	38	24	25	28	33
Essential/Must Have	10	19	25	21	8	10	9	17	21	13	10	13	18
Two story family room													
Do not want	42	21	10	16	47	43	37	30	19	38	42	33	28
Indifferent	25	24	20	26	22	28	28	25	23	23	23	27	22
Desirable	22	37	39	44	21	20	26	28	34	25	25	25	31
Essential/Must Have	11	19	31	13	10	8	9	17	24	13	11	15	18
Flex/multipurpose spaces													
Do not want	14	13	7	10	21	14	12	7	9	18	18	9	8
Indifferent	31	20	25	25	29	32	32	30	25	29	28	30	29
Desirable	44	44	44	52	40	44	46	47	47	41	42	47	46
Essential/Must Have	11	22	25	13	10	10	10	17	19	13	11	14	17
Sun room													
Do not want	17	16	7	13	22	16	15	14	9	17	17	14	12
Indifferent	26	24	23	27	24	28	25	28	23	24	27	26	26
Desirable	44	41	42	49	43	44	47	40	47	41	46	44	46
Essential/Must Have	13	19	28	12	11	12	14	18	20	17	10	16	17
Media room													
Do not want	29	16	9	15	36	27	23	19	16	29	31	23	16
Indifferent	31	23	22	26	28	36	32	32	21	26	33	31	26
Desirable	29	38	41	45	26	28	32	32	41	31	26	31	40
Essential/Must Have	12	23	27	14	10	9	13	17	22	14	10	15	18
Exercise room													
Do not want	27	14	8	16	35	27	22	17	11	28	29	22	12
Indifferent	29	17	24	23	25	35	30	28	23	26	30	28	25
Desirable	32	46	44	45	29	30	38	38	42	33	30	36	41
Essential/Must Have	12	23	24	16	11	8	10	18	24	14	10	14	22
Game room													
Do not want	32	17	11	17	36	33	27	24	18	30	29	28	22
Indifferent	30	21	29	28	28	33	36	27	24	25	34	29	27
Desirable	26	38	34	36	27	23	25	33	34	30	26	29	32
Essential/Must Have	11	24	26	19	9	11	12	15	24	15	11	14	18

Q38. How would the following various designs and features influence your purchase decision?
(Percent of respondents)

	All Home Buyers	Geography (Nine Census Divisions)									Buyer Type	
		New England	Middle Atlantic	East North Central	West North Central	South Atlantic	East South Central	West South Central	Mountain	Pacific	First-time	Repeat
SPECIALTY ROOMS OR FEATURES												
Home office												
Do not want	12	10	11	15	7	15	18	11	9	10	16	12
Indifferent	20	16	21	24	19	19	21	20	22	19	21	20
Desirable	43	42	42	42	47	42	38	46	46	41	41	43
Essential/Must Have	25	32	27	19	27	24	23	24	23	30	23	25
Mudroom												
Do not want	17	10	14	16	12	21	20	18	13	22	26	16
Indifferent	25	14	26	22	21	29	29	26	29	25	30	25
Desirable	42	50	40	48	51	38	36	40	44	36	34	43
Essential/Must Have	16	26	21	14	16	11	16	15	15	18	11	16
Drop zone (shoes, coats, etc.)												
Do not want	12	5	9	14	7	15	14	13	13	12	12	12
Indifferent	26	21	27	26	22	26	32	30	25	20	27	25
Desirable	45	51	45	42	51	45	41	44	49	47	44	46
Essential/Must Have	17	23	19	18	20	14	13	12	13	21	17	17
Study/den/library												
Do not want	15	11	15	20	12	15	13	12	16	12	16	14
Indifferent	23	21	24	23	24	23	24	23	20	21	26	22
Desirable	44	45	45	39	44	46	41	51	46	41	42	44
Essential/Must Have	18	23	17	17	20	16	22	14	18	25	16	19
Breakfast nook												
Do not want	15	11	15	20	12	14	14	15	17	11	14	15
Indifferent	28	25	28	31	30	27	27	29	29	27	27	28
Desirable	43	52	43	39	38	47	44	44	38	42	47	42
Essential/Must Have	14	12	14	10	21	11	15	12	16	20	12	14
Wine cellar												
Do not want	41	34	40	49	32	47	36	41	40	31	32	42
Indifferent	24	31	23	25	21	24	28	25	20	19	32	22
Desirable	23	24	23	15	31	20	21	23	28	32	24	23
Essential/Must Have	12	11	14	10	17	9	15	11	12	18	12	13
Vaulted/cathedral ceiling												
Do not want	18	16	17	24	16	18	23	15	16	13	19	18
Indifferent	26	19	29	27	23	27	26	29	24	24	31	26
Desirable	41	47	38	36	45	43	37	43	44	44	38	42
Essential/Must Have	14	17	15	12	16	12	13	13	15	19	12	15

Q38. How would the following various designs and features influence your purchase decision?
(Percent of respondents)

	Age of Household Head					Generation (year born)				Household Composition			
	Under 35 years old	35 to 44 years old	45 to 54 years old	55 to 64 years old	65 years old or older	Gen Z (1997 or later)	Millenni-als(1981-1996)	Gen X (1965-1980)	Boomers (1946-1964)	Married couple w children	Married couple no children	Single parent	One person
SPECIALTY ROOMS OR FEATURES													
Home office													
Do not want	8	8	10	14	15	12	7	11	16	8	12	16	19
Indifferent	20	18	19	21	22	27	17	18	22	19	22	21	21
Desirable	42	42	42	43	44	34	43	43	43	43	46	37	40
Essential/Must Have	30	33	30	22	19	28	33	28	19	30	20	27	20
Mudroom													
Do not want	12	11	14	20	22	14	11	14	22	12	20	21	25
Indifferent	26	25	23	26	27	30	23	25	26	21	31	22	29
Desirable	39	42	43	45	39	33	43	43	41	45	38	40	38
Essential/Must Have	23	23	19	9	13	23	23	18	11	22	12	17	8
Drop zone (shoes, coats, etc.)													
Do not want	9	7	12	13	16	12	6	11	15	8	13	14	18
Indifferent	22	20	23	30	28	24	19	24	29	20	31	23	33
Desirable	41	49	48	45	44	35	49	47	44	49	44	43	39
Essential/Must Have	28	25	17	12	12	29	26	17	12	22	12	20	10
Study/den/library													
Do not want	9	9	14	18	17	11	8	14	19	11	13	16	24
Indifferent	23	20	21	27	22	26	20	22	23	18	26	26	25
Desirable	40	48	45	41	45	34	49	43	44	46	48	38	40
Essential/Must Have	27	23	20	15	15	29	24	21	14	25	13	21	10
Breakfast nook													
Do not want	10	8	12	18	19	12	8	13	19	11	14	19	22
Indifferent	26	23	29	30	30	30	23	27	32	22	37	23	32
Desirable	42	45	43	44	42	35	46	44	42	47	41	42	39
Essential/Must Have	22	25	16	8	8	23	24	17	8	20	8	16	7
Wine cellar													
Do not want	17	18	37	51	55	18	16	37	54	26	55	35	58
Indifferent	26	26	27	23	20	28	25	27	20	24	22	26	22
Desirable	35	35	21	19	18	30	38	22	18	31	18	24	15
Essential/Must Have	22	21	15	6	8	25	21	15	7	19	6	15	6
Vaulted/cathedral ceiling													
Do not want	12	10	16	20	23	14	9	16	22	13	17	18	27
Indifferent	30	24	23	26	28	35	24	23	28	23	30	25	29
Desirable	36	44	45	44	38	29	44	45	40	44	44	38	36
Essential/Must Have	23	22	16	10	10	22	23	16	10	20	9	19	8

Q38. How would the following various designs and features influence your purchase decision?
(Percent of respondents)

	Race/Ethnicity				Home Buyers' Income Bracket					Price Expected to Pay			
	Cauca-sian	African-American	Hispanic	Asian	Under $50,000	$50,000 to $74,999	$75,000 to $99,999	$100,000 to $149,999	$150,000 or more	Less than $150,000	$150,000 to $249,999	$250,000 to $499,999	$500,000 or more
SPECIALTY ROOMS OR FEATURES													
Home office													
Do not want	13	11	5	11	21	13	10	7	6	19	14	10	5
Indifferent	20	16	25	18	24	25	19	18	14	23	28	19	13
Desirable	43	38	42	51	39	44	47	40	46	39	43	43	46
Essential/Must Have	23	35	29	20	16	18	24	34	34	18	14	28	36
Mudroom													
Do not want	17	25	13	17	27	18	17	10	11	21	22	14	12
Indifferent	26	22	21	23	28	30	24	26	18	27	29	25	22
Desirable	42	37	40	46	35	39	45	45	47	39	36	43	48
Essential/Must Have	14	16	25	14	10	13	14	19	23	13	13	17	19
Drop zone (shoes, coats, etc.)													
Do not want	13	11	8	7	19	13	10	9	8	16	14	11	9
Indifferent	27	22	20	25	26	30	27	28	19	24	31	26	20
Desirable	45	45	47	48	41	45	49	44	49	43	42	46	51
Essential/Must Have	15	22	25	20	13	13	14	19	24	16	13	17	21
Study/den/library													
Do not want	16	12	9	9	24	17	13	7	10	20	19	13	6
Indifferent	23	21	24	21	25	29	24	21	15	26	27	23	16
Desirable	45	42	41	44	37	42	48	50	47	38	40	48	49
Essential/Must Have	16	25	27	26	14	12	15	22	27	16	14	17	28
Breakfast nook													
Do not want	16	15	10	13	24	13	14	11	8	21	16	12	11
Indifferent	30	22	21	26	28	37	28	28	23	27	34	29	24
Desirable	43	45	42	43	40	40	47	43	46	37	42	45	47
Essential/Must Have	11	18	27	18	8	9	11	18	22	15	8	14	18
Wine cellar													
Do not want	48	27	14	22	52	49	43	36	24	43	43	43	28
Indifferent	23	25	24	23	22	26	26	23	23	21	25	22	27
Desirable	19	29	35	41	18	18	21	26	33	21	21	24	28
Essential/Must Have	9	19	27	14	8	7	10	15	21	14	11	10	17
Vaulted/cathedral ceiling													
Do not want	19	15	11	13	29	16	19	14	8	23	22	16	10
Indifferent	27	27	20	26	25	37	29	25	19	25	29	28	22
Desirable	41	39	46	42	38	35	38	45	50	38	39	44	46
Essential/Must Have	12	19	23	19	9	12	14	16	22	14	10	13	22

Q38. How would the following various designs and features influence your purchase decision?
(Percent of respondents)

	All Home Buyers	Geography (Nine Census Divisions)									Buyer Type	
		New England	Middle Atlantic	East North Central	West North Central	South Atlantic	East South Central	West South Central	Mountain	Pacific	First-time	Repeat
SPECIALTY ROOMS OR FEATURES												
Wet bar												
Do not want	31	31	30	38	28	34	27	31	29	23	24	32
Indifferent	27	35	26	29	22	28	28	31	26	23	32	27
Desirable	29	22	28	22	34	28	32	27	35	36	30	29
Essential/Must Have	13	11	16	11	16	10	13	11	10	17	13	13
Recessed lighting throughout house												
Do not want	10	6	9	15	10	10	12	8	5	7	14	9
Indifferent	25	27	25	25	25	27	24	25	20	26	31	25
Desirable	47	44	44	44	51	46	46	50	52	44	42	47
Essential/Must Have	19	23	22	16	14	17	18	16	23	22	13	19
Laundry chute												
Do not want	28	27	21	32	22	33	29	31	25	23	20	29
Indifferent	27	25	31	23	27	24	28	30	32	25	28	26
Desirable	32	36	32	32	33	30	32	28	30	34	38	31
Essential/Must Have	14	12	15	13	17	13	10	12	13	19	15	14
Garage storage												
Do not want	5	2	7	6	3	5	5	4	4	5	6	5
Indifferent	14	10	15	11	18	14	20	16	15	15	19	14
Desirable	50	53	49	47	48	54	44	54	47	49	49	50
Essential/Must Have	31	34	30	37	31	27	31	26	34	31	26	31
Elevator												
Do not want	47	42	42	53	35	54	42	52	47	37	45	47
Indifferent	20	14	17	21	20	19	22	22	22	21	23	20
Desirable	21	29	27	16	28	19	23	15	18	26	23	21
Essential/Must Have	12	15	14	10	17	9	13	11	13	16	10	13
Pet washing station												
Do not want	34	33	33	45	24	38	28	33	29	28	33	34
Indifferent	24	18	23	19	28	25	21	29	32	24	29	24
Desirable	29	38	31	25	28	27	32	25	28	32	30	28
Essential/Must Have	13	11	13	11	20	10	19	12	11	16	8	14
In-law suite												
Do not want	31	30	32	37	22	36	30	29	28	24	25	32
Indifferent	25	25	25	25	28	23	26	28	24	25	29	25
Desirable	31	35	31	26	31	31	30	33	34	31	35	30
Essential/Must Have	13	10	12	12	18	9	14	10	14	19	11	13

Q38. How would the following various designs and features influence your purchase decision?
(Percent of respondents)

	Age of Household Head					Generation (year born)				Household Composition			
	Under 35 years old	35 to 44 years old	45 to 54 years old	55 to 64 years old	65 years old or older	Gen Z (1997 or later)	Millenni-als(1981-1996)	Gen X (1965-1980)	Boomers (1946-1964)	Married couple w children	Married couple no children	Single parent	One person
SPECIALTY ROOMS OR FEATURES													
Wet bar													
Do not want	14	14	27	38	42	17	13	26	42	19	42	28	44
Indifferent	30	27	26	27	28	32	28	26	27	24	29	29	27
Desirable	36	35	34	28	22	31	36	33	24	38	22	29	22
Essential/Must Have	20	24	14	7	8	20	23	15	7	19	7	15	7
Recessed lighting throughout house													
Do not want	9	7	6	12	11	11	6	8	12	7	9	10	15
Indifferent	24	22	22	25	30	27	21	23	27	21	28	28	30
Desirable	42	45	50	49	46	38	47	48	47	48	50	44	44
Essential/Must Have	25	26	22	14	13	24	26	21	14	25	13	18	11
Laundry chute													
Do not want	12	11	22	38	38	13	10	23	39	17	38	22	44
Indifferent	23	26	27	27	27	26	24	28	26	25	30	22	31
Desirable	42	41	34	27	25	36	43	34	26	37	26	40	19
Essential/Must Have	23	22	17	8	10	24	23	16	9	21	6	17	7
Garage storage													
Do not want	6	3	5	5	5	8	3	5	6	4	5	4	8
Indifferent	19	16	15	13	13	23	16	15	14	15	14	19	14
Desirable	44	50	48	53	51	39	48	50	50	49	48	48	53
Essential/Must Have	31	32	32	29	30	30	32	30	30	33	33	29	26
Elevator													
Do not want	26	28	43	59	56	27	27	43	58	31	61	43	63
Indifferent	22	22	22	15	20	21	21	22	18	20	19	23	17
Desirable	30	29	22	18	16	27	31	22	17	28	15	20	15
Essential/Must Have	22	21	12	8	8	25	21	14	8	20	5	14	5
Pet washing station													
Do not want	15	15	29	40	49	17	15	28	46	21	50	35	46
Indifferent	24	28	22	23	24	26	26	23	24	24	21	22	21
Desirable	37	35	35	29	19	30	37	35	22	35	23	26	26
Essential/Must Have	24	22	13	8	8	26	22	14	7	19	6	17	8
In-law suite													
Do not want	17	12	25	35	46	17	13	24	44	19	42	29	46
Indifferent	26	26	24	27	24	30	25	26	24	24	30	23	23
Desirable	35	39	38	31	21	33	38	38	24	38	21	33	26
Essential/Must Have	22	22	12	6	9	20	23	12	8	18	7	15	5

Q38. How would the following various designs and features influence your purchase decision?
(Percent of respondents)

	Race/Ethnicity				Home Buyers' Income Bracket					Price Expected to Pay			
	Cauca-sian	African-American	Hispanic	Asian	Under $50,000	$50,000 to $74,999	$75,000 to $99,999	$100,000 to $149,999	$150,000 or more	Less than $150,000	$150,000 to $249,999	$250,000 to $499,999	$500,000 or more
SPECIALTY ROOMS OR FEATURES													
Wet bar													
Do not want	36	20	12	19	43	35	30	26	18	34	35	31	22
Indifferent	28	29	22	28	25	33	34	27	23	27	31	27	26
Desirable	26	34	42	36	24	23	26	31	40	27	25	29	36
Essential/Must Have	10	17	25	18	8	9	9	17	19	12	9	13	16
Recessed lighting throughout house													
Do not want	10	10	7	6	17	9	6	7	6	15	13	7	5
Indifferent	26	23	24	21	30	33	27	24	15	30	28	26	17
Desirable	47	45	43	55	40	46	50	47	53	40	45	48	52
Essential/Must Have	17	22	27	18	14	12	18	22	26	15	15	18	27
Laundry chute													
Do not want	33	20	7	19	38	30	24	25	18	28	31	28	21
Indifferent	28	20	23	26	21	34	31	26	25	21	27	29	28
Desirable	28	38	44	39	30	28	33	32	34	35	31	30	33
Essential/Must Have	11	21	25	16	10	8	12	16	22	15	11	13	18
Garage storage													
Do not want	5	6	3	5	8	3	5	4	3	10	5	3	3
Indifferent	13	16	22	18	16	14	15	16	11	20	18	12	12
Desirable	51	48	43	54	52	56	46	47	48	47	50	52	49
Essential/Must Have	31	29	32	23	24	27	34	34	37	23	27	34	37
Elevator													
Do not want	55	34	13	25	57	56	48	42	30	48	48	49	37
Indifferent	19	19	23	24	17	21	24	21	18	18	24	18	21
Desirable	17	28	38	34	18	16	20	20	31	22	19	21	25
Essential/Must Have	9	19	26	17	8	7	7	16	21	12	9	12	17
Pet washing station													
Do not want	38	35	13	24	43	37	39	31	22	33	38	35	27
Indifferent	25	20	28	18	24	27	25	23	23	27	28	23	22
Desirable	27	29	35	40	24	26	26	31	36	28	26	28	35
Essential/Must Have	11	16	24	18	9	9	11	16	20	12	8	14	16
In-law suite													
Do not want	36	23	13	16	41	37	34	26	18	34	38	29	23
Indifferent	26	22	21	27	24	28	29	25	22	23	28	25	26
Desirable	28	37	38	42	26	26	28	34	40	30	24	33	35
Essential/Must Have	10	18	29	15	9	8	10	15	20	13	10	13	15

Q38. How would the following various designs and features influence your purchase decision?
(Percent of respondents)

	All Home Buyers	Geography (Nine Census Divisions)									Buyer Type	
		New England	Middle Atlantic	East North Central	West North Central	South Atlantic	East South Central	West South Central	Mountain	Pacific	First-time	Repeat
SPECIALTY ROOMS OR FEATURES												
Glass wall(s)												
Do not want	42	37	36	47	34	48	41	44	45	31	38	42
Indifferent	24	24	28	24	21	26	22	28	21	22	30	24
Desirable	22	27	23	17	27	18	26	17	22	32	22	22
Essential/Must Have	12	12	12	12	18	8	11	10	12	16	10	12
Soundproof walls/floors												
Do not want	11	13	14	13	8	10	19	10	8	7	10	11
Indifferent	23	27	23	24	23	23	22	22	25	19	27	22
Desirable	47	40	40	47	47	51	40	53	48	49	41	48
Essential/Must Have	19	20	24	16	23	16	19	15	19	25	21	19
TECHNOLOGY FEATURES												
Wireless home security system												
Do not want	8	10	8	14	9	8	7	7	6	6	7	9
Indifferent	22	18	22	22	24	23	23	18	28	20	21	22
Desirable	47	44	46	42	47	50	50	49	49	47	48	47
Essential/Must Have	23	27	24	23	19	19	20	27	17	28	24	22
Wired home security system												
Do not want	12	15	13	19	13	11	8	11	8	7	11	12
Indifferent	27	33	26	25	28	33	27	24	33	19	22	28
Desirable	41	30	38	37	38	42	47	45	38	49	48	40
Essential/Must Have	20	22	22	19	21	14	17	20	21	25	20	20
Security cameras												
Do not want	7	11	6	10	11	6	9	5	6	6	5	7
Indifferent	17	16	15	19	21	18	16	20	14	12	14	17
Desirable	50	47	46	46	44	51	47	52	54	54	51	49
Essential/Must Have	26	26	33	25	24	25	29	23	26	28	30	26
Programmable thermostat												
Do not want	6	7	8	7	10	5	10	5	5	4	8	6
Indifferent	16	23	14	11	19	17	18	16	13	16	21	15
Desirable	49	36	52	47	45	50	46	51	50	51	48	49
Essential/Must Have	29	34	27	35	27	27	26	28	33	29	23	30
Wired home audio system												
Do not want	15	17	16	20	15	15	12	15	14	10	15	15
Indifferent	32	34	33	33	26	34	39	33	32	28	31	33
Desirable	37	35	33	33	40	38	33	39	39	41	40	36
Essential/Must Have	16	14	18	15	19	13	16	13	16	21	14	16

Q38. How would the following various designs and features influence your purchase decision?
(Percent of respondents)

	Age of Household Head					Generation (year born)				Household Composition			
	Under 35 years old	35 to 44 years old	45 to 54 years old	55 to 64 years old	65 years old or older	Gen Z (1997 or later)	Millenni-als(1981-1996)	Gen X (1965-1980)	Boomers (1946-1964)	Married couple w children	Married couple no children	Single parent	One person
SPECIALTY ROOMS OR FEATURES													
Glass wall(s)													
Do not want	19	23	36	54	53	19	22	36	54	26	55	38	59
Indifferent	26	24	25	24	24	28	23	26	23	23	27	27	21
Desirable	33	32	26	16	16	30	33	25	16	32	14	22	14
Essential/Must Have	21	22	13	5	7	22	22	13	6	19	5	13	6
Soundproof walls/floors													
Do not want	9	7	8	13	14	11	7	8	14	7	12	12	17
Indifferent	20	22	21	24	24	22	21	22	24	20	26	22	23
Desirable	43	46	49	50	46	37	47	50	47	48	49	44	47
Essential/Must Have	28	25	21	13	16	30	26	21	15	25	13	22	13
TECHNOLOGY FEATURES													
Wireless home security system													
Do not want	7	5	7	8	12	9	5	7	10	7	9	7	11
Indifferent	18	18	23	22	25	21	17	22	24	20	28	20	23
Desirable	46	47	43	53	45	41	48	44	49	46	46	47	49
Essential/Must Have	29	31	28	17	17	29	31	27	17	28	17	26	18
Wired home security system													
Do not want	9	7	13	11	16	11	7	12	14	10	12	12	17
Indifferent	20	21	27	34	28	26	18	27	30	22	35	25	31
Desirable	44	45	41	41	39	36	47	41	40	43	38	44	38
Essential/Must Have	28	27	19	14	17	27	28	20	16	25	15	19	14
Security cameras													
Do not want	5	5	7	6	10	9	4	6	8	6	8	6	8
Indifferent	16	14	18	14	20	20	15	16	18	15	20	18	17
Desirable	46	48	47	56	49	39	49	49	52	49	52	46	53
Essential/Must Have	32	33	28	24	22	32	32	29	22	31	20	30	23
Programmable thermostat													
Do not want	8	5	5	6	7	12	4	5	7	5	6	7	9
Indifferent	18	16	13	16	16	21	16	14	16	15	17	15	16
Desirable	47	48	50	51	48	43	49	50	48	48	47	47	51
Essential/Must Have	27	31	32	27	29	24	31	31	29	32	31	31	24
Wired home audio system													
Do not want	10	8	10	16	23	13	8	10	20	10	17	17	21
Indifferent	26	25	29	39	36	26	24	31	37	28	38	28	38
Desirable	40	41	44	35	30	36	42	41	33	40	35	38	31
Essential/Must Have	25	26	16	9	11	25	26	18	10	22	9	17	10

Q38. How would the following various designs and features influence your purchase decision?
(Percent of respondents)

	Race/Ethnicity				Home Buyers' Income Bracket					Price Expected to Pay			
	Cauca-sian	African-American	Hispanic	Asian	Under $50,000	$50,000 to $74,999	$75,000 to $99,999	$100,000 to $149,999	$150,000 or more	Less than $150,000	$150,000 to $249,999	$250,000 to $499,999	$500,000 or more
SPECIALTY ROOMS OR FEATURES													
Glass wall(s)													
Do not want	48	33	12	25	54	49	42	36	26	43	45	43	31
Indifferent	24	26	23	25	22	29	30	24	21	21	27	26	22
Desirable	18	24	40	37	18	17	18	25	32	23	20	20	31
Essential/Must Have	9	17	24	14	7	5	10	15	21	12	8	12	16
Soundproof walls/floors													
Do not want	12	9	6	8	17	12	7	9	7	15	12	11	5
Indifferent	23	22	24	22	24	26	25	21	20	24	27	22	20
Desirable	49	45	39	44	45	47	50	50	46	43	47	48	51
Essential/Must Have	16	23	31	26	14	16	18	21	27	18	14	19	24
TECHNOLOGY FEATURES													
Wireless home security system													
Do not want	9	5	6	6	14	8	7	7	4	14	10	6	6
Indifferent	23	18	20	21	23	27	22	19	21	21	23	24	18
Desirable	47	47	46	51	45	46	52	48	46	46	49	46	48
Essential/Must Have	21	31	28	22	19	19	19	26	29	19	18	24	28
Wired home security system													
Do not want	13	8	6	11	18	11	12	9	9	17	17	8	10
Indifferent	29	24	19	21	29	30	30	28	20	26	26	32	19
Desirable	40	45	44	48	39	44	40	40	44	41	42	40	44
Essential/Must Have	18	23	30	20	14	16	18	23	27	17	16	20	27
Security cameras													
Do not want	8	5	4	5	12	6	6	6	4	12	8	5	6
Indifferent	17	14	18	20	17	19	18	16	15	18	18	19	11
Desirable	51	46	45	49	49	49	48	50	51	46	51	50	50
Essential/Must Have	24	35	33	27	21	26	28	28	30	24	23	26	33
Programmable thermostat													
Do not want	6	7	5	9	10	6	7	3	5	10	7	4	6
Indifferent	15	19	20	16	18	19	15	17	11	20	18	14	11
Desirable	50	43	45	46	50	51	48	47	47	48	53	49	48
Essential/Must Have	29	31	31	28	23	24	30	34	37	22	22	34	35
Wired home audio system													
Do not want	17	11	7	11	24	16	16	9	7	22	18	13	10
Indifferent	35	26	22	29	32	38	36	36	24	27	35	37	26
Desirable	35	40	43	40	33	33	37	36	45	34	33	37	43
Essential/Must Have	13	24	27	20	11	12	10	20	24	17	14	14	22

Q38. How would the following various designs and features influence your purchase decision?
(Percent of respondents)

	All Home Buyers	Geography (Nine Census Divisions)									Buyer Type	
		New England	Middle Atlantic	East North Central	West North Central	South Atlantic	East South Central	West South Central	Mountain	Pacific	First-time	Repeat
TECHNOLOGY FEATURES												
Wireless home audio system												
Do not want	13	15	13	21	13	13	15	10	10	9	10	14
Indifferent	28	32	24	27	24	32	35	28	28	27	30	28
Desirable	41	35	41	36	45	42	33	47	45	45	43	41
Essential/Must Have	17	18	21	17	19	14	17	15	17	19	17	17
Outdoor speakers & audio controls												
Do not want	20	22	16	24	20	22	18	19	18	16	17	20
Indifferent	26	24	28	29	21	26	31	25	29	21	26	26
Desirable	38	41	39	31	36	39	38	40	40	42	42	38
Essential/Must Have	16	14	17	15	23	13	13	15	13	21	15	16
Home theatre												
Do not want	26	32	27	32	25	29	26	24	23	18	19	27
Indifferent	26	25	27	21	17	29	22	31	27	26	27	26
Desirable	33	27	30	32	41	30	37	32	32	36	39	32
Essential/Must Have	15	16	16	15	17	12	15	12	17	20	15	15
Lighting control system												
Do not want	11	13	11	17	9	12	13	11	8	5	11	11
Indifferent	26	28	24	25	21	27	31	29	26	25	21	27
Desirable	45	45	41	42	48	47	40	47	48	48	50	45
Essential/Must Have	18	13	25	16	22	14	16	13	18	22	19	17
Energy management system/display												
Do not want	12	16	9	16	12	13	11	10	11	8	11	12
Indifferent	26	23	26	29	24	28	26	30	26	22	27	26
Desirable	45	47	46	38	44	46	43	48	43	48	47	45
Essential/Must Have	17	13	19	17	20	13	19	12	20	22	15	17
Whole house control/automation												
Do not want	14	18	12	16	14	14	15	18	11	13	14	14
Indifferent	28	26	27	30	25	31	28	31	25	26	32	28
Desirable	41	40	42	39	45	43	41	38	47	39	39	42
Essential/Must Have	16	16	19	15	17	13	16	14	16	23	15	16
Central vacuum system												
Do not want	18	16	16	24	15	17	19	24	18	13	15	19
Indifferent	29	25	31	28	24	30	32	30	28	29	30	29
Desirable	38	39	35	34	51	40	35	33	41	39	42	38
Essential/Must Have	15	20	18	15	10	12	14	13	13	19	13	15

Q38. How would the following various designs and features influence your purchase decision?
(Percent of respondents)

	Age of Household Head					Generation (year born)				Household Composition			
	Under 35 years old	35 to 44 years old	45 to 54 years old	55 to 64 years old	65 years old or older	Gen Z (1997 or later)	Millennials(1981-1996)	Gen X (1965-1980)	Boomers (1946-1964)	Married couple w children	Married couple no children	Single parent	One person
TECHNOLOGY FEATURES													
Wireless home audio system													
Do not want	8	7	9	14	21	10	7	9	19	9	15	15	20
Indifferent	20	21	26	32	33	22	20	26	32	24	36	23	30
Desirable	44	45	45	43	35	42	45	44	39	44	40	44	36
Essential/Must Have	28	26	20	11	11	26	27	20	11	23	9	18	13
Outdoor speakers & audio controls													
Do not want	8	8	12	23	32	8	8	13	29	11	27	22	28
Indifferent	21	22	24	30	28	22	22	25	29	24	29	22	28
Desirable	45	46	46	36	29	43	47	44	31	43	33	38	34
Essential/Must Have	26	24	18	11	11	28	24	18	11	21	11	18	9
Home theatre													
Do not want	11	11	16	32	41	14	10	17	38	14	36	27	43
Indifferent	22	23	23	29	28	24	21	24	29	23	34	18	24
Desirable	41	42	42	29	22	37	44	40	25	41	23	35	24
Essential/Must Have	25	24	19	10	9	25	25	19	9	22	7	20	9
Lighting control system													
Do not want	7	6	8	12	17	10	5	8	15	7	13	13	17
Indifferent	18	20	23	31	30	20	19	24	30	23	33	23	25
Desirable	49	49	49	44	41	45	51	47	41	47	42	44	46
Essential/Must Have	26	25	20	13	13	25	26	20	13	23	12	20	13
Energy management system/display													
Do not want	10	5	10	12	17	13	6	11	15	8	15	10	15
Indifferent	24	21	25	32	27	29	20	25	29	20	34	27	31
Desirable	43	47	45	46	43	38	47	46	44	49	39	41	43
Essential/Must Have	24	27	19	11	12	20	27	19	12	23	11	22	11
Whole house control/automation													
Do not want	9	7	11	15	21	11	7	11	19	9	17	14	22
Indifferent	24	23	26	31	31	26	22	26	30	23	36	22	31
Desirable	41	45	45	44	36	38	45	44	40	45	37	45	36
Essential/Must Have	25	26	18	10	12	24	26	18	11	23	10	19	10
Central vacuum system													
Do not want	10	7	14	23	26	11	7	15	25	11	24	19	28
Indifferent	26	25	28	31	31	27	26	27	31	27	35	22	29
Desirable	43	43	42	35	34	41	42	41	35	41	34	42	33
Essential/Must Have	22	25	16	11	9	20	25	17	9	21	7	18	10

Q38. How would the following various designs and features influence your purchase decision?
(Percent of respondents)

	Race/Ethnicity				Home Buyers' Income Bracket					Price Expected to Pay			
	Cauca-sian	African-American	Hispanic	Asian	Under $50,000	$50,000 to $74,999	$75,000 to $99,999	$100,000 to $149,999	$150,000 or more	Less than $150,000	$150,000 to $249,999	$250,000 to $499,999	$500,000 or more
TECHNOLOGY FEATURES													
Wireless home audio system													
Do not want	15	10	6	10	22	15	13	9	5	21	16	11	6
Indifferent	31	20	20	24	28	34	31	31	21	27	32	30	22
Desirable	40	45	47	44	38	38	41	42	47	36	38	42	51
Essential/Must Have	14	26	26	21	12	13	15	19	26	17	14	17	21
Outdoor speakers & audio controls													
Do not want	22	15	10	15	31	20	18	16	10	24	25	18	13
Indifferent	28	18	23	20	25	30	30	26	22	25	29	28	21
Desirable	37	46	36	47	32	37	37	40	45	35	34	38	45
Essential/Must Have	13	21	31	18	12	13	15	18	23	15	12	16	21
Home theatre													
Do not want	31	14	9	13	37	29	28	21	15	29	35	24	19
Indifferent	27	21	22	22	26	34	26	25	20	25	24	28	23
Desirable	30	39	40	49	27	27	34	36	41	30	30	33	39
Essential/Must Have	12	26	28	16	10	11	11	18	24	16	10	15	19
Lighting control system													
Do not want	12	8	6	11	20	10	9	7	6	20	13	7	9
Indifferent	28	23	19	21	25	30	28	27	22	25	27	29	19
Desirable	45	44	45	48	41	46	47	45	48	39	47	46	50
Essential/Must Have	15	25	29	19	14	14	16	21	23	16	13	18	23
Energy management system/display													
Do not want	13	8	7	11	19	9	12	8	7	18	16	9	8
Indifferent	29	22	21	14	29	35	25	26	18	29	32	25	20
Desirable	44	47	42	63	39	42	50	44	52	38	40	47	52
Essential/Must Have	15	23	29	12	13	14	13	21	23	15	13	19	20
Whole house control/automation													
Do not want	16	11	7	10	24	15	13	10	7	22	18	11	8
Indifferent	30	20	23	25	30	35	29	26	22	26	30	29	25
Desirable	40	45	43	49	34	39	44	46	46	36	40	44	46
Essential/Must Have	14	23	28	17	12	10	13	18	25	16	12	16	21
Central vacuum system													
Do not want	21	13	7	12	27	17	18	15	12	22	20	17	14
Indifferent	30	27	24	30	28	30	31	32	25	27	30	30	28
Desirable	37	38	46	43	35	41	39	35	41	38	40	38	38
Essential/Must Have	13	22	23	15	10	12	12	18	22	13	10	15	20

Q38. How would the following various designs and features influence your purchase decision?
(Percent of respondents)

	All Home Buyers	Geography (Nine Census Divisions)									Buyer Type	
		New England	Middle Atlantic	East North Central	West North Central	South Atlantic	East South Central	West South Central	Mountain	Pacific	First-time	Repeat
TECHNOLOGY FEATURES												
Multi-zone HVAC system												
Do not want	10	7	11	14	10	9	12	12	7	6	14	10
Indifferent	22	22	22	25	22	21	22	25	24	18	23	22
Desirable	47	46	41	44	46	50	49	46	48	51	46	47
Essential/Must Have	21	25	26	18	22	19	17	18	21	24	17	21
Charging station for electric car												
Do not want	26	24	22	31	19	30	28	34	20	14	25	26
Indifferent	26	18	25	28	21	25	31	32	29	21	27	26
Desirable	33	34	32	26	41	34	29	24	36	42	34	32
Essential/Must Have	16	24	20	14	19	11	12	11	15	24	15	16
Smart washer/dryer (controlled remotely)												
Do not want	19	22	17	26	20	20	21	21	16	12	14	20
Indifferent	29	30	27	30	23	29	23	34	32	28	28	29
Desirable	35	34	38	29	39	37	41	34	33	37	41	35
Essential/Must Have	16	14	18	16	18	14	16	12	19	23	16	16
Smart refrigerator (contr. remotely)												
Do not want	20	26	19	27	19	21	21	20	16	13	14	21
Indifferent	30	34	26	29	24	30	32	33	37	28	30	30
Desirable	33	25	39	27	39	35	36	31	31	34	41	32
Essential/Must Have	17	16	16	17	18	14	11	16	16	25	15	17
Smart oven (controlled remotely)												
Do not want	20	22	19	29	20	20	20	19	16	14	15	21
Indifferent	31	35	27	31	25	33	28	33	30	30	31	31
Desirable	34	27	38	28	41	34	38	32	37	36	42	33
Essential/Must Have	15	15	16	12	13	13	13	16	17	20	12	15
Smart irrigation system (computer-controlled)												
Do not want	19	18	20	28	18	18	19	20	11	12	18	19
Indifferent	28	34	29	27	22	30	34	27	20	26	29	27
Desirable	39	35	33	35	41	38	37	39	50	44	44	38
Essential/Must Have	15	13	19	10	19	14	10	14	19	19	10	16
Video doorbell												
Do not want	8	10	7	11	12	6	8	4	8	6	8	8
Indifferent	19	23	16	17	22	20	17	21	19	16	18	19
Desirable	48	42	50	46	41	50	51	47	50	50	46	48
Essential/Must Have	26	25	27	26	25	24	24	27	23	28	29	25

Q38. How would the following various designs and features influence your purchase decision?
(Percent of respondents)

	Age of Household Head					Generation (year born)				Household Composition			
	Under 35 years old	35 to 44 years old	45 to 54 years old	55 to 64 years old	65 years old or older	Gen Z (1997 or later)	Millenni-als(1981-1996)	Gen X (1965-1980)	Boomers (1946-1964)	Married couple w children	Married couple no children	Single parent	One person
TECHNOLOGY FEATURES													
Multi-zone HVAC system													
Do not want	9	6	9	11	12	11	6	9	12	8	10	12	14
Indifferent	23	21	22	22	23	26	20	22	22	19	25	23	24
Desirable	43	47	48	49	46	38	47	47	48	48	48	45	47
Essential/Must Have	25	26	21	18	18	25	26	22	18	26	17	21	15
Charging station for electric car													
Do not want	15	12	25	34	30	18	12	25	31	17	31	27	36
Indifferent	24	24	29	25	26	25	23	29	26	23	30	23	25
Desirable	38	38	32	29	31	37	39	31	31	38	29	34	28
Essential/Must Have	22	25	14	12	13	20	25	15	12	23	10	15	11
Smart washer/dryer (controlled remotely)													
Do not want	9	7	15	26	27	9	7	15	26	11	27	18	28
Indifferent	23	23	27	30	34	27	22	27	33	25	35	23	33
Desirable	42	45	41	33	27	38	45	39	30	41	28	41	30
Essential/Must Have	27	26	17	11	12	25	26	18	11	24	10	18	9
Smart refrigerator (contr. remotely)													
Do not want	9	8	14	26	29	10	8	15	28	12	27	19	30
Indifferent	23	24	31	31	33	26	22	30	33	25	36	24	33
Desirable	41	41	37	31	27	38	42	35	29	39	26	39	28
Essential/Must Have	28	27	19	12	10	27	27	20	11	24	11	18	9
Smart oven (controlled remotely)													
Do not want	10	8	15	26	29	13	8	17	27	12	28	19	30
Indifferent	24	23	29	31	36	24	24	28	35	24	36	27	37
Desirable	40	43	39	32	27	38	43	37	30	42	28	38	25
Essential/Must Have	25	25	17	11	8	25	26	18	9	22	8	17	7
Smart irrigation system (computer-controlled)													
Do not want	10	7	16	26	24	12	7	16	25	13	21	19	26
Indifferent	25	26	27	29	28	27	25	28	28	24	33	27	27
Desirable	43	43	40	36	36	39	45	40	36	43	35	36	36
Essential/Must Have	22	23	16	9	12	22	24	16	11	20	10	17	11
Video doorbell													
Do not want	6	6	6	7	10	8	5	6	9	7	9	6	8
Indifferent	19	16	18	20	19	22	15	18	19	17	22	18	19
Desirable	43	46	46	50	51	39	47	46	51	48	48	47	47
Essential/Must Have	32	32	29	23	20	31	33	30	20	29	21	29	25

Q38. How would the following various designs and features influence your purchase decision?
(Percent of respondents)

	Race/Ethnicity				Home Buyers' Income Bracket					Price Expected to Pay			
	Caucasian	African-American	Hispanic	Asian	Under $50,000	$50,000 to $74,999	$75,000 to $99,999	$100,000 to $149,999	$150,000 or more	Less than $150,000	$150,000 to $249,999	$250,000 to $499,999	$500,000 or more
TECHNOLOGY FEATURES													
Multi-zone HVAC system													
Do not want	10	11	8	10	18	7	10	7	6	16	14	7	6
Indifferent	22	22	22	20	25	30	22	18	18	27	26	22	16
Desirable	47	44	43	53	45	46	48	51	46	40	46	49	50
Essential/Must Have	20	22	27	17	13	18	20	25	30	17	15	22	29
Charging station for electric car													
Do not want	30	20	7	9	37	32	22	18	15	35	30	24	13
Indifferent	27	22	21	27	25	34	29	29	17	25	31	27	20
Desirable	30	35	45	47	28	24	37	34	42	29	29	32	42
Essential/Must Have	13	22	28	17	11	10	13	19	26	11	10	17	25
Smart washer/dryer (controlled remotely)													
Do not want	23	9	6	11	29	22	19	14	10	25	24	17	12
Indifferent	31	25	23	20	28	33	29	30	26	24	31	31	29
Desirable	33	43	41	47	32	34	37	36	39	36	33	36	37
Essential/Must Have	13	23	30	22	11	11	14	21	25	15	12	16	23
Smart refrigerator (contr. remotely)													
Do not want	24	7	8	13	30	21	21	14	12	24	26	18	14
Indifferent	32	25	23	25	28	36	30	31	26	26	30	32	29
Desirable	30	47	39	42	31	31	33	33	38	34	30	34	36
Essential/Must Have	14	21	29	20	11	11	15	22	24	16	14	16	22
Smart oven (controlled remotely)													
Do not want	24	8	8	12	30	23	20	15	10	25	28	17	12
Indifferent	33	25	23	23	31	36	31	31	25	27	30	32	30
Desirable	30	47	44	47	28	31	36	36	41	33	31	36	37
Essential/Must Have	13	20	25	18	11	9	13	19	23	15	11	15	20
Smart irrigation system (computer-controlled)													
Do not want	21	13	8	11	32	19	16	11	10	27	24	15	10
Indifferent	29	22	24	27	25	34	32	31	21	27	27	30	25
Desirable	37	46	43	49	34	36	39	39	47	33	38	39	45
Essential/Must Have	13	19	25	13	9	11	14	20	22	13	11	16	20
Video doorbell													
Do not want	8	4	7	8	12	3	9	7	5	11	10	6	5
Indifferent	18	19	21	19	19	22	18	18	17	22	17	19	15
Desirable	50	40	40	50	49	50	48	48	46	44	51	48	50
Essential/Must Have	24	37	32	23	20	25	24	28	32	22	22	27	30

Q38. How would the following various designs and features influence your purchase decision?
(Percent of respondents)

	All Home Buyers	Geography (Nine Census Divisions)									Buyer Type	
		New England	Middle Atlantic	East North Central	West North Central	South Atlantic	East South Central	West South Central	Mountain	Pacific	First-time	Repeat
OUTDOOR FEATURES												
Front porch												
Do not want	4	4	4	4	6	3	6	2	4	6	3	4
Indifferent	15	17	16	13	19	14	15	13	21	11	14	15
Desirable	53	49	51	50	52	57	43	56	54	55	55	53
Essential/Must Have	28	29	30	33	23	25	36	28	21	28	28	28
Rear porch												
Do not want	6	3	7	4	8	6	8	4	7	9	5	6
Indifferent	17	9	14	21	22	16	15	14	19	18	21	16
Desirable	52	62	52	49	51	55	52	53	53	48	48	53
Essential/Must Have	25	26	27	26	19	22	25	29	21	26	26	25
Patio												
Do not want	4	3	4	3	7	3	5	3	3	3	6	3
Indifferent	11	13	11	11	13	12	13	9	8	13	13	11
Desirable	56	57	57	51	57	60	53	56	59	52	50	56
Essential/Must Have	30	27	29	35	23	26	29	32	30	32	31	29
Deck												
Do not want	6	2	7	5	6	4	8	5	8	8	5	6
Indifferent	16	13	13	13	18	16	18	16	22	16	15	16
Desirable	54	56	52	52	54	57	49	59	48	53	53	54
Essential/Must Have	25	29	28	30	22	23	26	20	23	24	27	25
Exterior lighting												
Do not want	4	2	3	6	2	3	6	3	4	3	5	3
Indifferent	14	19	15	15	23	9	17	12	16	15	16	14
Desirable	51	49	50	48	43	58	44	53	54	49	47	51
Essential/Must Have	31	30	32	32	31	29	33	32	26	34	32	31
Landscaping												
Do not want	4	1	4	5	4	3	7	5	2	4	6	4
Indifferent	16	12	15	16	17	16	13	14	16	20	25	14
Desirable	51	61	54	49	53	52	48	53	57	42	46	52
Essential/Must Have	29	25	27	30	26	29	31	29	25	34	23	30
Outdoor fireplace												
Do not want	16	19	13	19	12	18	15	13	15	17	20	16
Indifferent	25	13	28	26	28	25	24	28	23	21	24	25
Desirable	43	50	40	42	44	44	44	44	44	41	40	44
Essential/Must Have	16	17	20	13	16	13	17	14	17	22	15	16

Q38. How would the following various designs and features influence your purchase decision?
(Percent of respondents)

	Age of Household Head					Generation (year born)				Household Composition			
	Under 35 years old	35 to 44 years old	45 to 54 years old	55 to 64 years old	65 years old or older	Gen Z (1997 or later)	Millenni-als(1981-1996)	Gen X (1965-1980)	Boomers (1946-1964)	Married couple w children	Married couple no children	Single parent	One person
OUTDOOR FEATURES													
Front porch													
Do not want	4	3	3	4	5	6	3	3	5	4	4	4	4
Indifferent	16	11	15	16	15	16	13	14	16	14	16	12	16
Desirable	47	52	51	57	55	47	50	51	55	50	57	50	54
Essential/Must Have	33	34	31	24	25	31	35	31	24	31	23	33	26
Rear porch													
Do not want	6	3	5	6	8	8	3	6	7	5	6	6	8
Indifferent	15	19	14	15	20	19	17	14	18	15	19	19	17
Desirable	48	50	53	57	51	44	49	54	54	52	52	46	56
Essential/Must Have	31	28	28	21	22	29	30	27	22	27	23	29	19
Patio													
Do not want	5	4	3	4	3	6	4	4	3	4	3	4	3
Indifferent	13	14	11	10	11	13	13	11	11	12	10	13	13
Desirable	47	50	54	62	57	48	48	55	60	52	58	50	60
Essential/Must Have	35	33	32	25	28	33	35	30	26	32	29	33	24
Deck													
Do not want	5	5	5	6	6	6	5	6	6	6	5	5	8
Indifferent	18	15	13	14	18	22	14	14	16	14	16	18	19
Desirable	48	50	56	58	53	44	51	55	55	52	57	46	56
Essential/Must Have	30	30	26	22	22	29	31	26	22	29	23	31	18
Exterior lighting													
Do not want	5	4	4	3	4	7	4	4	3	4	3	6	3
Indifferent	17	14	14	11	16	23	13	14	15	16	14	13	12
Desirable	46	52	49	58	48	41	51	51	51	49	53	47	54
Essential/Must Have	32	31	33	28	32	30	33	32	30	31	30	34	31
Landscaping													
Do not want	6	4	4	3	5	7	4	4	4	4	3	6	4
Indifferent	17	16	12	17	16	19	16	14	17	15	16	13	17
Desirable	47	48	53	57	50	45	47	53	53	50	51	51	53
Essential/Must Have	30	33	31	24	29	28	34	30	26	31	30	30	26
Outdoor fireplace													
Do not want	7	8	11	17	26	9	7	11	23	8	20	18	26
Indifferent	20	20	22	27	29	20	19	23	28	21	29	22	28
Desirable	45	47	49	45	36	44	47	47	39	49	41	43	35
Essential/Must Have	28	26	18	12	9	27	27	19	10	22	10	18	11

Q38. How would the following various designs and features influence your purchase decision?
(Percent of respondents)

	Race/Ethnicity				Home Buyers' Income Bracket					Price Expected to Pay			
	Cauca-sian	African-American	Hispanic	Asian	Under $50,000	$50,000 to $74,999	$75,000 to $99,999	$100,000 to $149,999	$150,000 or more	Less than $150,000	$150,000 to $249,999	$250,000 to $499,999	$500,000 or more
OUTDOOR FEATURES													
Front porch													
Do not want	3	4	5	11	4	3	3	5	5	4	4	3	6
Indifferent	15	11	17	16	14	16	17	17	12	15	17	12	17
Desirable	54	49	49	51	58	55	51	49	51	53	55	55	48
Essential/Must Have	28	36	29	22	24	26	29	30	32	28	23	29	29
Rear porch													
Do not want	6	6	5	7	7	6	5	6	5	8	7	4	6
Indifferent	16	16	19	28	17	17	17	18	16	18	18	16	17
Desirable	54	45	49	46	54	54	55	48	51	50	55	55	48
Essential/Must Have	24	33	27	19	22	23	23	29	28	25	20	25	28
Patio													
Do not want	3	4	6	8	6	3	2	2	4	6	4	2	3
Indifferent	10	11	17	15	13	9	13	12	9	14	15	10	8
Desirable	58	52	48	51	60	59	56	51	52	55	59	56	52
Essential/Must Have	29	33	30	26	21	29	29	35	36	24	21	32	37
Deck													
Do not want	6	6	5	7	7	6	4	5	5	6	6	4	5
Indifferent	14	17	21	21	18	16	13	16	13	17	16	16	13
Desirable	56	45	48	53	55	56	57	50	52	54	57	54	52
Essential/Must Have	24	32	26	19	19	22	26	29	29	23	21	25	30
Exterior lighting													
Do not want	3	6	3	4	6	2	2	3	3	6	5	2	2
Indifferent	13	13	25	21	15	14	14	15	14	18	18	13	11
Desirable	54	46	36	52	53	53	52	46	50	49	51	53	50
Essential/Must Have	30	36	35	23	26	31	33	36	33	27	27	33	37
Landscaping													
Do not want	4	6	4	6	8	3	2	2	2	6	6	2	3
Indifferent	15	18	17	22	19	18	16	12	14	22	18	14	10
Desirable	53	44	47	51	54	52	53	49	49	49	56	52	48
Essential/Must Have	29	31	31	21	20	28	29	37	35	22	19	33	39
Outdoor fireplace													
Do not want	17	16	9	16	26	19	13	13	7	22	17	15	10
Indifferent	26	24	17	24	24	28	27	25	21	21	30	24	24
Desirable	43	41	47	42	40	41	47	41	48	40	42	45	45
Essential/Must Have	14	19	27	18	11	12	13	20	24	17	11	16	21

Q38. How would the following various designs and features influence your purchase decision?
(Percent of respondents)

	All Home Buyers	Geography (Nine Census Divisions)									Buyer Type	
		New England	Middle Atlantic	East North Central	West North Central	South Atlantic	East South Central	West South Central	Mountain	Pacific	First-time	Repeat
OUTDOOR FEATURES												
Outdoor grill (built-in)												
Do not want	12	13	9	16	12	12	13	10	11	11	11	12
Indifferent	23	26	20	28	23	22	21	22	27	20	23	23
Desirable	46	42	48	40	45	47	49	51	46	44	45	46
Essential/Must Have	19	19	23	16	19	19	17	17	16	24	20	19
Outdoor kitchen (cooking, refrigeration, & sink)												
Do not want	19	22	19	24	17	19	19	18	21	15	19	19
Indifferent	25	22	25	28	26	27	29	22	27	21	27	25
Desirable	38	42	37	36	36	40	40	44	35	37	37	39
Essential/Must Have	17	14	20	12	21	15	12	16	17	26	17	17
Lot with trees												
Do not want	8	3	9	10	8	7	8	5	6	9	11	7
Indifferent	19	15	20	21	12	20	20	18	19	20	23	18
Desirable	48	53	50	42	49	47	45	54	53	43	44	48
Essential/Must Have	26	29	21	27	31	26	27	23	22	28	22	26
Lawn sprinklers												
Do not want	13	16	15	20	12	8	16	11	12	9	12	13
Indifferent	23	26	20	25	25	22	24	24	20	22	27	22
Desirable	43	37	41	36	42	48	39	44	45	44	40	43
Essential/Must Have	22	22	24	18	22	22	21	21	23	25	20	22
ACCESSIBILITY FEATURES												
A full bath on the main level												
Do not want	4	5	6	6	5	3	4	4	5	4	5	4
Indifferent	15	13	18	15	18	13	18	12	20	17	18	15
Desirable	47	46	47	43	43	47	53	51	44	48	46	47
Essential/Must Have	33	36	29	36	34	37	25	33	31	31	31	34
Doorways at least 3 ft. wide												
Do not want	5	7	4	6	5	4	6	6	4	5	6	5
Indifferent	22	25	25	25	23	21	18	15	25	20	25	21
Desirable	50	46	50	46	53	55	52	55	51	44	50	51
Essential/Must Have	23	22	21	22	19	20	24	24	20	31	19	23
Hallways at least 4 ft. wide												
Do not want	6	4	6	4	6	7	7	6	5	6	8	6
Indifferent	23	20	26	27	23	24	19	19	23	23	24	23
Desirable	50	51	47	47	53	50	52	56	53	46	50	50
Essential/Must Have	21	25	21	21	18	19	22	19	19	25	18	21

Q38. How would the following various designs and features influence your purchase decision?
(Percent of respondents)

	Age of Household Head					Generation (year born)				Household Composition			
	Under 35 years old	35 to 44 years old	45 to 54 years old	55 to 64 years old	65 years old or older	Gen Z (1997 or later)	Millenni-als(1981-1996)	Gen X (1965-1980)	Boomers (1946-1964)	Married couple w children	Married couple no children	Single parent	One person
OUTDOOR FEATURES													
Outdoor grill (built-in)													
Do not want	6	6	9	12	19	6	6	8	17	6	15	15	19
Indifferent	18	18	19	26	27	20	17	20	27	20	24	20	28
Desirable	47	47	48	48	42	46	47	48	43	49	48	43	41
Essential/Must Have	29	28	24	14	12	29	29	23	12	25	13	22	12
Outdoor kitchen (cooking, refrigeration, & sink)													
Do not want	11	7	15	20	30	13	8	14	27	10	23	24	34
Indifferent	20	22	21	31	27	21	21	23	29	21	31	22	25
Desirable	42	47	45	38	29	39	47	43	32	45	34	38	32
Essential/Must Have	26	23	20	11	13	27	24	20	13	24	12	17	10
Lot with trees													
Do not want	7	6	8	8	9	7	5	7	9	6	8	9	11
Indifferent	18	19	19	19	19	18	19	20	20	17	21	20	19
Desirable	46	48	47	50	46	46	49	45	49	49	44	45	48
Essential/Must Have	29	27	26	23	26	29	27	28	23	28	26	26	23
Lawn sprinklers													
Do not want	8	6	11	16	16	10	5	12	17	8	12	15	21
Indifferent	22	23	21	25	22	23	22	22	23	20	28	27	18
Desirable	43	43	44	43	41	41	44	43	43	45	41	33	45
Essential/Must Have	27	28	24	16	20	26	29	23	18	27	18	25	16
ACCESSIBILITY FEATURES													
A full bath on the main level													
Do not want	5	5	6	5	3	6	4	6	3	5	3	4	5
Indifferent	19	17	17	15	12	24	17	16	13	16	12	20	17
Desirable	47	45	46	52	45	43	46	49	47	49	42	46	46
Essential/Must Have	29	33	31	28	40	27	33	29	36	30	43	30	32
Doorways at least 3 ft. wide													
Do not want	5	5	7	5	4	5	5	6	4	5	4	7	5
Indifferent	21	21	24	23	20	24	19	24	21	20	22	22	27
Desirable	45	51	49	56	49	41	51	49	52	51	51	48	50
Essential/Must Have	29	24	20	16	26	29	24	21	23	25	23	23	18
Hallways at least 4 ft. wide													
Do not want	6	7	5	5	6	8	5	6	6	5	6	5	8
Indifferent	20	22	23	25	24	18	22	24	23	21	24	26	28
Desirable	45	48	54	55	46	43	48	52	50	50	52	47	48
Essential/Must Have	29	24	18	14	23	31	25	18	21	25	18	22	16

Q38. How would the following various designs and features influence your purchase decision?
(Percent of respondents)

	Race/Ethnicity				Home Buyers' Income Bracket					Price Expected to Pay			
	Cauca-sian	African-American	Hispanic	Asian	Under $50,000	$50,000 to $74,999	$75,000 to $99,999	$100,000 to $149,999	$150,000 or more	Less than $150,000	$150,000 to $249,999	$250,000 to $499,999	$500,000 or more
OUTDOOR FEATURES													
Outdoor grill (built-in)													
Do not want	13	8	7	11	19	13	8	11	6	16	15	9	11
Indifferent	24	17	22	22	26	25	27	22	17	24	27	24	17
Desirable	46	45	46	48	43	45	49	43	50	43	45	48	46
Essential/Must Have	17	30	26	19	13	17	16	23	27	17	13	20	26
Outdoor kitchen (cooking, refrigeration, & sink)													
Do not want	22	15	10	15	31	22	17	15	9	25	25	17	13
Indifferent	27	19	21	26	27	26	26	28	21	24	26	27	21
Desirable	37	44	39	42	32	40	41	36	45	35	38	40	40
Essential/Must Have	14	22	30	18	11	12	16	21	25	16	11	16	27
Lot with trees													
Do not want	7	14	7	14	12	8	7	4	6	10	8	5	8
Indifferent	19	22	18	21	19	23	20	20	14	21	23	18	16
Desirable	49	44	41	47	48	48	48	45	49	45	47	50	46
Essential/Must Have	26	20	34	18	21	21	25	31	31	25	23	26	30
Lawn sprinklers													
Do not want	14	9	7	9	20	12	10	10	8	18	19	10	6
Indifferent	23	20	24	24	25	25	26	19	18	28	27	20	18
Desirable	43	42	41	47	39	43	41	47	43	36	40	47	44
Essential/Must Have	20	29	28	20	15	20	22	24	30	18	15	23	32
ACCESSIBILITY FEATURES													
A full bath on the main level													
Do not want	4	4	4	7	5	2	6	4	5	5	5	3	6
Indifferent	14	17	20	22	12	17	16	20	15	16	16	16	13
Desirable	46	48	50	48	53	46	45	40	47	50	51	44	46
Essential/Must Have	35	32	26	23	31	35	34	36	33	29	28	38	35
Doorways at least 3 ft. wide													
Do not want	5	7	4	3	6	3	6	5	4	6	7	4	4
Indifferent	22	15	20	30	21	24	26	23	19	21	22	21	23
Desirable	51	50	52	44	54	50	48	45	52	52	52	51	47
Essential/Must Have	22	28	24	22	19	23	20	27	25	20	20	23	26
Hallways at least 4 ft. wide													
Do not want	6	7	5	6	7	6	5	6	4	9	6	5	4
Indifferent	25	18	17	24	22	29	28	21	19	21	26	25	19
Desirable	50	51	48	51	53	45	48	48	52	51	49	50	50
Essential/Must Have	19	24	30	19	18	20	19	24	25	19	19	20	26

Q38. How would the following various designs and features influence your purchase decision?
(Percent of respondents)

	All Home Buyers	Geography (Nine Census Divisions)									Buyer Type	
		New England	Middle Atlantic	East North Central	West North Central	South Atlantic	East South Central	West South Central	Mountain	Pacific	First-time	Repeat
ACCESSIBILITY FEATURES												
Bathroom aids (grab bars, etc.)												
Do not want	11	11	10	10	9	11	15	10	10	10	14	10
Indifferent	25	27	25	27	24	24	26	25	27	23	29	25
Desirable	41	43	41	38	47	43	41	41	42	38	38	41
Essential/Must Have	23	20	25	25	21	22	18	24	20	29	19	24
Lower kitchen cabinets												
Do not want	13	10	16	13	16	13	20	10	11	12	11	13
Indifferent	29	22	31	31	27	32	27	25	30	27	33	29
Desirable	39	41	36	36	40	37	39	46	40	38	38	39
Essential/Must Have	19	26	17	20	17	18	14	20	19	22	17	19
Lower countertops												
Do not want	19	17	22	20	16	19	21	17	15	17	16	19
Indifferent	34	32	36	34	35	37	31	34	39	29	33	34
Desirable	32	35	29	33	33	33	34	33	30	33	37	32
Essential/Must Have	15	16	13	14	16	11	14	16	16	21	14	15
Non-slip floor surfaces												
Do not want	5	1	6	7	5	5	7	3	5	3	6	5
Indifferent	21	26	23	23	25	21	19	17	18	21	23	21
Desirable	50	45	49	46	45	50	55	60	50	47	47	50
Essential/Must Have	24	28	22	25	25	24	19	20	28	29	25	24
An entrance without steps												
Do not want	6	5	6	5	6	6	6	6	4	6	10	5
Indifferent	27	25	28	28	28	26	26	28	26	25	32	26
Desirable	46	45	46	41	49	46	49	47	43	47	37	47
Essential/Must Have	22	26	20	25	17	22	19	19	27	22	21	22
GREEN FEATURES												
Insulation higher than required by code												
Do not want	5	4	5	7	4	4	8	5	4	6	9	5
Indifferent	23	15	23	23	24	24	25	24	22	19	28	22
Desirable	50	58	51	47	42	51	43	56	52	50	47	50
Essential/Must Have	22	22	21	23	30	21	24	16	22	26	17	23
ENERGY STAR rating for whole home												
Do not want	4	4	2	8	3	3	6	4	3	4	4	4
Indifferent	18	18	19	15	22	19	17	17	19	17	25	17
Desirable	51	47	52	48	48	53	51	53	59	46	45	52
Essential/Must Have	27	30	27	29	27	26	26	26	20	34	26	27

Q38. How would the following various designs and features influence your purchase decision?
(Percent of respondents)

	Age of Household Head					Generation (year born)				Household Composition			
	Under 35 years old	35 to 44 years old	45 to 54 years old	55 to 64 years old	65 years old or older	Gen Z (1997 or later)	Millenni-als(1981-1996)	Gen X (1965-1980)	Boomers (1946-1964)	Married couple w children	Married couple no children	Single parent	One person
ACCESSIBILITY FEATURES													
Bathroom aids (grab bars, etc.)													
Do not want	11	10	13	13	7	13	11	14	8	9	9	13	15
Indifferent	25	25	32	26	20	26	23	29	24	24	28	23	26
Desirable	37	38	37	44	44	34	38	38	44	42	42	40	38
Essential/Must Have	28	27	18	17	28	28	28	18	24	25	21	25	21
Lower kitchen cabinets													
Do not want	8	8	15	15	15	8	9	14	14	8	18	9	20
Indifferent	25	27	26	36	29	29	25	28	31	26	33	27	31
Desirable	41	39	42	37	37	39	40	40	38	41	35	43	36
Essential/Must Have	25	26	17	13	19	25	27	17	17	24	15	21	14
Lower countertops													
Do not want	10	10	18	24	22	13	9	19	22	11	27	15	27
Indifferent	27	28	32	40	38	26	29	31	39	30	39	34	40
Desirable	39	39	35	29	28	37	39	34	28	38	25	37	24
Essential/Must Have	24	23	15	8	12	24	24	16	10	21	9	14	10
Non-slip floor surfaces													
Do not want	5	6	6	4	4	6	6	6	4	5	4	6	5
Indifferent	22	21	23	20	21	24	20	22	20	19	24	20	25
Desirable	42	45	51	58	48	38	46	50	53	48	51	48	51
Essential/Must Have	30	28	21	18	26	32	28	22	23	28	20	26	20
An entrance without steps													
Do not want	9	6	6	6	4	13	7	6	4	6	6	6	4
Indifferent	26	28	30	29	23	26	27	30	25	24	25	33	31
Desirable	40	40	44	48	49	37	40	44	50	44	51	39	47
Essential/Must Have	24	26	20	17	23	23	26	21	21	26	18	22	18
GREEN FEATURES													
Insulation higher than required by code													
Do not want	8	5	6	4	4	11	5	6	4	6	4	6	5
Indifferent	25	23	24	24	20	27	22	25	21	21	23	24	22
Desirable	43	46	49	54	52	40	49	48	53	49	52	49	52
Essential/Must Have	24	26	21	17	24	23	25	21	22	25	21	21	20
ENERGY STAR rating for whole home													
Do not want	7	4	3	3	4	10	4	3	4	4	4	6	3
Indifferent	26	16	17	19	17	31	17	18	17	17	19	20	16
Desirable	42	51	53	54	50	37	50	51	52	51	50	48	53
Essential/Must Have	26	30	27	24	29	22	29	27	27	28	27	26	28

Q38. How would the following various designs and features influence your purchase decision?
(Percent of respondents)

	Race/Ethnicity				Home Buyers' Income Bracket					Price Expected to Pay			
	Cauca-sian	African-American	Hispanic	Asian	Under $50,000	$50,000 to $74,999	$75,000 to $99,999	$100,000 to $149,999	$150,000 or more	Less than $150,000	$150,000 to $249,999	$250,000 to $499,999	$500,000 or more
ACCESSIBILITY FEATURES													
Bathroom aids (grab bars, etc.)													
Do not want	11	9	7	8	12	10	10	13	8	11	10	10	11
Indifferent	26	21	20	26	19	30	26	27	27	22	22	27	25
Desirable	39	44	47	47	45	40	44	36	39	43	45	41	37
Essential/Must Have	23	26	26	19	24	20	20	24	26	24	23	22	26
Lower kitchen cabinets													
Do not want	15	11	6	13	13	15	12	15	13	12	12	13	15
Indifferent	30	24	24	29	29	31	34	30	25	27	32	30	27
Desirable	37	44	42	44	42	39	37	35	39	41	40	39	35
Essential/Must Have	18	21	28	14	17	15	18	21	24	20	16	18	23
Lower countertops													
Do not want	21	15	7	12	19	19	22	19	16	19	19	18	20
Indifferent	38	25	24	25	35	41	37	35	26	32	36	36	32
Desirable	29	41	40	48	32	30	29	29	38	32	34	32	32
Essential/Must Have	12	19	28	14	14	10	12	17	20	17	11	14	17
Non-slip floor surfaces													
Do not want	5	5	4	6	5	3	6	5	5	5	5	5	6
Indifferent	22	16	17	26	19	23	26	23	19	21	19	23	21
Desirable	51	43	45	45	55	51	47	45	48	51	52	49	47
Essential/Must Have	21	37	34	23	21	24	21	27	28	23	24	23	27
An entrance without steps													
Do not want	6	9	4	6	6	3	7	6	6	7	5	6	4
Indifferent	28	22	21	30	24	32	30	28	24	26	27	26	27
Desirable	45	45	49	47	49	47	44	43	43	46	47	47	41
Essential/Must Have	21	24	27	18	20	17	19	24	27	21	20	21	27
GREEN FEATURES													
Insulation higher than required by code													
Do not want	5	9	6	7	9	5	2	3	5	9	7	3	4
Indifferent	22	22	25	24	24	27	23	22	18	28	23	22	17
Desirable	52	46	38	50	51	49	52	48	50	44	53	50	53
Essential/Must Have	21	24	30	19	17	20	23	27	27	19	17	24	26
ENERGY STAR rating for whole home													
Do not want	3	5	4	9	6	4	3	2	4	7	4	3	4
Indifferent	17	17	21	22	19	18	15	21	16	22	18	16	16
Desirable	52	45	43	53	51	51	56	47	50	46	55	53	48
Essential/Must Have	27	33	31	16	24	27	26	30	30	25	23	28	32

Q38. How would the following various designs and features influence your purchase decision?
(Percent of respondents)

	All Home Buyers	Geography (Nine Census Divisions)									Buyer Type	
		New England	Middle Atlantic	East North Central	West North Central	South Atlantic	East South Central	West South Central	Mountain	Pacific	First-time	Repeat
GREEN FEATURES												
ENERGY STAR rated appliances												
Do not want	4	4	3	6	3	4	5	3	2	3	7	3
Indifferent	16	13	14	13	20	15	22	18	21	16	24	15
Desirable	50	51	49	50	48	53	43	54	51	48	46	51
Essential/Must Have	30	31	34	31	29	28	30	25	26	33	23	31
Efficient lighting that uses less energy than traditional bulbs												
Do not want	5	4	6	7	6	3	9	5	4	5	6	5
Indifferent	21	20	21	21	19	20	26	21	24	20	27	20
Desirable	50	47	49	47	52	54	40	57	55	47	48	51
Essential/Must Have	24	29	25	26	23	23	25	18	16	28	20	24
Tankless water heater												
Do not want	8	8	7	12	6	8	13	7	7	6	10	8
Indifferent	27	26	27	28	30	28	29	23	26	25	30	27
Desirable	46	50	48	42	48	45	46	50	47	41	46	46
Essential/Must Have	19	16	18	18	16	18	12	20	20	28	14	20
Solar water heating/electric system												
Do not want	11	13	13	17	13	11	12	8	9	6	10	11
Indifferent	28	22	26	31	22	32	30	31	29	19	32	27
Desirable	44	49	45	38	47	43	46	46	45	47	44	44
Essential/Must Have	17	17	15	15	18	14	11	15	17	28	13	17
Geothermal heating/cooling												
Do not want	11	10	12	16	9	13	12	10	9	7	11	11
Indifferent	34	31	30	34	31	40	39	35	31	33	34	34
Desirable	40	46	42	39	37	37	37	42	45	40	42	40
Essential/Must Have	14	13	17	11	23	10	12	13	15	20	13	15
Roof mounted, electricity generating wind turbine												
Do not want	22	24	21	31	15	26	19	18	17	14	17	22
Indifferent	32	34	32	29	37	36	34	31	31	28	37	32
Desirable	33	27	32	28	39	30	32	37	38	40	35	33
Essential/Must Have	13	15	14	12	9	8	14	14	13	19	12	13
Net Zero home												
Do not want	8	5	11	11	5	8	9	8	6	6	9	8
Indifferent	32	28	28	35	34	34	33	33	34	24	36	31
Desirable	45	50	44	39	43	46	44	47	45	49	42	45
Essential/Must Have	16	17	17	14	17	13	14	13	16	22	13	16

Q38. How would the following various designs and features influence your purchase decision?
(Percent of respondents)

	Age of Household Head					Generation (year born)				Household Composition			
	Under 35 years old	35 to 44 years old	45 to 54 years old	55 to 64 years old	65 years old or older	Gen Z (1997 or later)	Millennials(1981-1996)	Gen X (1965-1980)	Boomers (1946-1964)	Married couple w children	Married couple no children	Single parent	One person
GREEN FEATURES													
ENERGY STAR rated appliances													
Do not want	7	5	3	3	3	11	5	3	3	4	3	6	3
Indifferent	25	16	16	17	13	30	17	17	14	16	16	18	13
Desirable	43	48	51	53	51	37	48	49	53	50	50	46	53
Essential/Must Have	25	31	29	27	33	22	30	30	30	30	30	30	31
Efficient lighting that uses less energy than traditional bulbs													
Do not want	7	5	6	5	5	10	4	6	5	5	5	7	5
Indifferent	23	20	18	24	20	25	20	20	20	19	24	21	21
Desirable	44	48	50	56	50	42	48	50	53	49	49	50	54
Essential/Must Have	26	27	25	16	26	24	28	24	22	26	22	22	20
Tankless water heater													
Do not want	8	4	11	6	10	10	5	10	8	6	10	8	9
Indifferent	27	21	27	32	27	31	21	29	28	23	31	29	29
Desirable	43	48	44	47	45	35	50	42	46	47	44	43	45
Essential/Must Have	22	26	18	14	18	23	24	19	18	23	15	21	17
Solar water heating/electric system													
Do not want	8	7	8	14	14	9	7	9	14	8	13	13	15
Indifferent	26	22	29	31	28	28	22	29	28	22	34	25	32
Desirable	42	44	47	42	46	37	45	44	46	47	42	43	40
Essential/Must Have	24	27	15	13	12	26	26	18	12	23	10	19	13
Geothermal heating/cooling													
Do not want	8	7	9	14	14	12	6	9	15	8	15	11	14
Indifferent	28	26	34	44	34	28	26	35	38	28	39	33	39
Desirable	41	44	42	34	40	38	44	41	37	44	35	40	40
Essential/Must Have	22	24	15	7	12	22	24	14	10	20	11	15	7
Roof mounted, electricity generating wind turbine													
Do not want	10	9	17	29	29	12	9	18	28	15	30	18	28
Indifferent	26	26	33	37	34	28	25	32	36	27	37	33	35
Desirable	41	41	36	29	29	37	42	35	29	40	26	33	31
Essential/Must Have	23	25	14	6	8	23	24	15	7	19	7	15	6
Net Zero home													
Do not want	7	7	7	12	7	10	7	8	8	7	10	7	10
Indifferent	28	23	32	34	35	30	24	33	34	26	38	33	33
Desirable	41	45	42	44	47	36	45	40	48	47	41	43	46
Essential/Must Have	23	25	18	10	11	23	24	19	9	21	11	17	12

Q38. How would the following various designs and features influence your purchase decision?
(Percent of respondents)

	Race/Ethnicity				Home Buyers' Income Bracket					Price Expected to Pay			
	Cauca-sian	African-American	Hispanic	Asian	Under $50,000	$50,000 to $74,999	$75,000 to $99,999	$100,000 to $149,999	$150,000 or more	Less than $150,000	$150,000 to $249,999	$250,000 to $499,999	$500,000 or more
GREEN FEATURES													
ENERGY STAR rated appliances													
Do not want	4	5	4	5	5	4	2	3	3	7	3	2	4
Indifferent	15	18	19	20	17	18	15	17	14	20	16	15	16
Desirable	51	43	48	50	52	49	51	49	49	47	55	53	43
Essential/Must Have	30	34	29	25	26	29	32	31	34	26	26	30	38
Efficient lighting that uses less energy than traditional bulbs													
Do not want	5	6	5	8	8	4	3	4	5	8	5	3	7
Indifferent	21	20	21	18	22	23	20	20	19	22	24	20	17
Desirable	51	53	47	52	49	54	58	49	46	48	50	54	46
Essential/Must Have	23	21	27	23	21	20	19	27	30	22	21	23	30
Tankless water heater													
Do not want	8	9	6	8	13	8	8	5	6	11	9	7	6
Indifferent	28	26	24	25	30	34	24	25	23	31	29	27	22
Desirable	46	45	43	50	43	43	50	48	46	41	48	47	47
Essential/Must Have	18	20	27	17	15	15	19	22	25	17	15	19	26
Solar water heating/electric system													
Do not want	13	11	5	7	16	10	11	9	9	15	12	9	10
Indifferent	29	27	21	24	27	33	28	29	23	27	30	30	21
Desirable	43	45	46	52	45	44	44	41	46	42	46	45	46
Essential/Must Have	15	18	28	17	12	13	17	21	22	16	12	16	24
Geothermal heating/cooling													
Do not want	13	10	5	9	15	11	9	11	9	13	13	10	10
Indifferent	37	26	24	27	35	41	36	35	27	33	37	35	31
Desirable	38	45	43	49	40	37	41	39	42	39	41	41	37
Essential/Must Have	12	19	28	15	10	10	13	16	22	14	9	13	22
Roof mounted, electricity generating wind turbine													
Do not want	25	17	10	11	27	23	20	21	16	21	25	21	20
Indifferent	33	28	31	28	33	36	39	31	26	30	34	34	27
Desirable	31	36	38	49	31	31	31	35	38	37	31	32	37
Essential/Must Have	11	19	21	13	9	10	10	14	20	12	11	13	16
Net Zero home													
Do not want	9	8	3	8	11	7	5	6	8	12	8	6	8
Indifferent	33	29	27	29	34	37	33	29	26	32	33	34	25
Desirable	44	41	49	44	44	44	49	45	43	40	46	46	46
Essential/Must Have	14	22	22	19	11	12	13	20	22	16	13	15	20

Q38. How would the following various designs and features influence your purchase decision?
(Percent of respondents)

	All Home Buyers	Geography (Nine Census Divisions)									Buyer Type	
		New England	Middle Atlantic	East North Central	West North Central	South Atlantic	East South Central	West South Central	Mountain	Pacific	First-time	Repeat
GREEN FEATURES												
Roof partially or completely covered by plants												
Do not want	34	30	36	40	29	41	32	33	25	22	27	34
Indifferent	27	27	25	25	22	26	31	29	31	28	32	26
Desirable	28	33	28	26	32	23	24	29	29	33	32	27
Essential/Must Have	12	11	12	10	17	10	13	9	15	17	9	12
Water-conserving bathroom faucets (flow rate below the federal conservation standard)												
Do not want	12	11	10	15	11	12	14	10	10	9	12	11
Indifferent	26	19	26	29	24	26	32	27	26	25	27	26
Desirable	43	49	45	38	44	44	42	47	43	37	46	42
Essential/Must Have	20	21	20	17	21	18	12	16	21	29	15	20
Water-conserving shower heads (flow rate below the federal conservation standard)												
Do not want	12	9	12	14	12	14	16	12	10	10	16	12
Indifferent	25	18	23	29	23	24	29	24	31	24	28	25
Desirable	44	54	47	38	41	44	42	50	42	43	41	44
Essential/Must Have	19	20	18	20	24	18	13	14	17	22	14	19
Water-conserving toilets (volume below fed. conservation standard)												
Do not want	10	8	10	12	11	10	16	11	9	8	11	10
Indifferent	26	23	24	32	21	25	30	23	29	22	27	25
Desirable	44	45	47	35	46	45	38	47	42	46	45	43
Essential/Must Have	20	24	18	21	22	20	16	19	20	24	17	21
Barrels/cisterns to collect rainwater for irrigation, toilet flushing, etc.												
Do not want	18	15	17	21	16	21	25	16	12	13	15	18
Indifferent	31	23	35	33	23	36	27	30	36	24	32	31
Desirable	36	49	33	34	43	32	33	41	35	38	39	36
Essential/Must Have	15	13	15	13	17	11	15	13	17	25	14	15
Components made of recycled mats.												
Do not want	10	10	10	15	9	11	12	10	7	6	12	10
Indifferent	38	32	40	37	39	44	44	41	36	26	42	37
Desirable	38	42	35	36	34	35	28	40	35	50	37	38
Essential/Must Have	14	16	15	12	18	10	16	9	23	19	9	15

Q38. How would the following various designs and features influence your purchase decision?
(Percent of respondents)

	Age of Household Head					Generation (year born)				Household Composition			
	Under 35 years old	35 to 44 years old	45 to 54 years old	55 to 64 years old	65 years old or older	Gen Z (1997 or later)	Millenni-als(1981-1996)	Gen X (1965-1980)	Boomers (1946-1964)	Married couple w children	Married couple no children	Single parent	One person
GREEN FEATURES													
Roof partially or completely covered by plants													
Do not want	13	14	29	44	46	15	13	29	45	20	48	29	44
Indifferent	28	26	28	28	26	31	26	27	27	25	28	28	29
Desirable	39	37	31	23	20	34	39	31	21	37	18	28	20
Essential/Must Have	21	23	12	5	9	21	22	13	7	18	6	16	7
Water-conserving bathroom faucets (flow rate below the federal conservation standard)													
Do not want	7	7	11	13	14	10	6	11	13	8	19	12	13
Indifferent	23	25	28	30	24	26	23	30	26	24	26	23	31
Desirable	45	45	43	42	41	42	46	42	42	46	38	43	40
Essential/Must Have	24	24	18	14	21	23	25	17	18	23	17	22	16
Water-conserving shower heads (flow rate below the federal conservation standard)													
Do not want	9	8	12	14	15	10	8	12	14	8	19	13	15
Indifferent	24	24	28	28	22	28	23	29	24	23	24	23	30
Desirable	42	42	44	46	45	37	43	43	46	48	41	42	40
Essential/Must Have	25	26	17	12	18	26	26	16	16	21	16	23	15
Water-conserving toilets (volume below fed. conservation standard)													
Do not want	8	7	11	13	11	8	7	12	11	7	15	8	13
Indifferent	26	25	26	30	23	30	25	27	25	24	26	26	28
Desirable	43	43	43	43	45	38	44	42	45	45	42	43	42
Essential/Must Have	24	25	20	15	21	24	25	20	19	24	16	23	17
Barrels/cisterns to collect rainwater for irrigation, toilet flushing, etc.													
Do not want	10	10	16	22	22	12	10	15	22	12	20	19	26
Indifferent	26	24	32	36	32	27	24	31	34	25	40	31	31
Desirable	40	40	37	34	34	36	42	37	35	42	28	32	35
Essential/Must Have	23	26	16	8	11	24	25	16	10	21	11	18	8
Components made of recycled mats.													
Do not want	9	7	11	10	12	12	6	11	11	8	13	12	12
Indifferent	28	29	34	47	41	31	28	35	44	29	46	38	45
Desirable	39	42	38	35	36	34	44	37	36	42	33	35	35
Essential/Must Have	23	22	17	8	11	23	22	17	10	21	8	15	8

Q38. How would the following various designs and features influence your purchase decision?
(Percent of respondents)

	Race/Ethnicity				Home Buyers' Income Bracket					Price Expected to Pay			
	Cauca-sian	African-American	Hispanic	Asian	Under $50,000	$50,000 to $74,999	$75,000 to $99,999	$100,000 to $149,999	$150,000 or more	Less than $150,000	$150,000 to $249,999	$250,000 to $499,999	$500,000 or more
GREEN FEATURES													
Roof partially or completely covered by plants													
Do not want	39	27	11	17	41	40	35	29	23	33	37	34	29
Indifferent	28	22	22	31	27	29	29	27	23	24	29	28	25
Desirable	24	33	42	39	23	24	28	30	34	30	25	27	31
Essential/Must Have	9	18	24	13	9	7	9	14	20	12	9	12	16
Water-conserving bathroom faucets (flow rate below the federal conservation standard)													
Do not want	13	10	7	5	14	11	11	11	10	13	10	10	13
Indifferent	27	22	22	24	28	32	28	25	20	27	29	27	21
Desirable	43	46	38	48	43	43	44	39	45	42	46	44	40
Essential/Must Have	17	22	33	23	16	14	17	25	25	18	15	19	26
Water-conserving shower heads (flow rate below the federal conservation standard)													
Do not want	14	12	7	8	15	11	14	10	11	14	11	12	12
Indifferent	26	20	22	27	27	31	27	21	21	26	27	26	21
Desirable	44	44	44	48	45	42	41	45	45	45	48	44	42
Essential/Must Have	17	24	27	17	14	16	17	23	23	15	14	19	25
Water-conserving toilets (volume below fed. conservation standard)													
Do not want	12	9	5	7	12	10	11	9	10	11	10	10	10
Indifferent	27	20	22	26	28	31	27	24	20	28	28	25	22
Desirable	43	45	45	49	43	42	45	43	45	43	44	45	42
Essential/Must Have	19	26	28	18	18	16	18	23	26	18	18	20	26
Barrels/cisterns to collect rainwater for irrigation, toilet flushing, etc.													
Do not want	20	17	5	12	23	17	19	15	13	20	19	16	17
Indifferent	33	28	21	29	29	39	32	31	27	27	31	34	28
Desirable	34	34	47	44	37	34	35	36	37	38	39	34	36
Essential/Must Have	13	20	27	14	11	10	14	18	22	15	11	16	20
Components made of recycled mats.													
Do not want	11	13	7	10	14	13	8	9	7	12	13	9	8
Indifferent	41	32	21	33	40	45	41	36	30	35	40	41	33
Desirable	36	39	42	40	37	35	39	37	39	38	37	36	41
Essential/Must Have	12	17	29	18	9	8	13	17	24	14	11	14	18

Q38. How would the following various designs and features influence your purchase decision?
(Percent of respondents)

	All Home Buyers	Geography (Nine Census Divisions)									Buyer Type	
		New England	Middle Atlantic	East North Central	West North Central	South Atlantic	East South Central	West South Central	Mountain	Pacific	First-time	Repeat
GREEN FEATURES												
Components made from locally produced materials												
Do not want	8	9	8	12	11	7	10	8	5	5	10	8
Indifferent	37	30	37	37	30	45	39	38	39	30	37	37
Desirable	40	48	40	39	41	36	41	43	40	44	40	40
Essential/Must Have	14	13	15	12	19	11	10	12	15	21	13	14
Components built using certified sustainably harvested lumber												
Do not want	9	8	10	12	10	8	10	9	5	6	9	9
Indifferent	35	27	33	39	31	41	36	35	39	23	38	34
Desirable	41	47	40	35	39	39	40	43	42	50	39	41
Essential/Must Have	15	18	17	14	19	12	13	13	14	21	14	15
Prefabricated components (like panelized wall sections or roof & floor trusses												
Do not want	13	9	13	16	11	15	18	13	7	10	12	13
Indifferent	42	43	43	42	36	48	40	39	45	35	42	42
Desirable	32	39	30	30	40	25	31	38	33	37	36	32
Essential/Must Have	13	9	15	12	14	11	11	10	15	18	10	13
Certification home is above ***water*** efficiency standards												
Do not want	6	5	7	7	5	5	10	4	5	6	8	6
Indifferent	26	25	25	27	26	26	28	28	31	22	28	26
Desirable	49	53	48	46	43	52	44	54	48	47	47	49
Essential/Must Have	19	18	20	20	26	18	18	14	17	24	16	20
Certification home is above ***energy*** efficiency standards												
Do not want	6	7	5	7	6	4	11	5	5	6	7	6
Indifferent	25	26	21	27	23	26	26	24	29	20	32	24
Desirable	49	42	52	43	47	52	45	54	50	51	46	50
Essential/Must Have	20	25	22	23	24	18	17	16	16	23	15	21

Q38. How would the following various designs and features influence your purchase decision?
(Percent of respondents)

	Age of Household Head					Generation (year born)				Household Composition			
	Under 35 years old	35 to 44 years old	45 to 54 years old	55 to 64 years old	65 years old or older	Gen Z (1997 or later)	Millennials(1981-1996)	Gen X (1965-1980)	Boomers (1946-1964)	Married couple w children	Married couple no children	Single parent	One person
GREEN FEATURES													
Components made from locally produced materials													
Do not want	9	6	6	9	10	11	6	7	9	6	8	13	9
Indifferent	27	28	38	43	42	29	28	37	42	30	49	32	44
Desirable	40	42	40	40	40	37	42	39	41	43	36	39	40
Essential/Must Have	25	23	15	8	9	23	24	17	8	21	6	16	7
Components built using certified sustainably harvested lumber													
Do not want	8	6	8	11	9	11	6	10	9	7	10	12	11
Indifferent	27	24	36	40	38	29	24	35	38	27	43	37	41
Desirable	42	43	41	40	41	38	45	39	42	45	37	37	38
Essential/Must Have	22	27	15	10	11	22	25	16	11	21	11	15	9
Prefabricated components (like panelized wall sections or roof & floor trusses													
Do not want	9	8	11	15	17	12	7	12	16	9	17	14	17
Indifferent	30	28	43	51	45	31	28	42	47	31	56	34	51
Desirable	40	40	32	30	28	36	41	33	29	40	22	37	25
Essential/Must Have	21	24	14	5	10	20	24	14	9	20	5	16	6
Certification home is above ***water*** efficiency standards													
Do not want	6	5	6	6	6	9	4	6	6	6	7	7	5
Indifferent	23	23	22	29	29	26	22	24	28	22	32	25	28
Desirable	46	47	52	49	48	40	48	50	49	49	47	45	51
Essential/Must Have	25	25	19	16	17	25	25	20	17	24	15	23	16
Certification home is above ***energy*** efficiency standards													
Do not want	6	6	6	6	6	8	5	6	6	5	7	6	5
Indifferent	26	21	24	26	25	31	21	24	25	20	28	26	28
Desirable	44	48	49	54	49	39	48	48	51	51	46	45	51
Essential/Must Have	24	25	22	14	20	23	25	21	18	24	18	22	17

Q38. How would the following various designs and features influence your purchase decision?
(Percent of respondents)

	Race/Ethnicity				Home Buyers' Income Bracket					Price Expected to Pay			
	Caucasian	African-American	Hispanic	Asian	Under $50,000	$50,000 to $74,999	$75,000 to $99,999	$100,000 to $149,999	$150,000 or more	Less than $150,000	$150,000 to $249,999	$250,000 to $499,999	$500,000 or more
GREEN FEATURES													
Components made from locally produced materials													
Do not want	8	11	7	6	13	9	6	6	6	11	11	6	6
Indifferent	40	30	23	37	38	43	42	35	31	35	39	38	36
Desirable	40	40	45	40	40	37	41	41	42	38	39	42	42
Essential/Must Have	12	19	25	17	9	11	12	17	21	16	10	14	17
Components built using certified sustainably harvested lumber													
Do not want	9	11	4	6	13	10	7	6	5	13	10	6	8
Indifferent	38	29	23	29	36	43	35	32	29	32	39	36	31
Desirable	40	40	44	51	39	37	44	44	42	38	40	43	42
Essential/Must Have	13	20	28	14	12	10	13	17	23	17	11	15	20
Prefabricated components (like panelized wall sections or roof & floor trusses													
Do not want	14	16	7	9	16	16	10	11	10	15	14	13	10
Indifferent	46	33	25	30	46	50	44	38	33	38	43	45	36
Desirable	29	37	43	44	28	27	34	35	38	33	32	30	37
Essential/Must Have	11	15	25	17	10	7	11	17	19	14	11	12	18
Certification home is above ***water*** efficiency standards													
Do not want	6	8	4	9	8	6	4	5	5	10	7	4	5
Indifferent	27	21	27	22	29	30	25	26	21	27	29	26	20
Desirable	50	45	42	51	48	50	54	45	49	47	48	50	50
Essential/Must Have	17	26	27	18	15	15	17	24	25	16	15	20	25
Certification home is above ***energy*** efficiency standards													
Do not want	6	7	6	9	8	5	3	5	6	10	5	4	5
Indifferent	25	20	24	21	27	30	27	23	17	28	28	24	18
Desirable	51	46	43	49	49	49	53	48	50	46	49	51	51
Essential/Must Have	18	27	27	22	16	17	17	23	28	16	17	20	27

Q38. How would the following various designs and features influence your purchase decision?
(Percent of respondents)

	All Home Buyers	Geography (Nine Census Divisions)									Buyer Type	
		New England	Middle Atlantic	East North Central	West North Central	South Atlantic	East South Central	West South Central	Mountain	Pacific	First-time	Repeat
INDOOR AIR QUALITY												
Home dehumidification system												
Do not want	7	2	6	9	5	7	8	5	11	5	6	7
Indifferent	27	17	22	24	21	30	29	33	33	30	29	27
Desirable	48	58	52	49	52	48	47	49	41	41	50	48
Essential/Must Have	18	23	21	17	23	14	17	14	15	23	15	18
Electronic air cleaner												
Do not want	7	12	7	9	6	8	9	6	6	4	6	7
Indifferent	29	31	25	34	23	30	29	27	27	26	30	28
Desirable	46	41	49	40	50	46	47	53	49	45	48	46
Essential/Must Have	18	16	19	17	21	15	15	14	18	25	16	18
Low VOC materials (paint, flooring, adhesives)												
Do not want	7	8	7	11	5	6	10	6	5	4	7	7
Indifferent	30	29	31	31	27	36	32	30	28	24	37	30
Desirable	45	42	45	40	51	43	39	50	46	46	41	45
Essential/Must Have	18	22	17	18	18	15	19	14	21	25	15	19
Whole house mechanical ventilation												
Do not want	7	6	6	12	7	6	9	5	4	5	6	7
Indifferent	30	22	30	35	27	34	28	32	32	24	33	30
Desirable	46	49	44	40	47	46	46	52	47	47	47	46
Essential/Must Have	17	23	20	13	19	14	18	12	17	24	14	17
Certification home has above-standard indoor environmental quality												
Do not want	6	4	6	9	5	3	9	4	6	5	6	6
Indifferent	24	22	24	28	16	26	26	21	24	21	29	23
Desirable	49	54	50	44	53	51	44	56	49	47	43	50
Essential/Must Have	21	20	20	20	26	20	21	18	21	27	22	21
Certification home is above health and wellness standards												
Do not want	5	3	5	9	6	4	10	4	4	4	6	5
Indifferent	23	20	20	26	24	24	18	24	27	22	25	23
Desirable	50	57	54	45	49	51	44	56	47	48	50	50
Essential/Must Have	21	21	20	20	21	21	28	16	22	25	19	22

Q38. How would the following various designs and features influence your purchase decision?
(Percent of respondents)

	Age of Household Head					Generation (year born)				Household Composition			
	Under 35 years old	35 to 44 years old	45 to 54 years old	55 to 64 years old	65 years old or older	Gen Z (1997 or later)	Millenni-als(1981-1996)	Gen X (1965-1980)	Boomers (1946-1964)	Married couple w children	Married couple no children	Single parent	One person
INDOOR AIR QUALITY													
Home dehumidification system													
Do not want	7	5	6	7	8	10	4	7	7	5	8	9	8
Indifferent	24	25	26	29	29	23	23	28	29	22	33	29	30
Desirable	45	46	48	53	47	42	48	47	49	50	48	41	49
Essential/Must Have	25	25	20	10	16	25	25	19	14	23	11	21	13
Electronic air cleaner													
Do not want	6	4	6	9	9	8	4	7	8	5	10	8	9
Indifferent	23	24	27	36	29	25	22	29	31	23	37	29	28
Desirable	45	44	48	45	47	44	46	45	47	48	44	40	50
Essential/Must Have	25	28	18	10	15	23	29	18	13	25	9	22	13
Low VOC materials (paint, flooring, adhesives)													
Do not want	7	5	6	7	8	8	5	7	8	5	8	7	7
Indifferent	28	30	30	35	29	32	27	32	30	25	35	34	34
Desirable	42	42	47	47	44	37	44	45	45	47	43	37	42
Essential/Must Have	24	23	17	12	20	23	23	16	17	22	14	22	17
Whole house mechanical ventilation													
Do not want	5	5	6	7	8	6	5	8	7	5	7	8	9
Indifferent	26	25	29	37	31	29	23	30	33	23	37	34	34
Desirable	44	45	45	45	48	40	48	43	47	47	46	38	45
Essential/Must Have	24	25	20	11	13	25	24	19	13	24	10	21	12
Certification home has above-standard indoor environmental quality													
Do not want	6	4	5	6	6	8	5	6	6	5	6	6	6
Indifferent	21	23	24	26	23	24	20	26	24	20	27	27	26
Desirable	46	45	49	52	51	40	48	47	51	49	51	43	51
Essential/Must Have	27	27	22	16	19	28	28	21	19	26	17	24	16
Certification home is above health and wellness standards													
Do not want	6	5	4	6	5	8	4	5	5	4	6	6	6
Indifferent	22	20	23	25	25	27	18	25	24	20	25	28	25
Desirable	46	46	48	55	52	39	49	46	53	50	52	43	53
Essential/Must Have	26	29	25	14	19	27	29	24	17	26	17	24	16

Q38. How would the following various designs and features influence your purchase decision?
(Percent of respondents)

	Race/Ethnicity				Home Buyers' Income Bracket					Price Expected to Pay			
	Cauca-sian	African-American	Hispanic	Asian	Under $50,000	$50,000 to $74,999	$75,000 to $99,999	$100,000 to $149,999	$150,000 or more	Less than $150,000	$150,000 to $249,999	$250,000 to $499,999	$500,000 or more
INDOOR AIR QUALITY													
Home dehumidification system													
Do not want	7	7	4	7	10	7	5	6	5	9	6	6	6
Indifferent	29	21	21	23	31	30	29	26	22	28	28	28	23
Desirable	48	49	47	53	45	49	50	48	50	46	51	49	47
Essential/Must Have	16	24	28	17	15	15	16	20	23	18	15	17	23
Electronic air cleaner													
Do not want	8	7	4	6	11	6	3	6	7	12	6	5	6
Indifferent	31	18	21	25	31	30	30	29	23	28	37	28	23
Desirable	46	49	47	49	43	50	53	45	44	41	45	50	47
Essential/Must Have	15	25	27	20	15	13	13	21	25	19	12	17	25
Low VOC materials (paint, flooring, adhesives)													
Do not want	7	8	4	9	10	6	6	6	5	10	7	5	5
Indifferent	33	25	22	27	32	36	33	28	24	33	35	30	25
Desirable	44	44	46	49	43	42	47	46	46	40	43	47	46
Essential/Must Have	16	23	28	16	15	16	14	20	25	17	14	18	24
Whole house mechanical ventilation													
Do not want	7	6	3	6	9	7	6	6	5	10	5	7	4
Indifferent	33	20	22	26	33	33	34	27	26	31	34	29	29
Desirable	45	51	47	52	45	47	45	47	45	42	47	48	45
Essential/Must Have	15	23	28	16	13	13	15	20	24	17	14	16	23
Certification home has above-standard indoor environmental quality													
Do not want	6	6	6	6	8	5	5	5	3	10	4	4	5
Indifferent	25	20	22	25	26	28	24	23	18	28	28	21	20
Desirable	51	41	46	50	49	51	51	47	50	43	51	52	51
Essential/Must Have	19	34	27	20	17	16	20	24	29	19	17	22	24
Certification home is above health and wellness standards													
Do not want	5	5	4	6	7	5	5	5	4	8	4	4	5
Indifferent	24	18	26	20	24	27	23	23	20	26	26	22	20
Desirable	51	47	42	54	51	51	52	47	50	48	49	54	49
Essential/Must Have	19	29	28	19	18	17	20	25	26	18	21	20	26

Q38. How would the following various designs and features influence your purchase decision?
(Percent of respondents)

	All Home Buyers	Geography (Nine Census Divisions)									Buyer Type	
		New England	Middle Atlantic	East North Central	West North Central	South Atlantic	East South Central	West South Central	Mountain	Pacific	First-time	Repeat
COMMUNITY FEATURES												
Gated to control access												
Do not want	19	20	22	30	19	15	19	18	16	13	17	19
Indifferent	28	25	29	29	22	28	30	30	31	27	30	28
Desirable	37	41	34	28	38	42	37	36	37	38	40	36
Essential/Must Have	16	14	15	13	21	14	14	17	16	22	14	16
Golf course												
Do not want	35	37	39	40	29	39	37	36	27	27	32	36
Indifferent	31	29	26	31	27	29	31	34	37	35	36	30
Desirable	24	28	22	22	30	24	23	21	24	27	24	24
Essential/Must Have	10	7	12	7	14	8	9	9	11	11	8	10
Swimming pool												
Do not want	18	18	20	25	20	18	15	14	16	14	15	18
Indifferent	25	26	24	26	21	22	28	33	22	26	28	25
Desirable	40	36	40	37	37	42	44	40	41	40	43	40
Essential/Must Have	17	20	17	12	22	18	14	13	21	20	14	17
Access to public transportation												
Do not want	17	13	12	22	17	20	20	21	13	10	14	18
Indifferent	32	27	31	34	27	34	34	32	35	30	32	32
Desirable	35	37	40	29	39	35	34	36	36	37	36	35
Essential/Must Have	15	23	16	14	17	11	12	11	16	22	19	15
Daycare center												
Do not want	35	34	33	41	27	41	39	35	31	27	30	36
Indifferent	32	32	30	32	26	33	29	33	36	32	36	31
Desirable	23	24	25	21	28	19	23	23	21	26	27	22
Essential/Must Have	11	11	12	6	19	7	9	10	13	15	7	11
Outdoor maintenance service												
Do not want	16	16	16	23	13	15	18	19	13	11	15	16
Indifferent	29	21	28	31	27	29	29	30	33	27	34	28
Desirable	39	39	40	33	43	40	37	39	34	42	37	39
Essential/Must Have	16	24	17	13	18	15	15	12	20	20	13	17
Good primary/secondary public schools												
Do not want	18	20	15	22	16	20	21	19	13	14	17	18
Indifferent	32	28	35	33	29	32	28	29	35	32	34	31
Desirable	33	34	32	28	33	34	35	35	34	35	34	33
Essential/Must Have	17	18	18	17	22	14	16	17	17	19	15	18

Q38. How would the following various designs and features influence your purchase decision?
(Percent of respondents)

	Age of Household Head					Generation (year born)				Household Composition			
	Under 35 years old	35 to 44 years old	45 to 54 years old	55 to 64 years old	65 years old or older	Gen Z (1997 or later)	Millenni-als(1981-1996)	Gen X (1965-1980)	Boomers (1946-1964)	Married couple w children	Married couple no children	Single parent	One person
COMMUNITY FEATURES													
Gated to control access													
Do not want	12	11	17	24	24	13	10	17	24	14	26	19	22
Indifferent	27	25	31	29	28	29	25	29	27	25	29	28	32
Desirable	38	42	37	34	36	36	42	36	35	40	33	36	36
Essential/Must Have	23	22	16	14	13	22	23	17	13	21	12	17	11
Golf course													
Do not want	18	22	29	43	46	18	20	31	45	23	46	36	48
Indifferent	27	28	35	34	29	28	27	32	31	28	32	30	33
Desirable	36	32	26	19	19	34	35	26	19	35	16	21	14
Essential/Must Have	19	19	10	4	6	21	18	11	5	14	5	13	5
Swimming pool													
Do not want	9	7	14	19	28	10	7	15	25	12	25	17	27
Indifferent	22	23	27	28	24	26	22	26	25	23	27	25	25
Desirable	45	46	41	41	35	37	49	40	37	44	35	42	36
Essential/Must Have	24	24	18	12	14	27	23	19	13	21	13	17	12
Access to public transportation													
Do not want	10	11	18	21	19	10	10	18	20	15	20	17	19
Indifferent	28	27	34	34	34	29	26	34	33	25	41	26	40
Desirable	41	42	32	33	34	39	43	32	34	41	30	36	30
Essential/Must Have	21	21	16	11	13	21	21	16	13	20	10	21	11
Daycare center													
Do not want	12	16	33	46	45	13	14	33	45	23	49	33	50
Indifferent	29	27	35	33	33	31	28	32	34	28	35	28	31
Desirable	38	38	23	18	13	36	39	25	15	32	12	27	14
Essential/Must Have	21	19	9	4	9	20	19	11	7	17	4	12	5
Outdoor maintenance service													
Do not want	11	9	16	23	17	12	8	17	19	12	21	15	17
Indifferent	27	31	33	27	27	31	29	31	28	25	33	31	29
Desirable	39	39	35	37	41	33	41	36	40	42	34	37	43
Essential/Must Have	23	22	16	12	14	23	22	16	13	21	12	17	11
Good primary/secondary public schools													
Do not want	10	6	17	23	24	13	6	17	24	11	24	18	25
Indifferent	23	23	29	37	36	22	22	30	36	25	41	26	39
Desirable	41	41	34	30	28	41	40	34	29	39	28	33	28
Essential/Must Have	27	30	20	10	11	25	31	19	11	26	7	22	7

Q38. How would the following various designs and features influence your purchase decision?
(Percent of respondents)

	Race/Ethnicity				Home Buyers' Income Bracket					Price Expected to Pay			
	Cauca-sian	African-American	Hispanic	Asian	Under $50,000	$50,000 to $74,999	$75,000 to $99,999	$100,000 to $149,999	$150,000 or more	Less than $150,000	$150,000 to $249,999	$250,000 to $499,999	$500,000 or more
COMMUNITY FEATURES													
Gated to control access													
Do not want	22	14	11	13	27	21	19	15	11	27	20	17	14
Indifferent	30	23	18	27	27	36	26	27	26	26	29	29	28
Desirable	35	42	46	38	36	33	39	38	38	34	38	36	39
Essential/Must Have	14	22	25	22	10	11	16	19	25	14	13	18	18
Golf course													
Do not want	41	27	15	19	47	42	35	29	23	38	38	35	29
Indifferent	31	35	27	33	32	35	32	30	26	30	36	30	27
Desirable	21	24	39	39	16	19	25	26	36	20	19	26	31
Essential/Must Have	8	14	18	9	6	4	8	15	15	11	6	9	14
Swimming pool													
Do not want	20	14	8	15	25	20	17	15	11	21	22	16	15
Indifferent	26	21	22	23	25	30	30	24	19	26	30	25	21
Desirable	39	44	41	47	37	37	39	39	46	38	36	42	42
Essential/Must Have	15	20	29	14	12	13	14	21	24	15	12	18	22
Access to public transportation													
Do not want	19	12	7	13	21	19	15	14	14	21	21	15	14
Indifferent	35	23	21	29	32	38	34	35	25	32	32	35	27
Desirable	34	40	40	40	32	32	38	35	40	32	34	36	39
Essential/Must Have	11	25	31	18	15	10	12	16	21	15	13	14	20
Daycare center													
Do not want	41	24	11	15	43	43	35	30	24	37	36	35	30
Indifferent	33	29	26	35	32	34	35	34	26	30	33	32	31
Desirable	18	34	36	39	18	18	23	22	32	22	23	23	25
Essential/Must Have	8	12	27	11	7	5	7	15	18	10	8	10	14
Outdoor maintenance service													
Do not want	19	11	5	10	23	17	14	15	10	22	19	13	13
Indifferent	30	25	23	25	30	38	30	28	21	31	32	29	22
Desirable	37	43	45	47	35	35	40	37	46	33	38	40	44
Essential/Must Have	14	21	27	18	11	11	15	20	24	14	12	17	21
Good primary/secondary public schools													
Do not want	21	13	9	8	26	18	16	14	13	23	20	16	14
Indifferent	34	22	24	32	35	41	34	26	24	33	32	32	30
Desirable	30	43	42	39	28	29	35	35	40	29	34	34	35
Essential/Must Have	15	21	25	22	11	12	15	25	23	15	14	18	22

Q38. How would the following various designs and features influence your purchase decision?
(Percent of respondents)

	All Home Buyers	Geography (Nine Census Divisions)									Buyer Type	
		New England	Middle Atlantic	East North Central	West North Central	South Atlantic	East South Central	West South Central	Mountain	Pacific	First-time	Repeat
COMMUNITY FEATURES												
Dog park												
Do not want	23	20	22	27	20	27	22	21	18	17	23	23
Indifferent	30	24	30	33	30	28	29	31	33	27	32	29
Desirable	34	40	32	30	38	31	36	38	34	38	34	34
Essential/Must Have	14	16	16	10	12	14	12	10	15	18	11	14
Community garden												
Do not want	20	19	20	25	14	22	21	25	16	12	21	20
Indifferent	33	29	33	34	26	38	30	33	36	32	34	33
Desirable	34	38	32	29	42	32	39	32	31	40	36	34
Essential/Must Have	13	14	14	12	17	9	10	10	16	17	9	13
Walking/joggin trails												
Do not want	12	7	11	16	10	13	16	14	7	7	11	12
Indifferent	23	21	23	27	22	24	18	24	24	20	26	23
Desirable	49	56	49	42	48	49	52	53	48	48	47	49
Essential/Must Have	17	16	17	15	21	15	13	9	21	25	16	17
Designated bike lanes												
Do not want	20	17	25	24	16	20	23	24	14	13	22	20
Indifferent	32	28	30	36	30	35	28	33	33	27	40	31
Desirable	34	42	31	29	40	34	39	30	37	39	30	35
Essential/Must Have	13	13	14	11	14	11	10	12	17	20	8	14
BikeShare/CarShare services												
Do not want	26	22	26	32	19	29	26	29	19	19	25	26
Indifferent	36	30	39	36	34	39	37	35	39	34	38	36
Desirable	26	34	24	23	30	24	27	26	28	33	30	26
Essential/Must Have	11	14	12	8	16	8	11	11	14	15	7	12
Electric vehicle charging station												
Do not want	24	23	23	29	18	26	30	33	18	13	24	24
Indifferent	30	30	25	32	24	32	30	29	36	28	34	29
Desirable	32	33	35	26	37	31	31	29	29	38	31	32
Essential/Must Have	14	14	16	12	21	11	10	8	17	20	11	14
Park area												
Do not want	11	11	9	16	11	10	15	13	9	7	10	11
Indifferent	23	11	21	26	20	26	25	22	17	24	26	22
Desirable	49	57	51	45	50	50	44	47	58	48	50	49
Essential/Must Have	17	21	19	13	19	14	16	18	16	20	14	17

Q38. How would the following various designs and features influence your purchase decision?
(Percent of respondents)

	Age of Household Head					Generation (year born)				Household Composition			
	Under 35 years old	35 to 44 years old	45 to 54 years old	55 to 64 years old	65 years old or older	Gen Z (1997 or later)	Millenni-als(1981-1996)	Gen X (1965-1980)	Boomers (1946-1964)	Married couple w children	Married couple no children	Single parent	One person
COMMUNITY FEATURES													
Dog park													
Do not want	11	12	18	27	32	11	11	18	31	14	32	25	29
Indifferent	23	25	32	30	32	27	24	31	31	28	33	23	32
Desirable	41	43	35	35	27	38	44	35	30	40	25	35	32
Essential/Must Have	25	20	15	8	9	24	21	16	8	18	10	16	7
Community garden													
Do not want	13	11	20	27	22	13	10	21	24	13	25	23	26
Indifferent	26	28	34	32	39	27	27	33	36	28	41	32	37
Desirable	39	37	35	35	30	38	40	33	32	39	29	32	30
Essential/Must Have	22	24	12	6	9	22	23	13	8	20	5	13	7
Walking/joggin trails													
Do not want	8	6	12	13	15	10	6	12	14	7	13	14	17
Indifferent	22	22	23	25	23	25	21	23	23	22	23	25	24
Desirable	44	49	50	53	46	41	50	49	49	51	49	41	48
Essential/Must Have	25	22	15	10	17	24	23	16	14	20	14	20	11
Designated bike lanes													
Do not want	14	13	19	25	24	15	13	20	24	15	23	21	28
Indifferent	28	28	33	32	35	32	27	31	34	26	35	34	38
Desirable	37	37	34	35	32	31	39	35	33	40	32	29	27
Essential/Must Have	21	22	14	8	10	22	22	15	9	19	10	17	7
BikeShare/CarShare services													
Do not want	15	14	25	34	31	16	14	25	31	18	31	28	35
Indifferent	31	31	38	39	38	33	30	36	40	30	45	30	41
Desirable	35	35	27	22	22	30	37	28	22	35	18	29	19
Essential/Must Have	19	21	10	5	9	21	20	11	8	17	6	13	5
Electric vehicle charging station													
Do not want	15	15	24	30	28	17	14	25	28	17	28	27	34
Indifferent	27	25	32	32	31	26	26	30	32	25	35	29	30
Desirable	37	38	32	28	29	37	38	32	30	38	29	28	27
Essential/Must Have	21	22	12	10	12	21	22	13	11	20	8	16	9
Park area													
Do not want	10	6	11	11	13	12	6	11	12	8	13	14	11
Indifferent	19	21	28	23	22	22	19	26	23	20	24	24	26
Desirable	45	48	44	55	51	41	50	44	53	49	52	40	54
Essential/Must Have	26	24	18	11	14	26	25	18	12	22	12	22	9

Q38. How would the following various designs and features influence your purchase decision?
(Percent of respondents)

	Race/Ethnicity				Home Buyers' Income Bracket					Price Expected to Pay			
	Cauca-sian	African-American	Hispanic	Asian	Under $50,000	$50,000 to $74,999	$75,000 to $99,999	$100,000 to $149,999	$150,000 or more	Less than $150,000	$150,000 to $249,999	$250,000 to $499,999	$500,000 or more
COMMUNITY FEATURES													
Dog park													
Do not want	25	24	10	13	29	26	24	19	14	25	23	21	19
Indifferent	31	20	27	29	30	34	30	28	27	30	30	32	25
Desirable	33	37	41	41	31	30	34	36	40	30	37	33	39
Essential/Must Have	11	19	22	16	10	10	11	16	19	14	9	14	17
Community garden													
Do not want	23	23	5	9	30	23	18	16	12	26	22	18	14
Indifferent	35	24	26	35	31	41	36	35	27	31	36	35	30
Desirable	32	39	41	41	31	29	37	32	41	32	32	34	38
Essential/Must Have	10	15	27	15	8	7	10	17	20	11	10	13	18
Walking/joggin trails													
Do not want	13	10	6	5	19	13	10	9	5	18	15	9	6
Indifferent	24	21	23	18	25	29	24	20	19	27	27	23	18
Desirable	49	46	45	61	44	48	48	50	55	42	43	53	54
Essential/Must Have	14	23	26	17	13	11	19	21	21	13	16	16	22
Designated bike lanes													
Do not want	23	17	7	13	28	23	23	15	11	26	23	18	14
Indifferent	34	30	23	30	34	41	32	31	24	32	38	32	26
Desirable	32	34	45	44	30	29	32	36	44	29	30	36	42
Essential/Must Have	11	18	25	14	9	6	14	18	21	13	9	14	18
BikeShare/CarShare services													
Do not want	30	19	9	15	33	29	25	23	17	30	26	25	20
Indifferent	39	30	26	37	37	45	41	34	29	33	41	38	32
Desirable	23	35	40	35	22	20	25	28	36	24	24	27	33
Essential/Must Have	8	16	25	13	8	7	8	15	17	12	9	11	15
Electric vehicle charging station													
Do not want	28	17	10	8	35	32	21	17	13	33	29	22	14
Indifferent	31	26	28	25	31	32	34	31	23	29	32	32	24
Desirable	30	39	35	47	25	27	32	36	41	25	29	33	40
Essential/Must Have	11	18	27	20	9	9	12	17	22	13	10	13	21
Park area													
Do not want	12	8	9	8	17	12	10	8	7	15	13	9	8
Indifferent	24	21	19	22	25	27	20	23	18	27	26	21	18
Desirable	50	46	48	51	46	50	51	46	54	43	47	52	55
Essential/Must Have	14	25	25	19	11	11	18	23	21	15	14	18	19

Q38. How would the following various designs and features influence your purchase decision?
(Percent of respondents)

	All Home Buyers	Geography (Nine Census Divisions)									Buyer Type	
		New England	Middle Atlantic	East North Central	West North Central	South Atlantic	East South Central	West South Central	Mountain	Pacific	First-time	Repeat
COMMUNITY FEATURES												
Playgrounds												
Do not want	24	24	23	29	21	27	27	22	22	18	19	25
Indifferent	30	31	31	30	24	31	28	31	34	31	32	30
Desirable	32	33	30	30	34	31	33	36	30	35	38	32
Essential/Must Have	13	12	16	11	21	10	11	11	13	16	11	13
Baseball or soccer fields												
Do not want	32	28	30	37	27	36	32	35	27	25	27	32
Indifferent	33	33	34	36	27	35	33	32	35	29	38	33
Desirable	23	27	22	19	27	20	27	22	21	31	26	23
Essential/Must Have	12	11	14	8	19	9	9	11	17	14	9	12
Tennis court												
Do not want	30	23	31	36	30	33	28	31	24	23	27	30
Indifferent	34	28	32	33	26	35	37	39	38	35	36	34
Desirable	25	38	24	22	30	24	27	22	25	28	29	25
Essential/Must Have	11	11	13	9	14	8	8	8	12	14	8	11
Pickleball court												
Do not want	32	33	32	38	24	34	34	37	25	26	33	32
Indifferent	33	27	31	34	33	36	28	34	31	33	39	32
Desirable	25	28	26	19	28	23	26	22	31	30	23	25
Essential/Must Have	10	12	10	9	15	7	12	7	13	12	5	11
Lake												
Do not want	14	12	16	18	13	13	16	12	14	13	15	14
Indifferent	27	22	24	27	28	28	25	30	30	27	29	27
Desirable	46	52	46	43	42	50	51	48	41	41	45	46
Essential/Must Have	13	14	14	12	17	9	8	10	15	19	12	13
Clubhouse												
Do not want	25	29	27	32	25	25	28	25	18	20	25	26
Indifferent	32	32	29	29	27	33	33	37	38	30	36	31
Desirable	30	25	31	28	30	31	33	26	28	32	29	30
Essential/Must Have	13	14	14	10	18	10	6	12	16	18	10	13
Green rating for subdivisiion												
Do not want	16	14	17	23	11	13	21	18	13	11	15	16
Indifferent	35	32	34	38	37	38	32	33	35	30	37	35
Desirable	36	35	33	29	36	38	35	39	35	39	36	36
Essential/Must Have	14	19	16	10	15	11	12	11	17	19	13	14

Q38. How would the following various designs and features influence your purchase decision?
(Percent of respondents)

	Age of Household Head					Generation (year born)				Household Composition			
	Under 35 years old	35 to 44 years old	45 to 54 years old	55 to 64 years old	65 years old or older	Gen Z (1997 or later)	Millenni-als(1981-1996)	Gen X (1965-1980)	Boomers (1946-1964)	Married couple w children	Married couple no children	Single parent	One person
COMMUNITY FEATURES													
Playgrounds													
Do not want	11	8	20	32	34	12	8	21	33	15	35	19	38
Indifferent	26	24	32	35	31	29	23	31	32	24	39	27	34
Desirable	39	48	32	28	25	36	47	33	26	41	20	39	23
Essential/Must Have	24	20	15	6	10	22	22	15	8	20	6	14	6
Baseball or soccer fields													
Do not want	14	15	25	41	43	17	13	26	43	20	44	30	43
Indifferent	28	29	40	35	32	29	27	38	33	28	37	34	36
Desirable	38	35	24	18	15	35	39	23	16	33	14	21	16
Essential/Must Have	20	21	11	6	9	19	21	13	8	19	5	15	5
Tennis court													
Do not want	16	17	24	38	39	16	16	25	39	20	38	31	43
Indifferent	29	30	39	37	33	31	28	37	34	29	41	31	36
Desirable	33	35	29	18	21	30	36	27	21	35	17	26	15
Essential/Must Have	22	19	9	6	7	23	20	11	6	16	5	12	5
Pickleball court													
Do not want	18	18	30	40	40	19	17	30	41	22	41	33	43
Indifferent	29	32	36	33	33	30	30	34	32	27	34	32	39
Desirable	34	34	24	23	19	31	36	25	20	35	19	24	14
Essential/Must Have	19	16	10	4	8	21	17	10	7	16	6	11	4
Lake													
Do not want	9	8	11	14	21	9	8	12	18	10	16	19	17
Indifferent	26	24	28	28	28	28	23	28	28	24	31	23	29
Desirable	44	46	49	50	42	42	48	47	45	48	44	43	48
Essential/Must Have	21	22	12	8	9	20	21	13	9	18	8	15	6
Clubhouse													
Do not want	12	13	23	33	32	11	12	23	32	18	31	29	36
Indifferent	30	29	36	31	32	33	28	35	32	27	35	30	33
Desirable	38	40	27	29	24	35	41	27	26	37	25	27	24
Essential/Must Have	20	19	14	7	11	21	19	14	10	18	9	15	6
Green rating for subdivisiion													
Do not want	10	11	16	19	18	11	9	17	17	12	18	18	17
Indifferent	28	29	35	38	38	29	29	33	38	28	42	32	40
Desirable	39	39	37	33	34	36	40	36	35	41	30	32	34
Essential/Must Have	23	22	12	10	11	23	22	14	10	18	10	18	9

Q38. How would the following various designs and features influence your purchase decision?
(Percent of respondents)

	Race/Ethnicity				Home Buyers' Income Bracket					Price Expected to Pay			
	Cauca-sian	African-American	Hispanic	Asian	Under $50,000	$50,000 to $74,999	$75,000 to $99,999	$100,000 to $149,999	$150,000 or more	Less than $150,000	$150,000 to $249,999	$250,000 to $499,999	$500,000 or more
COMMUNITY FEATURES													
Playgrounds													
Do not want	29	14	8	14	33	28	20	21	17	27	25	23	21
Indifferent	33	25	20	27	31	35	35	28	25	29	35	30	29
Desirable	28	43	46	42	28	30	31	35	38	32	30	32	36
Essential/Must Have	10	19	26	17	9	7	14	15	20	12	10	15	14
Baseball or soccer fields													
Do not want	37	25	12	18	42	34	33	28	20	36	31	31	26
Indifferent	35	30	23	34	32	40	37	34	27	30	38	34	31
Desirable	20	30	36	35	19	19	21	24	33	22	20	23	28
Essential/Must Have	9	16	29	13	7	7	10	15	20	12	11	12	14
Tennis court													
Do not want	35	22	12	17	40	39	34	23	15	34	36	30	19
Indifferent	36	28	24	33	35	38	35	34	31	30	38	35	33
Desirable	21	34	42	34	19	18	25	29	35	25	19	25	33
Essential/Must Have	8	17	21	16	6	6	7	14	19	10	8	10	15
Pickleball court													
Do not want	36	29	16	20	45	40	30	25	18	39	36	30	23
Indifferent	34	35	24	39	33	38	37	32	28	29	37	34	31
Desirable	23	26	36	29	16	17	23	29	39	22	17	28	32
Essential/Must Have	8	10	24	11	6	6	10	13	15	10	10	9	14
Lake													
Do not want	15	17	9	16	20	16	11	13	9	16	16	14	9
Indifferent	29	22	23	27	26	34	30	27	23	23	30	28	26
Desirable	46	46	44	46	44	43	47	46	48	47	43	46	49
Essential/Must Have	11	16	24	11	10	7	13	14	20	14	11	12	16
Clubhouse													
Do not want	29	23	11	16	35	30	25	21	15	31	27	23	20
Indifferent	34	29	24	25	33	37	32	35	25	30	35	32	30
Desirable	28	30	36	46	23	27	30	31	39	24	26	32	35
Essential/Must Have	10	18	28	14	9	6	13	14	21	14	11	13	15
Green rating for subdivisiion													
Do not want	18	13	7	12	23	16	15	13	10	21	19	13	13
Indifferent	37	27	31	31	37	43	36	31	29	34	39	36	29
Desirable	35	41	36	40	31	31	37	42	38	32	33	37	40
Essential/Must Have	11	19	26	18	9	11	11	15	22	13	9	14	19

Q38. How would the following various designs and features influence your purchase decision?
(Percent of respondents)

	All Home Buyers	Geography (Nine Census Divisions)									Buyer Type	
		New England	Middle Atlantic	East North Central	West North Central	South Atlantic	East South Central	West South Central	Mountain	Pacific	First-time	Repeat
COMMUNITY FEATURES												
Exercise room												
Do not want	21	23	20	27	21	23	21	19	20	10	16	21
Indifferent	30	25	25	32	26	32	34	36	29	30	37	30
Desirable	34	36	36	29	38	33	35	34	34	40	34	34
Essential/Must Have	15	16	19	13	16	12	10	11	17	20	13	15
Typically suburban (all single-family detached houses)												
Do not want	11	11	10	14	8	11	14	12	8	9	14	11
Indifferent	25	26	24	31	28	20	23	23	26	30	30	25
Desirable	46	43	48	38	45	50	45	49	50	44	42	47
Essential/Must Have	18	20	18	16	20	18	18	17	16	18	13	18
High density (community with smaller lots and attached or multifamily buildings)												
Do not want	32	28	30	39	27	35	35	32	34	26	26	33
Indifferent	31	34	31	33	24	35	28	34	25	28	36	31
Desirable	26	30	26	21	33	22	26	24	29	30	28	25
Essential/Must Have	11	9	13	7	16	8	11	9	12	17	11	11
Infill (in the center of an older, established neighborhood)												
Do not want	18	21	19	22	16	20	23	19	14	10	18	18
Indifferent	40	36	38	44	31	44	31	37	42	42	38	40
Desirable	31	33	30	26	35	28	33	36	32	31	34	30
Essential/Must Have	11	10	13	8	18	8	13	8	12	16	11	11
Near retail space (grocery, drug stores, etc.)												
Do not want	9	9	7	12	8	7	11	13	9	7	7	9
Indifferent	21	25	21	21	21	21	22	17	22	23	24	21
Desirable	48	47	49	44	47	53	41	47	44	48	49	47
Essential/Must Have	22	19	23	22	24	19	26	22	24	23	20	22
Other mixed use (homes near office or other commercial buildings)												
Do not want	29	26	28	33	24	33	32	30	26	19	25	29
Indifferent	35	27	33	37	30	35	34	37	37	33	38	34
Desirable	25	32	27	22	28	23	25	22	26	32	30	25
Essential/Must Have	11	15	12	7	18	8	9	11	11	15	8	11

Q38. How would the following various designs and features influence your purchase decision?
(Percent of respondents)

	Age of Household Head					Generation (year born)				Household Composition			
	Under 35 years old	35 to 44 years old	45 to 54 years old	55 to 64 years old	65 years old or older	Gen Z (1997 or later)	Millenni-als(1981-1996)	Gen X (1965-1980)	Boomers (1946-1964)	Married couple w children	Married couple no children	Single parent	One person
COMMUNITY FEATURES													
Exercise room													
Do not want	9	10	18	24	29	11	8	17	27	14	25	22	31
Indifferent	26	26	32	33	31	28	26	31	31	25	36	28	33
Desirable	41	40	34	35	29	36	43	35	32	40	30	33	29
Essential/Must Have	24	23	17	8	11	24	23	16	10	20	10	17	7
Typically suburban (all single-family detached houses)													
Do not want	8	8	10	14	12	10	6	12	13	9	12	11	15
Indifferent	26	24	27	24	25	29	23	26	25	23	27	26	29
Desirable	43	47	44	48	46	40	48	43	48	46	46	44	45
Essential/Must Have	23	21	18	14	16	21	23	19	14	22	15	20	11
High density (community with smaller lots and attached or multifamily buildings)													
Do not want	14	16	29	44	40	13	15	30	42	24	44	25	42
Indifferent	29	28	33	32	32	29	28	32	32	24	35	34	38
Desirable	37	38	26	20	19	36	38	26	20	35	16	27	16
Essential/Must Have	21	17	12	4	8	21	19	12	7	17	5	14	5
Infill (in the center of an older, established neighborhood)													
Do not want	13	11	16	23	22	14	11	16	22	14	23	19	24
Indifferent	30	33	40	42	45	31	31	39	44	31	51	33	47
Desirable	37	37	33	29	26	35	38	32	27	37	22	36	23
Essential/Must Have	21	19	11	6	7	20	19	13	7	18	5	12	6
Near retail space (grocery, drug stores, etc.)													
Do not want	8	7	9	11	9	11	6	9	9	8	10	10	9
Indifferent	22	21	23	23	19	23	20	22	21	20	24	22	20
Desirable	42	46	45	50	50	39	47	45	50	46	50	45	51
Essential/Must Have	28	26	24	16	22	27	27	23	20	26	16	23	20
Other mixed use (homes near office or other commercial buildings)													
Do not want	14	15	23	37	38	15	14	23	37	20	37	29	40
Indifferent	28	27	36	40	36	30	27	37	38	28	41	36	36
Desirable	37	40	28	17	18	37	40	28	19	34	18	24	19
Essential/Must Have	21	17	12	6	8	19	20	12	7	18	4	11	5

Q38. How would the following various designs and features influence your purchase decision?
(Percent of respondents)

	Race/Ethnicity				Home Buyers' Income Bracket					Price Expected to Pay			
	Cauca-sian	African-American	Hispanic	Asian	Under $50,000	$50,000 to $74,999	$75,000 to $99,999	$100,000 to $149,999	$150,000 or more	Less than $150,000	$150,000 to $249,999	$250,000 to $499,999	$500,000 or more
COMMUNITY FEATURES													
Exercise room													
Do not want	23	15	8	15	31	25	18	15	11	28	26	17	12
Indifferent	33	21	23	25	30	38	33	28	26	28	34	31	28
Desirable	31	43	46	46	28	28	36	39	41	29	32	36	40
Essential/Must Have	13	21	23	14	11	9	13	18	22	14	8	16	20
Typically suburban (all single-family detached houses)													
Do not want	12	8	7	10	18	11	9	7	8	17	12	8	9
Indifferent	26	23	25	24	25	27	30	27	20	29	30	22	24
Desirable	46	48	45	49	44	50	44	44	49	40	43	49	50
Essential/Must Have	16	21	24	16	13	13	17	21	24	14	15	21	18
High density (community with smaller lots and attached or multifamily buildings)													
Do not want	37	23	14	17	39	35	33	30	24	33	30	33	31
Indifferent	33	30	19	34	32	41	36	28	24	32	37	29	28
Desirable	21	32	43	35	21	18	22	29	36	24	23	27	28
Essential/Must Have	8	14	23	14	9	6	10	13	16	12	10	10	13
Infill (in the center of an older, established neighborhood)													
Do not want	20	19	9	13	22	20	17	18	14	22	18	17	17
Indifferent	43	31	29	36	43	48	43	36	32	36	45	40	37
Desirable	28	34	39	41	27	25	30	33	36	30	28	32	32
Essential/Must Have	9	17	23	10	7	8	10	13	17	12	10	11	14
Near retail space (grocery, drug stores, etc.)													
Do not want	10	8	6	9	12	8	7	9	8	13	10	7	8
Indifferent	22	16	20	23	21	23	24	22	18	23	21	22	19
Desirable	49	44	43	48	48	50	50	44	47	45	51	48	47
Essential/Must Have	20	32	31	20	20	18	19	26	27	18	18	24	26
Other mixed use (homes near office or other commercial buildings)													
Do not want	33	21	10	16	38	32	29	25	17	31	31	29	22
Indifferent	36	33	26	36	35	40	39	32	30	33	40	33	34
Desirable	22	32	38	34	19	21	24	29	34	23	22	27	29
Essential/Must Have	8	15	26	14	8	7	8	13	19	13	8	11	14

Q38. How would the following various designs and features influence your purchase decision?
(Percent of respondents)

	All Home Buyers	Geography (Nine Census Divisions)									Buyer Type	
		New England	Middle Atlantic	East North Central	West North Central	South Atlantic	East South Central	West South Central	Mountain	Pacific	First-time	Repeat
COMMUNITY FEATURES												
Walkable community (with walkways connecting homes, shopping, public spaces and transportation)												
Do not want	12	10	10	17	9	10	16	16	9	7	11	12
Indifferent	23	20	26	25	19	25	22	21	21	21	25	23
Desirable	47	55	45	43	51	46	45	47	51	50	45	48
Essential/Must Have	18	15	19	15	20	19	17	16	20	22	19	18
Community with a Homeonwers Association												
Do not want	34	34	27	42	28	40	33	34	34	26	33	34
Indifferent	27	29	30	28	22	24	23	32	26	26	31	26
Desirable	26	24	30	19	34	27	33	21	22	30	25	26
Essential/Must Have	13	13	14	11	16	10	10	12	18	18	11	13
Responses	3,008	141	358	414	236	651	224	290	278	416	521	2,487

Q39. If a home office is essential or desirable to you, about how large would you prefer this room to be?
(Percent of respondents)

	All Home Buyers	Geography (Nine Census Divisions)									Buyer Type	
		New England	Middle Atlantic	East North Central	West North Central	South Atlantic	East South Central	West South Central	Mountain	Pacific	First-time	Repeat
Small (less than 100 square feet)	19	19	20	23	20	20	15	17	18	19	24	19
Medium (100 to 150 square feet)	59	69	56	58	56	59	53	61	70	55	61	59
Large (more than 150 square feet)	22	12	24	19	24	21	33	22	13	26	15	23
Responses	2,073	108	256	268	167	449	137	190	188	310	343	1,730

Q38. How would the following various designs and features influence your purchase decision?
(Percent of respondents)

	Age of Household Head					Generation (year born)				Household Composition			
	Under 35 years old	35 to 44 years old	45 to 54 years old	55 to 64 years old	65 years old or older	Gen Z (1997 or later)	Millenni-als(1981-1996)	Gen X (1965-1980)	Boomers (1946-1964)	Married couple w children	Married couple no children	Single parent	One person
COMMUNITY FEATURES													
Walkable community (with walkways connecting homes, shopping, public spaces and transportation)													
Do not want	11	7	15	13	11	13	7	14	11	9	13	13	13
Indifferent	21	22	22	21	27	23	20	23	24	22	25	20	27
Desirable	41	46	48	52	47	39	46	45	50	47	47	49	47
Essential/Must Have	27	26	16	14	15	25	28	17	15	22	15	18	14
Community with a Homeonwers Association													
Do not want	16	19	33	43	42	16	18	33	42	23	43	32	47
Indifferent	27	27	29	25	26	30	26	28	25	22	32	28	28
Desirable	35	33	26	25	21	33	35	25	24	35	17	24	20
Essential/Must Have	22	21	12	8	11	21	21	13	9	20	8	16	5
Responses	934	610	503	436	525	428	932	741	772	1,278	527	391	473

Q39. If a home office is essential or desirable to you, about how large would you prefer this room to be?
(Percent of respondents)

	Age of Household Head					Generation (year born)				Household Composition			
	Under 35 years old	35 to 44 years old	45 to 54 years old	55 to 64 years old	65 years old or older	Gen Z (1997 or later)	Millenni-als(1981-1996)	Gen X (1965-1980)	Boomers (1946-1964)	Married couple w children	Married couple no children	Single parent	One person
Small (less than 100 square feet)	17	17	18	17	24	16	17	16	24	16	18	23	26
Medium (100 to 150 square feet)	57	61	52	63	60	62	58	55	61	56	65	56	59
Large (more than 150 square feet)	26	23	30	20	15	22	25	29	16	27	17	21	15
Responses	665	446	359	281	322	266	706	529	468	946	354	252	298

Q38. How would the following various designs and features influence your purchase decision?
(Percent of respondents)

	Race/Ethnicity				Home Buyers' Income Bracket					Price Expected to Pay			
	Cauca-sian	African-American	Hispanic	Asian	Under $50,000	$50,000 to $74,999	$75,000 to $99,999	$100,000 to $149,999	$150,000 or more	Less than $150,000	$150,000 to $249,999	$250,000 to $499,999	$500,000 or more
COMMUNITY FEATURES													
Walkable community (with walkways connecting homes, shopping, public spaces and transportation)													
Do not want	13	12	6	7	16	11	12	8	9	17	12	10	8
Indifferent	24	18	21	19	25	28	21	24	18	24	29	22	18
Desirable	46	46	52	56	46	49	48	45	49	44	46	49	50
Essential/Must Have	17	24	21	17	14	11	19	22	25	15	13	19	24
Community with a Homeonwers Association													
Do not want	40	26	11	18	44	42	35	28	20	37	39	33	27
Indifferent	27	26	26	25	26	33	29	24	23	27	31	26	24
Desirable	24	29	36	37	20	20	25	31	35	23	20	29	30
Essential/Must Have	10	18	27	20	9	5	11	16	22	13	10	13	19
Responses	1,997	390	341	280	907	549	427	552	573	718	531	1,155	530

Q39. If a home office is essential or desirable to you, about how large would you prefer this room to be?
(Percent of respondents)

	Race/Ethnicity				Home Buyers' Income Bracket					Price Expected to Pay			
	Cauca-sian	African-American	Hispanic	Asian	Under $50,000	$50,000 to $74,999	$75,000 to $99,999	$100,000 to $149,999	$150,000 or more	Less than $150,000	$150,000 to $249,999	$250,000 to $499,999	$500,000 or more
Small (less than 100 square feet)	20	17	19	7	26	27	16	17	13	22	24	19	15
Medium (100 to 150 square feet)	60	47	59	67	59	58	65	63	53	57	61	62	53
Large (more than 150 square feet)	20	35	22	26	16	16	19	20	33	21	15	18	32
Responses	1,356	282	233	202	534	361	308	409	461	433	321	848	432

Appendix B

Survey Questionnaire

1. Do you own or rent your current residence? ☐ Own ☐ Rent

2. Do you typically work from home at least 2 days a week? ☐ Yes ☐ No ☐ N/A

3. How long have you lived in this home?

☐ Less than four years ☐ 4 to 9 years ☐ 10 years or more

4. Do you plan to purchase a home within?

☐ Next 12 months ☐ 1 to 3 years ☐ More than 3 years ☐ No plans to purchase ☐ Not sure

5. How many homes have you owned (including your present home)?

☐ None ☐ One ☐ Two ☐ Three ☐ Four or more

6. Which type of home do you currently live in? What type would be your first choice if you were buying a home?

	Current Home	First Choice if Buying
Single-family detached	☐	☐
Townhouse/single-family attached	☐	☐
Multifamily Apartment	☐	☐
Manufactured (mobile) home	☐	☐
Other	☐	☐

[For whom 1st Choice is SFD]

7. If location, home size and finish quality were the same, what price discount would incentivize you to buy a townhome instead of a detached single-family home?

☐ 5% to 10% ☐ 11% to 20% ☐ 21% to 30% ☐ More than 30%

☐ None (wouldn't buy a townhouse regardless of discount)

8. What is the maximum mortgage interest rate you would accept on a loan to buy a home?

☐ Under 3% ☐ 3.0% to 4.9% ☐ 5.0% to 6.9% ☐ 7.0% or higher

☐ Interest rate doesn't play a role in my home purchase decisions

9. If you were buying a home, what would your first preference be?

☐ A brand new home offered by a builder
☐ An existing home
☐ A home custom built on a lot you own
☐ Other
☐ Not sure/Don't know

10. If you were buying a new home, what are the top three areas you would pay more to upgrade?

☐ Gourmet kitchen (high end appliances, cabinets, counters)
☐ Upgraded master bath (freestanding tub, rainfall shower)
☐ Outdoor features (deck, fencing, patio)
☐ Other
☐ Upgraded front exterior material
☐ Finished basement
☐ Hardwood floor for entire house
☐ None

11. What material would you prefer for framing the exterior walls of your home?

☐ Wood ☐ Steel (additional $15,000) ☐ Concrete (additional $35,000) ☐ No preference

12. Which would you prefer for the exterior design of your new home? (Pictures are broad examples)

☐ **Modern** (bold, boxy, flat roofs) *Photo by Tsutsumida Pictures*)	☐ **Contemporary** (clean lines, sloped roofs, expansive windows) *Photo by ImageArts Productions*)	☐ **Traditional** (rooted in historic styles) *Photo by Donald Stasenka*)	☐ **Transitional** (contemporary design with traditional cues) *Photo by Mark Boisclair Photography*)	☐ **Other**	☐ **No strong preference for exterior design**

13. In what type of area would you prefer to buy a home?

☐ Rural ☐ Outlying suburb ☐ Close in suburb
☐ Central city–downtown ☐ Central city–outside downtown

14. What is the farthest distance you would travel one-way between home and work?

☐ < 5 miles ☐ 5-10 miles ☐ 11-20 miles ☐ 21-50 miles ☐ Over 50 miles

15. Are you planning on watching virtual home tours during the home purchase process (or did you watch if you bought a home in the last three years)?

☐ Yes ☐ No ☐ Don't know/not sure

16. What price would you expect to pay (or did you pay if you bought a home in the last three years)?

☐ Less than $100,000
☐ $100,000 - $149,999
☐ $150,000 - $249,999
☐ $250,000 - $349,999
☐ $350,000 - $499,999
☐ $500,000 - $999,999
☐ $1 million and over
☐ Not sure/Don't know

17. What is the square footage of finished area of your present home and how many square feet would you like to have?

	Present home	Would Like to Have
Less than 1,200 square feet	☐	☐
1,200 – 1,599 square feet	☐	☐
1,600 – 1,999 square feet	☐	☐
2,000 – 2,499 square feet	☐	☐
2,500 – 2,999 square feet	☐	☐
3,000 – 3,999 square feet	☐	☐
4,000 square feet or more	☐	☐

18. What is your preference for lot size?

☐ 2+ acres
☐ 1 acre
☐ 1/2 acre
☐ 1/4 acre
☐ 1/8 acre
☐ No preference

19. If you were having trouble finding a home in your ideal price range, which of the following potential compromises would you be willing to accept in order to be able to afford it? (Check All That Apply).

- ☐ Smaller house
- ☐ Smaller lot
- ☐ Unfinished spaces
- ☐ Fewer rooms
- ☐ Fewer energy-efficient features (when not mandated by code)
- ☐ Farther from urban core
- ☐ Substitution of expensive materials for less expensive options
- ☐ Fewer exterior amenities (e.g. porches, decks, patios, pools, etc.)
- ☐ More modular or pre-fabricated housing construction components
- ☐ Denser development
- ☐ Other

[If "Smaller house" is chosen in Q19]
20. What areas would you be willing to make smaller?

☐ Kitchen ☐ Bedrooms ☐ Bathrooms ☐ Closets ☐ Family room
☐ Living room ☐ Dining room ☐ Home office ☐ Garage ☐ Other

21. How many home offices (or spaces dedicated to work/study from home) would you prefer to have?

☐ None ☐ One ☐ Two ☐ More than two

22a. Which of the following <u>kitchen-dining room</u> arrangements do you prefer?

☐ Completely open ☐ In separate areas of the house
☐ Partially open (separated by half wall, arch, counter, etc.)
☐ Side-by side separate rooms ☐ Home without a dining room

22b. Which of the following <u>kitchen-family room</u> arrangements do you prefer?

☐ Completely open ☐ In separate areas of the house
☐ Partially open (separated by half wall, arch, counter, etc.)
☐ Side-by side separate rooms ☐ Home without a family room

22c. Which of the following <u>dining room-family room</u> arrangements do you prefer?

☐ Completely open ☐ In separate areas of the house
☐ Partially open (separated by half wall, arch, counter, etc.)
☐ Side-by side separate rooms ☐ N/A, don't want one or both of the rooms

23. Excluding any basement, which of these floor plan types would you prefer, assuming each plan had the same amount of floor space/living area?

☐ Single-story ☐ Two-story ☐ Three-story ☐ Split-level

24. What type of basement would you prefer?

- ☐ No basement
- ☐ Half basement (additional $22,500)
- ☐ A full basement (additional $45,000)

25. How many bedrooms would you like to have in a new home?

☐ 1 ☐ 2 ☐ 3 ☐ 4 ☐ 5 or more

26. Where would you like to have your clothes washer and dryer in a new home?

☐ Basement ☐ On the first floor ☐ Other
☐ Garage ☐ On the second or higher floor

27. Please indicate the number of bathrooms you prefer, assuming an additional cost of $25,000 for each full bathroom.

☐ 1 ☐ 2 ☐ 3 ☐ 4 or more
☐ 1 ½ ☐ 2 ½ ☐ 3 ½

28. Which type of parking facility would you prefer with your new home, taking into account the probable differences in cost?

☐ 1 - carport ($10,000) ☐ 2 - car garage ($50,000)
☐ 2 - carport ($18,000) ☐ 3+ car garage ($70,000)
☐ 1 - car garage ($30,000) ☐ None

29. Would you prefer to purchase a home designed to house multiple generations (you, plus two younger and/or older generations?

☐ Yes ☐ No ☐ Not Sure/Don't know

30. Which energy source do you prefer for the following systems?

	Gas	Electric	Have no preference/ Don't know
Air Heating/Cooling system	☐	☐	☐
Water heating system	☐	☐	☐
Cooking	☐	☐	☐

31. Please indicate the reasons for your preference of energy source for cooking (if any). Check all that apply.

☐ Saves money
☐ Is easier/better to cook with
☐ Improves air quality in the home
☐ Is reliable
☐ Is available where I want to live
☐ Produces low levels of greenhouse gas emissions to operate
☐ Other (please specify):____________________

32. Would you consider buying an all-electric home (i.e., not connected to gas lines)?

☐ Yes ☐ No ☐ Maybe/Not sure

33. How concerned are you about the impact of your home on the environment?

☐ Not concerned
☐ Concerned about environment, but not a consideration in house purchase
☐ Want "environment-friendly" home, but would not pay more
☐ Would pay more for "environment-friendly" home

34. How much extra would you pay up front, in the purchase price for your next home, if it would save $1,000 every year in utility costs? $____________________

35. Are you aware of any of the following specific green certification programs for homes?

ENERGY STAR	Yes ☐	No ☐
Green Globes	Yes ☐	No ☐
HERS (Home Energy Rating System)	Yes ☐	No ☐
Indoor AirPLUS	Yes ☐	No ☐
LEED for Homes	Yes ☐	No ☐
Living Building Challenge	Yes ☐	No ☐
NGBS (National Green Building Standard)	Yes ☐	No ☐
PHIUS (Passive House Institute US)	Yes ☐	No ☐
WaterSense	Yes ☐	No ☐
ZERH (Zero Energy Ready Homes)	Yes ☐	No ☐

36. When purchasing a new home, which would you prefer?

a.☐ All the amenities and features included in the base price of the home	**OR**	☐ A basic home with all amenities offered as options at extra cost
c. ☐ Home on a cul de sac or other street design with limited traffic flow	**OR**	☐ Home on a continuous, interconnected street with more efficient traffic flow
d. ☐ Wider sidewalks and streets	**OR**	☐ Narrower sidewalks and streets with more green space
e. ☐ Home oriented to make efficient use of the sun's energy for heating and cooling	**OR**	☐ Home oriented to optimize the attractiveness of the home as viewed from the street
f. ☐ A heating and cooling system designed to meet your current needs efficiently	**OR**	☐ A heating and cooling system larger than currently needed with some excess capacity for possible future needs
g. ☐ Conventional landscaping with a traditional lawn, trees shrubs, etc.	**OR**	☐ Low maintenance landscaping with plants that grow in the local climate with minimal watering, weeding or mowing
h. ☐ Features and finishes made of more expensive materials that last longer	**OR**	☐ Features and finishes made of materials that cost less but need to be replaced more often
i. ☐ Upgraded interior finishes (e.g., flooring/counters/trim)	**OR**	☐ Green features (e.g., energy/water efficiency/indoor air quality)

37. For the same amount of money, which of the following would you choose?

a.☐ A bigger house with fewer amenities	**OR**	☐ A smaller house with high quality products and amenities
b.☐ A much larger family room and no living room	**OR**	☐ Family room and living room about equal in size
c.☐ Larger than average kitchen and smaller living area spaces	**OR**	☐ Typical kitchen and living area spaces
d. ☐ One primary bedroom suite (larger than average bedroom directly connected to a bath) plus three standard bedrooms	**OR**	☐ Two primary bedroom suites plus one standard bedroom

38. How would the following various designs and features influence your purchase decision? Please rate each design or feature as follows:

Do not want - not likely to buy a home with this design or feature.
Indifferent - wouldn't influence decision.
Desirable - would be seriously influenced to purchase a home because this design or feature was included.
Essential/Must have - unlikely to purchase a home without this design or feature.

	Do not Want	Indifferent	Desirable	Essential/ Must have
Windows				
Low-e insulating glass	☐	☐	☐	☐
Gas filled (Argon or Krypton) insulating glass	☐	☐	☐	☐
Triple-pane insulating glass	☐	☐	☐	☐
ENERGY STAR rated windows	☐	☐	☐	☐
Bay or bow windows	☐	☐	☐	☐
Greenhouse windows	☐	☐	☐	☐
Skylights	☐	☐	☐	☐
Floor-to-ceiling windows	☐	☐	☐	☐
Exterior Doors				
Double main entry door	☐	☐	☐	☐
Entry door with decorative glass panels	☐	☐	☐	☐
Sliding patio door	☐	☐	☐	☐
Hinged/French patio door	☐	☐	☐	☐
Front Exterior Siding				
Vinyl/Vinyl covered aluminum	☐	☐	☐	☐
Wood/Wood product	☐	☐	☐	☐
Fiber Cement	☐	☐	☐	☐
Stucco	☐	☐	☐	☐
Brick	☐	☐	☐	☐
Stone	☐	☐	☐	☐
Flooring for Living Spaces on Main Floor				
Bamboo	☐	☐	☐	☐
Carpet	☐	☐	☐	☐
Cork	☐	☐	☐	☐
Hardwood	☐	☐	☐	☐
Laminate	☐	☐	☐	☐
Tile	☐	☐	☐	☐
Decorative and Other Features				
Ceiling crown molding	☐	☐	☐	☐
Tray ceiling	☐	☐	☐	☐
Chair rails	☐	☐	☐	☐
Built-in shelving	☐	☐	☐	☐
Built-in kitchen seating	☐	☐	☐	☐
Exposed beams	☐	☐	☐	☐
Wood burning fireplace	☐	☐	☐	☐
Gas Fireplace	☐	☐	☐	☐
Ceiling fan	☐	☐	☐	☐

Kitchen Features

	Do not Want	Indifferent	Desirable	Essential/ Must have
Glass front on at least one cabinet	☐	☐	☐	☐
Central island	☐	☐	☐	☐
Central island with range	☐	☐	☐	☐
Double island	☐	☐	☐	☐
Induction cooktop	☐	☐	☐	☐
Steam oven	☐	☐	☐	☐
Walk-in pantry	☐	☐	☐	☐
Butler's pantry	☐	☐	☐	☐
Double sink (side-by-side)	☐	☐	☐	☐
Recessed lighting	☐	☐	☐	☐
Instant hot water dispenser	☐	☐	☐	☐
Drinking water filtration	☐	☐	☐	☐
Trash compactor	☐	☐	☐	☐
Table space for eating	☐	☐	☐	☐
Breakfast bar	☐	☐	☐	☐
Warming drawer	☐	☐	☐	☐
Pull-out shelves	☐	☐	☐	☐
Wine cooler	☐	☐	☐	☐
Special use storage (wine rack, spice drawer, pots & pans cabinet etc.)	☐	☐	☐	☐
Recycling center	☐	☐	☐	☐
Sensor-operated faucets	☐	☐	☐	☐
Desk/Computer area	☐	☐	☐	☐
Solid surface countertop (Corian etc.)	☐	☐	☐	☐
Ceramic tile countertop	☐	☐	☐	☐
Granite/Natural stone countertop	☐	☐	☐	☐
Laminate countertop	☐	☐	☐	☐
Quartz/Engineered stone countertop	☐	☐	☐	☐
Customized backsplash	☐	☐	☐	☐

Bath Features

Both shower stall & tub in primary bath (connected to primary bedroom)	☐	☐	☐	☐
Only a shower stall in primary bath	☐	☐	☐	☐
Whirlpool tub in primary bath	☐	☐	☐	☐
Private toilet compartment in primary bath	☐	☐	☐	☐
Multiple shower heads in primary bath	☐	☐	☐	☐
Body spray panel in primary bath (shower head(s) plus spray massage jets)	☐	☐	☐	☐

Skylight in primary bath	☐	☐	☐	☐
Linen closet in primary bath	☐	☐	☐	☐
Dual toilets in primary bath	☐	☐	☐	☐
Double vanity in primary bath	☐	☐	☐	☐
Granite vanity	☐	☐	☐	☐
Cultured marble vanity	☐	☐	☐	☐
Dressing/make-up area	☐	☐	☐	☐
His & Her baths	☐	☐	☐	☐
Toilet, tub, &sink - white	☐	☐	☐	☐
Toilet, tub, &sink - color	☐	☐	☐	☐
Ceramic tile walls	☐	☐	☐	☐
Bidet	☐	☐	☐	☐

Specialty Rooms or Features

Delivery vestibule	☐	☐	☐	☐
Great room (Kitchen/Family room/Living room combined)	☐	☐	☐	☐
Laundry room	☐	☐	☐	☐
Dining room	☐	☐	☐	☐
Separate living room	☐	☐	☐	☐
Separate family room	☐	☐	☐	☐
Two story entry foyer	☐	☐	☐	☐
Two story family room	☐	☐	☐	☐
Flex/multipurpose spaces	☐	☐	☐	☐
Sun room	☐	☐	☐	☐
Media room	☐	☐	☐	☐
Exercise room	☐	☐	☐	☐
Game room	☐	☐	☐	☐
Home office	☐	☐	☐	☐
Mudroom	☐	☐	☐	☐
Drop zone (shoes, coats, etc.)	☐	☐	☐	☐
Study/den/library	☐	☐	☐	☐
Breakfast nook	☐	☐	☐	☐
Wine cellar	☐	☐	☐	☐
Vaulted/cathedral ceiling	☐	☐	☐	☐
Wet bar	☐	☐	☐	☐
Recessed lighting throughout house	☐	☐	☐	☐
Laundry chute	☐	☐	☐	☐
Garage storage	☐	☐	☐	☐
Elevator	☐	☐	☐	☐
Pet washing station	☐	☐	☐	☐
In-law suite	☐	☐	☐	☐
Glass wall(s)	☐	☐	☐	☐
Soundproof walls/floors	☐	☐	☐	☐

Technology Features

Wireless home security system	☐	☐	☐	☐
Wired home security system	☐	☐	☐	☐
Security cameras	☐	☐	☐	☐
Programmable thermostat	☐	☐	☐	☐
Wired home audio system	☐	☐	☐	☐

Wireless home audio system	☐	☐	☐	☐
Outdoor speakers & audio controls	☐	☐	☐	☐
Home Theatre	☐	☐	☐	☐
Lighting control system	☐	☐	☐	☐
Energy management system/display	☐	☐	☐	☐
Whole house control/automation system	☐	☐	☐	☐
Central vacuum system	☐	☐	☐	☐
Multi-zone HVAC system	☐	☐	☐	☐
Charging station for electric car	☐	☐	☐	☐
Smart washer/dryer (controlled remotely)	☐	☐	☐	☐
Smart refrigerator (controlled remotely)	☐	☐	☐	☐
Smart oven (controlled remotely)	☐	☐	☐	☐
Smart irrigation system (computer-controlled)	☐	☐	☐	☐
Video doorbell	☐	☐	☐	☐

Outdoor Features

Front porch	☐	☐	☐	☐
Rear porch	☐	☐	☐	☐
Patio	☐	☐	☐	☐
Deck	☐	☐	☐	☐
Exterior lighting	☐	☐	☐	☐
Landscaping	☐	☐	☐	☐
Outdoor fireplace	☐	☐	☐	☐
Outdoor grill (built-in)	☐	☐	☐	☐
Outdoor kitchen (cooking, refrigeration, & sink)	☐	☐	☐	☐
Lot with trees	☐	☐	☐	☐
Lawn sprinklers	☐	☐	☐	☐

Accessibility Features

	Do not Want	Indifferent	Desirable	Essential/ Must have
A full bath on the main level	☐	☐	☐	☐
Doorways at least 3 ft. wide	☐	☐	☐	☐
Hallways at least 4 ft. wide	☐	☐	☐	☐
Bathroom aids, such as grab bars or seating in shower	☐	☐	☐	☐
Lower kitchen cabinets	☐	☐	☐	☐
Lower countertops	☐	☐	☐	☐
Non-slip floor surfaces	☐	☐	☐	☐
An entrance without steps	☐	☐	☐	☐

Green Features

	Do not Want	Indifferent	Desirable	Essential/ Must have
Insulation higher than required by code	☐	☐	☐	☐
ENERGY STAR rating for whole home	☐	☐	☐	☐
ENERGY STAR rated appliances	☐	☐	☐	☐
Efficient lighting that uses less energy than traditional bulbs	☐	☐	☐	☐
Tankless water heater	☐	☐	☐	☐
Solar water heating/electric system	☐	☐	☐	☐
Geothermal heating/cooling	☐	☐	☐	☐
Roof mounted, electricity generating wind turbine	☐	☐	☐	☐
"Net Zero" energy home (produces as much energy from renewable sources as it consumes)	☐	☐	☐	☐
Roof partially or completely covered by plants	☐	☐	☐	☐
Water-conserving bathroom faucets (flow rate below the federal conservation standard)	☐	☐	☐	☐
Water-conserving shower heads (flow rate below the federal conservation standard)	☐	☐	☐	☐
Water-conserving toilets (flush volume below the federal conservation standard)	☐	☐	☐	☐
Barrels/cisterns to collect rainwater for irrigation, toilet flushing, etc.	☐	☐	☐	☐
Home components made of recycled materials.	☐	☐	☐	☐
Components made from locally produced materials	☐	☐	☐	☐
Components built using certified sustainably harvested lumber	☐	☐	☐	☐
Prefabricated components (like panelized wall sections or roof & floor trusses)	☐	☐	☐	☐
Certification home is above water efficiency standards	☐	☐	☐	☐
Certification home is above energy efficiency standards	☐	☐	☐	☐

Indoor Air Quality

Home dehumidification system	☐	☐	☐	☐
Electronic air cleaner	☐	☐	☐	☐
Low VOC materials (paint, flooring, adhesives)	☐	☐	☐	☐
Whole house mechanical ventilation	☐	☐	☐	☐
Certification home has above-standard indoor environmental quality	☐	☐	☐	☐
Certification home is above health and wellness standards	☐	☐	☐	☐

Community Features

	Do not Want	Indifferent	Desirable	Essential/ Must have
Gated to control access	☐	☐	☐	☐
Golf course	☐	☐	☐	☐
Swimming pool	☐	☐	☐	☐
Access to public transportation	☐	☐	☐	☐
Daycare center	☐	☐	☐	☐
Outdoor maintenance service	☐	☐	☐	☐
Good primary/secondary public schools	☐	☐	☐	☐
Dog park	☐	☐	☐	☐
Community garden	☐	☐	☐	☐
Walking/jogging trail	☐	☐	☐	☐
Designated bike lane	☐	☐	☐	☐
BikeShare/CarShare services	☐	☐	☐	☐
Electric vehicle charging station	☐	☐	☐	☐
Park area	☐	☐	☐	☐
Playground	☐	☐	☐	☐
Baseball or soccer field	☐	☐	☐	☐
Tennis court	☐	☐	☐	☐
Pickleball court	☐	☐	☐	☐
Lake	☐	☐	☐	☐
Clubhouse	☐	☐	☐	☐
Green rating for subdivision	☐	☐	☐	☐
Exercise room	☐	☐	☐	☐
Typically suburban (all single-family detached houses)	☐	☐	☐	☐
High density (smaller lots and attached or multifamily buildings)	☐	☐	☐	☐
Infill (in the center of an older, established neighborhood)	☐	☐	☐	☐
Near retail space (grocery, drug stores etc.)	☐	☐	☐	☐
Other mixed use (homes near office or other commercial buildings)	☐	☐	☐	☐

Walkable community (with walkways connecting homes, shopping, and public spaces and transportation)	☐	☐	☐	☐
Community with a Homeowners Association	☐	☐	☐	☐

39. If a home office is essential or desirable to you, about how large would you prefer this room to be?

☐Small (< 100 square feet) ☐Medium (100 to 150 square feet) ☐Large (> 150 square feet)

D1. What is your gender?

☐ Male
☐ Female

D2. Which of the following best represents your total annual household income?

☐ Under $50,000
☐ $50,000 but less than $75,000
☐ $75,000 but less than $100,000
☐ $100,000 but less than $150,000
☐ $150,000 but less than $200,000
☐ $200,000 or more
☐ Prefer not to say

D3. Please indicate your racial background. Check all that apply.

☐ White (Non-Hispanic)
☐ African-American (Non-Hispanic)
☐ Asian/Pacific Islander
☐ American Indian/Alaska Native
☐ Other
☐ Prefer not to say

D4. Are you of Hispanic, Latino or Spanish origin?

☐ Yes
☐ No
☐ Prefer not to say

D5. In which state is your current residence located? List of states.

D6. What is your age? List of years 18 through 85+

D7. What is the composition of your household?

☐ Married couple with children
☐ Married couple without children
☐ Single parent
☐ One person household
☐ Other